A Nation in Debt: Economists Debate the Federal Budget Deficit

A Nation in Debt: Economists Debate the Federal Budget Deficit

Edited by

Richard H. Fink
President, Citizens for a Sound Economy

and

Jack C. High
Director, Center for the Study of Market Processes
George Mason University

University Publications of America, Inc.
44 North Market Street, Frederick, Maryland 21701

Copyright © 1987 by Richard H. Fink and Jack C. High
Library of Congress Cataloging-in-Publication Data

A Nation in debt.

   1. Budget deficits—United States.   2. Debts, Public—
United States.   3. Budget—Law and legislation—United
States.   I. Fink, Richard H.   II. High, Jack C.
HJ2052.N36   1987   339.5'23'0973   86–28252
ISBN 0-89093-963-2
ISBN 0-89093-964-0 (pbk).

Printed in the United States of America

TABLE OF CONTENTS

ACKNOWLEDGMENTS

The editors would like to express their thanks to the following authors for their generous cooperation:

James M. Buchanan, whose "The Moral Dimension of Debt Financing" was reprinted with the permission of the author from *Economic Inquiry*, Vol. 13, no. 1, January 1985, pp. 1–6. Also reprinted in *Liberty, Market, and the State* (Brighton, England: Wheatsheaf Press, and New York: New York University Press, 1985), pp. 189–194.

Robert Eisner and Paul Pieper, whose "How to Make Sense of the Deficit" was reprinted with the permission of the authors from *The Public Interest*, no. 78, Winter 1985, pp. 101–118.

Martin Feldstein, whose "The Job of Reducing the Federal Deficit" was reprinted with the permission of the author from the *Wall Street Journal*.

John Kenneth Galbraith, whose "The Budget and the Bust" was reprinted with the permission of the author from *The New Republic*, March 17, 1982, p. 9.

E.G. West, whose "Public Debt Burden and Cost Theory" was reprinted with the permission of the author and the publisher from *Economic Inquiry*, Vol. 13, no. 2, June 1975, pp. 179–190.

We would also like to thank:

Randolph Boehm and Jeff Shulman of University Publications of America for helping to make this project a reality; Peter Boettke and Jerome Ellig for providing valuable assistance in tracking down and sifting through articles; Colleen Morretta and Deborah Kramer for keeping the project on time and organized; Mary Ellen Beisner for typing the manuscript of the Introduction; and Pamela Heard and Nancy Mitchell for painstakingly proofreading the galleys.

Finally, the Center for the Study of Market Processes at George Mason University provided additional research support.

CONTRIBUTORS

Part I

Karl Marx (1818–1883) is the intellectual father of Marxism. Considered by many to have been the most severe critic of the capitalist system, he authored *Capital* and *The Communist Manifesto*.

Adam Smith (1723–1790) is commonly regarded as the founder of modern economic science. Smith's *An Inquiry into the Nature and Causes of the Wealth of Nations,* published in 1776, drew attention to the possibility that the self-interested actions of individuals can generate unintended beneficial social consequences.

Part II

Alvin Hansen (1887–1975) was one of the chief propagators of Keynesian ideas in the United States. He served as president of the American Economic Association in 1938. A professor at Harvard University, he wrote *A Guidebook to Keynes*.

John Maynard Keynes (1883–1946) was perhaps the most influential economist of this century. His *General Theory of Employment, Interest, and Money* provided an economic rationale for activist fiscal and monetary policies. He was one of the chief architects of the post-World War II Bretton Woods monetary agreement.

Abba Lerner (1903–1982) was a distinguished fellow and past vice president of the American Economic Association. He is regarded as the founder of "functional finance."

Ludwig von Mises (1881–1973) was a distinguished fellow of the American Economic Association and leading 20th-century figure in the "Austrian school" of economics. He was the founder of the Austrian Institute for Business Cycle Research; his publications in economics include *The Theory of Money and Credit* and *Human Action*.

Part III

James Buchanan, a Nobel laureate, is a distinguished fellow of the American Economic Association and university distinguished professor, department of economics, George Mason University. General director of the Center for the Study of Public Choice, he is considered the founding father of the "public choice" school of economics. His numerous publications include *Liberty, Market, and State, The Power to Tax* (with G. Brennan), *Democracy in Deficit: The Political*

Legacy of Lord Keynes (with R. Wagner), *Cost and Choice, The Limits of Liberty,* and *The Calculus of Consent* (with G. Tullock).

Robert Eisner is William R. Kennan Professor of Economics, Northwestern University. He is president of the American Economic Association and the author of *How Real is the Deficit?* and *Factors in Business Investment.*

Milton Friedman, a Nobel laureate, is a senior research fellow at the Hoover Institution and professor emeritus, department of economics, University of Chicago. He served as president of the American Economic Association in 1967. His books range from detailed academic studies like *A Monetary History of the United States* (with A. Schwartz) to the best-selling *Free to Choose.*

Rose Friedman, also an economist, is co-author, with Milton Friedman, of *Free to Choose* and *Tyranny of the Status Quo.*

John Kenneth Galbraith is professor emeritus, department of economics, Harvard University. He served as president of the American Economic Association in 1972. He is the author of numerous books, including *The Affluent Society* and *The New Industrial State.*

Friedrich von Hayek, a Nobel laureate, is professor emeritus, University of Chicago and University of Freiburg im Breisgau, West Germany. His work in economics includes *Prices and Production* and *The Pure Theory of Capital.* Interdisciplinary studies include *Law, Legislation, and Liberty* (3 Vols.), *The Constitution of Liberty,* and *The Road to Serfdom.*

Paul J. Pieper is a professor of economics, University of Illinois at Chicago. He conducts research on the impact of deficits on the economy and price measurements.

Paul Craig Roberts holds the William E. Simon Chair of Political Economy at Georgetown University's Center for Strategic and International Studies. He was assistant secretary of the treasury for economic policy during the first year of the Reagan administration and was the chief architect of the original Kemp-Roth tax cut bill as a Senate staff economist. He is the author of *Alienation and the Soviet Economy* and *Marx's Theory of Exchange, Alienation, and Crisis.*

James Tobin, a Nobel laureate, is Sterling Professor of Economics, Yale University. He served on President Kennedy's Council of Economic Advisers. He is the author of *Asset Accumulation and Economic Activity* and *The New Economics, One Decade Later.*

Edwin G. West is a professor of economics, Carleton University. He is the author of *Education and the State, Education and the Industrial Revolution,* and *Adam Smith: The Man and His Works.*

Part IV

Norman S. Fieleke is vice president and economist at the Federal Reserve Bank of Boston, specializing in international economics.

Thomas M. Humbert is budget analyst to Congressman Jack Kemp (R-NY). He is a former senior policy analyst and Walker Fellow in Economics at the Heritage Foundation.

Paul A. Volcker is chairman of the Federal Reserve Board. He is past president of the New York District Federal Reserve Bank.

Part V

Henry Hazlitt is a former editor of the *New York Times* and business columnist for *Newsweek*. He has written 18 books, including *Economics in One Lesson* and *From Bretton Woods to World Inflation*.

Alvin Rabushka is a senior fellow at Stanford University's Hoover Institution. He is the author of 14 books, including *Low Tax, Simple Tax, Flat Tax* (with R. Hall) and *From Adam Smith to the Wealth of America*.

Herbert Stein is a senior fellow at the American Enterprise Institute. He was chairman of President Nixon's Council of Economic Advisers.

Robert D. Tollison is director of the Center for the Study of Public Choice and professor of economics, George Mason University. He headed the Federal Trade Commission's Bureau of Economics from 1981 to 1983 and is a past president of the Southern Economic Association. He is co-author and co-editor of *Toward a Theory of the Rent-Seeking Society*.

Richard E. Wagner is a professor of economics, Florida State University. With J. Buchanan, he co-authored *Democracy in Deficit: The Political Legacy of Lord Keynes*.

Part VI

Peter Boettke is a research fellow at the Center for the Study of Market Processes, George Mason University, and managing editor of *Market Process*.

Stuart Butler is director of domestic policy studies at the Heritage Foundation. He is the author of *Privatizing Federal Spending*.

Timothy B. Clark covers government budget and financial issues for the *National Journal*.

Jerome Ellig is a research fellow at the Center for the Study of Market Processes, George Mason University, and staff economist for Citizens for a Sound Economy, a Washington-based public interest consumer organization.

Martin Feldstein is president of the National Bureau of Economic Research and professor of economics, Harvard University. He is a recipient of the American Economic Association's John Bates Clark Award, given annually to the outstanding economist under 40. He is a former chairman of President Reagan's Council of Economic Advisers.

Alice M. Rivlin is director of economic studies at the Brookings Institution and a former president of the American Economic Association. She is also a former director of the Congressional Budget Office. She is the editor of *Economic Choices* and author of *Systematic Thinking for Social Action*.

Part VII

William P. Orzechowski is director of federal budget policy for the U.S. Chamber of Commerce. His articles on budget and tax policy have appeared in the *Wall Street Journal*, *Economic Outlook*, and the *Cato Journal*.

Cesar V. Conda is a staff economist at the U.S. Chamber of Commerce specializing in federal budget policy. His articles have appeared in the *Wall Street Journal*, *Washington Times*, *Economic Outlook*, and *Human Events*.

ABOUT THE EDITORS

Richard H. Fink is founder, president, and chief executive officer of Citizens for a Sound Economy, a 250,000-member citizens' public advocacy organization. He also founded and formerly directed the Center for the Study of Market Processes at George Mason University in Fairfax, Virginia. Mr. Fink is the editor of *Supply Side Economics: A Critical Appraisal* and author of articles appearing in such journals as the *American Economic Review* and *Contemporary Policy Issues*. He is a member of the Federal Reserve Board's Consumer Advisory Council.

Mr. Fink received his bachelor's degree in economics from Rutgers University, graduating magna cum laude, Phi Beta Kappa. He received his master's degree in economics from U.C.L.A. At New York University he was awarded Scaife and Mohrman graduate fellowships for academic excellence.

Jack C. High received a B.A. from the University of Utah and a Ph.D. in economics from U.C.L.A. He has taught at California State University at Long Beach, and is currently an assistant professor of economics at George Mason University, where he also directs the Center for the Study of Market Processes. Professor High has published in *Barron's*, *Economic Inquiry*, the *Journal of Post Keynesian Economics*, the *CATO Journal*, *Contemporary Policy Issues*, and several scholarly volumes on economics. He is currently completing a book comparing economic theories of price adjustment.

INTRODUCTION

Economists and the National Deficit

Time was when the United States government lived within its means. Throughout the nineteenth century and into the twentieth, the government's balance sheet was mostly black ink. There were red years, of course—during the Civil War (1861–1865) the accumulated deficit was $523,000, and during WWI (1917–1919) it ran to $23 million. But usually government receipts were sufficient to cover expenditures.

All that changed beginning in 1931. In the 50 years since, the federal government has managed a surplus only seven times. Even more striking are the sizes of recent increases. The deficit for 1980, the year President Reagan was elected, was $59.6 billion. For 1982, it was $110.6 billion; for 1983, $195.4 billion. The accumulated deficit is currently approaching $2 trillion. Small wonder that balancing the budget has become a topic on every tongue and, for some, our most pressing national priority.

What are the causes of the mounting deficit? What are its effects? How are we to evaluate these effects? What, if anything, should be done? These are questions that concern today's citizens and policymakers. Quite naturally, these same questions have concerned economists for a very long time. As with most national economic issues, answers to these questions differ both among laymen and professionals.

This volume presents the thinking of a wide array of economists on government deficits. In these pages Smith and Marx, Keynes and Mises, Friedman and Tobin, Galbraith and Buchanan all have their say.

Economists from the classical period (1770–1870), the Keynesian Revolution (1930s and 1940s), and the modern era argue about causes and consequences of deficit financing. Nor does the controversy stop with theory. Economists have differing views on what should be done. Some argue for constitutional reform, some for legislative reform, some for no reform at all.

Concern over the budget deficit has involved more than words. Today, several Washington groups are trying to implement various reform measures. The volume ends with a report of who is doing what about the budget deficit.

By presenting a variety of viewpoints in a historical context, we hope to inform the interested reader and stimulate further thought about the federal budget deficit. We hope that the reader will be able to form better judgments on the causes and effects of deficits, and on the efficacy of reform proposals.

Historical Background

Adam Smith attributes the public debt to three influences—the desire of government officials to spend, the unpopularity of increasing taxes, and the willingness of capitalists to lend. Thus he sees government debt as an accompaniment of commercial or capitalist society.

Smith did not look with favor on government debt. He thought that increasing deficits would "in the long-run probably ruin all the great nations of Europe" (p. 4). Moreover, he believed that the ability of governments to borrow increased their willingness to wage war. If governments had to raise money by taxing rather than borrowing, "Wars would in general be more speedily concluded, and less wantonly undertaken. . . . The foresight of the heavy and unavoidable burdens of war would hinder the people from wantonly calling for it when there was no real interest to fight for" (p. 15).

Smith argued that government, like a private citizen, will eventually default on its loans if its debt keeps increasing. However, governments can default in a way that private creditors cannot—by inflation. "The raising of the denomination of the coin has been the most usual expedient by which a real public bankruptcy has been disguised," he wrote (p. 18).

In sum, Smith criticizes government debt rather harshly. Government borrowing encourages profligacy and waste during peace and leads to reckless waging of war. Debt results in higher taxes and inflation, which rewards spendthrifts and punishes savers. Debt weakens the productive capacity of a people and eventually weakens or destroys even wealthy nations.

Karl Marx agrees with Smith that public debt is the creature of capitalist society and harms the general populace. However, Marx's condemnation of public debt is bound up with his views on exploitation.

Lending to the government is an easy way for lenders to augment their capital without the necessity of exposing it to "the troubles and risks inseparable from its employment in industry or even in usury" (p. 38).

The public debt brings on a number of consequences that Marx condemns because they ultimately result in the exploitation of labor. First, it creates a class of "lazy annuitants." Second, it results in central bankers, who are granted special privileges in return for lending to the state. Third, it encourages more taxation and tax collectors in order to pay the national debt. Fourth, it artificially stimulates manufacturing, which leads to greater exploitation of the workers. In consequence, Marx, like Smith before him, was opposed to public debt.

The modern justification for public debt emerges with *John Maynard Keynes*. In the chapter from Keynes's *General Theory* that we have included, Keynes does not address the deficit specifically. But he does express ideas that justify deficit financing. Keynes believes that a shortfall in consumer spending, rather than a shortfall in savings, impedes investment: "For we have seen that, up to the point that full employment prevails, the growth of capital depends not at all on a low propensity to consume but is, on the contrary, held back by it . . ." (p. 44). The task of the government, when there is unemployment, is to borrow and spend. Although Keynes does not explicitly say that in the section reprinted here, he does elsewhere, in chapter 10 of the *General Theory*. When there is unemployment, " 'wasteful' loan expenditure [i.e., government expense financed by debt] may nevertheless enrich the community on balance. Pyramid building, earthquakes, even wars may serve to increase wealth. . . ."

In urging the government to run up the deficit, even if the expenditure is for something useless, Keynes breaks with the writings of Smith and Marx. He thinks that such expenditure, rather than impoverishing the general populace, enriches it.

Alvin Hansen places the Keynesian view in historical context. Adam Smith's opinion that government should not finance expenditures by borrowing was shared by many social philosophers, including Thomas Aquinas, Jean Bodin, and David Hume. Thomas Hobbes dissented; he thought the growing expenditures of government required borrowing on occasion.

As to the actual history of government deficits, Hansen concurs with Smith and Marx that deficits were greatest during war. Wars remained the primary impetus to deficits until the Great Depression of the 1930s. Then, out of necessity, government began expending huge sums for relief. Consequently, "Government debt was everywhere mounting and fiscal policy was being drafted willy-nilly to serve as an instrument to increase the volume of employment" (p. 57).

Hansen's brief history suggests that Keynes's *General Theory* gave a rationale for what governments, in an attempt to combat the depression, were doing anyway.

Abba Lerner states the Keynesian position boldly. During periods of unemployment, government spending, whether financed through borrowing or printing money, must always be beneficial, irrespective of the amount of the debt. His argument "means that the absolute size of the national debt does not matter at all, and that however large the interest payments that have to be made, these do not constitute any burden upon society as a whole" (p. 64).

Lerner openly criticizes the tradition of financial prudence handed down by classical economists. "In brief," he writes, "functional finance rejects completely the traditional doctrines of 'sound finance' and the principle of trying to balance the budget over a solar year or any other arbitrary period" (p. 60).

Functional finance is predicated on the principle that there can be either inflation or unemployment in our economy, but not both. If there is inflation, the government should increase taxes and cut back its spending; if there is unemployment, the government should decrease taxes and increase its spending. Implicit in the argument is that a free economy cannot function by itself without having one or the other. Only the government can balance saving and expenditure so that there is neither.

Although the influence of Keynes and his followers was very great from 1940 onward, not all economists were convinced. *Ludwig von Mises* scorned Keynes as "the new prophet of inflationism" who believed that credit expansion performs the " 'miracle . . . of turning a stone into bread' " (p. 68).

Mises criticizes Keynes and his followers for not bothering to refute the long tradition of arguments against deficit financing and credit expansion. He writes, "Their critique aims at a body of doctrine created by their own illusions, which has no resemblance to the theories expounded by serious economists. They pass over in silence all that economists have said about the inevitable outcome of credit expansion" (p. 71).

According to Mises, economists before Keynes knew very well what caused depression and mass unemployment. These were the consequences of government banks expanding the money supply, which set in motion a boom-bust cycle, and labor unions holding wage rates above their market clearing levels.

For Mises, the Keynesian prescription of deficit financing was the cause of unemployment and depression, not the cure. He pronounced the Keynesian policies unworkable and predicted their failure.

Modern Controversy

Smith, Marx, Keynes, Mises, et al. form a historical backdrop against which the modern controversy over the deficit takes place. The diverse opinions expressed by modern economists extend, refine, and modify the ideas set forth during the classical and Keynesian periods.

James Tobin, like Lerner, argues that the size of the budget deficit is irrelevant, or at least greatly exaggerated. Deficits are not driving up interest rates and crowding out private borrowing and investment. Rather, "The deficit is mostly result, not cause, of recent and current high interest rates and the depression caused by those rates . . ." (p. 79). Tobin calls for credit expansion to lower interest rates and stimulate recovery, which will increase tax revenues and eventually reduce the deficit. Thus Tobin falls squarely in the Keynesian tradition of using credit expansion to stimulate the economy.

Paul Craig Roberts echoes Tobin's view that deficits are not the cause of high interest rates. He writes, "In recent years economists have begun to search for empirical evidence that deficits cause inflation and higher interest rates. So far they have not been able to find any" (p. 83).

If government borrowing does not cause high interest rates, what does? According to Roberts, "The empirical evidence shows that monetary policy is to blame" (p. 85).

Roberts (p. 85) points to two influences of monetary policy. First, unanticipated growth in the money supply creates the expectation of future inflation, which adds a premium to the interest rate. Second, an unanticipated cutback in the money supply creates excess demand for lendable funds and drives up the short-term interest rate.

Roberts concludes that economic policy should not be based on "unsubstantiated fears" that the budget deficit will crowd out private investment and retard growth.

Robert Eisner and *Paul Pieper* advance two arguments, both of which conclude that we should not worry about the size of the current deficit.

First, they feel that government deficits are beneficial during periods of unemployment. They state that "if we own government savings bonds, Treasury bills, or notes we feel richer. We value our holdings of government debt more highly than the 'present value' we attach to the uncertain future tax burden which may be associated with them, and the wealthier we feel . . . the more we feel free to spend. To the extent that more spending is desirable, because we are in a recession, more government debt is actually beneficial, however paradoxical it may seem" (pp. 87–88).

Eisner and Pieper also argue that the size of the deficit is overstated because of accounting practices.

They point out that there is no capital account in the government's budget. If a firm borrows $100,000 and spends it to build equipment, the debt is offset by the value of the equipment. Not so with the government. "As a result, all federal expenditures for such things as public buildings, roads, harbors, post offices, trucks, and computers become a part of the deficit, as if they were government consumption rather than investment in hard assets" (p. 88).

Eisner and Pieper also criticize debt figures for being computed at par values rather than market values. If government issues $100,000 in bonds at 10 percent, and the interest rate subsequently rises to 20 percent, the market value of the bonds will fall. Yet the government debt is still figured at the par value of $100,000. This, say Eisner and Pieper, is a mistake which overstates the size of the deficit.

Recalculating U.S. debt according to their accounting practices, Eisner and Pieper find that the $1.2 trillion debt of 1980 is really only $447.5 billion, a substantial difference. Moreover, when the deficit is further adjusted for inflation, they conclude that what appear to be deficits under the current accounting methods are actually surpluses under theirs.

Not all economists concur with the finding that government deficits are either unimportant or beneficial. *James Buchanan* condemns them as downright harmful. "For let us make no mistake about it," he says in his 1983 presidential address to the Western Economic Association, "this is precisely what the debt financing of public consumption is: an 'eating up' of national capital" (p. 105).

Buchanan focuses on the moral precepts that held government deficits in check prior to the 1930s but which broke down during the Keynesian era.

Buchanan believes that the natural proclivities of citizens and politicians favor deficit financing. "Constituents enjoy receiving the benefits of public outlays, and they deplore paying taxes. Elected politicians attempt to satisfy constituents" (p. 105). What kept this proclivity in check, says Buchanan, was a respect for the national stock of capital, a respect that was the product of cultural evolution. That changed with Keynes, who "may be viewed as a successful revolutionary who destroyed the Victorian precepts" (p. 104).

Although Keynes's policy seemed logical at the time, Buchanan believes that it broke down the moral barrier that preserved our capital stock, which will be eroded if we do not succeed in erecting barriers again. He feels that a constitutional amendment to balance the budget is the best chance we have for this.

One of the arguments that the debt doesn't matter is that "we owe it to ourselves." What one person owes is another person's gain; therefore, the national debt constitutes no real burden.

E.G. West analyzes this and other problems of the debt burden by asking what the "cost" of the debt is both individually and in the aggregate. He does not believe that we can write off the debt problem simply because we owe it to ourselves.

"Imagine," writes West, "an American population of Smiths and Joneses. Assume that the Joneses are the debt holders. As taxpayers called upon to service the debt, each Smith family is inescapably burdened . . . To be told that this burden will be less because each Mr. Jones is 'one of ourselves' is of no consolation. The Smiths have to service the debt just as if they had borrowed from a Canadian or an Australian Mr. Jones" (pp. 110–111).

West goes on to argue that whenever government incurs a debt, someone bears a cost. "The cost arises simply because the decision is made; foregone opportunities are experienced. Both domestic and foreign debt involve such present costs (opportunity costs). Future settlements (outlays) are of course associated in all cases; and these are made by future taxpayers to bond holders . . ." (p. 111).

West then analyzes how costs are distributed when government expenditures are financed through taxes and through borrowing. Again he identifies the Smiths who are taxed to pay the Joneses who are bondholders.

Milton and *Rose Friedman* do not praise government deficits, but neither do they believe that red ink is the main problem with the budget. For them, "Taxes and spending are the real culprits, not deficits and debt . . . *The federal budget would have been roughly balanced, or gained a surplus in 1980, 1981, and 1982, had total spending been held down to the same percentage of the national income as in 1979*" (p. 130, their italics). Much of their writing documents the growth of government spending in America, especially the marked increase in federal spending, which has grown from 3 percent of national income in 1900 to 28 percent in 1980.

They identify three harmful effects of the deficit. First, it enables politicians to spend without the necessity of simultaneously imposing a tax. Second, government borrowing uses funds "that would otherwise be available for building houses or factories or machines" (p. 120). Third, if the government finances the deficit through creating money, "it imposes a hidden tax of inflation—each dollar you have will buy less" (p. 120).

John Kenneth Galbraith finds himself, somewhat surprisingly, in accord with the Friedmans and others on evaluation of the budget deficit. Looking at the large deficit of 1983, he says, "The sound instinct of the American people is that deficits of this magnitude are unwise and dangerous" (p. 136).

Galbraith worries about the effect that monetary policy will have on the deficit. Tight monetary policy means less money available for business loans, less output, and lower tax revenues, which will increase the size of the deficit. Credit-sensitive industries, such as housing, automobiles, and construction, will suffer more than others and will therefore generate less revenues.

Galbraith also worries that deficits and tight monetary policy will drive up interest rates and discourage private investment, which is harmful: " . . . it is from borrowing for investment that we get improvement in productivity" (p. 138).

As a remedy for the deficit, Galbraith would like military spending to be cut back. Part of the $100 billion per year that are spent in military investment "could be used for private capital investment" (p. 140). He would also like taxes raised. He believes that "higher taxes are far better for the economy than higher interest rates. Investment, productivity, and economic growth are consistent, or can be made consistent, with higher taxes" (p. 141).

For *Friedrich von Hayek*, the main danger of the budget deficit is that it will be financed by creating money, which causes unemployment.

Hayek, like Buchanan, condemns the Keynesian doctrine for breaking down the barriers that held government spending in check. "Spending money and having budget deficits were suddenly represented as virtues" (p. 146).

The flaw in the Keynesian prescription, argues Hayek, is that inflation causes unemployment, rather than curing it. He writes, ". . . in the long run such inflation inevitably creates much *more* unemployment than the amount it was originally designed to prevent" (p. 148).

Newly created money makes it possible for some employers to offer higher wages to workers, thus making particular jobs more attractive. But the effect is temporary. As the new money works its way through the economic system, the artificially high wages readjust, and workers who took the jobs made attractive through the injection of new money are thrown out of work.

This consequence of inflation, says Hayek, is unavoidable. "We ought to have no illusion that we can escape the consequences of the mistakes we have made. Any attempt to preserve the jobs made profitable by inflation would lead to a complete destruction of the market order" (p. 149).

For Hayek, the unpleasant consequence of past inflation is present unemployment. Any attempts to avoid this consequence through more inflation will only lead to worse unemployment and suffering later. Thus, Hayek concludes, "The first necessity now is to stop the increase in the quantity of money . . . and this cannot happen soon enough" (p. 150).

International Consequences

The federal budget deficit influences interest rates, private investment, monetary policy, and, *Paul Volcker* argues, the trade deficit as well. He sees the budget deficit contributing to the trade deficit and believes that both deficits hurt the prospects for long-term growth.

Financing the budget deficit in 1983 "amounted to three-quarters of our net new domestic savings" (p. 157). If this condition continues, "not much of our domestic savings will be left over for the investment we need" (p. 157).

The effect on private investment has been ameliorated through foreign investment, which has flowed into the U.S. because of high interest rates. Says Volcker, "In effect, the growing capital inflow has, directly and indirectly, helped to finance the internal budget, by the same token helping to moderate the pressures of the budget deficit on the domestic financial markets" (p. 157).

But foreign investment has another effect. It increases the demand for dollars, drives up their price, and undercuts America's ability to export goods. It increases our trade deficit. Assessing this situation, Volcker says, "We simply can't have it both ways—on the one hand, look abroad for increasing help in financing the credits related to our budget deficit, our housing, and our investment, and on the other hand, expect to narrow the growing gap in our trade accounts" (p. 157).

Volcker argues vigorously for reducing both deficits. He writes, "Our common sense tells us that enormous and potentially rising budget deficits, and the high and rising deficits in our trade accounts, are wrong—they cannot be indefinitely prolonged . . . the time to take the initiative is now, when we can influence markets constructively—when we can demonstrate that we are in control of our own financial destiny. Real progress toward reducing the budget deficit is needed to clear away the dangers" (p. 161).

Thomas Humbert disagrees sharply with Volcker's conclusions about the government deficit and the trade deficit. He first argues that trade deficits are substantially overstated because they do not include American export of services. Examining the trade accounts for the first three quarters of 1983, he writes, "While the merchandise deficit was a record $41.6 billion, it was offset by a surplus of services, amounting to $21.8 billion. The near record service surplus kept the three quarter 1983 current account deficit to $25.5 billion" (p. 164).

Humbert also argues that U.S. budget deficits do not cause high interest rates or weaken the value of the dollar. Statistical studies show no correlation between the budget deficit and high interest rates, nor between budget deficits and capital flows, nor between budget deficits and a strong dollar.

He concludes that trade deficits and a strong dollar do not forebode an economic downturn. They do not cause unemployment, merely a redirection of employment. Moreover, imports confer the benefit of enabling consumers to buy goods cheaper and thus raise the U.S. standard of living. The danger of the budget and trade deficits, Humbert feels, is that they could goad politicians into unwise policies, such as raising taxes, or inflating, or imposing tariffs and quotas.

Norman Fieleke discusses some of the issues brought up by both Volcker and Humbert, and supports both authors on particular points.

He concisely states the link derived from economic theory between the budget deficit and the trade deficit. He says, " . . . an increase in government borrowing in a country will, other things equal, put upward pressure on interest rates . . . in that country, thereby attracting foreign investment. As foreign investors acquire the country's currency, in order to invest there, they bid up the price of that currency in the foreign exchange markets. The higher price of the country's currency will discourage foreigners from purchasing its goods but will encourage residents of the country to use their now more valuable currency to purchase foreign goods, so that the country's current account will move toward a deficit" (pp. 173–174).

Fieleke shows a statistical correlation between the budget deficit and the trade deficit, and between the budget deficit and the value of the dollar. However, he also warns that the correlations are sensitive to the assumptions made in computing the statistics, and tells us that "strong conclusions should not be drawn from them alone" (p. 175).

Fieleke thinks that the trade deficit has "exerted a restraining influence on economic activity [in the United States], as the nation's exports have fallen off in relation to its import purchases," but he does not believe the United States has lost its competitive edge: " . . . the trade balance by itself is not a valid indicator of competitiveness. Other more comprehensive measures suggest that the United States remains a powerful competitor" (p. 177). The United States's share of world output increased even during the large trade deficits of 1982 and 1983, indicating that American businesses are still effective competitors.

Fieleke is not alarmed by the size of the trade deficit. Over the long term, it will gradually diminish as the value of the dollar falls in international markets.

Reform

The controversy over the deficit has naturally produced agitation for reform, which we have divided into "constitutional" and "legislative."

The most prominent constitutional reform is an amendment requiring Congress to balance the budget each year. *Richard Wagner* and *Robert Tollison* present a detailed and carefully reasoned analysis favoring such an amendment.

Wagner and Tollison draw from and elaborate on many of the arguments which appear in the earlier sections. They note the proclivity of politicians to spend, but not to tax, the combination of which leads to deficit financing. They argue that government borrowing is harmful because it crowds out private investment, and the latter is more productive than the former. They elaborate on the Hayekian theme that monetizing the debt will misdirect investment, causing economic instability and unemployment.

Because of the economically harmful effects of deficits, Wagner and Tollison think the budget should be balanced. But they display little confidence in the ability of politicians to do this through legislation: " . . . how reasonable is it," they ask, "to rely upon the normal processes of congressional decision-making? It is these very processes that have brought about our chronic deficits" (p. 191).

A constitutional amendment to balance the budget would force politicians to do what they will not do on their own: it would require them to finance what they spend through taxes. "Tax finance forces legislators to take responsibility for their budgetary decisions; if they approve a greater utilization of resources through government, they must at the same time impose the higher taxes necessary to transfer command over the resources from taxpayers to government. Borrowing or money creation weakens this responsibility. . . . A balanced budget requirement would promote responsibility or accountability in budgetary decision-making" (p. 194).

Although they favor a balanced budget amendment, Wagner and Tollison do not regard it as a panacea. They carefully consider what the amendment must contain if it is to achieve fiscal responsibility.

They are particularly concerned that politicians not be allowed to avoid fiscal responsibility through off-budget expenditures. These include expenditures for "commercial" enterprises, such as the Tennessee Valley Authority, and for loan guarantees, such as the Farm Credit Administration. They also feel that "emergencies," which would allow for deficits, should be carefully defined, and should require a two-thirds majority of each chamber.

Alvin Rabushka goes even farther in advocating a balanced budget amendment. He wants not only a balanced budget but a constitutional restraint on taxes as well. Consequently, he favors Senate Joint Resolution 58, which passed the Senate with a two-thirds majority in 1982.

Section 1 of the resolution mandates that "Prior to each fiscal year, the Congress shall adopt a statement of receipts and outlays for that year in which total outlays are no greater than total receipts" (p. 224).

Section 2 of the resolution requires that "Total receipts for any fiscal year . . . shall not increase by a rate greater than the rate of increase in national income in the last calendar year . . . " (p. 226).

The combined effects of Sections 1 and 2, Rabushka points out, "establish a *de facto* spending limit. Thus neither taxes nor spending can grow more rapidly than the economy" (p. 227).

The Senate resolution also contains provisions for overriding the spending limit, but an override requires a vote of Congress. Importantly, the spending limit cannot be evaded by expenditures on off-budget items. Rabushka notes, "An important feature of Section 1 is that it imposes upon the Congress and the President a mandate to prevent total actual outlays, which include both on- and off-budget items, from exceeding statement outlays" (p. 225).

Although the Senate resolution imposes no sanctions on Congress if it fails to abide by it, Rabushka nevertheless believes the amendment would be beneficial. He says, "By establishing a focus upon two or three critical votes each year relating to the total level of taxation or the size of the deficits, in place of the present piecemeal focus on hundreds of separate spending measures, the amendment will enable the electorate to better identify those members of Congress most responsible for higher levels of spending, taxing, and deficits with their harmful effects on inflation, interest rates, and unemployment" (p. 228).

Henry Hazlitt does not support a balanced budget amendment in general and specifically opposes the Senate resolution favored by Rabushka. Of Senate Joint Resolution 58 Hazlitt says, "The trouble with such an amendment is not merely that it would be too cumbersome and restrictive, but that it misses the real problem. The basic problem is not the deficit itself, but the excessive government spending that causes the deficit" (p. 232).

Hazlitt proposes two of his own amendments that, he argues, will cut government spending. The first gives the President a line item veto. He writes, "At present he [the President] has only the power of vetoing an entire bill. This, in practice, makes his veto power, on appropriation bills, unusable. For Congress is able consistently to circumvent the intention of this constitutional provision by combining in a single bill appropriations it knows the President won't like with appropriations it knows he must have. . . . A constitutional amendment giving the President the power to reduce or veto individual items in appropriation bills would give him the real power to curb congressional spending that the framers of the Constitution intended him to have" (p. 233).

Hazlitt believes that this amendment by itself might suffice to control excessive government spending, but if not, its combination with a second amendment surely would.

Hazlitt's second amendment would restrict the origin of appropriations bills to the House. He argues, "The record shows that in departmental and other omnibus appropriation bills, the Senate in nearly every case increases the appropriations provided by the House. . . . The solution seems to be a constitutional amendment that would take from the Senate any power to initiate appropriations or to increase an appropriation by the House . . ." (p. 233).

Herbert Stein also opposes a balanced budget amendment, but for different reasons than Hazlitt.

Stein believes that deficits have two opposing effects on the economy. In the short run, deficits will "raise the rate of increase of nominal GNP and the price level and also . . . raise output and employment." However, in the long run, "the larger the deficit is . . . the slower will be the growth of private productive investment" (p. 236).

According to Stein, deficits slow down private investment by crowding out private borrowing. Consequently, "The larger the government deficit is, the smaller private investment will be . . ." (p. 238).

Stein believes the size of the deficit should be based on its long-run impact on investment and economic growth. He writes, " . . . it seems clear that in thinking about the desirable size of the deficit or surplus, one should be thinking primarily about the desired rate of growth of national output and productivity. But once that has been said it is hard to say more. There is no objective way to determine how much the nation should forgo current government services and private consumption in order to make the future national income greater" (p. 240).

Since the proper rate of growth is neither objectively determined nor fixed once and for all, Stein opposes a balanced budget amendment, which would lock economic growth into a fixed rate. He says, "The desirable size of the surplus or deficit is not fixed forever. That is why it should not be incorporated in a constitutional amendment. The choice of a surplus or deficit target is a political decision to be made from time to time in the light of long-run growth considerations" (p. 241).

There is obvious disagreement among economists as to whether a balanced budget amendment to the Constitution should be implemented. This disagreement extends into legislative proposals to curb rapidly growing expenditures and debt.

Legislative proposals fall into two categories—those which aim at increasing taxes and those which aim at reducing expenditures.

Timothy Clark takes a hard look at political realities and concludes that the only way the deficit can be reduced is through the first category—increasing taxes.

Although one might think that a Republican President would be willing and able to cut expenditures on domestic programs, thereby reducing the deficit, Clark believes otherwise. "The huge social insurance programs that have driven that growth [of domestic spending] are essentially off-limits to budget cutters" (p. 243). Moreover, "Republicans have almost reached the limit of their willingness to countenance other domestic budget cuts" (p. 243).

Nor does Clark believe that defense spending will be cut. Although the defense budget contains more discretionary spending than other parts of the budget, "there seems little prospect of sharply slowing the defense buildup that started at the beginning of the decade; Reagan would resist it, and even the House Democrats do not seem inclined to approve huge cuts" (p. 247).

With no prospect for substantially cutting government spending, Clark concludes that "the large deficits will continue unless taxes are raised" (p. 252).

Contrary to Clark, *Martin Feldstein* believes cuts in social programs are the best means of reducing the deficit. He says, "The issue is whether Congress and the administration will have the political fortitude to make the necessary legislative changes, especially in Social Security and the other 'entitlement' or cash-transfer programs" (p. 255).

Feldstein urges Washington to reduce spending on these programs to their levels in the 1970s. He points out, "In 1960, federal civilian spending accounted for 9 percent of gross national product. That increased to 13 percent by 1970 and 17 percent by 1980. Returning such spending to 1970's share of GNP . . . would reduce outlays by 4 percent of GNP or $160 billion at the 1984 level, enough to eliminate the entire deficit" (p. 256).

Feldstein also warns against increasing taxes, even in the face of large deficits. Low taxes are necessary incentives for saving and investment, on which the health of the economy depends. Says Feldstein, " . . . the legitimate fear of a permanent deficit cannot justify a reversal of the 1981 tax cuts or a permanent increase in taxes from other sources" (p. 257).

Alice Rivlin looks to a combination of spending cuts and tax increases to reduce the deficit.

For domestic spending cuts, she proposes a two-step process. Freeze domestic spending for one year, and then scale back projected expenditures for social security, medicare, government retirement benefits, and agriculture.

Rivlin also points to defense cuts that can be made without endangering national security. For example, she says, "Several big ticket weapons systems—including the MX missile, the B1B bomber, the Army's AH-64 attack helicopter, and the Navy's F-15 fighter aircraft—largely duplicate the capabilities of other systems. Trimming such redundancy could save about $23 billion in fiscal year 1985, and more in subsequent years" (p. 264).

According to Rivlin, budget cutting is not enough. Taxes must also be raised. "To bring the budget into approximate balance by 1989 would require substantial additions to revenues . . . a revenue increase of about $100 billion would be required to close the remaining budgetary gap" (p. 264). Rivlin recommends increases in both tax rates and the tax base as means of raising more government revenues.

Stuart Butler recommends a rather different path for reaching a balanced budget. He proposes that government reduce its spending by turning over many of its programs to the private sector.

Butler argues that his strategy to reduce spending is eminently workable, because it employs the same political incentives that cause expenditures to increase in the first place. His plan merely reverses these incentives, getting them to work in the opposite direction.

Government programs increase because of what Butler calls a "federal ratchet." Government programs usually begin modestly, with relatively small expenditures allocated to them. But once a program is under way, interest groups coalesce to urge expansion of the program. The members of these groups include the recipients of government expenditures, the near recipients (i.e., those who almost qualify for funds, and would qualify with a minor change in the law), the program's administrators, and its public and/or private suppliers. These groups have much to gain by an expansion of government expenditure and concentrate their efforts on obtaining more money. The taxpayer, who will foot the bill, has little to lose on any one program, and so will not oppose the special interests with the required force. The result is a ratchet, which forces government spending to climb.

Butler proposes to reverse the "federal ratchet" by turning government programs over to private initiatives where appropriate. He says, "The privatization strategy recognizes the existence of the Federal spending ratchet and seeks to replace it with a private ratchet. Instead of trying to win an unwinnable war of attrition on the budget, privatization calls for the government to become a 'facilitator,' rather than a provider, of goods and services for society" (p. 268).

As Butler sees it, the key to achieving privatization lies in "the conscious creation of coalitions of beneficiaries, providers, and administrators to press for an expanded private-sector role in delivering services, just as the public-sector coalitions now lobby for increased Federal spending" (p. 269).

Butler uses Social Security to illustrate the federal ratchet and IRA's to illustrate the private ratchet. He writes, "Enacted in 1935 to provide a modest supplementary retirement income, Social Security has mushroomed into an enormous program that includes disability income, hospital insurance, spousal benefits, and even allowances for students" (p. 269).

In 1981 Congress passed legislation permitting Americans to open tax-deductible Individual Retirement Accounts. As a result, says Butler, "Congress planted the seeds of a private Social Security alternative. It was not long before the political dynamics of privatization began to be felt. Even before the new law went into effect, banks and other financial institutions began a massive campaign to encourage the public to open IRA's. The privatization coalition was born" (p. 269).

Butler sees similar possibilities for coalitions in transportation, waste disposal, and community services for the poor.

Peter Boettke and Jerome Ellig also see the deficit as primarily an expenditure problem, and expand on Butler's privatization as a solution.

Boettke and Ellig use the historical record to argue that deficits are not reduced through tax increases. They write, "Since 1969, the last year in which a budget surplus occurred, the trends in federal receipts, expenditures, and deficits have all moved in the same direction—up" (p. 278). To reduce expenditures, they recommend taking away the privileged monopoly position of government in providing services. "If America is to reap the full benefits of privatization," write Boettke and Ellig, "government services should be thrown open to competition from the private sector. To the extent that profit-seeking entrepreneurs and nonprofit organizations find ways to provide them, the government will be relieved of additional financial burdens" (p. 274).

Boettke and Ellig discuss at some length one industry they think should be opened to competition—banking. They want to remove the government's monopoly issue of currency, and institute a system of competitive currency supply, a system known as free banking. Although such a system might seem unworkable at first glance, recent theoretical research shows that it is quite feasible, and Boettke and Ellig point to the historical system of Scotland. For 150 years, Scotland operated without a government bank, and all private banks were free to issue their own currency. The result was a stable monetary system, free from the booms, busts, bank failures, and inflation of government monetary regimes.

Boettke and Ellig believe that "restoration of private note issue combined with elimination of the Fed's money-creation power would insulate the money supply from capricious government manipulation while still providing an elastic supply of currency" (p. 284).

William Orzechowski and *Cesar Conda* describe the workings of the budget process and discuss some of the organizations in Washington that are working against large deficits.

Orzechowski and Conda place a large part of the blame for deficits on the Congressional Budget and Impoundment Control Act of 1974. The intent of the Act was to increase overall budget planning by Congress; the result has been congressional budget resolutions that have understated actual expenditures by an average of $28 billion per year over the past five years.

Orzechowski and Conda list several reasons why Congress does not stay within its budget resolutions. Projected expenditures are deliberately understated; the costs of mandatory programs are intentionally underestimated; Congress passes low-priority budget items first, knowing that political pressure will enable them to later overspend projections when high-priority programs are considered.

Public disapproval of large expenditures and deficits is beginning to show effects in Washington. A number of interest groups opposed to federal budget policies are forming, and while their numbers are still small, they are nevertheless growing.

Among the groups listed by Orzechowski and Conda are the U.S. Chamber of Commerce, National Association of Manufacturers, National Taxpayers Union, National Tax Limitation Committee, Citizens for a Sound Economy, Heritage Foundation, and the Cato Institute. These groups support several measures designed to reduce the deficit, including a balanced budget, tax limitation, a line-item veto, and various privatization projects.

Although these antideficit groups have not yet succeeded in reducing government expenditures and debt, they have had some legislative victories. Perhaps the most notable is their influence in the passage of Senate Joint Resolution 58, which limited taxes and spending, and passed the Senate with a two-thirds majority in 1982. These groups are also gaining allies and sponsors in Congress. Robert Dole and Phil Gramm in the Senate and Larry Craig and Richard Armey in the House are among the members of Congress fighting deficits and expenditures.

The success of these Washington interest groups will depend on their leadership and the support they receive from businesses and private citizens. The interest groups fighting public expenditures are substantially outnumbered by the interest groups seeking to increase them. According to Orzechowski and Conda, there are about 2,000 interest groups in Washington today, an increase of 135 percent since 1975. Lobbying for and obtaining government expenditure is obviously a healthy industry. The battle to control expenditures and deficits in the years ahead will be strongly contested.

Chapter 1: THE CLASSICAL MASTERS

In this chapter from the Wealth of Nations, *Smith presents the classical principles of public finance: a government is responsible for running its financial affairs with the same prudence an individual takes in running his own financial affairs. Budget deficits are to be avoided except in time of war or other emergency.*

OF PUBLIC DEBTS
Adam Smith

In that rude state of society which precedes the extension of commerce and the improvement of manufactures, when those expensive luxuries which commerce and manufactures can alone introduce, are altogether unknown, the person who possesses a large revenue, I have endeavoured to show in the third book of this Inquiry,[1] can spend or enjoy that revenue in no other way than by maintaining nearly as many people as it can maintain. A large revenue may at all times be said to consist in the command of a large quantity of the necessaries of life. In that rude state of things it is commonly paid in a large quantity of those necessaries, in the materials of plain food and coarse clothing, in corn and cattle, in wool and raw hides. When neither commerce nor manufactures furnish any thing for which the owner can exchange the greater part of those materials which are over and above his own consumption, he can do nothing with the surplus but feed and clothe nearly as many people as it will feed and clothe. A hospitality in which there is no luxury, and a liberality in which there is no ostentation, occasion, in this situation of things, the principal expences of the rich and the great. But these, I have likewise endeavoured to show in the same book,[2] are expences by which people are not very apt to ruin themselves. There is not, perhaps, any selfish pleasure so frivolous, of which the pursuit has not sometimes ruined even sensible men. A passion for cock-fighting has ruined many. But the instances, I believe, are not very numerous of people who have been ruined by a hospitality or liberality of this kind; though the hospitality of luxury and the liberality of ostentation have ruined many. Among our feudal ancestors, the long time during which estates used to continue in the same family, sufficiently demonstrates the general disposition of people to live within their income. Though the rustic hospitality, constantly exercised by the great land-holders, may not, to us in the present times, seem

Reprinted with permission of the publisher from *An Inquiry Into the Nature and Causes of the Wealth of Nations*. Edwin Canaan, Ed. Chicago: University of Chicago Press, 1976, pp. 441–86.

consistent with that order, which we are apt to consider as inseparably connected with good economy, yet we must certainly allow them to have been at least so far frugal as not commonly to have spent their whole income. A part of their wool and raw hides they had generally an opportunity of selling for money. Some part of this money, perhaps, they spent in purchasing the few objects of vanity and luxury, with which the circumstances of the times could furnish them; but some part of it they seem commonly to have hoarded. They could not well indeed do anything else but hoard whatever money they saved. To trade was disgraceful to a gentleman, and to lend money at interest, which at that time was considered as usury and prohibited by law, would have been still more so. In those times of violence and disorder, besides, it was convenient to have a hoard of money at hand, that in case they should be driven from their own home, they might have something of known value to carry with them to some place of safety. The same violence, which made it convenient to hoard, made it equally convenient to conceal the hoard. The frequency of treasure-trove, or of treasure found of which no owner was known, sufficiently demonstrates the frequency in those times both of hoarding and of concealing the hoard. Treasure-trove was then considered as an important branch of the revenue of the sovereign.[3] All the treasure-trove of the kingdom would scarce perhaps in the present times make an important branch of the revenue of a private gentleman of a good estate.

The same disposition to save and to hoard prevailed in the sovereign, as well as in the subjects. Among nations to whom commerce and manufactures are little known, the sovereign, it has already been observed in the fourth book,[4] is in a situation which naturally disposes him to the parsimony requisite for accumulation. In that situation the expence even of a sovereign cannot be directed by that vanity which delights in the gaudy finery of a court. The ignorance of the times affords but few of the trinkets in which that finery consists. Standing armies are not then necessary, so that the expence even of a sovereign, like that of any other great lord, can be employed in scarce any thing but bounty to his tenants, and hospitality to his retainers. But bounty and hospitality very seldom lead to extravagance; though vanity almost always does.[5] All the ancient sovereigns of Europe accordingly, it has already been observed, had treasures. Every Tartar chief in the present times is said to have one.

In a commercial country abounding with every sort of expensive luxury, the sovereign, in the same manner as almost all the great proprietors in his dominions, naturally spends a great part of his revenue in purchasing those luxuries. His own and the neighbouring countries supply him abundantly with all the costly trinkets which compose the splendid, but insignificant pageantry of a court. For the sake of an inferior pageantry of the same kind, his nobles dismiss their retainers, make their tenants independent, and become gradually themselves as insignificant as the greater part of the wealthy burghers in his dominions. The same frivolous passions, which influence their conduct, influence his. How can it be supposed that he should be the only rich man in his dominions who is insensible to pleasures of this kind? If he does not, what he is very likely to do, spend upon those pleasures so great a part of his revenue as to debilitate very much the defensive power of the state, it cannot well be expected that he should not spend upon them all that part of it which is over and above what is necessary for supporting that defensive power. His ordinary expence becomes equal to his ordinary revenue, and it is well if it does not frequently exceed it. The amassing of treasure can no longer be expected, and when extraordinary exigencies require extraordinary expences, he must necessarily call upon his subjects for an extraordinary aid. The present and the late king of Prussia are the only great princes of Europe, who, since the death of Henry IV of France in 1610, are supposed to have amassed any considerable treasure.[6] The parsimony which leads to accumulation has become almost as rare in republican as in monarchical governments. The Italian republics, the United Provinces of the Netherlands, are all in debt. The canton of Berne is the single republic in Europe which has amassed any considerable treasure.[7] The other Swiss republics have not. The taste for some sort of pageantry, for splendid buildings, at least, and other public ornaments, frequently prevails as much in the apparently sober senate-house of a little republic, as in the dissipated court of the greatest king.

The want of parsimony in time of peace, imposes the necessity of contracting debt in time of war. When war comes, there is no money in the treasury but what is necessary for carrying on the ordinary expence of the peace establishment. In war an establishment of three or four times that expence becomes necessary for the defence of the state, and consequently a revenue three or four times greater than the peace revenue. Supposing that the sovereign should have, what he scarce ever has, the immediate means of augmenting his revenue in proportion to the augmentation of his expence, yet still the produce of the taxes, from which this increase of revenue must be drawn, will not begin to come into the treasury till perhaps ten or twelve months after they are imposed. But the moment in which war begins, or rather the moment in which it appears likely to begin, the army must be augmented, the fleet must be fitted out, the garrisoned towns must be put into a posture of defence; that army, that fleet, those garrisoned towns must be furnished with arms, ammunition, and provisions. An immediate and great expence must be incurred in that moment of immediate danger, which will not wait for the gradual and slow returns of the new taxes. In this exigency government can have no other resource but in borrowing.

The same commercial state of society which, by the operation of moral causes, brings government in this manner into the necessity of borrowing, produces in the subjects both an ability and an inclination to lend. If it commonly brings along with it the necessity of borrowing, it likewise brings along[8] with it the facility of doing so.

A country abounding with merchants and manufacturers, necessarily abounds with a set of people through whose hands not only their own capitals, but the capitals of all those who either lend them money, or trust them with goods, pass as frequently, or more frequently, than the revenue of a private man, who, without trade or business, lives upon his income, passes through his hands. The revenue of such a man can regularly pass through his hands only once in a year. But the whole amount of the capital and credit of a merchant, who deals in a trade of which the returns are very quick, may sometimes pass through his hands two, three, or four times in a year. A country abounding with merchants and manufacturers, therefore, necessarily abounds with a set of people who have it at all times in their power to advance, if they chuse to do so, a very large sum of money to government. Hence the ability in the subjects of a commercial state to lend.

Commerce and manufactures can seldom flourish long in any state which does not enjoy a regular administration of justice, in which the people do not feel themselves secure in the possession of their property, in which the faith of contracts is not supported by law, and in which the authority of the state is not supposed to be regularly employed in enforcing the payment of debts from all those who are able to pay. Commerce and manufactures, in short, can seldom flourish in any state in which there is not a certain degree of confidence in the justice of government. The same confidence which disposes great merchants and manufacturers, upon ordinary occasions, to trust their property to the protection of a particular government; disposes them, upon extraordinary occasions, to trust that government with the use of their property. By lending money to government, they do not even for a moment diminish their ability to carry on their trade and manufactures. On the contrary, they commonly augment it. The necessities of the state render government upon most occasions willing to borrow upon terms extremely advantageous to the lender. The security which it grants to the original creditor, is made transferable to any other creditor, and, from the universal confidence in the justice of the state, generally sells in the market for more than was originally paid for it. The merchant or monied man makes money by lending money to government, and instead of diminishing, increases his trading capital. He generally considers it as a favour, therefore, when the administration admits him to a share in the first subscription for a new loan. Hence the inclination or willingness in the subjects of a commercial state to lend.

The government of such a state is very apt to repose itself upon this ability and willingness of its subjects to lend it their money on extraordinary occasions. It foresees the facility of borrowing, and therefore dispenses itself from the duty of saving.

In a rude state of society there are no great mercantile or manufacturing capitals. The individuals, who hoard whatever money they can save, and who conceal their hoard, do so from a distrust of the justice of government, from a fear that if it was known that they had a hoard, and where that hoard was to be found, they would quickly be plundered. In such a state of things few people would be able, and nobody would be willing, to lend their money to government on extraordinary exigencies. The sovereign feels that he must provide for such exigencies by saving, because he foresees the absolute impossibility of borrowing. This foresight increases still further his natural disposition to save.

The progress of the enormous debts which at present oppress, and will in the long-run probably ruin, all the great nations of Europe, has been pretty uniform. Nations, like private men, have generally begun to borrow upon what may be called personal credit, without assigning or mortgaging any particular fund for the payment of the debt; and when this resource has failed them, they have gone on to borrow upon assignments or mortgages of particular funds.

What is called the unfunded debt of Great Britain, is contracted in the former of those two ways. It consists partly in a debt which bears, or is supposed to bear, no interest, and which resembles the debts that a private man contracts upon account; and partly in a debt which bears interest, and which resembles what a private man contracts upon his bill or promissory note. The debts which are due either for extraordinary services, or for services either not provided for, or not paid at the time when they are performed; part of the extraordinaries of the army, navy, and ordnance, the arrears of subsidies to foreign princes, those of seamen's wages, &c. usually constitute a debt of the first kind. Navy and Exchequer bills, which are issued sometimes in payment of a part of such debts and sometimes for other purposes, constitute a debt of the second kind; Exchequer bills bearing interest from the day on which they are issued, and navy bills six months after they are issued. The bank of England, either by voluntarily discounting those bills at their current value, or by agreeing with government for certain considerations to circulate Exchequer bills, that is, to receive them at par, paying the interest which happens to be due upon them, keeps up their value and facilitates their circulation, and thereby frequently enables government to contract a very large debt of this kind. In France, where there is no bank, the state bills (billets d'état[9]) have sometimes sold at sixty and seventy per cent. discount. During the great recoinage in King William's time, when the bank of England thought proper to put a stop to its usual transactions, Exchequer bills and tallies are said to have sold from twenty-five to sixty per cent. discount;[10] owing partly, no doubt, to the supposed instability of the new government established by the Revolution, but partly too to the want of the support of the bank of England.

When this resource is exhausted, and it becomes necessary, in order to raise money, to assign or mortgage some particular branch of the public revenue for the payment of the debt, government has upon different occasions done this in two different ways. Sometimes it has made this assignment or mortgage for a short period of time only, a year, or a few years, for example; and sometimes for perpetuity. In the one case, the fund was supposed sufficient to pay, within the limited time, both principal and interest of the money borrowed. In the other, it was supposed sufficient to pay the interest only, or a perpetual annuity equivalent to the interest, government being at liberty to redeem at any time this annuity, upon paying back the principal sum borrowed. When money was raised in the one way, it was said to be raised by anticipation; when in the other, by perpetual funding, or, more shortly, by funding.

In Great Britain the annual land and malt taxes are regularly anticipated every year, by virtue of a borrowing clause constantly inserted into the acts which impose them. The bank of England generally advances at an interest, which since the Revolution has varied from eight to three per cent. the sums for which those taxes are granted, and receives payment as their produce gradually comes in. If there is a deficiency, which there always is, it is provided for in the supplies of the ensuing year. The only considerable branch of the public revenue which yet remains unmortgaged is thus regularly spent before it comes in. Like an improvident[11] spendthrift, whose pressing occasions will not allow him to wait for the regular payment of his revenue, the state is in the constant practice of borrowing of its own factors and agents, and of paying interest for the use of its own money.

In the reign of king William, and during a great part of that of queen Anne, before we had become so familiar as we are now with the practice of perpetual funding, the greater part of the new taxes were imposed but for a short period of time (for four, five, six, or seven years only), and a great part of the grants of every year consisted in loans upon anticipations of the produce of those taxes. The produce being frequently insufficient for paying within the limited term the principal and interest of the money borrowed, deficiencies arose, to make good which it became necessary to prolong the term.

In 1697, by the 8th of William III.c.20. the deficiencies of several taxes were charged upon what was then called the first general mortgage or fund, consisting of a prolongation to the first of August, 1706, of several different taxes, which would have expired within a shorter term, and of which the produce was accumulated into one general fund. The deficiencies charged upon this prolonged term amounted to 5,160,459 1. 14s. 9-1/4d.[12]

In 1701, those duties, with some others, were still further prolonged for the like purposes till the first of August, 1710, and were called the second general mortgage or fund.[13] The deficiencies charged upon it amounted to 2,055,999 1. 7s. 11-1/2d.

In 1707, those duties were still further prolonged, as a fund for new loans, to the first of August, 1712, and were called the third general mortgage or fund. The sum borrowed upon it was 983,254 1. 11s. 9-1/4d.

In 1708, those duties were all (except the old subsidy of tonnage and poundage, of which one moiety only was made a part of this fund, and a duty upon the importation of Scotch linen, which had been taken off by the articles of union) still further continued, as a fund for new loans, to the first of August, 1714, and were called the fourth general mortgage or fund.[14] The sum borrowed upon it was 925,176 1. 9s. 2-1/4d.[15]

In 1709, those duties were all (except the old subsidy of tonnage and poundage, which was now left out of this fund altogether) still further continued for the same purpose to the first of August, 1716 and were called the fifth general mortgage or fund.[16] The sum borrowed upon it was 922,029 1. 6s. 0d.

In 1710, those duties were again prolonged to the first of August, 1720, and were called the sixth general mortgage or fund.[17] The sum borrowed upon it was 1,296,552 1. 9s. 11-3/4d.

In 1711, the same duties (which at this time were thus subject to four different anticipations), together with several others, were continued for ever, and made a fund for paying the interest of the capital of the South Sea company, which had that year advanced to government, for paying debts and making good deficiencies, the sum of 9,177,967 1. 15s. 4d.;[18] the greatest loan which at that time had ever been made.

Before this period, the principal, so far as I have been able to observe, the only taxes which in order to pay the interest of a debt had been imposed for perpetuity, were those for paying the interest of the money which had been advanced to government by the Bank and East India Company, and of what it was expected would be advanced, but which was never advanced, by a projected land bank. The bank fund at this time amounted to 3,375,027 l. 17s. 10-1/2d. for which was paid an annuity or interest of 206,501 l. 13s. 5d.[19] The East India fund amounted to 3,200,000 l. for which was paid an annuity or interest of 160,000 l;[20] the bank fund being at six per cent.,[21] the East India fund at five per cent. interest.

In 1715, by the first of George I. c. 12. the different taxes which had been mortgaged for paying the bank annuity, together with several others which by this act were likewise rendered perpetual, were accumulated into one common fund called The Aggregate Fund, which was charged, not only with the payments[22] of the bank annuity, but with several other annuities and burdens of different kinds. This fund was afterwards augmented by the third of George I. c. 8. and by the fifth of George I. c. 3. and the different duties which were then added to it were likewise rendered perpetual.[23]

In 1717, by the third of George I. c. 7.[24] several other taxes were rendered perpetual, and accumulated into another common fund, called The General Fund, for the payment of certain annuities, amounting in the whole to 724,849 l. 6s. 10-1/2d.

In consequence of those different acts, the greater part of the taxes which before had been anticipated only for a short term of years, were rendered perpetual as a fund for paying, not the capital, but the interest only, of the money which had been borrowed upon them by different successive anticipations.

Had money never been raised but by anticipation, the course of a few years would have liberated the public revenue, without any other attention of government besides that of not overloading the fund by charging it with more debt than it could pay within the limited term, and of not anticipating a second time before the expiration of the first anticipation. But the greater part of European governments have been incapable of those attentions. They have frequently overloaded the fund even upon the first anticipation; and when this happened not to be the case, they have generally taken care to overload it, by anticipating a second and a third time before the expiration of the first anticipation. The fund becoming in this manner altogether insufficient for paying both principal and interest of the money borrowed upon it, it became necessary to charge it with the interest only, or a perpetual annuity equal to the interest, and such unprovident anticipations necessarily gave birth to the more ruinous practice of perpetual funding. But though this practice necessarily puts off the liberation of the public revenue from a fixed period to one so indefinite that it is not very likely ever to arrive, yet as a greater sum can in all cases be raised by this new practice than by the old one of anticipations, the former, when men have once become familiar with it, has in the great exigencies of the state been universally preferred to the latter. To relieve the present exigency is always the object which principally interests those immediately concerned in the administration of public affairs. The future liberation of the public revenue, they leave to the care of posterity.

During the reign of queen Anne, the market rate of interest had fallen from six to five per cent., and in the twelfth year of her reign five per cent. was declared to be the highest rate which could lawfully be taken for money borrowed upon private security.[25] Soon after the greater part of the temporary taxes of Great Britain had been rendered perpetual, and distributed into the Aggregate, South Sea, and General Funds, the creditors of the public, like those of private persons, were induced to accept of five per cent. for the interest of their money,[26] which occasioned a saving of one per cent. upon the capital of the greater part of the debts which had been thus funded for perpetuity, or of one-sixth of the greater part of the annuities which were paid out of the three great funds above mentioned. This saving left a considerable surplus in the produce of the different taxes which had been accumulated into those funds, over and above what was necessary for paying the annuities which were now charged upon them, and laid the foundation of what has since been called the Sinking Fund. In 1717, it amounted to 323,434 l. 7s. 7-1/2d.[27] In 1727, the interest of the greater part of the public debts was still further reduced to four per cent.;[28] and in 1753[29] and 1757, to three and a half and three per cent.; which reductions still further augmented the sinking fund.

A sinking fund, though instituted for the payment of old, facilitates very much the contracting of new debts. It is a subsidiary fund always at hand to be mortgaged in aid of any other doubtful fund, upon which money is proposed to be raised in any exigency of the state. Whether the sinking fund of Great Britain has been more frequently applied to the one or to the other of those two purposes, will sufficiently appear by and by.

Besides those two methods of borrowing, by anticipations and by perpetual funding, there are two other methods, which hold a sort of middle place between them. These are, that of borrowing upon annuities for terms of years, and that of borrowing upon annuities for lives.

During the reigns of king William and queen Anne, large sums were frequently borrowed upon annuities for terms of years, which were sometimes longer and sometimes shorter. In 1693, an act was passed for borrowing one million upon an annuity of fourteen per cent.,[30] or of 140,000 l. a year, for sixteen years. In 1691, an act was passed for borrowing a million upon annuities for lives, upon terms which in the present times would appear very advantageous. But the subscription was not filled up. In the following year[31] the deficiency was made good by borrowing upon annuities for lives at fourteen per cent., or at little more than seven years purchase. In 1695, the persons who had purchased those annuities were allowed to exchange them for others of ninety-six years, upon paying into the Exchequer sixty-three pounds in the hundred; that is, the difference between fourteen per cent. for life, and fourteen per cent. for ninety-six years, was sold for sixty-three pounds, or for four and a half years purchase. Such was the supposed instability of government, that even these terms procured few purchasers. In the reign of queen Anne, money was upon different occasions borrowed both upon annuities for lives, and upon annuities for terms of thirty-two, of eighty-nine, of ninety-eight, and of ninety-nine years. In 1719, the proprietors of the annuities for thirty-two years were induced to accept in lieu of them South Sea stock to the amount of eleven and a half years purchase of the annuities, together with an additional quantity of stock equal to the arrears which happened then to be due upon them.[32] In 1720, the greater part of the other annuities for terms of years both long and short were subscribed into the same fund. The long annuities at that time amounted to 666,821 l. 8s. 3-1/2d. a year.[33] On the 5th of January, 1775, the remainder of them, or what was not subscribed at that time, amounted only to 136,453l. 12s. 8d.

During the two wars which begun in 1739 and in 1755, little money was borrowed either upon annuities for terms of years, or upon those for lives. An annuity for ninety-eight or ninety-nine years, however, is worth nearly as much money as a perpetuity, and should, therefore, one might think, be a fund for borrowing nearly as much. But those who, in order to make family settlements, and to provide for remote futurity, buy into the public stocks, would not care to purchase into one of which the value was continually diminishing; and such people make a very considerable proportion both of the proprietors and purchasers of stock.

An annuity for a long term of years, therefore, though its intrinsic value may be very nearly the same with that of a perpetual annuity, will not find nearly the same number of purchasers. The subscribers to a new loan, who mean generally to sell their subscription as soon as possible, prefer greatly a perpetual annuity redeemable by parliament, to an irredeemable annuity for a long term of years of only equal amount. The value of the former may be supposed always the same, or very nearly the same; and it makes, therefore, a more convenient transferable stock than the latter.

During the two last mentioned wars, annuities, either for terms of years or for lives, were seldom granted but as premiums to the subscribers to a new loan, over and above the redeemable annuity or interest upon the credit of which the loan was supposed to be made. They were granted, not as the proper fund upon which the money was borrowed; but as an additional encouragement to the lender.

Annuities for lives have occasionally been granted in two different ways; either upon separate lives, or upon lots of lives, which in French are called Tontines, from the name of their inventor. When annuities are granted upon separate lives, the death of every individual annuitant disburthens the public revenue so far as it was affected by his annuity. When annuities are granted upon tontines, the liberation of the public revenue does not commence till the death of all the annuitants comprehended in one lot, which may sometimes consist of twenty or thirty persons, of whom the survivors succeed to the annuities of all those who die before them; the last survivor succeeding to the annuities of the whole lot. Upon the same revenue more money can always be raised by tontines than by annuities for separate lives. An annuity, with a right of survivorship, is really worth more than an equal annuity for a separate life, and from the confidence which every man naturally has in his own good fortune, the principle upon which is founded the success of all lotteries, such an annuity generally sells for something more than it is worth. In countries where it is usual for government to raise money by granting annuities, tontines are upon this account generally preferred to annuities for separate lives. The expedient which will raise most money, is almost always preferred to that which is likely to bring about in the speediest manner the liberation of the public revenue.

In France, a much greater proportion of the public debts consists in annuities for lives than in England. According to a memoir presented by the parliament of Bourdeaux to the king in 1764, the whole public debt of France is estimated at twenty-four hundred millions of livres; of which the capital for which annuities for lives had been granted, is supposed to amount to three hundred millions, the eighth part of the whole public debt. The annuities themselves are computed to amount to thirty millions a year, the fourth part of one hundred and twenty millions, the supposed interest of that whole debt. These estimations, I know very well, are not exact, but having been presented by so very respectable a body as approximations to the truth, they may, I apprehend, be considered as such. It is not the different degrees of anxiety in the two governments of France and England for the liberation of the public revenue, which occasions this difference in their respective modes of borrowing. It arises altogether from the different views and interests of the lenders.

In England, the seat of government being in the greatest mercantile city in the world, the merchants are generally the people who advance money to government. By advancing it they do not mean to diminish, but, on the contrary, to increase their mercantile capitals; and unless they expected to sell with some profit their share in the subscription for a new loan, they never would subscribe. But if by advancing their money they were to purchase, instead of perpetual annuities, annuities for lives only, whether their own or those of other people, they would not always be so likely to sell them with a profit. Annuities upon their own lives they would always sell with loss; because no man will give for an annuity upon the life of another, whose age and state of health are nearly the same with his own, the same price which he would give for one upon his own. An annuity upon the life of a third person, indeed, is, no doubt, of equal value to the buyer and the seller; but its real value begins to diminish from the moment it is granted, and continues to do so more and more as long as it subsists. It can never, therefore, make so convenient a transferable stock as a perpetual annuity, of which the real value may be supposed always the same, or very nearly the same.

In France the seat of government not being in a great mercantile city, merchants do not make so great a proportion of the people who advance money to government. The people concerned in the finances, the farmers general, the receivers of the taxes which are not in farm, the court bankers, &c. make the greater part of those who advanced their money in all public exigencies. Such people are commonly men of mean birth, but of great wealth, and frequently of great pride. They are too proud to marry their equals, and women of quality disdain to marry them. They frequently resolve, therefore, to live bachelors, and having neither any families of their own, nor much regard for those of their relations, whom they are not always very fond of acknowledging, they desire only to live in splendour during their own time, and are not unwilling that their fortune should end with themselves. The number of rich people, besides, who are either averse to marry, or whose condition of life renders it either improper or inconvenient for them to do so, is much greater in France than in England. To such people, who have little or no care for posterity, nothing can be more convenient than to exchange their capital for a revenue, which is to last just as long,[34] and no longer than they wish it to do.

The ordinary expence of the greater part of modern governments in time of peace being equal or nearly equal to their ordinary revenue, when war comes, they are both unwilling and unable to increase their revenue in proportion to the increase of their expence. They are unwilling, for fear of offending the people, who by so great and so sudden an increase of taxes, would soon be disgusted with the war; and they are unable, from not well knowing what taxes would be sufficient to produce the revenue wanted. The facility of borrowing delivers them from the embarrassment which this fear and inability would otherwise occasion. By means of borrowing they are enabled, with a very moderate increase of taxes, to raise, from year to year, money sufficient for carrying on the war, and by the practice of perpetual funding they are enabled, with the smallest possible increase of taxes, to raise annually the largest possible sum of money. In great empires the people who live in the capital, and in the provinces remote from the scene of action, feel, many of them, scarce any inconveniency from the war; but enjoy, at their ease, the amusement of reading in the newspapers the exploits of their own fleets and armies. To them this amusement compensates the small difference between the taxes which they pay on account of the war, and those which they had been accustomed to pay in time of peace. They are commonly dissatisfied with the return of peace, which puts an end to their amusement, and to a thousand visionary hopes of conquest and national glory, from a longer continuance of the war.

The return of peace, indeed, seldom relieves them from the greater part of the taxes imposed during the war. These are mortgaged for the interest of the debt contracted in order to carry it on. If, over and above paying the interest of this debt, and defraying the ordinary expence of government, the old revenue, together with the new taxes, produce some surplus revenue, it may perhaps be converted into a sinking fund for paying off the debt. But, in the first place, this sinking fund, even supposing it should be applied to no other purpose, is generally altogether inadequate for paying, in the course of any period during which it can reasonably be expected that peace should continue, the whole debt contracted during the war; and, in the second place, this fund is almost always applied to other purposes.

The new taxes were imposed for the sole purpose of paying the interest of the money borrowed upon them. If they produce more, it is generally something which was neither intended nor expected, and is therefore seldom very considerable. Sinking funds have generally arisen, not so much from any surplus of the taxes which was over and above what was necessary for paying the interest or annuity originally charged upon them, as from a subsequent reduction of that interest. That of Holland in 1655, and that of the ecclesiastical state in 1685, were both formed in this manner.[35] Hence the usual insufficiency of such funds.

During the most profound peace, various events occur which require an extraordinary expence, and government finds it always more convenient to defray this expence by misapplying the sinking fund than by imposing a new tax. Every new tax is immediately felt more or less by the people. It occasions always some murmur, and meets with some opposition. The more taxes may have been multiplied, the higher they may have been raised upon every different subject of taxation; the more loudly the people complain of every new tax, the more difficult it becomes too either to find out new subjects of taxation, or to raise much higher the taxes already imposed upon the old. A momentary suspension of the payment of debt is not immediately felt by the people, and occasions neither murmur nor complaint. To borrow of the sinking fund is always an obvious and easy expedient for getting out of the present difficulty. The more the public debts may have been accumulated, the more necessary it may have become to study to reduce them, the more dangerous, the more ruinous it may be to misapply any part of the sinking fund; the less likely is the public debt to be reduced to any considerable degree, the more likely, the more certainly is the sinking fund to be misapplied towards defraying all the extraordinary expences which occur in time of peace. When a nation is already overburdened with taxes, nothing but the necessities of a new war, nothing but either the animosity of national vengeance, or the anxiety for national security, can induce the people to submit, with tolerable patience, to a new tax. Hence the usual misapplication of the sinking fund.

In Great Britain, from the time that we had first recourse to the ruinous expedient of perpetual funding, the reduction of the public debt in time of peace, has never borne any proportion to its accumulation in time of war. It was in the war which began in 1688, and was concluded by the treaty of Ryswick in 1697, that the foundation of the present enormous debt of Great Britain was first laid.

On the 31st of December 1697, the public debts of Great Britain, funded and unfunded, amounted to 21,515,742 1. 13s. 8-1/2d. A great part of those debts had been contracted upon short anticipations, and some part upon annuities for lives; so that before the 31st of December 1701, in less than four years, there had partly been paid off, and partly reverted to the public, the sum of 5,121,041 1. 12s. 0-3/4d. a greater reduction of the public debt than has ever since been brought about in so short a period of time. The remaining debt, therefore, amounted only to 16,394,701 1. 1s. 7-1/4d.

In the war which began in 1702, and which was concluded by the treaty of Utrecht, the public debts were still more accumulated. On the 31st of December 1714, they amounted to 53,681,076 1. 5s. 6-1/12d. The subscription into the South Sea fund of the short and long[36] annuities increased the capital of the public debts, so that on the 31st of December 1722, it amounted to 55,282,978 1. 1s. 3-5/6d. The reduction of the debt began in 1723, and went on so slowly that, on the 31st of December 1739, during seventeen years of profound peace, the whole sum paid off was no more than 8,328,354 1. 17s. 11-3/12d. the capital of the public debt at that time amounting to 46,954,623 1. 3s. 4-7/12d.

The Spanish war, which began in 1739, and the French war which soon followed it, occasioned a further increase of the debt, which, on the 31st of December 1748, after the war had been concluded by the treaty of Aix la Chapelle, amounted to 78,293,313 1. 1s. 10-3/4d. The most profound peace of seventeen years continuance had taken no more than 8,328,354 1. 17s. 11-3/12d. from it. A war of less than nine years continuance added 31,338,689 1. 18s. 6-1/6d. to it.[37]

During the administration of Mr. Pelham, the interest of the public debt was reduced, or at least measures were taken for reducing it, from four to three per cent.;[38] the sinking fund was increased, and some part of the public debt was paid off. In 1755, before the breaking out of the late war, the funded debt of Great Britain amounted to 72,289,673 1.[39] On the 5th of January 1763, at the conclusion of the peace, the funded debt amounted to 122,603,336 1. 8s. 2-1/4d.[40] The unfunded debt has been stated at 13,927,589 1. 2s. 2d. But the expence occasioned by the war did not end with the conclusion of the peace;[41] so that though, on the 5th of January 1764, the funded debt was increased (partly by a new loan, and partly by funding a part of the unfunded debt)[42] to 129,586,789 1. 10s. 1-3/4d.[43] there still remained (accordingly to the very well informed author of the Considerations on the Trade and Finances of Great Britain)[44] an unfunded debt which was brought to account in that and the following year, of 9,975,017 1. 12s. 2-15/44d. In 1764, therefore, the public debt in Great Britain, funded and unfunded together, amounted, according to this author, to 139,561,807 1. 2s. 4d.[45] The annuities for lives too, which had been granted as premiums to the subscribers to the new loans in 1757, estimated at fourteen years purchase, were valued at 472,500 1.; and the annuities for long terms of years, granted as premiums likewise, in 1761 and 1762, estimated at 27-1/2 years purchase, were valued at 6,826,875 1.[46] During a peace of about seven years continuance, the prudent and truly patriot administration of Mr. Pelham, was not able to pay off an old debt of six millions. During a war of nearly the same continuance, a new debt of more than seventy-five millions was contracted.

On the 5th of January 1775, the funded debt of Great Britain amounted to 124,996,086 1. 1s. 6-1/4d. The unfunded, exclusive of a large civil list debt, to 4,150,236 1. 3s. 11-7/8d. Both together, to 129,146,322 1. 5s. 6d. According to this account the whole debt paid off during eleven years profound peace amounted only to 10,415,474 1. 16s. 9-7/8d. Even this small reduction of debt, however, has not been all made from the savings out of the ordinary revenue of the state. Several extraneous sums, altogether independent of that ordinary revenue, have contributed towards it. Amongst[47] these we may reckon an additional shilling in the pound land tax for three years; the two millions received from the East India company, as indemnification for their territorial acquisitions; and the one hundred and ten thousand pounds received from the bank for the renewal of their charter. To these must be added several other sums which, as they arose out of the late war, ought perhaps to be considered as deductions from the expences of it. The principal are,

	1.	s.	d.
The produce of French prizes	690,449	18	9
Composition for French prisoners	670,000	0	0
What has been received from the sale of the ceded islands[48]	95,500	0	0
Total	1,455,949	18	9

If we add to this sum the balance of the earl of Chatham's and Mr. Calcraft's accounts, and other army savings of the same kind, together with what has been received from the bank, the East India company, and the additional shilling in the pound land tax; the whole must be a good deal more than five millions. The debt, therefore, which since the peace has been paid out of the savings from the ordinary revenue of the state, has not, one year with another, amounted to half a million a year. The sinking fund has, no doubt, been considerably augmented since the peace, by the debt which has been paid off, by the reduction of the redeemable four per cents. to three per cents., and by the annuities for lives which have fallen in, and, if peace were[49] to continue, a million, perhaps, might now be annually spared out of it towards the discharge of the debt. Another million, accordingly, was paid in the course of last year; but, at the same time, a large civil list debt was left unpaid, and we are now involved in a new war which, in its progress, may prove as expensive as any of our former wars.[50] The new debt which will probably be contracted before the end of the next campaign, may perhaps be nearly equal to all the old debt which has been paid off from the savings out of the ordinary revenue of the state. It would be altogether chimerical, therefore, to expect that the public debt should ever be completely discharged by any savings which are likely to be made from that ordinary revenue as it stands at present.

The public funds of the different indebted nations of Europe, particularly those of England, have by one author been represented as the accumulation of a great capital superadded to the other capital of the country, by means of which its trade is extended, its manufactures multiplied, and its lands cultivated and improved much beyond what they could have been by means of that other capital only.[51] He does not consider that the capital which the first creditors of the public advanced to government, was, from the moment in which they advanced it, a certain portion of the annual produce turned away from serving in the function of a capital, to serve in that of a revenue; from maintaining productive labourers to maintain unproductive ones, and to be spent and wasted, generally in the course of the year, without even the hope of any future reproduction. In return for the capital which they advanced they obtained, indeed, an annuity in the public funds in most cases of more than equal value. This annuity, no doubt, replaced to them their capital, and enabled them to carry on their trade and business to the same or perhaps to a greater extent than before; that is, they were enabled either to borrow of other people a new capital upon the credit of this annuity, or by selling it to get from other people a new capital of their own, equal or superior to that which they had advanced to government. This new capital, however, which they in this manner either bought or borrowed of other people, must have existed in the country before, and must have been employed as all capitals are, in maintaining productive labour. When it came into the hands of those who had advanced their money to government, though it was in some respects a new capital to them, it was not so to the country; but was only a capital withdrawn from certain employments in order to be turned towards others. Though it replaced to them what they had advanced to government, it did not replace it to the country. Had they not advanced this capital to government, there would have been in the country two capitals, two portions of the annual produce, instead of one, employed in maintaining productive labour.

When for defraying the expense of government a revenue is raised within the year from the produce of free or unmortgaged taxes, a certain portion of the revenue of private people is only turned away from maintaining one species of unproductive labour, towards maintaining another. Some part of what they pay in those taxes might no doubt have been accumulated into capital, and consequently employed in maintaining productive labour; but the greater part would probably have been spent and consequently employed in maintaining unproductive labour. The public expence, however, when defrayed in this manner, no doubt hinders more or less the further accumulation of new capital; but it does not necessarily occasion the destruction of any actually existing capital.

When the public expence is defrayed by funding, it is defrayed by the annual destruction of some capital which had before existed in the country; by the perversion of some portion of the annual produce which had before been destined for the maintenance of productive labour, towards that of unproductive labour. As in this case, however, the taxes are lighter than they would have been, had a revenue sufficient for defraying the same expence been raised within the year; the private revenue of individuals is necessarily less burdened, and consequently their ability to save and accumulate some part of that revenue into capital is a good deal less impaired. If the method of funding destroy[52] more old capital, it at the same time hinders less the accumulation or acquisition of new capital, than that of defraying the public expence by a revenue raised within the year. Under the system of funding, the frugality and industry of private people can more easily repair the breaches which the waste and extravagance of government may occasionally make in the general capital of the society.

It is only during the continuance of war, however, that the system of funding has this advantage over the other system. Were the expence of war to be defrayed always by a revenue raised within the year, the taxes from which that extraordinary revenue was drawn would last no longer than the year. The ability of private people to accumulate, though less during the war, would have been greater during the peace than under the system of funding. War would not necessarily have occasioned the destruction of any old capitals, and peace would have occasioned the accumulation of many more new. Wars would in general be more speedily concluded, and less wantonly undertaken. The people feeling, during the continuance of the war, the complete burden of it, would soon grow weary of it, and government, in order to humour them, would not be under the necessity of carrying it on longer than it was necessary to do so. The foresight of the heavy and unavoidable burdens of war would hinder the people from wantonly calling for it when there was no real or solid interest to fight for. The seasons during which the ability of private people to accumulate was somewhat impaired, would occur more rarely, and be of shorter continuance. Those on the contrary, during which that ability was in the highest vigour, would be of much longer duration than they can well be under the system of funding.

When funding, besides, has made a certain progress, the multiplication of taxes which it brings along with it sometimes impairs as much the ability of private people to accumulate even in time of peace, as the other system would in time of war. The peace revenue of Great Britain amounts at present to more than ten millions a year. If free and unmortgaged, it might be sufficient, with proper management and without contracting a shilling of new debt, to carry on the most vigorous war. The private revenue of the inhabitants of Great Britain is at present as much encumbered in time of peace, their ability to accumulate is[53] as much impaired as it would have been in the time of the most expensive war, had the pernicious system of funding never been adopted.

In the payment of the interest of the public debt, it has been said, it is the right hand which pays the left.[54] The money does not go out of the country. It is only a part of the revenue of one set of the inhabitants which is transferred to another; and the nation is not a farthing the poorer. This apology is founded altogether in the sophistry of the mercantile system, and after the long examination which I have already bestowed upon that system, it may perhaps be unnecessary to say any thing further about it. It supposes, besides, that the whole public debt is owing to the inhabitants of the country, which happens not to be true; the Dutch, as well as several other foreign nations, having a very considerable share in our public funds. But though the whole debt were owing to the inhabitants of the country, it would not upon that account be less pernicious.

Land and capital stock are the two original sources of all revenue both private and public. Capital stock pays the wages of productive labour, whether employed in agriculture, manufactures, or commerce. The management of those two original sources of revenue belongs to two different sets of people; the proprietors of land, and the owners or employers of capital stock.

The proprietor of land is interested for the sake of his own revenue to keep his estate in as good condition as he can, by building and repairing his tenants' houses, by making and maintaining the necessary drains and enclosures, and all those other expensive improvements which it properly belongs to the landlord to make and maintain. But by different land-taxes the revenue of the landlord may be so much diminished; and by different duties upon the necessaries and conveniences of life, that diminished revenue may be rendered of so little real value, that he may find himself altogether unable to make or maintain those expensive improvements. When the landlord, however, ceases to do his part, it is altogether impossible that the tenant should continue to do his. As the distress of the landlord increases, the agriculture of the country must necessarily decline.

When, by different taxes upon the necessaries and conveniences of life, the owners and employers of capital stock find, that whatever revenue they derive from it, will not, in a particular country, purchase the same quantity of those necessaries and conveniences which an equal revenue would in almost any other, they will be disposed to remove to some other. And when, in order to raise those taxes, all or the greater part of merchants and manufacturers, that is, all or the greater part of the employers of great capitals, come to be continually exposed to the mortifying and vexatious visits of the tax-gatherers, this disposition to remove will soon be changed into an actual removal. The industry of the country will necessarily fall with the removal of the capital which supported it, and the ruin of trade and manufactures will follow the declension of agriculture.

To transfer from the owners of those two great sources of revenue, land and capital stock, from the persons immediately interested in the good condition of every particular portion of land, and in the good management of every particular portion of capital stock, to another set of persons (the creditors of the public, who have no such particular interest), the greater part of the revenue arising from either, must, in the long-run, occasion both the neglect of land, and the waste or removal of capital stock. A creditor of the public has no doubt a general interest in the prosperity of the agriculture, manufactures, and commerce of the country; and consequently in the good condition of its lands, and in the good management of its capital stock. Should there be any general failure or declension in any of these things, the produce of the different taxes might no longer be sufficient to pay him the annuity or interest which is due to him. But a creditor of the public, considered merely as such, has no interest in the good condition of any particular portion of land, or in the good management of any particular portion of capital stock. As a creditor of the public he has no knowledge of any such particular portion. He has no inspection of it. He can have no care about it. Its ruin may in some[55] cases be unknown to him, and cannot directly affect him.

The practice of funding has gradually enfeebled every state which has adopted it. The Italian republics seem to have begun it. Genoa and Venice, the only two remaining which can pretend to an independent existence, have both been enfeebled by it. Spain seems to have learned the practice from the Italian republics, and (its taxes being probably less judicious than theirs) it has, in proportion to its natural strength, been still more enfeebled. The debts of Spain are of very old standing. It was deeply in debt before the end of the sixteenth century, about a hundred years before England owed a shilling. France, notwithstanding all its natural resources, languishes under an oppressive load of the same kind. The republic of the United Provinces is as much enfeebled by its debts as either Genoa or Venice. Is it likely that in Great Britain alone a practice, which has brought either weakness or desolation into every other country, should prove altogether innocent?

The system of taxation established in those different countries, it may be said, is inferior to that of England. I believe it is so. But it ought to be remembered, that when the wisest government has exhausted all the proper subjects of taxation, it must, in cases of urgent necessity, have recourse to improper ones.[56] The wise republic of Holland has upon some occasions been obliged to have recourse to taxes as inconvenient as the greater part of those of Spain. Another war begun before any considerable liberation of the public revenue had been brought about, and growing in its progress as expensive as the last war, may, from irresistible necessity, render the British system of taxation as oppressive as that of Holland, or even as that of Spain. To the honour of our present system of taxation, indeed, it has hitherto given so little embarrassment to industry, that, during the course even of the most expensive wars, the frugality and good conduct of individuals seem[57] to have been able, by saving and accumulation, to repair all the breaches which the waste and extravagance of government had made in the general capital of the society. At the conclusion of the late war, the most expensive that Great Britain ever waged, her agriculture was as flourishing, her manufacturers as numerous and as fully employed, and her commerce as extensive, as they had ever been before. The capital, therefore, which supported all those different branches of industry, must have been equal to what it had ever been before. Since the peace, agriculture has been still further improved, the rents of houses have risen in every town and village of the country, a proof of the increasing wealth and revenue of the people; and the annual amount of the greater part of the old taxes, of the principal branches of the excise and customs in particular, has been continually increasing, an equally clear proof of an increasing consumption, and consequently of an increasing produce, which could alone support that consumption. Great Britain seems to support with ease, a burden which, half a century ago, nobody believed her capable of supporting. Let us not, however, upon this account rashly conclude that she is capable of supporting any burden; nor even be too confident that she could support, without great distress, a burden a little greater than what has already been laid upon her.

When national debts have once been accumulated to a certain degree, there is scarce, I believe, a single instance of their having been fairly and completely paid. The liberation of the public revenue, if it has ever been brought about at all, has always been brought about by a bankruptcy; sometimes by an avowed one, but always by a real one, though frequently by a pretended payment.[58]

The raising of the denomination of the coin has been the most usual expedient by which a real public bankruptcy has been disguised under the appearance of a pretended payment. If a sixpence, for example, should either by act of parliament or royal proclamation be raised to the denomination of a shilling, and twenty sixpences to that of a pound sterling; the person who under the old denomination had borrowed twenty shillings, or near four ounces of silver, would, under the new, pay with twenty sixpences, or with something less than two ounces. A national debt of about a hundred and twenty-eight millions, nearly the capital of the funded and unfunded debt of Great Britain, might in this manner be paid with about sixty-four millions of our present money. It would indeed be a pretended payment only, and the creditors of the public would really be defrauded of ten shillings in the pound of what was due to them. The calamity too would extend much further than to the creditors of the public, and those of every private person would suffer a proportionable loss; and this without any advantage, but in most cases with a great additional loss, to the creditors of the public. If the creditors of the public indeed were generally much in debt to other people, they might in some measure compensate their loss by paying their creditors in the same coin in which the public had paid them. But in most countries the creditors of the public are, the greater part of them, wealthy people, who stand more in the relation of creditors than in that of debtors towards the rest of their fellow-citizens. A pretended payment of this kind, therefore, instead of alleviating, aggravates in most cases the loss of the creditors of the public; and without any advantage to the public, extends the calamity to a great number of other innocent people. It occasions a general and most pernicious subversion of the fortunes of private people; enriching in most cases the idle and profuse debtor at the expence of the industries and frugal creditor, and transporting a great part of the national capital from the hands which were likely to increase and improve it, to those which are likely to dissipate and destroy it. When it becomes necessary for a state to declare itself bankrupt, in the same manner as when it becomes necessary for an individual to do so, a fair, open, and avowed bankruptcy is always the measure which is both least dishonourable to the debtor, and least hurtful to the creditor. The honour of a state is surely very poorly provided for, when, in order to cover the disgrace of a real bankruptcy, it has recourse to a juggling trick of this kind, so easily seen through, and at the same time so extremely pernicious.

Almost all states, however, ancient as well as modern, when reduced to this necessity, have, upon some occasions, played this very juggling trick. The Romans, at the end of the first Punic war, reduced the As, the coin or denomination by which they computed the value of all their other coins, from containing twelve ounces of copper to contain only two ounces: that is, they raised two ounces' of copper to a denomination which had always before expressed the value of twelve ounces. The republic was, in this manner, enabled to pay the great debts which it had contracted with the sixth part of what it really owed. So sudden and so great a bankruptcy, we should in the present times be apt to imagine, must have occasioned a very violent popular clamour. It does not appear to have occasioned any. The law which enacted it was, like all other laws relating to the coin, introduced and carried through the assembly of the people by a tribune, and was probably a very popular law. In Rome, as in all the other ancient republics, the poor people were constantly in debt to the rich and the great, who, in order to secure their votes at the annual elections, used to lend them money at exorbitant interest, which, being never paid, soon accumulated into a sum too great either for the debtor to pay, or for any body else to pay for him. The debtor, for fear of a very severe execution, was obliged, without any further gratuity, to vote for the candidate whom the creditor recommended. In spite of all the laws against bribery and corruption, the bounty of the candidates, together with the occasional distributions of corn, which were ordered by the senate, were the principal funds from which, during the latter[59] times of the Roman republic, the poorer citizens derived their subsistence. To deliver themselves from this subjection to their creditors, the poorer citizens were continually calling out either for an entire abolition of debts, or for what they called New Tables; that is, for a law which should entitle them to a complete acquittance, upon paying only a certain proportion of their accumulated debts. The law which reduced the coin of all denominations to a sixth part of its former value, as it enabled them to pay their debts with a sixth part of what they really owed, was equivalent to the most advantageous new tables. In order to satisfy the people, the rich and the great were, upon several different occasions, obliged to consent to laws both for abolishing debts, and for introducing new tables; and they probably were induced to consent to this law, partly for the same reason, and partly that, by liberating the public revenue, they might restore vigour to that government of which they themselves had the principal direction. An operation of this kind would at once reduce a debt of a hundred and twenty-eight millions to twenty-one millions three hundred and thirty-three thousand three hundred and thirty-three pounds six shillings and eight pence. In the course of the second Punic war the As was still further reduced, first, from two ounces of copper to one ounce; and afterwards from one ounce to half an ounce; that is, to the twenty-fourth part of its original value.[60] By combining the three Roman operations into one, a debt of a hundred and twenty-eight millions of our present money, might in this manner be reduced all at once to a debt of five millions three hundred and thirty-three thousand three hundred and thirty-three pounds six shillings and eight-pence. Even the enormous debt of Great Britain might in this manner soon be paid.

By means of such expedients the coin of, I believe, all nations has been gradually reduced more and more below its original value, and the same nominal sum has been gradually brought to contain a smaller and a smaller quantity of silver.

Nations have sometimes, for the same purpose, adulterated the standard of their coin; that is, have mixed a greater quantity of alloy in it. If in the pound weight of our silver coin, for example, instead of eighteen penny-weight, according to the present standard, there was mixed eight ounces of alloy; a pound sterling, or twenty shillings of such coin, would be worth little more than six shillings and eight-pence of our present money. The quantity of silver contained in six shillings and eight-pence of our present money, would thus be raised very nearly to the denomination of a pound sterling. The adulteration of the standard has exactly the same effect with what the French call an augmentation, or a direct raising of the denomination of the coin.

An augmentation, or a direct raising of the denomination of the coin, always is, and from its nature must be, an open and avowed operation. By means of it pieces of a smaller weight and bulk are called by the same name which had before been given to pieces of a greater weight and bulk. The adulteration of the standard, on the contrary, has generally been a concealed operation. By means of it pieces were issued from the mint of the same denominations, and, as nearly as could be contrived, of the same weight, bulk, and appearance, with pieces which had been current before of much greater value. When king John of France,[61] in order to pay his debts, adulterated his coin, all the officers of his mint were sworn to secrecy. Both operations are unjust. But a simple augmentation is an injustice of open violence; whereas an adulteration is an injustice of treacherous fraud. This latter operation, therefore, as soon as it has been discovered, and it could never be concealed very long, has always excited much greater indignation that the former. The coin after any considerable augmentation has very seldom been brought back to its former weight; but after the greatest adulterations it has almost always been brought back to its former fineness. It has scarce ever happened that the fury and indignation of the people could otherwise be appeased.

In the end of the reign of Henry VIII. and in the beginning of that of Edward VI. the English coin was not only raised in its denomination, but adulterated in its standard. The like frauds were practised in Scotland during the minority of James VI. They have occasionally been practised in most other countries.

That the public revenue of Great Britain can ever[62] be completely liberated, or even that any considerable progress can ever be made towards that liberation, while the surplus of that revenue, or what is over and above defraying the annual expence of the peace establishment, is so very small, it seems altogether in vain to expect. That liberation, it is evident, can never be brought about without either some very considerable augmentation of the public revenue, or some equally considerable reduction of the public expence.

A more equal land tax, a more equal tax upon the rent of houses, and such alterations in the present system of customs and excise as those which have been mentioned in the foregoing chapter, might, perhaps, without increasing the burden of the greater part of the people, but only distributing the weight of it more equally upon the whole, produce a considerable augmentation of revenue. The most sanguine projector, however, could scarce flatter himself that any augment-ation of this kind would be such as could give any reasonable hopes, either of liberating the public revenue altogether, or even of making such progress towards that liberation in time of peace, as either to prevent or to compensate the further accumulation of the public debt in the next war.

By extending the British system of taxation to all the different provinces of the empire inhabited by people of either[63] British or European extraction, a much greater augmentation of revenue might be expected. This, however, could scarce, perhaps, be done, consistently with the principles of the British constitution, without admitting into the British parliament, or if you will into the states-general of the British empire, a fair and equal representation of all those different provinces, that of each province bearing the same proportion to the produce of its taxes, as the representation of Great Britain might bear to the produce of the taxes levied upon Great Britain. The private interest of many powerful individuals, the confirmed prejudices of great bodies of people seem, indeed, at present, to oppose to so great a change such obstacles as it may be very difficult, perhaps altogether impossible, to surmount. Without, however, pretending to determine whether such a union be practicable or impracticable, it may not, perhaps, be improper, in a speculative work of this kind, to consider how far the British system of taxation might be applicable to all the different provinces of the empire; what revenue might be expected from it if so applied, and in what manner a general union of this kind might be likely to affect the happiness and prosperity of the different provinces comprehended within it. Such a speculation can at worst be regarded but as a new Utopia, less amusing certainly, but not more useless and chimerical than the old one.

The land-tax, the stamp-duties, and the different duties of customs and excise, constitute the four principal branches of the British taxes.

Ireland is certainly as able, and our American and West Indian plantations more able to pay a land-tax than Great Britain. Where the landlord is subject neither to tithe nor poors rate, he must certainly be more able to pay such a tax, than where he is subject to both those other burdens. The tithe, where there is no modus, and where it is levied in kind, diminishes more what would otherwise be the rent of the landlord, than a land-tax which really amounted to five shillings in the pound. Such a tithe will be found in most cases to amount to more than a fourth part of the real rent of the land, or of what remains after replacing completely the capital of the farmer, together with his reasonable profit. If all moduses and all impropriations were taken away, the complete church tithe of Great Britain and Ireland could not well be estimated at less than six or seven millions. If there was no tithe either in Great Britain or Ireland, the landlords could afford to pay six or seven millions additional land-tax, without being more burdened than a very great part of them are at present. America pays no tithe, and could therefore very well afford to pay a land-tax. The lands in America and the West Indies, indeed, are in general not tenanted nor[64] leased out to farmers. They could not therefore be assessed according to any rent-roll. But neither were the lands of Great Britain, in the 4th of William and Mary, assessed according to any rent-roll, but according to a very loose and inaccurate estimation. The lands in America might be assessed either in the same manner, or according to an equitable valuation in consequence of an accurate survey, like that which was lately made in the Milanese, and in the dominions of Austria, Prussia, and Sardinia.[65]

Stamp-duties, it is evident, might be levied without any variation in all countries where the forms of law process, and the deeds by which property both real and personal is transferred, are the same or nearly the same.

The extension of the custom-house laws of Great Britain to Ireland and the plantations, provided it was accompanied, as in justice it ought to be, with an extension of the freedom of trade, would be in the highest degree advantageous to both. All the invidious restraints which at present oppress the trade of Ireland, the distinction between the enumerated and non-enumerated commodities of America, would be entirely at an end.[66] The countries north of Cape Finisterre would be as open to every part of the produce of America, as those south of that Cape are to some parts of that produce at present. The trade between all the different parts of the British empire would, in consequence of this uniformity in the custom-house laws, be as free as the coasting trade of Great Britain is at present. The British empire would thus afford within itself an immense internal market for every part of the produce of all its different provinces. So great an extension of market would soon compensate both to Ireland and the plantations, all that they could suffer from the increase of the duties of customs.

The excise is the only part of the British system of taxation, which would require to be varied in any respect according as it was applied to the different provinces of the empire. It might be applied to Ireland without any variation; the produce and consumption of that kingdom being exactly of the same nature with those of Great Britain. In its application to America and the West Indies, of which the produce and consumption are so very different from those of Great Britain, some modification might be necessary, in the same manner as in its application to the cyder and beer counties of England.

A fermented liquor, for example, which is called beer, but which, as it is made of melasses, bears very little resemblance to our beer, makes a considerable part of the common drink of the people in America. This liquor, as it can be kept only for a few days, cannot, like our beer, be prepared and stored up for sale in great breweries; but every private family must brew it for their own use, in the same manner as they cook their victuals. But to subject every private family to the odious visits and examination of the tax-gatherers, in the same manner as we subject the keepers of alehouses and the brewers for public sale, would be altogether inconsistent with liberty. If for the sake of equality it was thought necessary to lay a tax upon this liquor, it might be taxed by taxing the material of which it is made, either at the place of manufacture, or, if the circumstances of the trade rendered such an excise improper, by laying a duty upon its importation into the colony in which it was to be consumed. Besides the duty of one penny a gallon imposed by the British parliament upon the importation of melasses into America; there is a provincial tax of this kind upon their importation into Massachusets Bay, in ships belonging to any other colony, of eight-pence the hogshead; and another upon their importation, from the northern colonies, into South Carolina, of five-pence the gallon. Or if neither of these methods was found convenient, each family might compound for its consumption of this liquor, either according to the number of persons of which it consisted, in the same manner as private families compound for the malt-tax in England; or according to the different ages and sexes of those persons, in the same manner as several different taxes are levied in Holland; or nearly as Sir Matthew Decker proposes that all taxes upon consumable commodities should be levied in England.[67] This mode of taxation, it has already been observed, when applied to objects of a speedy consumption, is not a very convenient one. It might be adopted, however, in cases where no better could be done.

Sugar, rum, and tobacco, are commodities which are no where necessaries of life, which are become objects of almost universal consumption, and which are therefore extremely proper subjects of taxation. If a union with the colonies were[68] to take place, those commodities might be taxed either before they go out of the hands of the manufacturer or grower; or if this mode of taxation did not suit the circumstances of those persons, they might be deposited in public warehouses both at the place of manufacture, and at all the different ports of the empire to which they might afterwards be transported, to remain there, under the joint custody of the owner and the revenue officer, till such time as they should be delivered out either to the consumer, to the merchant retailer for home-consumption, or to the merchant exporter, the tax not to be advanced till such delivery. When delivered out for exportation, to go duty free; upon proper security being given that they should really be exported out of the empire. These are perhaps the principal commodities with regard to which a union with the colonies might require some considerable change in the present system of British taxation.

What might be the amount of the revenue which this system of taxation extended to all the different provinces of the empire might produce, it must, no doubt, be altogether impossible to ascertain with tolerable exactness. By means of this system there is annually levied in Great Britain, upon less than eight millions of people, more than ten millions of revenue. Ireland contains more than two millions of people, and according to the accounts laid before the congress,[69] the twelve associated provinces of America contain more than three. Those accounts, however, may have been exaggerated, in order, perhaps, either to encourage their own people, or to intimidate those of this country, and we shall suppose therefore that our North American and West Indian colonies taken together contain no more than three millions; or that the whole British empire, in Europe and America, contains no more than thirteen millions of inhabitants. If upon less than eight millions of inhabitants this system of taxation raises a revenue of more than ten millions sterling; it ought upon thirteen millions of inhabitants to raise a revenue of more than sixteen millions two hundred and fifty thousand pounds sterling. From this revenue, supposing that this system could produce it, must be deducted, the revenue usually raised in Ireland and the plantations for defraying the expence of their respective civil governments. The expence of the civil and military establishment of Ireland, together with the interest of the public debt, amounts, at a medium of the two years which ended March 1775, to something less than seven hundred and fifty thousand pounds a year. By a very exact account[70] of the revenue of the principal colonies of America and the West Indies, it amounted, before the commencement of the present[71] disturbances, to a hundred and forty-one thousand eight hundred pounds. In this account, however, the revenue of Maryland, of North Carolina, and of all our late acquisitions both upon the continent and in the islands, is omitted, which may perhaps make a difference of thirty or forty thousand pounds. For the sake of even numbers therefore, let us suppose that the revenue necessary for supporting the civil government of Ireland and the plantations, may amount to a million. There would remain consequently a revenue of fifteen millions two hundred and fifty thousand pounds, to be applied towards defraying the general expence of the empire, and towards paying the public debt. But if from the present revenue of Great Britain a million could in peaceable times be spared towards the payment of that debt, six millions two hundred and fifty thousand pounds could very well be spared from this improved revenue. This great sinking fund too might be augmented every year by the interest of the debt which had been discharged the year before, and might in this manner increase so very rapidly, as to be sufficient in a few years to discharge the whole debt, and thus to restore completely the at present debilitated and languishing vigour of the empire. In the mean time the people might be relieved from some of the most burdensome taxes; from those which are imposed either upon the necessaries of life, or upon the materials of manufacture. The labouring poor would thus be enabled to live better, to work cheaper, and to send their goods cheaper to market. The cheapness of their goods would increase the demand for them, and consequently for the labour of those who produced them. This increase in the demand for labour, would both increase the numbers and improve the circumstances of the labouring poor. Their consumption would increase, and together with it the revenue arising from all those articles of their consumption upon which the taxes might be allowed to remain.

The revenue arising from this system of taxation, however, might not immediately increase in proportion to the number of people who were subjected to it. Great indulgence would for some time be due to those provinces of the empire which were thus subjected to burthens to which they had not before been accustomed, and even when the same taxes came to be levied every where as exactly as possible, they would not every where produce a revenue proportioned to the numbers of the people. In a poor country the consumption of the principal commodities subject to the duties of customs and excise is very small; and in a thinly inhabited country the opportunities of smuggling are very great. The consumption of malt liquors among the inferior ranks of people in Scotland is very small, and the excise upon malt, beer, and ale, produces less there than in England in proportion to the numbers of the people and the rate of the duties, which upon malt is different on account of a supposed difference of quality. In these particular branches of the excise, there is not, I apprehend, much more smuggling in the one country than in the other. The duties upon the distillery, and the greater part of the duties of customs, in proportion to the numbers of people in the respective countries, produce less in Scotland than in England, not only on account of the smaller consumption of the taxed commodities, but of the much greater facility of smuggling. In Ireland, the inferior ranks of people are still poorer than in Scotland, and many parts of the country arc almost as thinly inhabited. In Ireland, therefore, the consumption of the taxed commodities might, in proportion to the number of the people, be still less than in Scotland, and the facility of smuggling nearly the same. In America and the West Indies the white people even of the lowest rank are in much better circumstances than those of the same rank in England, and their consumption of all the luxuries in which they usually indulge themselves is probably much greater. The blacks, indeed, who make the greater part of the inhabitants both of the southern colonies upon the continent and of the West India[72] islands, as they are in a state of slavery, are, no doubt, in a worse condition than the poorest people either in Scotland or Ireland. We must not, however, upon that account, imagine that they are worse fed, or that their consumption of articles which might be subjected to moderate duties, is less than that even of the lower ranks of people in England. In order that they may work well, it is the interest of their master that they should be fed well and kept in good heart, in the same manner as it is his interest that his working cattle should be so. The blacks accordingly have almost every where their allowance of rum and of melasses or spruce beer, in the same manner as the white servants; and this allowance would not probably be withdrawn, though those articles should be subjected to moderate duties. The consumption of the taxed commodities, therefore, in proportion to the number of inhabitants, would probably be as great in America and the West Indies as in any part of the British empire. The opportunities of smuggling indeed, would be much greater; America, in proportion to the extent of the country, being much more thinly inhabited than either Scotland or

Ireland. If the revenue, however, which is at present raised by the different duties upon malt and malt liquors, were[73] to be levied by a single duty upon malt, the opportunity of smuggling in the most important branch of the excise would be almost entirely taken away: And if the duties of customs, instead of being imposed upon almost all the different articles of importation, were confined to a few of the most general use and consumption, and if the levying of those duties were subjected to the excise laws, the opportunity of smuggling, though not so entirely taken away, would be very much diminished. In consequence of those two, apparently, very simple and easy alterations, the duties of customs and excise might probably produce a revenue as great in proportion to the consumption of the most thinly inhabited province, as they do at present in proportion to that of the most populous.

The Americans, it has been said, indeed, have no gold or silver money; the interior commerce of the country being carried on by a paper currency, and the gold and silver which occasionally come among them being all sent to Great Britain in return for the commodities which they receive from us. But without gold and silver, it is added, there is no possibility of paying taxes. We already get all the gold and silver which they have. How is it possible to draw from them what they have not?

The present scarcity of gold and silver money in America is not the effect of the poverty of that country, or of the inability of the people there to purchase those metals. In a country where the wages of labour are so much higher, and the price of provisions so much lower than in England, the greater part of the people must surely have wherewithal to purchase a greater quantity, if it were[74] either necessary or convenient for them to do so. The scarcity of those metals therefore, must be the effect of choice, and not of necessity.

It is for transacting either domestic or foreign business, that gold and silver money is either necessary or convenient.

The domestic business of every country, it has been shewn in the second book of this Inquiry,[75] may, at least in peaceable times, be transacted by means of a paper currency, with nearly the same degree of conveniency as by gold and silver money. It is convenient for the Americans, who could always employ with profit in the improvement of their lands a greater stock than they can easily get, to save as much as possible the expence of so costly an instrument of commerce as gold and silver, and rather to employ that part of their surplus produce which would be necessary for purchasing those metals, in purchasing the instruments of trade, the materials of clothing, several parts of household furniture, and the iron-work necessary for building and extending their settlements and plantations; in purchasing, not dead stock, but active and productive stock. The colony governments find it for their interest to supply the[76] people with such a quantity of paper-money as is fully sufficient and generally more than sufficient for transacting their domestic business. Some of those governments, that of Pennsylvania particularly, derive a revenue from lending this paper-money to their subjects at an interest of so much per cent. Others, like that of Massachusett's Bay, advance upon extraordinary emergencies a paper-money of this kind for defraying the public expence, and afterwards, when it suits the conveniency of the colony, redeem it at the depreciated value to which it gradually falls. In 1747[77] that colony paid, in this manner, the greater part of its public debts, with the tenth part of the money for which its bills had been granted. It suits the conveniency of the planters to save the expence of employing gold and silver money in their domestic transactions; and it suits the conveniency of the colony governments to supply them with a medium, which, though attended with some very considerable disadvantages, enables them to save that expense. The redundancy of paper-money necessarily banishes gold and silver from the domestic transactions of the colonies, for the same reason that it has banished those metals from the greater part of the domestic transactions in[78] Scotland; and in both countries it is not the poverty, but the enterprizing and projecting spirit of the people, their desire of employing all the stock which they can get as active and productive stock, which has occasioned this redundancy of paper-money.

In the exterior commerce which the different colonies carry on with Great Britain, gold and silver are more or less employed, exactly in proportion as they are more or less necessary. Where those metals are not necessary, they seldom appear. Where they are necessary, they are generally found.

In the commerce between Great Britain and the tobacco colonies, the British goods are generally advanced to the colonists at a pretty long credit, and are afterwards paid for in tobacco, rated at a certain price. It is more convenient for the colonists to pay in tobacco than in gold and silver. It would be more convenient for any merchant to pay for the goods which his correspondents had sold to him in some other sort of goods which he might happen to deal in, than in money. Such a merchant would have no occasion to keep any part of his stock by him unemployed, and in ready money, for answering occasional demands. He could have, at all times, a larger quantity of goods in his shop or warehouse, and he could deal to a greater extent. But it seldom happens to be convenient for all the correspondents of a merchant to receive payment for the goods which they sell to him, in goods of some other kind which he happens to deal in. The British merchants who trade to Virginia and Maryland happen to be a particular set of correspondents, to whom it is more convenient to receive payment for the goods which they sell to those colonies in tobacco than in gold and silver. They expect to make a profit by the sale of the tobacco. They could make none by that of the gold and silver. Gold and silver, therefore, very seldom appear in the commerce between Great Britain and the tobacco colonies. Maryland and Virginia have as little occasion for those metals in their foreign as in their domestic commerce. They are said, accordingly, to have less gold and silver money than any other colonies in America. They are reckoned, however, as thriving, and consequently as rich, as any of their neighbours.

In the northern colonies, Pennsylvania, New York, New Jersey, the four governments of New England, &c. the value of their own produce which they export to Great Britain is not equal to that of the manufactures which they import for their own use, and for that of some of the other colonies to which they are the carriers. A balance, therefore, must be paid to the mother country in gold and silver, and this balance they generally find.

In the sugar colonies the value of the produce annually exported to Great Britain is much greater than that of all the goods imported from thence. If the sugar and rum annually sent to the mother country were paid for in those colonies, Great Britain would be obliged to send out every year a very large balance in money, and the trade to the West Indies would, by a certain species of politicians, be considered as extremely disadvantageous. But it so happens, that many of the principal proprietors of the sugar plantations reside in Great Britain. Their rents are remitted to them in sugar and rum, the produce of their estates. The sugar and rum which the West India merchants purchase in those colonies upon their own account, are not equal in value to the goods which they annually sell there. A balance therefore must necessarily[79] be paid to them in gold and silver, and this balance too is generally found.

The difficulty and irregularity of payment from the different colonies to Great Britain, have not been at all in proportion to the greatness or smallness of the balances which were respectively due from them. Payments have in general been more regular from the northern than from the tobacco colonies, though the former have generally paid a pretty large balance in money, while the latter have either paid[80] no balance, or a much smaller one. The difficulty of getting payment from our different sugar colonies has been greater or less in proportion, not so much to the extent of the balances respectively due from them, as to the quantity of uncultivated land which they contained; that is, to the greater or smaller temptation which the planters have been under of over-trading, or of undertaking the settlement and plantation of greater quantities of waste land than suited the extent of their capitals. The returns from the great island of Jamaica, where there is still much uncultivated land, have, upon this account, been in general more irregular and uncertain, than those from the smaller islands of Barbados, Antigua, and St. Christophers, which have for these many years been completely cultivated, and have, upon that account, afforded less field for the speculations of the planter. The new acquisitions of Grenada, Tobago, St. Vincents, and Dominica,[81] have opened a new field for speculations of this kind; and the returns from those islands have of late been as irregular and uncertain as those from the great island of Jamaica.

It is not, therefore, the poverty of the colonies which occasions, in the greater part of them, the present scarcity of gold and silver money. Their great demand for active and productive stock makes it convenient for them to have as little dead stock as possible; and disposes them upon that account to content themselves with a cheaper, though less commodious instrument of commerce than gold and silver. They are thereby enabled to convert the value of that gold and silver into the instruments of trade, into the materials of clothing, into household furniture, and into the iron work necessary for building and extending their settlements and plantations. In those branches of business which cannot be transacted without gold and silver money, it appears, that they can always find the necessary quantity of those metals; and if they frequently do not find it, their failure is generally the effect, not of their necessary poverty, but of their unnecessary and excessive enterprize. It is not because they are poor that their payments are irregular and uncertain; but because they are too eager to become excessively rich. Though all that part of the produce of the colony taxes, which was over and above what was necessary for defraying the expence of their own civil and military establishments, were to be remitted to Great Britain in gold and silver, the colonies have abundantly wherewithal to purchase the requisite quantity of those metals. They would in this case be obliged, indeed, to exchange a part of their surplus produce, with which they now purchase active and productive stock, for dead stock. In transacting their domestic business they would be obliged to employ a costly instead of a cheap instrument of commerce; and the expence of purchasing this costly instrument might damp somewhat the vivacity and ardour of their excessive enterprize in the improvement of land. It might not, however, be necessary to remit any part of the American revenue in gold and silver. It might be remitted in bills drawn upon and accepted by particular merchants or companies in Great Britain, to whom a part of the surplus produce of America had been consigned, who would pay into the treasury the American revenue in money, after having themselves received the value of it in goods; and the whole business might frequently be transacted without exporting a single ounce of gold or silver[82] from America.

It is not contrary to justice that both Ireland and America should contribute towards the discharge of the public debt of Great Britain. That debt has been contracted in support of the government established by the Revolution, a government to which the protestants of Ireland owe, not only the whole authority which they at present enjoy in their own country, but every security which they possess for their liberty, their property, and their religion; a government to which several of the colonies of America owe their present charters, and consequently their present constitution, and to which all the colonies of America owe the liberty, security, and property which they have ever since enjoyed. That public debt has been contracted in the defence, not of Great Britain alone, but of all the different provinces of the empire; the immense debt contracted in the late war in particular, and a great part of that contracted in the war before, were both properly contracted in defence of America.

By a union with Great Britain, Ireland would gain, besides the freedom of trade, other advantages much more important, and which would much more than compensate any increase of taxes that might accompany that union. By the union with England, the middling and inferior ranks of people in Scotland gained a complete deliverance from the power of an aristocracy which had always before oppressed them. By a union with Great Britain, the greater part of the people of all ranks in Ireland would gain an equally complete deliverance from a much more oppressive aristocracy; an aristocracy not founded, like that of Scotland, in the natural and respectable distinctions of birth and fortune; but in the most odious of all distinctions, those of religious and political prejudices; distinctions which, more than any other, animate both the insolence of the oppressors and the hatred and indignation of the oppressed, and which commonly render the inhabitants of the same country more hostile to one another than those of different countries ever are. Without a union with Great Britain, the inhabitants of Ireland are not likely for many ages to consider themselves as one people.

No oppressive aristocracy has ever prevailed in the colonies. Even they, however, would, in point of happiness and tranquility, gain considerably by a union with Great Britain. It would, at least, deliver them from those rancorous and virulent factions which are inseparable from small democracies, and which have so frequently divided the affections of their people, and disturbed the tranquility of their governments, in their form so nearly democratical. In the case of a total separation from Great Britain, which, unless prevented by a union of this kind, seems very likely to take place, those factions would be ten times more virulent than ever. Before the commencement of the present disturbances, the coercive power of the mother-country had always been able to restrain those factions from breaking out into any thing worse than gross brutality and insult. If that coercive power were[83] entirely taken away, they would probably soon break out into open violence and bloodshed. In all great countries which are united under one uniform government, the spirit of party commonly prevails less in the remote provinces than in the centre of the empire. The distance of those provinces from the capital, from the principal seat of the great scramble of faction and ambition, makes them enter less into the views of any of the contending parties, and renders them more indifferent and impartial spectators of the conduct of all. The spirit of party prevails less in Scotland than in England. In the case of a union it would probably prevail less in Ireland than in Scotland, and the colonies would probably soon enjoy a degree of concord and unanimity at present unknown in any part of the British empire. Both Ireland and the colonies, indeed, would be subjected to heavier taxes than any which they at present pay. In consequence, however, of a diligent and faithful application of the public revenue towards the discharge of the national debt, the greater part of those taxes might not be of long continuance, and the public revenue of Great Britain might soon be reduced to what was necessary for maintaining a moderate peace establishment.

The territorial acquisitions of the East India company, the undoubted right of the crown, that is, of the state and people of Great Britain, might be rendered another source of revenue more abundant, perhaps, than all those already mentioned. Those countries are represented as more fertile, more extensive; and, in proportion to their extent, much richer and more populous than Great Britain. In order to draw a great revenue from them, it would not probably be necessary to introduce any new system of taxation into countries which are already sufficiently and more than sufficiently taxed. It might, perhaps, be more proper to lighten, than to aggravate, the burden of those unfortunate countries, and to endeavour to draw a revenue from them, not by imposing new taxes, but by preventing the embezzlement and misapplication of the greater part of those which they already pay.

If it should be found impracticable for Great Britain to draw any considerable augmentation of revenue from any of the resources above mentioned; the only resource which can remain to her is a diminution of her expence. In the mode of collecting, and in that of expending the public revenue; though in both there may be still room for improvement; Great Britain seems to be at least as oeconomical as any of her neighbours. The military establishment which she maintains for her own defence in time of peace, is more moderate than that of any European state which can pretend to rival her either in wealth or in power. None of those articles, therefore, seem to admit of any considerable reduction of expence. The expence of the peace establishment of the colonies was, before the commencement of the present disturbances, very considerable, and is an expence which may, and if no revenue can be drawn from them, ought certainly to be saved altogether. This constant expence in time of peace, though very great, is insignificant in comparison with what the defence of the colonies has cost us in time of war. The last war, which was undertaken altogether on account of the colonies, cost Great Britain, it has already been observed, upwards of ninety millions.[84] The Spanish war of 1739 was principally undertaken on their account; in which, and in the French war that was the consequence of it, Great Britain spent upwards of forty millions, a great part of which ought justly to be charged to the colonies. In those two wars the colonies cost Great Britain much more than double the sum which the national debt amounted to before the commencement of the first of them. Had it not been for those wars that debt might, and probably would by this time, have been completely paid; and had it not been for the colonies, the former of those wars might not, and the latter certainly would not have been undertaken. It was because the colonies were supposed to be provinces of the British empire, that this expence was laid out upon them. But countries which contribute neither revenue nor military force towards the support of the empire, cannot be considered as provinces. They may perhaps be considered as appendages, as a sort of splendid and showy equipage of the empire. But if the empire can no longer support the expence of keeping up this equipage, it ought certainly to lay it down; and if it cannot raise its revenue in proportion to its expence, it ought, at least, to accommodate its expence to its revenue. If the colonies, notwithstanding their refusal to submit to British taxes, are still to be considered as provinces of the British empire, their defence in some future war may cost Great Britain as great an expence as it ever has done in any former war. The rulers of Great Britain have, for more than a century past, amused the people with the imagination that they possessed a great empire on the west side of the Atlantic. This empire, however, has hitherto existed in imagination only. It has hitherto been, not an empire, but the project of an empire; not a gold mine, but the project of a gold mine; a project which has cost, which continues to cost, and which, if pursued in the same way as it has been hitherto, is likely to cost, immense expence, without being likely to bring any profit; for the effects of the monopoly of the colony trade, it has been shewn,[85] are, to the great body of the people, mere loss instead of profit. It is surely now time that our rulers should either realize this golden dream, in which they have been indulging themselves, perhaps, as well as the people; or, that they should awake from it themselves, and endeavour to awaken the people. If the project cannot be completed, it ought to be given up. If any of the provinces of the British empire cannot be made to contribute towards the support of the whole empire, it is surely time that Great Britain should free herself from the expence of defending those provinces in time of war, and of supporting any part of their civil or military establishments in time of peace, and endeavour to accommodate her future views and designs to the real mediocrity of her circumstances.

Notes

1. [Above, vol. i., pp. 433, 434.]
2. [Above, vol. i., p. 440.]
3. [Cp. vol. i., p. 301.]
4. [Above, vol. i., p. 468.]
5. [Repeated *verbatim* from vol. i., p. 468]
6. [Above, vol. i., p. 463.]
7. [Above, p. 344.]
8. [Ed. 5 omits 'along,' doubtless by a misprint.]
9. See Examen des Reflexions politiques sur les Finances. [P. J. Duvernev. *Examen du livre intitule Reflexions politiques sur les finances et le commerce* (by Du Tot), tom. i., p. 225.]
10. [James Postlethwayt, *History of the Public Revenue*, 1759, pp. 14, 15, mentions discounts of 25 and 55 per cent. The discount varied with the priority of the tallies and did not measure the national credit in general, but the probability of particular taxes bringing in enough to pay the amounts charged upon them. See also above, vol. i., p. 338.]
11. [Ed. I reads 'unprovident,' as do all editions below, p. 450.]
12. [Postlethwayt, *op. cit.*, p. 38. Ed. 5 misprints '9-1/2d.']
13. [*Ibid.*, p. 40.]
14. [*Ibid.*, p. 59.]
15. [*Ibid.*, pp. 63, 64.]
16. [Postlethwayt, *op. cit.*, p. 68.]
17. [*Ibid.*, p. 71.]
18. [*Ibid.*, p. 311.]
19. [*Ibid.*, pp. 301–303, and see above, vol. i., p. 339.]
20. [*Ibid.*, pp. 319, 320.]
21. [The odd L4,000 of the L206,501 13s. 5d. was for expenses of management. See above, vol. i., p. 339.]
22. [Ed. 1 reads 'payment,' perhaps correctly.]
23. [Postlethwayt, *History of the Public Revenue*, p. 305.]
24. [This Act belongs to 1716, not 1717.]
25. [Above, vol. i., pp. 99, 100.]
26. [In 1717, under the provisions of 3 Geo. I., c. 7. Postlethwayt, *History of the Public Revenue*, pp. 120, 145.]
27. [Anderson, *Commerce*, A.D. 1717.]
28. [*Ibid.*, A.D. 1727.]
29. [This should be 1750. *Ibid.*, A.D. 1749.]
30. [5 and 6 W. and M., c. 7.]
31. [4 W. and M., c. 3.]
32. [Anderson, *Commerce*, A.D. 1719.]
33. [*Ibid.*, A.D. 1720.]
34. [Ed. 1 reads 'just as long as'.]
35. [Anderson, *Commerce*, mentions these reductions under their dates, and recalls them in reference to the British reduction in 1717.]
36. [Ed. 1. reads 'long and short'.]
37. See James Postlethwayt's history of the public revenue. [Pp. 42, 143–145, 147, 224, 300. The reference covers the three paragraphs in the text above.]
38. [Above, p. 451.]
39. [*Present State of the Nation* (above, vol. i., p. 465), p. 28.]
40. [Anderson, *Commerce*, postscript *ad init.*]
41. ['*But the expenses of the war did not cease with its operations.*'—*Considerations* (see a few lines below), p. 4.]
42. [*Ibid.*, p. 5.]
43. [The account is given in the Continuation of Anderson's *Commerce*, A.D. 1764, vol. iv., p. 58, in ed. of 1801. The '3/4d.' should '1/4d.']

44. [*Considerations on the Trade and Finances of this Kingdom and on the measures of administration with respect to those great national objects since the conclusion of the peace*, by Thomas Whately, 1766 (often ascribed to George Grenville), p. 22.]

45. [This is the amount obtained by adding the two items mentioned, and is the reading of ed. 1. Eds. 2–5 all read 'L139,516,807 2s. 4d.', which is doubtless a misprint. The total is not given in *Considerations*.]

46. [*Considerations*, p. 4.]

47. [Ed. 1 reads 'Among'.]

48. [Above, p. 90, note 5.]

49. [Eds. 1–3 read 'was'.]

50. It has proved more expensive than any of our former wars; and has involved us in an additional debt of more than one hundred millions. During a profound peace of eleven years, little more than ten millions of debt was paid; during a war of seven years, more than one hundred millions was contracted. [This note appears first in ed. 3.]

51. Garnier's note, *Recherches etc.*, tom. iv., p. 501, is 'Pinto: *Traité de la Circulation et du Crédit*,' a work published in 1771 ('Amsterdam'), 'par l'auteur de l'essai sur le luxe,' of which see esp. pp. 44, 45, 209–211. But an English essay of 1731 to the same effect is quoted by Melon, *Essai Politique sur le Commerce*, chap. xxiii., ed. of 1761, p. 296, and Melon seems to be referred to below, p. 463. Cp. *Lectures*, p. 210.]

52. [Eds. 1–3 read the indicative, 'destroys'.]

53. [Misprinted 'it' in ed. 5.]

54. ['Les Dettes d'un Etat sont des dettes de la main droite à la main gauche, dont le corps ne se trouvera point affaibli, s'il a la quantité d'aliments nécessaires, et s'il sait les distribuer.'—Melon, *Essai politique sur le Commerce*, chap. xxiii., ed. of 1761, p. 296.]

55. [Ed. 1 reads 'most'.]

56. [Above, p. 439.]

57. [Eds. 1 and 2 read 'seems'.]

58. [Raynal says 'L'evidence autorise seulement à dire que les gouvernements qui pour le malheur des peuples ont adopté le détestable système des emprunts doivent tôt ou tard l'abjurer: et que l'abus qu'ils en ont fait les forcera vraisemblablement à être infidèles.'—*Histoire philosophique*, Amsterdam, 1773, tom. iv., p. 274.]

59. [Eds. I and 2 read 'later'; cp. above, p. 410.]

60. [This chapter of Roman history is based on a few sentences in Pliny, *H.N.*, lib. xxxiii., cap. iii. Modern criticism has discovered the facts to be not nearly so simple as they are represented in the text.]

61. See du Cange Glossary, voce Moneta; the Benedictine edition. [This gives a table of the alterations made in the coin and refers to Le Blanc, *Traite historique des Monnoyes de France*, 1792, in which the fact that the officers were adjured by their oaths to keep the matter secret is mentioned on p. 218, but the adjuration is also quoted in the more accessible Melon, *Essai politique sur le Commerce*, chap. xiii., ed. of 1761, p. 177.]

62. [Misprinted 'never' in eds. 2–5.]

63. [Ed. 1 reads 'either of'.]

64. [Ed. 1 reads 'or'.]

65. [Above, pp. 353, 360, 361.]

66. [Above, p. 89.]

67. [Above, pp. 406, 407.]

68. [Eds. 1–3 read 'was'.]

69. [Given in the Continuation of Anderson's *Commerce*, A.D. 1774, vol. iv., p. 178, in ed. of 1801.]

70. [Above, p. 85.]

71. [Ed. 1 reads 'late'; cp. above, vol. i., p. 524.]

72. [Eds. 1 and 2 read 'West Indian'.]

73. [Eds. 1–3 read 'was' here and five lines below.]

74. [Eds. 1–3 read 'was'.]

75. [Above, vol. i., pp. 309–315.]

76. [Ed. 1 omits 'the'.]

77. See Hutchinson's Hist. of Massachusett's Bay, Vol. II., page 436 & seq. [*History of the Colony of Massachusets Bay*, 2nd ed., 1765–8.]

78. [Ed. 1 reads 'of'.]

79. [Ed. 1 reads 'must generally'.]

80. [Ed. 1 reads 'paid either'.]

81. [Above, p. 90, note 5.]

82. [Ed. 1 reads 'gold and silver'.]
83. [Eds. 1–3 read 'was'.]
84. [Above, vol. i., p. 463.]
85. [Above, pp. 103–146.]

[Brackets within the preceding notes have been retained from the University of Chicago edition.]

Marx argues that public debt is a creature of industrialization and that "public debt becomes the creed of capital." Thus, Marx sees the development of public debt as a method of exploitation.

GENESIS OF THE INDUSTRIAL CAPITALIST

Karl Marx

The genesis of the industrial[1] capitalist did not proceed in such a gradual way as that of the farmer. Doubtless many small guild-masters, and yet more independent small artisans, or even wage-labourers, transformed themselves into small capitalists, and (by gradually extending exploitation of wage-labour and corresponding accumulation) into full-blown capitalists. In the infancy of capitalist production, things often happened as in the infancy of medieval towns, where the question, which of the escaped serfs should be master and which servant, was in great part decided by the earlier or later date of their flight. The snail's-pace of this method corresponded in no wise with the commercial requirements of the new world-market that the great discoveries of the end of the 15th century created. But the middle age had handed down two distinct forms of capital, which mature in the most different economic social formations, and which, before the era of the capitalist mode of production, are considered as capital quand meme—usurer's capital and merchant's capital.

"At present, all the wealth of society goes first into the possession of the capitalist . . . . he pays the landowner his rent, the labourer his wages, the tax and tithe gatherer their claims, and keeps a large, indeed the largest, and a continually augmenting share, of the annual produce of labour for himself. The capitalist may now be said to be the first owner of all the wealth of the community, though no law has conferred on him the right to this property . . . . this change has been effected by the taking of interest on capital . . . . and it is not a little curious that all the lawgivers of Europe endeavoured to prevent this by statutes, viz., statutes against usury. . . . . The power of the capitalist over all the wealth of the country is a complete change in the right of property, and by what law, or series of laws, was it effected?"[2] The author should have remembered that revolutions are not made by laws.

Reprinted with permission of the publisher from *Capital,* Vol. I, Modern Library Edition. New York: Random House, 1906, pp. 822–34.

The money capital formed by means of usury and commerce was prevented from turning into industrial capital, in the country by the feudal constitution, in the towns by the guild organization.³ These fetters vanished with the dissolution of feudal society, with the expropriation and partial eviction of the country population. The new manufacturers were established at sea-ports, or in inland points beyond the control of the old municipalities and their guilds. Hence in England an embittered struggle of the corporate towns against these new industrial nurseries.

The discovery of gold and silver in America, the extirpation, enslavement and entombment in mines of the aboriginal population, the beginning of the conquest and looting of the East Indies, the turning of Africa into a warren for the commercial hunting of black-skins, signalised the rosy dawn of the era of capitalist production. These idyllic proceedings are the chief momenta of primitive accumulation. On their heels treads the commercial war of the European nations, with the globe for a theatre. It begins with the revolt of the Netherlands from Spain, assumes giant dimensions in England's anti-jacobin war, and is still going on in the opium wars against China, &c.

The different momenta of primitive accumulation distribute themselves now, more or less in chronological order, particularly over Spain, Portugal, Holland, France, and England. In England at the end of the 17th century, they arrive at a systematical combination, embracing the colonies, the national debt, the modern mode of taxation, and the protectionist system. These methods depend in part on brute force, *e.g.*, the colonial system. But they all employ the power of the State, the concentrated and organised force of society, to hasten, hothouse fashion, the process of transformation of the feudal mode of production into the capitalist mode, and to shorten the transition. Force is the midwife of every old society pregnant with a new one. It is itself an economic power.

Of the Christian colonial system, W. Howitt, a man who makes a specialty of Christianity, says: "The barbarities and desperate outrages of the so-called Christian race, throughout every region of the world, and upon every people they have been able to subdue, are not to be paralleled by those of any other race, however fierce, however untaught, and however reckless of mercy and of shame, in any age of the earth."⁴ The history of the colonial administration of Holland—and Holland was the head capitalistic nation of the 17th century—"is one of the most extraordinary relations of treachery, bribery, massacre, and meanness."⁵ Nothing is more characteristic than their system of stealing men, to get slaves for Java. The men stealers were trained for this purpose. The thief, the interpreter, and the seller, were the chief agents in this trade, native princes the chief sellers. The young people stolen, were thrown into the secret dungeons of Celebes, until they were ready for sending to the slave-ships. An official report says: "This one town of Macassar, *e.g.*, is full of secret prisons, one more horrible than the other, crammed with unfortunates, victims of greed and tyranny fettered in chains, forcibly torn from their families." To secure Malacca, the Dutch corrupted the Portuguese governor. He let them into the town in 1641. They hurried at once to his house and assassinated him, to "abstain" from the payment of £21,875, the price of his treason. Wherever they set foot, devastation and depopulation followed. Banjuwangi, a province of Java, in 1750 numbered over 80,000 inhabitants, in 1811 only 18,000. Sweet commerce!

The English East India Company, as is well known, obtained, besides the political rule in India, the exclusive monopoly of the tea-trade, as well as of the Chinese trade in general, and of the transport of goods to and from Europe. But the coasting trade of India and between the islands, as well as the internal trade of India, were the monopoly of the higher employés of the company. The monopolies of salt, opium, betel and other commodities, were inexhaustible mines of wealth. The employés themselves fixed the price and plundered at will the unhappy Hindus. The Governor-General took part in this private traffic. His favourite received contracts under conditions whereby they, cleverer than the alchemists, made gold out of nothing. Great fortunes sprang up like mushrooms in a day; primitive accumulation went on without the advance of a shilling. The trial of Warren Hastings swarms with such cases. Here is an instance. A contract for opium was given to a certain Sullivan at the moment of his departure on an official mission to a part of India far removed from the opium district. Sullivan sold his contract to one Binn for £40,000; Binn sold it the same day for £60,000, and the ultimate purchaser who carried out the contract declared that after all he realised an enormous gain. According to one of the lists laid before Parliament, the Company and its employés from 1757–1766 got £6,000,000 from the Indians as gifts. Between 1769 and 1770, the English manufactured a famine by buying up all the rice and refusing to sell it again, except at fabulous prices.[6]

The treatment of the aborigines was, naturally, most frightful in plantation-colonies destined for export trade only, such as the West Indies, and in rich and well-populated countries, such as Mexico and India, that were given over to plunder. But even in the colonies properly so-called, the Christian character of primitive accumulation did not belie itself. Those sober virtuosi of Protestantism, the Puritans of New England, in 1703, by decrees of their assembly set a premium of £40 on every Indian scalp and every captured red-skin: in 1720 a premium of £100 on every scalp; in 1744, after Massachusetts Bay had proclaimed a certain tribe as rebels, the following prices: for a male scalp of 12 years and upwards £100 (new currency), for a male prisoner £105, for women and children prisoners £50, for scalps of women and children £50. Some decades later, the colonial system took its revenge on the descendants of the pious pilgrim fathers, who had grown seditious in the meantime. At English instigation and for English pay they were tomahawked by red-skins. The British Parliament, proclaimed blood-hounds and scalping as "means that God and Nature had given into its hand."

The colonial system ripened, like a hot-house, trade and navigation. The "societies Monopolia" of Luther were powerful levers for concentration of capital. The colonies secured a market for the budding manufactures, and, through the monopoly of the market, an increased accumulation. The treasures captured outside Europe by undisguised looting, enslavement, and murder, floated back to the mother-country and were there turned into capital. Holland, which first fully developed the colonial system, in 1648 stood already in the acme of its commercial greatness. It was "in almost exclusive possession of the East Indian trade and the commerce between the south-east and north-west of Europe. Its fisheries, marine, manufactures, surpassed those of any other country. The total capital of the Republic was probably more important than that of all the rest of Europe put together." Gülich forgets to add that by 1648, the people of Holland were more overworked, poorer and more brutally oppressed than those of all the rest of Europe put together.

To-day industrial supremacy implies commercial supremacy. In the period of manufacture properly so-called, it is, on the other hand, the commercial supremacy that gives industrial predominance. Hence the preponderant rôle that the colonial system plays at that time. It was "the strange God" who perched himself on the altar cheek by jowl with the old Gods of Europe, and one fine day with a shove and a kick chucked them all of a heap. It proclaimed surplus-value making as the sole end and aim of humanity.

The system of public credit, *i.e.* of national debts, whose origin we discover in Genoa and Venice as early as the middle ages, took possession of Europe generally during the manufacturing period. The colonial system with its maritime trade and commercial wars served as a forcing-house for it. Thus it first took root in Holland. National debts, *i.e.*, the alienation of the state—whether despotic, constitutional or republican—marked with its stamp the capitalistic era. The only part of the so-called national wealth that actually enters into the collective possessions of modern peoples is—their national debt.[7] Hence, as a necessary consequence, the modern doctrine that a nation becomes the richer the more deeply it is in debt. Public credit becomes the *credo* of capital. And with the rise of national debt-making, want of faith in the national debt takes the place of the blasphemy against the Holy Ghost, which may not be forgiven.

The public debt becomes one of the most powerful levers of primitive accumulation. As with the stroke of an enchanter's wand, it endows barren money with the power of breeding and thus turns it into capital, without the necessity of its exposing itself to the troubles and risks inseparable from its employment in industry or even in usury. The state-creditors actually give nothing away, for the sum lent is transformed into public bonds, easily negotiable, which go on functioning in their hands just as so much hard cash would. But further, apart from the class of lazy annuitants thus created, and from the improvised wealth of the financiers, middlemen between the government and the nation—as also apart from the tax-farmers, merchants, private manufacturers, to whom a good part of every national loan renders the service of a capital fallen from heaven—the national debt has given rise to joint-stock companies, to dealings in negotiable effects of all kinds, and to agiotage, in a word to stock-exchange gambling and the modern bankocracy.

At their birth the great banks, decorated with national titles, were only associations of private speculators, who placed themselves by the side of governments, and, thanks to the privileges they received, were in a position to advance money to the state. Hence the accumulation of the national debt has no more infallible measure than the successive rise in the stock of these banks, whose full development dates from the founding of the Bank of England in 1694. The Bank of

England began with lending its money to the Government at 8%; at the same time it was empowered by Parliament to coin money out of the same capital, by lending it again to the public in the form of bank-notes. It was allowed to use these notes for discounting bills, making advances on commodities, and for buying the precious metals. It was not long ere this credit-money, made by the bank itself, became the coin in which the Bank of England made its loans to the state, and paid, on account of the state, the interest on the public debt. It was not enough that the bank gave with one hand and took back more with the other; it remained, even whilst receiving, the eternal creditor of the nation down to the last shilling advanced. Gradually it became inevitably the receptacle of the metallic hoard of the country, and the centre of gravity of all commercial credit. What effect was produced on their contemporaries by the sudden uprising of this brood of bankocrats, financiers, rentiers, brokers, stock-jobbers, &c, is proved by the writings of that time, *e.g.*, by Bolingbroke's.[8]

With the national debt arose an international credit system, which often conceals one of the sources of primitive accumulation in this or that people. Thus the villainies of the Venetian thieving system formed one of the secret bases of the capital-wealth of Holland to whom Venice in her decadence lent large sums of money. So also was it with Holland and England. By the beginning of the 18th century the Dutch manufactures were far outstripped. Holland had ceased to be the nation preponderant in commerce and industry. One of its main lines of business, therefore, from 1701–1776, is the lending out of enormous amounts of capital, especially to its great rival England. The same thing is going on to-day between England and the United States. A great deal of capital, which appears to-day in the United States without any certificate of birth, was yesterday, in England, the capitalised blood of children.

As the national debt finds its support in the public revenue, which must cover the yearly payments for interest, &c., the modern system of taxation was the necessary complement of the system of national loans. The loans enable the government to meet extraordinary expenses, without the tax-payers feeling it immediately, but they necessitate, as a consequence, increased taxes. On the other hand, the raising of taxation caused by the accumulation of debts contracted one after another, compels the government always to have recourse to new loans for new extraordinary expenses. Modern fiscality, whose pivot is formed by taxes on the most necessary means of subsistence (thereby increasing their price), thus contains within itself the germ of automatic progression. Over-taxation is not an incident, but rather a principle. In Holland, therefore, where this system was first inaugurated, the great patriot, De Witt, has in his "Maxims" extolled it as the best system for making the wage-labourer submissive, frugal, industrious, and over-burdened with labour. The destructive influence that it exercises on the condition of the wage-labourer concerns us less however, here, than the forcible expropriation resulting from it, of peasants, artisans, and in a word, all elements of the lower middle-class. On this there are not two opinions, even among the bourgeois economists. Its expropriating efficacy is still further heightened by the system of protection, which forms one of its integral parts.

The great part that the public debt, and the fiscal system corresponding with it, has played in the capitalisation of wealth and the expropriation of the masses, has led many writers, like Cobbett, Doubleday and others, to seek in this, incorrectly, the fundamental cause of the misery of the modern peoples.

The system of protection was an artificial means of manufacturing manufacturers, of expropriating independent labourers, of capitalising the national means of production and subsistence, of forcibly abbreviating the transition from the medieval to the modern mode of production. The European states tore one another to pieces about the patent of this invention, and, once entered into the service of the surplus-value makers, did not merely lay under contribution in the pursuit of this purpose their own people, indirectly through protective duties, directly through export premiums. They also forcibly rooted out, in their dependent countries, all industry, as *e.g.*, England did with the Irish woollen manufacture. On the continent of Europe, after Colbert's example, the process was much simplified. The primitive industrial capital, here, came in part directly out of the state treasury. "Why," cries Mirabeau, "why go so far to seek the cause of the manufacturing glory of Saxony before the war? 180,000,000 of debts contracted by the sovereigns!"[9]

Colonial system, public debts, heavy taxes, protection, commercial wars, &c., these children of the true manufacturing period, increase gigantically during the infancy of Modern Industry. The birth of the latter is heralded by a great slaughter of the innocents. Like the royal navy, the factories were recruited by means of the press-gang. Blasé as Sir F. M. Eden is as to the horrors of the expropriation of the agricultural population from the soil, from the last third of the 15th century to his own time; with all the self-satisfaction with which he rejoices in this process, "essential" for establishing capitalistic agriculture and "the due proportion between arable and pasture land"—he does not show, however, the same economic insight in respect to the necessity of child-stealing and child-slavery for the transformation of manufacturing exploitation into factory exploitation, and the establishment of the "true relation" between capital and labour-power. He says: "It may, perhaps, be worthy the attention of the public to consider, whether any manufacture, which, in order to be carried on successfully, requires that cottages and workhouses should be ransacked for poor children; that they should be employed by turns during the greater part of the night and robbed of that rest which, though indispensable to all, is most required by the young; and that numbers of both sexes, of different ages and dispositions, should be collected together in such a manner that the contagion of example cannot but lead to profligacy and debauchery; will add to the sum of individual or national felicity?"[10]

"In the counties of Derbyshire, Nottinghamshire, and more particularly in Lancashire," says Fielden, "the newly-invented machinery was used in large factories built on the sides of streams capable of turning the water-wheel. Thousands of hands were suddenly required in these places, remote from towns; and Lancashire, in particular, being, till then, comparatively thinly populated and barren, a population was all that she now wanted. The small and nimble fingers of little children being by very far the most in request, the custom instantly sprang up of procuring *apprentices* from the different parish workhouses of London, Birmingham, and elsewhere. Many, many thousands of these little, hapless creatures were sent down into the north, being from the age of 7 to the age of 13 or 14 years old. The custom was for the master to clothe his *apprentices* and to feed and lodge them in an "apprentice house" near the factory; overseers were appointed to see to the works, whose interest it was to work the children to the utmost, because their pay was in proportion to the quantity of work that they could exact. Cruelty was, of course, the consequence . . . . In many of the manufacturing districts, but particularly, I am afraid, in the guilty county to which I belong [Lancashire], cruelties the most heart-rending were practised upon the unoffending and friendless creatures who were thus consigned to the charge of master manufacturers; they were harassed to the brink of death by excess of labour . . . . were flogged, fettered and tortured in the most exquisite refinement of cruelty; . . . . they were in many cases starved to the bone while flogged to their work and . . . . even in some instances . . . . were driven to commit suicède . . . . The beautiful and romantic valleys of Derbyshire, Nottinghamshire and Lancashire, secluded from the public eye, became the dismal solitudes of torture, and of many a murder. The profits of manufacturers were enormous; but this only whetted the appetite that it should have satisfied, and therefore the manufacturers had recourse to an expedient that seemed to secure to them those profits without any possibility of limit; they began the practice of what is termed "night-working," that is, having tired one set of hands, by working them throughout the day, they had another set ready to go on working throughout the night; the day-set getting into the beds that the night-set had just quitted, and in their turn again, the night-set getting into the beds that the day-set quitted in the morning. It is a common tradition in Lancashire, that the beds *never get cold*:"[11]

With the development of capitalist production during the manufacturing period, the public opinion of Europe had lost the last remnant of shame and conscience. The nations bragged cynically of every infamy that served them as a means to capitalistic accumulation. Read, *e.g.*, the náive Annals of Commerce of the worthy A. Anderson. Here it is trumpetted forth as a triumph of English statecraft that at the Peace of Utrecht, England extorted from the Spaniards by the Asiento Treaty the privilege of being allowed to ply the negro-trade, until then only carried on between Africa and the English West Indies, between Africa and Spanish America as well. England thereby acquired the right of supplying Spanish America until 1743 with 4800 negroes yearly. This threw, at the same time, an official cloak over British smuggling. Liverpool waxed fat on the slave-trade. This was its method of primitive accumulation. And, even to the present day, Liverpool "respectability" is the Pindar of the slave-trade which—compare the work of Aikin [1795] already quoted—"has coincided with that spirit of bold adventure which has characterised the trade of Liverpool and rapidly carried it to its present state of prosperity; has occasioned vast employment for shipping and sailors, and greatly augmented the demand for the manufactures of the country" (p. 339). Liverpool employed in the slave trade, in 1730, 15 ships; in 1751, 53; in 1760, 74; in 1770, 96; and in 1792, 132.

Whilst the cotton industry introduced child-slavery in England, it gave in the United States a stimulus to the transformation of the earlier, more or less patriarchal slavery, into a system of commercial exploitation. In fact, the veiled slavery of the wage-earners in Europe needed, for its pedestal, slavery pure and simple in the new world.[12]

Tantae molis erat, to establish the "eternal laws of Nature" of the capitalist mode of production, to complete the process of separation between labourers and conditions of labour, to transform, at one pole, the social means of production and subsistence into capital, at the opposite pole, the mass of the population into wage-labourers, into "free labouring poor," that artificial product of modern society.[13] If money, according to Augier,[14] "comes into the world with a congenital blood-stain on one cheek," capital comes dripping from head to foot, from every pore, with blood and dirt.[15]

Notes

1. Industrial here in contradistinction to agricultural. In the "categoric" sense the farmer is an industrial capitalist as much as the manufacturer.

2. "The Natural and Artificial Rights of Property Contrasted." Lond., 1832, pp. 98–99. Author of the anonymous work: "Th. Hodgskin."

3. Even as late as 1794, the small-cloth makers of Leeds sent a deputation to Parliament, with a petition for a law to forbid any merchant from becoming a manufacturer. (Dr. Aikin. l. c.)

4. William Howitt: "Colonisation and Christianity: A Popular History of the Treatment of the Natives by the Europeans in all their Colonies." London, 1838, p. 9. On the treatment of the slaves there is a good compilation in Charles Comte, Traité de la Législation. 3me ed. Bruxelles, 1837. This subject one must study in detail, to see what the bourgeoisie makes of itself and of the labourer, wherever it can, without restraint, model the world after its own image.

5. Thomas Stamford Raffles, late Lieut.-Gov. of that island: "History of Java and its dependencies." Lond., 1817.

6. In the year 1866 more than a million Hindus died of hunger in the province of Orissa alone. Nevertheless, the attempt was made to enrich the Indian treasury by the price at which the necessaries of life were sold to the starving people.

7. William Cobbett remarks that in England all public institutions are designated "royal;" as compensation for this, however, there is the "national" debt.

8. "Si les Tartares inondaient l'Europe aujourd'hui, il faudrait bien des affaires pour leur faire entendre ce que c'est qu'un financier parmi nous." Montesquieu Esprit des lois, t. iv. p. 33, ed. Londres, 1769.

9. Mirabeau, l. c. t. vi., p. 101.

10. Eden, l. c., Vol. I., Book II., Ch. I., p. 421.

11. John Fielden, l. c. pp. 5, 6. On the earlier infamies of the factory system, cf. Dr. Aikin (1795) l. c. p. 219, and Gisborne: Enquiry into the Duties of Men, 1795, Vol. II. When the steam-engine transplanted the factories from the country waterfalls to the middle of towns, the "abstemious" surplus-value maker found the child-material ready to his hand, without being forced to seek slaves from the workhouses. When Sir R. Peel, (father of the "minister of plausibility"), brought in his bill for the protection of children, in 1815, Francis Horner, lumen of the Bullion Committee and intimate friend of Ricardo, said in the House of Commons: "It is notorious, that with a bankrupt's effects, a gang, if he might use the word, of these children had been put up to sale, and were advertised publicly as part of the property. A most atrocious instance had been brought before the Court of King's Bench two years before, in which a number of these boys, apprenticed by a parish in London to one manufacturer, had been transferred to another, and had been found by some benevolent persons in a state of absolute famine. Another case more horrible had come to his knowledge while on a [Parliamentary] Committee . . . that not many years ago, an agreement had been made between a London parish and a

Lancashire manufacturer, by which it was stipulated, that with every 20 sound children one idiot should be taken."

12. In 1790, there were in the English West Indies ten slaves for one free man, in the French fourteen for one, in the Dutch twenty-three for one. (Henry Brougham: An Inquiry into the Colonial Policy of the European Powers. Edin. 1803, vol. II. p. 74.)

13. The phrase, "labouring poor," is found in English legislation from the moment when the class of wage-labourers becomes noticeable. This term is used in opposition, on the one hand, to the "idle poor," beggars, etc., on the other to those labourers, who, pigeons not yet plucked, are still possessors of their own means of labour. From the Statute Book it passed into political economy, and was handed down by Culpeper, J. Child, etc., to Adam Smith and Eden. After this, one can judge of the good faith of the "execrable political cant-monger," Edmund Burke, when he called the expression, "labouring poor,"—"execrable political cant." This sycophant who, in the pay of the English oligarchy, played the romantic laudator temporis acti against the French Revolution, just as, in the pay of the North American Colonies, at the beginning of the American troubles, he had played the Liberal against the English oligarchy, was an out and out vulgar bourgeois. "The laws of commerce are the laws of Nature, and therefore the laws of God." (E. Burke, l. c., pp. 31, 32.) No wonder that, true to the laws of God and of Nature, he always sold himself in the best market. A very good portrait of this Edmund Burke, during his liberal time, is to be found in the writings of the Rev. Mr. Tucker. Tucker was a parson and a Tory, but, for the rest, an honourable man and a competent political economist. In face of the infamous cowardice of character that reigns to-day, and believes most devoutly in "the laws of commerce," it is our bounden duty again and again to brand the Burkes, who only differ from their successors in one thing—talent.

14. Marie Augier: Du Crédit Public. Paris, 1842.

15. "Capital is said by a Quarterly Reviewer to fly turbulence and strife, and to be timid, which is very true; but this is very incompletely stating the question. Capital eschews no profit, or very small profit, just as Nature was formerly said to abhor a vacuum. With adequate profit, capital is very bold. A certain 10 per cent. will ensure its employment anywhere; 20 per cent. certain will produce eagerness; 60 per cent., positive audacity; 100 per cent. will make it ready to trample on all human laws; 300 per cent., and there is not a crime at which it will scruple, nor a risk it will not run, even to the chance of its owner being hanged. If turbulence and strife will bring a profit, it will freely encourage both. Smuggling and the slave-trade have amply proved all that is here stated." (P.J. Dunning, l. c., p. 35.)

Chapter 2: THE KEYNESIAN REVOLUTION

Keynes asserts that "the outstanding faults of the economic society in which we live are its failure to provide full employment and its arbitrary and inequitable distribution of wealth and incomes." This situation came about, he believes, because classical economics failed to recognize that the market cannot, by itself, adequately maintain consumption demand and coordinate investment decisions. Government, then, must take an active role in promoting full employment through both fiscal and monetary policy.

CONCLUDING NOTES ON THE SOCIAL PHILOSOPHY TOWARDS WHICH THE GENERAL THEORY MIGHT LEAD

John Maynard Keynes

I

The outstanding faults of the economic society in which we live are its failure to provide for full employment and its arbitrary and inequitable distribution of wealth and incomes. The bearing of the foregoing theory on the first of these is obvious. But there are also two important respects in which it is relevant to the second.

Since the end of the nineteenth century significant progress towards the removal of very great disparities of wealth and income has been achieved through the instrument of direct taxation—income tax and surtax and death duties—especially in Great Britain. Many people would wish to see this process carried much further, but they are deterred by two considerations; partly by the fear of making skilful evasions too much worth while and also of diminishing unduly the motive towards risk-taking, but mainly, I think, by the belief that the growth of capital depends upon the strength of the motive towards individual saving and that for a large proportion of this growth we are dependent on the savings of the rich out of their superfluity. Our argument does not affect the first of these considerations. But it may considerably modify our attitude towards the second. For we have seen that, up to the point where full employment prevails, the growth of capital depends not at all on a low propensity to consume but is, on the contrary, held back by it; and only in conditions of full employment is a low propensity to consume conducive to the growth of capital. Moreover, experience suggests that in existing

Reprinted with permission of the publisher from *The General Theory of Employment, Interest, and Money*. New York: Harcourt Brace Jovanovich, 1937, pp. 372–84.

conditions saving by institutions and through sinking funds is more than adequate, and that measures for the redistribution of incomes in a way likely to raise the propensity to consume may prove positively favourable to the growth of capital.

The existing confusion of the public mind on the matter is well illustrated by the very common belief that the death duties are responsible for a reduction in the capital wealth of the country. Assuming that the State applies the proceeds of these duties to its ordinary outgoings so that taxes on incomes and consumption are correspondingly reduced or avoided, it is, of course, true that a fiscal policy of heavy death duties has the effect of increasing the community's propensity to consume. But inasmuch as an increase in the habitual propensity to consume will in general (*i.e.* except in conditions of full employment) serve to increase at the same time the inducement to invest, the inference commonly drawn is the exact opposite of the truth.

Thus our argument leads towards the conclusion that in contemporary conditions the growth of wealth, so far from being dependent on the abstinence of the rich, as is commonly supposed, is more likely to be impeded by it. One of the chief social justifications of great inequality of wealth is, therefore, removed. I am not saying that there are no other reasons, unaffected by our theory, capable of justifying some measure of inequality in some circumstances. But it does dispose of the most important of the reasons why hitherto we have thought it prudent to move carefully. This particularly affects our attitude towards death duties: for there are certain justifications for inequality of incomes which do not apply equally to inequality of inheritances.

For my own part, I believe that there is social and psychological justification for significant inequalities of incomes and wealth, but not for such large disparities as exist to-day. There are valuable human activities which require the motive of money-making and the environment of private wealth-ownership for their full fruition. Moreover, dangerous human proclivities can be canalised into comparatively harmless channels by the existence of opportunities for money-making and private wealth, which, if they cannot be satisfied in this way, may find their outlet in cruelty, the reckless pursuit of personal power and authority, and other forms of self-aggrandisement. It is better that a man should tyrannise over his bank balance than over his fellow-citizens; and whilst the former is sometimes denounced as being but a means to the latter, sometimes at least it is an alternative. But it is not necessary for the stimulation of these activities and the satisfaction of these proclivities that the game should be played for such high stakes as at present. Much lower stakes will serve the purpose equally well, as soon as the players are accustomed to them. The task of transmuting human nature must not be confused with the task of managing it. Though in the ideal commonwealth men may have been taught or inspired or bred to take no interest in the stakes, it may still be wise and prudent statesmanship to allow the game to be played, subject to rules and limitations, so long as the average man, or even a significant section of the community, is in fact strongly addicted to the money-making passion.

II

There is, however, a second, much more fundamental inference from our argument which has a bearing on the future of inequalities of wealth; namely, our theory of the rate of interest. The justification for a moderately high rate of interest has been found hitherto in the necessity of providing a sufficient inducement to save. But we have shown that the extent of effective saving is necessarily determined by the scale of investment and that the scale of investment is promoted by a *low* rate of interest, provided that we do not attempt to stimulate it in this way beyond the point which corresponds to full employment. Thus it is to our best advantage to reduce the rate of interest to that point relatively to the schedule of the marginal efficiency of capital at which there is full employment.

There can be no doubt that this criterion will lead to a much lower rate of interest than has ruled hitherto; and, so far as one can guess at the schedules of the marginal efficiency of capital corresponding to increasing amounts of capital, the rate of interest is likely to fall steadily, if it should be practicable to maintain conditions of more or less continuous full employment—unless, indeed, there is an excessive change in the aggregate propensity to consume (including the State).

I feel sure that the demand for capital is strictly limited in the sense that it would not be difficult to increase the stock of capital up to a point where its marginal efficiency had fallen to a very low figure. This would not mean that the use of capital instruments would cost almost nothing, but only that the return from them would have to cover little more than their exhaustion by wastage and obsolescence together with some margin to cover risk and the exercise of skill and judgment. In short, the aggregate return from durable goods in the course of their life would, as in the case of short-lived goods, just cover their labour-costs of production plus an allowance for risk and the costs of skill and supervision.

Now, though this state of affairs would be quite compatible with some measure of individualism, yet it would mean the euthanasia of the rentier, and, consequently, the euthanasia of the cumulative oppressive power of the capitalist to exploit the scarcity-value of capital. Interest to-day rewards no genuine sacrifice, any more than does the rent of land. The owner of capital can obtain interest because capital is scarce, just as the owner of land can obtain rent because land is scarce. But whilst there may be intrinsic reasons for the scarcity of land, there are no intrinsic reasons for the scarcity of capital. An intrinsic reason for such scarcity, in the sense of a genuine sacrifice which could only be called forth by the offer of a reward in the shape of interest, would not exist, in the long run, except in the event of the individual propensity to consume proving to be of such a character that net saving in conditions of full employment comes to an end before capital has become sufficiently abundant. But even so, it will still be possible for communal saving through the agency of the State to be maintained at a level which will allow the growth of capital up to the point where it ceases to be scarce.

I see, therefore, the rentier aspect of capitalism as a transitional phase which will disappear when it has done its work. And with the disappearance of its rentier aspect much else in it besides will suffer a sea-change. It will be, moreover, a great advantage of the order of events which I am advocating, that the euthanasia of the rentier, of the functionless investor, will be nothing sudden, merely a gradual but prolonged continuance of what we have seen recently in Great Britain, and will need no revolution.

Thus we might aim in practice (there being nothing in this which is unattainable) at an increase in the volume of capital until it ceases to be scarce, so that the functionless investor will no longer receive a bonus; and at a scheme of direct taxation which allows the intelligence and determination and executive skill of the financier, the entrepreneur *et hoc genus omne* (who are certainly so fond of their craft that their labour could be obtained much cheaper than at present), to be harnessed to the service of the community on reasonable terms of reward.

At the same time we must recognise that only experience can show how far the common will, embodied in the policy of the State, ought to be directed to increasing and supplementing the inducement to invest; and how far it is safe to stimulate the average propensity to consume, without forgoing our aim of depriving capital of its scarcity-value within one or two generations. It may turn out that the propensity to consume will be so easily strengthened by the effects of a falling rate of interest, that full employment can be reached with a rate of accumulation little greater than at present. In this event a scheme for the higher taxation of large incomes and inheritances might be open to the objection that it would lead to full employment with a rate of accumulation which was reduced considerably below the current level. I must not be supposed to deny the possibility, or even the probability, of this outcome. For in such matters it is rash to predict how the average man will react to a changed environment. If, however, it should prove easy to secure an approximation to full employment with a rate of accumulation not much greater than at present, an outstanding problem will at least have been solved. And it would remain for separate decision on what scale and by what means it is right and reasonable to call on the living generation to restrict their consumption, so as to establish, in course of time, a state of full investment for their successors.

III

In some other respects the foregoing theory is moderately conservative in its implications. For whilst it indicates the vital importance of establishing certain central controls in matters which are now left in the main to individual initiative, there are wide fields of activity which are unaffected. The State will have to exercise a guiding influence on the propensity to consume partly through its scheme of taxation, partly by fixing the rate of interest, and partly, perhaps, in other ways. Furthermore, it seems unlikely that the influence of banking policy on the rate of interest will be sufficient by itself to determine an optimum rate of investment. I conceive, therefore, that a somewhat comprehensive socialisation of investment will prove the only means of securing an approximation to full employment; though this need not exclude all manner of compromises and of devices by which public authority will co-operate with private initiative. But beyond this no obvious case is made out for a system of State Socialism which would embrace most of the economic life of the community. It is not the ownership of the instruments of production which it is important for the State to assume. If the State is able to determine the aggregate amount of resources devoted to augmenting the instruments and the basic rate of reward to those who own them, it will have accomplished all that is necessary. Moreover, the necessary measures of socialisation can be introduced gradually and without a break in the general traditions of society.

Our criticism of the accepted classical theory of economics has consisted not so much in finding logical flaws in its analysis as in pointing out that its tactic assumptions are seldom or never satisfied, with the result that it cannot solve the economic problems of the actual world. But if our central controls succeed in establishing an aggregate volume of output corresponding to full employment as nearly as is practicable, the classical theory comes into its own again from this point onwards. If we suppose the volume of output to be given, *i.e.* to be determined by forces outside the classical scheme of thought, then there is no objection to be raised against the classical analysis of the manner in which private self-interest will determine what in particular is produced, in what proportions the factors of production will be combined to produce it, and how the value of the final product will be distributed between them. Again, if we have dealt otherwise with the problem of thrift, there is no objection to be raised against the modern classical theory as to the degree of consilience between private and public advantage in conditions of perfect and imperfect competition respectively. Thus, apart from the necessity of central controls to bring about an adjustment between the propensity to consume and the inducement to invest, there is no more reason to socialise economic life than there was before.

To put the point concretely, I see no reason to suppose that the existing system seriously misemploys the factors of production which are in use. There are, of course, errors of foresight; but these would not be avoided by centralising decisions. When 9,000,000 men are employed out of 10,000,000 willing and able to work, there is no evidence that the labour of these 9,000,000 men is misdirected. The complaint against the present system is not that these 9,000,000 men ought to be employed on different tasks, but that tasks should be available for the remaining 1,000,000 men. It is in determining the volume, not the direction, of actual employment that the existing system has broken down.

Thus I agree with Gesell that the result of filling in the gaps in the classical theory is not to dispose of the "Manchester System", but to indicate the nature of the environment which the free play of economic forces requires if it is to realise the full potentialities of production. The central controls necessary to ensure full employment will, of course, involve a large extension of the traditional functions of government. Furthermore, the modern classical theory has itself called attention to various conditions in which the free play of economic forces may need to be curbed or guided. But there will still remain a wide field for the exercise of private initiative and responsibility. Within this field the traditional advantages of individualism will still hold good.

Let us stop for a moment to remind ourselves what these advantages are. They are partly advantages of efficiency—the advantages of decentralisation and of the play of self-interest. The advantage to efficiency of the decentralisation of decisions and of individual responsibility is even greater, perhaps, than the nineteenth century supposed; and the reaction against the appeal to self-interest may have gone too far. But, above all, individualism, if it can be purged of its defects and its abuses, is the best safeguard of personal liberty in the sense that, compared with any other system, it greatly widens the field for the exercise of personal choice. It is also the best safeguard of the variety of life, which emerges precisely from this extended field of personal choice, and the loss of which is the greatest of all the losses of the homogeneous or totalitarian state. For this variety preserves the traditions which embody the most secure and successful choices of former generations; it colours the present with the diversification of its fancy; and, being the handmaid of experiment as well as of tradition and of fancy, it is the most powerful instrument to better the future.

Whilst, therefore, the enlargement of the functions of government, involved in the task of adjusting to one another the propensity to consume and the inducement to invest, would seem to a nineteenth-century publicist or to a contemporary American financier to be a terrific encroachment on individualism, I defend it, on the contrary, both as the only practicable means of avoiding the destruction of existing economic forms in their entirety and as the condition of the successful functioning of individual initiative.

For if effective demand is deficient, not only is the public scandal of wasted resources intolerable, but the individual enterpriser who seeks to bring these resources into action is operating with the odds loaded against him. The game of hazard which he plays is furnished with many zeros, so that the players *as a whole* will lose if they have the energy and hope to deal all the cards. Hitherto the increment of the world's wealth has fallen short of the aggregate of positive individual savings; and the difference has been made up by the losses of those whose courage and initiative have not been supplemented by exceptional skill or unusual good fortune. But if effective demand is adequate, average skill and average good fortune will be enough.

The authoritarian state systems of to-day seem to solve the problem of unemployment at the expense of efficiency and of freedom. It is certain that the world will not much longer tolerate the unemployment which, apart from brief intervals of excitement, is associated—and, in my opinion, inevitably associated—with present-day capitalistic individualism. But it may be possible by a right analysis of the problem to cure the disease whilst preserving efficiency and freedom.

IV

I have mentioned in passing that the new system might be more favourable to peace than the old has been. It is worth while to repeat and emphasise that aspect.

War has several causes. Dictators and others such, to whom war offers, in expectation at least, a pleasurable excitement, find it easy to work on the natural bellicosity of their peoples. But, over and above this, facilitating their task of fanning the popular flame, are the economic causes of war, namely, the pressure of population and the competitive struggle for markets. It is the second factor, which probably played a predominant part in the nineteenth century, and might again, that is germane to this discussion.

I have pointed out in the preceding chapter that, under the system of domestic *laissez-faire* and an international gold standard such as was orthodox in the latter half of the nineteenth century, there was no means open to a government whereby to mitigate economic distress at home except through the competitive struggle for markets. For all measures helpful to a state of chronic or intermittent under-employment were ruled out, except measures to improve the balance of trade on income account.

Thus, whilst economists were accustomed to applaud the prevailing international system as furnishing the fruits of the international division of labour and harmonising at the same time the interests of different nations, there lay concealed a less benign influence; and those statesmen were moved by common sense and a correct apprehension of the true course of events, who believed that if a rich, old country were to neglect the struggle for markets its prosperity would droop and fail. But if nations can learn to provide themselves with full employment by their domestic policy (and, we must add, if they can also attain equilibrium in the trend of their population), there need be no important economic forces calculated to set the interes. of one country against that of its neighbours. There would still be room for the international division of labour and for international lending in appropriate conditions. But there would no longer be a pressing motive why one country need force its wares on another or repulse the offerings of its neighbour, not because this was necessary to enable it to pay for what it wished to purchase, but with the express object of upsetting the equilibrium of payments so as to develop a balance of trade in its own favour. International trade would cease to be what it is, namely, a desperate expedient to maintain employment at home by forcing sales on foreign markets and restricting purchases, which, if successful, will merely shift the problem of unemployment to the neighbour which is worsted in the struggle, but a willing and unimpeded exchange of goods and services in conditions of mutual advantage.

V

Is the fulfilment of these ideas a visionary hope? Have they insufficient roots in the motives which govern the evolution of political society? Are the interests which they will thwart stronger and more obvious than those which they will serve?

I do not attempt an answer in this place. It would need a volume of a different character from this one to indicate even in outline the practical measures in which they might be gradually clothed. But if the ideas are correct—a hypothesis on which the author himself must necessarily base what he writes—it would be a mistake, I predict, to dispute their potency over a period of time. At the present moment people are unusually expectant of a more fundamental diagnosis; more particularly ready to receive it; eager to try it out, if it should be even plausible. But apart from this contemporary mood, the ideas of economists and political philosophers, both when they are right and when they are wrong, are more powerful than is commonly understood. Indeed the world is ruled by little else. Practical men, who believe themselves to be quite exempt from any intellectual influences, are usually the slaves of some defunct economist. Madmen in authority, who hear voices in the air, are distilling their frenzy from some academic scribbler of a few years back. I am sure that the power of vested interests is vastly exaggerated compared with the gradual encroachment of ideas. Not, indeed, immediately, but after a certain interval; for in the field of economic and political philosophy there are not many who are influenced by new theories after they are twenty-five or thirty years of age, so that the ideas which civil servants and politicians and even agitators apply to current events are not likely to be the newest. But, soon or late, it is ideas, not vested interests, which are dangerous for good or evil.

In this article, Hansen traces the history of economic thought on fiscal policy. The traditional view of fiscal policy allowed the government to go into debt only in times of emergency. In fact, the wartime borrowing requirements of governments stimulated the growth and development of modern credit institutions. Hansen views unemployment as another emergency; hence, government is justified in using public debt as a tool of demand management in order to prevent or eliminate unemployment.

FISCAL POLICY, NEW AND OLD

Alvin Hansen

The changing ideas about the nature and use of public credit, from ancient times through the early modern period, constitute a fascinating chapter in the history of thought. Scholastic theologians, like Thomas Aquinas, were bitterly opposed to loans.[1] This attitude was due not merely to the official church opposition to the payment of interest, but to a belief that public debt was itself immoral. Political philosophers of the early modern period continued to regard the prior accumulation of treasures as superior to borrowing. Jean Bodin, for example, approved only six sources of state revenue: the public domain, conquest, gifts (which are "rare"), annual contributions of allies, customs, and taxes. Traffic in rights and titles he considered pernicious, and borrowing at high interest rates "the ruin of princes." Emergencies should be met by accumulated hoards, and only war provided justification for extraordinary levies or loans.[2]

Thomas Hobbes was more realistic in his approach. He recognized the limitations of revenue from the public domain alone. In view of the widening scope of governmental expenditures, the monarch must resort to taxation, and occasionally even to public credit.[3] Adam Smith reverted to the older tradition, parting company on this point with Hobbes. He maintained that only "the want of parsimony in time of peace imposes the necessity of contracting debt in time of war." He observed that with the growth of commerce and manufactures European monarchs have unfortunately lost their "disposition to save," while the upkeep of standing armies and needless luxuries absorb ordinary revenue. Individuals follow the example of the state by running into debt, and "the enormous debts . . . will in the long-run probably ruin all the great nations of Europe."[4]

Hume likewise compared contemporary financing with the ancient practice of accumulating hoards, much to the disadvantage of contemporary methods. "Our modern expedient," he wrote, "is to mortgage the public revenues . . . a practice which appears ruinous." In former times the "opening of the public treasure" in wartime at least "served as a temporary encouragement to industry, and atoned, in some degree, for the inevitable calamities of war." Loan-financed wars are doubly calamitous, for the similarity between the "circulation" of "stocks" and the "circulation" of goods and money is illusory. The taxes raised to pay interest on the loans are a check on industry. Government securities have all the disadvantages of paper credit, give rise to speculation, confer advantages on the city at the expense of the nation, make the country dependent upon foreign financiers, and encourage "a useless and inactive life."[5]

Wars and the Rise of Credit Institutions

Whatever the ideas of the political philosophers, the expansion of commerce and the undertaking of wars were from the very beginning of the Middle Ages closely associated with loan financing, both public and private. Through several centuries credit institutions were slowly developing to meet growing needs, leading ultimately to an organized capital market dominated by the stock exchanges and by large banks, operating on a fractional reserve basis. Through the development of these institutions it became possible to engage in extraordinary expenditures, such as those incurred in war, without imposing confiscatory taxes. The development of credit institutions made possible the financing of wars in a manner which added stimulus to the economy through the net additions of purchasing power injected into the community through the use of credit. To be sure, the dose of credit was frequently excessive, leading to price inflation. At any rate, public borrowing for war purposes removed the necessity for unduly severe and quasi-confiscatory exactions upon private wealth and income, and instead furnished a powerful stimulant to trade and enterprise. In so far as they were fought on foreign soil and with hired mercenaries, wars came to be regarded as by no means an unmixed evil. Indeed, the whole history from the late seventeenth century to the end of the Napoleonic Wars indicates a high correlation between: (a) the expenditures and use of public credit to which war gave rise, and (b) brisk trade, rising economic activity, and business prosperity. From the standpoint of the sovereign, wars were usually fought for dynastic reasons, for glory of empire, and frequently for acquisition of territory. The secondary consequences of wars during this earlier period in the history of capitalism are such as to give much support to the thesis that in this period in history wars stimulated the development of industrialism. This relatively complacent view of war was, however, shattered by the terrible experience of the first World War. Only in consequence of the disastrous effect on the economic system as a whole, and the revolutionary changes which emerged from the first World War, did there at last arise a conviction, in at least a large part of the Western world, that under modern conditions wars must be regarded as an economic, no less than a moral and social, disaster.

Thus, the emergence of private and especially public credit institutions aided the waging of expensive wars, and these, in turn, powerfully reinforced the development of the modern credit economy.

In 1761 the entire national debt in England was only £3 millions. By 1815 it amounted to over £800 millions. This enormous increase in the public debt created a haven of refuge—for capitalists both in England and abroad—for the investment of funds in a period of risk and uncertainty created by the international upheaval. The buying and selling of government obligations led to the development of the stock exchange, and throughout the eighteenth century dealings on the exchange were confined almost entirely to government securities. As late as 1843, 70 per cent of the securities listed on the London Stock Exchange consisted of securities of the English government, while an additional 10 per cent was composed of the debt obligations of foreign governments. Even as late as 1875 slightly over two thirds of the securities listed on the London Stock Exchange consisted of governmental securities.[6]

Moreover, in the very early stages of the development of modern industrialism public investments financed by public borrowing played a quite extraordinary role. In the case of the United States, internal improvements, such as turnpikes, canals, and, at the very beginning, railroads, were financed by lavish state expenditures. These wildly speculative promotional activities based on excessive optimism brought financial ruin, as is well known, to many American states and other local governmental units, leading to widespread defaults. But it must not be forgotten that, while individual investors—in very large part foreigners—lost their savings in these defaults, from a social standpoint these promotional developments played an important role in the emergence of the rapidly expanding industrialism. On the Continent of Europe the enormous financial needs incident to the development of modern systems of transportation, in particular the railroad, could not be financed from private sources under the prevailing state of financial institutional development. The great transportation undertakings, therefore, in contrast with the smaller requirements of manufacturing, were almost everywhere on the Continent financed by public borrowing and became established state enterprises. The tradition of an efficient bureaucratic civil service doubtless played an important role in the success of these ventures in contrast with the financially disastrous public ventures undertaken in America.

In England and the United States, however, and in the subsequent emergence of the manufacturing phases of modern industrialism on the Continent, governmental securities were increasingly supplanted, relatively speaking, by the emergence of the corporation and the issuance of private securities. Thus, the nineteenth century, particularly the last half, witnessed a prodigious growth of private corporate securities and the development (almost to the point of the exclusion of governmental credit as a factor in economic life) of private capitalism. In consequence of the first World War and its aftermath, and particularly as a result of the unprecedented unemployment incident to the Great Depression, public credit as an instrument of economic policy has again come powerfully to the fore. Thus, we witness a cycle in the role of public credit in the history of modern industrialism.

Starting with public credit playing a major role in the period of the early rise of private capitalism, we now again see a reemergence of the role of public credit in economic life.

We have noted how the emergence of public credit was related to the rise of war expenditures. Historically, this has been, and still remains, by far the major cause of the rise of public debt. The enormous increase in public revenues derived from taxes is, however, mainly a function of the widening scope of governmental activities, though in part it is a result of the growing necessity of financing from taxes the necessary interest payments on the public debt created mainly by war. Government services, starting from the limited function of giving protection to life and property, expanded under the requirements of a growing industrial system, the rapid agglomeration of population in huge cities, and the increasing problems of organization incident to these developments. Collective action had to be taken to protect against disaster from fire and flood; to provide for sanitation and hospitalization; to protect the public health and prevent the spread of contagious diseases; to provide methods of communication in the development of roads, postal services, and, in many countries, telegraph and telephone; to provide for protection against crime; and, increasingly with the rise of democracy, to provide on an ever more lavish scale for the education of the entire population. Services which, in large part, had formerly been provided by private agencies eventually had to be taken over by the government. Thus, provision for self-protection was transformed into a public police force. Settlement of private disputes through mutual arbitration or dueling was transferred to public courts, private education was transferred to public schools, private hospitals to public hospitals, and increasingly, particularly since the Great Depression, private charity has given way to enormous expenditures on public relief and social insurance. Moreover, the development of modern standards of living and a huge urban population have made necessary large expenditures on community consumers' capital in the form of playgrounds, recreational facilities, public schools, and public buildings of various types. Public activities have, therefore, spread from current services to the development of large expensive capital projects devoted to community consumption.

Public Finance Under Early Capitalism

The nineteenth century was preoccupied with the problem of attaining a volume of savings adequate for the requirements of a rapidly expanding economy. The dynamics of population growth and technological progress placed a premium upon freedom of enterprise and private initiative. Fiscal policy aimed at the least possible interference with the functioning of the private, capitalistic economy. The Jeffersonian ideal in America and the Gladstonian in England alike sought to minimize to the utmost the functions of governments so that, as far as possible, the entire disposable income might be expended by the individual citizen, whether for consumption or investment, for such ends as he might deem advisable. The productive resources of the community, it was believed, would be utilized most effectively if guided by a market responsive to the choices of individuals free to use as they wished their personal incomes. Public functions per se were regarded as a necessary evil. Taxes were "unproductive" expenditures, representing an unfortunate waste in the process of production. The flow of goods and services which the citizenry might enjoy could always be increased by tax reduction. Sound fiscal policy called for two things: (1) the reduction of public expenditures to the utmost possible limit, and (2) a tax structure which disturbed the pricing system as little as possible, including the pricing of the factors of production, thereby leaving intact the relative distribution of income as it would be in a tax-free society.

Such was the ideal of public finance in the heyday of private capitalism. The ideal was, of course, never fully realized. As the "high" capitalistic period receded before the advance of state interventionism, taxation was seized upon as a convenient and highly effective instrument for the regulation and control of economic life. Already in the mercantilist period taxation had been used as a police measure designed to prohibit certain activities regarded as undesirable, whether in the field of consumption or production.

Changing Role of Fiscal Policy

A far more revolutionary aim of social policy now appeared above the horizon, the full implications of which were at first not wholly visible. Indeed, it was introduced at first largely as a by-product of the imperious necessity of financing great wars and not in response to a well-thought-out social philosophy. While avowed socialists had their eyes fixed on the goal of social ownership of the means of production, the course of events had unexpectedly forged a powerful instrument for the socialization of income. The severe requirements of national defense had demonstrated the extraordinary possibilities of progressive income and inheritance taxation and had thus prepared the ground for the utilization of tax measures to accomplish far-reaching social ends, such as the more equal distribution of income and the expansion of collective consumption by the community as a whole.

In the meantime, devastating depressions brought to the foreground as never before the problem of business instability. Whereas it had been the concern of economic policy to raise the standard of living, now attention was centered on the promotion of security and stability. At first, main reliance was placed upon monetary policy, but the exigencies of the Great Depression compelled (or, at any rate, led to) enormous expenditures for the relief of the unemployed. These were made more willingly in the belief that they served the double purpose of giving relief and also of "curing" the depression. Thus, fiscal policy was forced into service as a compensatory device more by accident than by design. It was, therefore, not surprising that experience in the implementation of this policy turned up some rather surprising results. Part of the consequences, it appears, were due to the applications of orthodox canons of fiscal policy to a situation for which they were totally unsuited. It was the old story of putting new wine into old bottles.

Back of the menacing unfolding of violent industrial fluctuations there now appeared the specter of chronic unemployment. Many, perhaps most, competent observers professed to doubt its reality and conceived it to be an illusion springing from the distracted psychological atmosphere created by the Great Depression.

Discussions with respect to the phenomena of "long waves" and of structural changes in the economy, together with the increasing development of the theoretical tools of dynamic analysis, produced challenging hypotheses in explanation of chronic or secular unemployment. And while the debate progressed, all the leading governments of the world were continuing to pour out vast funds for armaments or for the relief of depression—whatever its character, whether temporary or secular. Government debt was everywhere mounting and fiscal policy was being drafted willy-nilly to serve as an instrument to increase the volume of employment.

There is thus emerging a new aim of fiscal policy, vigorously assailed by some and staunchly defended by others—the aim of ensuring the full employment of the factors of production. This policy involves greatly enlarged governmental expenditures. Some would finance these wholly from progressive taxation, once a full-income level had been achieved, and thus "balance the budget." Others would finance them partly from a progressive rise in the public debt. The possible limits of this development are certainly far wider than is usually supposed, owing partly to the low rates of interest which, under an appropriate Central Bank policy, are adequate to tempt idle funds into short-term government obligations, and partly to the fact that taxes raised to pay interest on a public debt domestically held flow back again to the community as a part of the income receipts of individuals. The larger aspects of this problem and its implications in terms of the distribution of income and the price structure will be discussed subsequently in this volume.

Notes

1. Cf. E. R. A. Seligman, article on "Public Finance," in the *Encyclopedia of the Social Sciences*, Vol. 12, p. 641.
2. *Six livres de la Republique*, Book VI. Chapter 2, especially pp. 655–56, 661, 671, 680–83, 690–92.
3. *English Works of Thomas Hobbes*, ed. Molesworth; Volume VI, Chapter 1. A Dialogue Between a Philosopher and a Student of the Common Laws of England, pp. 10–22.
4. *The Wealth of Nations*, Book V, Chapter 3, Stuart Edition, pp. 724–27.
5. *Essays and Treatises on Several Subjects*, Volume II, London, 1760. Essay "Of Public Credit," especially pp. 134–42.
6. G. W. Edwards, *The Evolution of Finance Capitalism*, Longmans, 1938.

Lerner argues that fiscal policy should be determined by the "needs" of the government and not some traditional wisdom which called for balanced budgets. "The central idea is that government fiscal polic[ies] . . . shall all be undertaken with an eye only to the results of these actions on the economy and not to any established traditional doctrine about what is sound or unsound."

FUNCTIONAL FINANCE AND THE FEDERAL DEBT

Abba P. Lerner

Apart from the necessity of winning the war, there is no task facing society today so important as the elimination of economic insecurity. If we fail in this after the war the present threat to democratic civilization will arise again. It is therefore essential that we grapple with this problem even if it involves a little careful thinking and even if the thought proves somewhat contrary to our preconceptions.

In recent years the principles by which appropriate government action can maintain prosperity have been adequately developed, but the proponents of the new principles have either not seen their full logical implications or shown an oversolicitousness which caused them to try to save the public from the necessary mental exercise. This has worked like a boomerang. Many of our publicly minded men who have come to see that deficit spending actually works still oppose the permanent maintenance of prosperity because in their failure to see how it all works they are easily frightened by fairy tales of terrible consequences.

I.

As formulated by Alvin Hansen and others who have developed and popularized it, the new fiscal theory (which was first put forward in substantially complete form by J. M. Keynes in England) sounds a little less novel and absurd to our preconditioned ears than it does when presented in its simplest and most logical form, with all the unorthodox implications expressly formulated. In some cases the less shocking formulation may be intentional, as a tactical device to gain serious attention. In other cases it is due not to a desire to sugar the pill but to the fact that the writers themselves have not seen all the unorthodox implications— perhaps subconsciously compromising with their own orthodox education. But now it is these compromises that are under fire. Now more than ever it is necessary to pose the theorems in the purest form. Only thus will it be possible to clear the air

Reprinted with permission of the publisher from *Social Research*, Vol. 10, February 1983, pp. 38–51.

of objections which really are concerned with awkwardnesses that appear only when the new theory is forced into the old theoretical framework.

Fundamentally the new theory, like almost every important discovery, is extremely simple. Indeed it is this simplicity which makes the public suspect it as too slick. Even learned professors who find it hard to abandon ingrained habits of thought have complained that it is "merely logical" when they could find no flaw in it. What progress the theory has made so far has been achieved not by simplifying it but by dressing it up to make it more complicated and accompanying the presentation with impressive but irrelevant statistics.

The central idea is that government fiscal policy, its spending and taxing, its borrowing and repayment of loans, its issue of new money and its withdrawal of money, shall all be undertaken with an eye only to the *results* of these actions on the economy and not to any established traditional doctrine about what is sound or unsound. This principle of judging only by *effects* has been applied in many other fields of human activity, where it is known as the method of science as opposed to scholasticism. The principle of judging fiscal measures by the way they work or function in the economy we may call *Functional Finance*.

The first financial responsibility of the government (since nobody else can undertake that responsibility) is to keep the total rate of spending in the country on goods and services neither greater nor less than that rate which at the current prices would buy all the goods that it is possible to produce. If total spending is allowed to go above this there will be inflation, and if it is allowed to go below this there will be unemployment. The government can increase total spending by spending more itself or by reducing taxes so that the taxpayers have more money left to spend. It can reduce total spending by spending less itself or by raising taxes so that taxpayers have less money left to spend. By these means total spending can be kept at the required level, where it will be enough to buy the goods that can be produced by all who want to work, and yet not enough to bring inflation by demanding (at current prices) *more* than can be produced.

In applying this first law of Functional Finance, the government may find itself collecting more in taxes than it is spending, or spending more than it collects in taxes. In the former case it can keep the difference in its coffers or use it to repay some of the national debt, and in the latter case it would have to provide the difference by borrowing or printing money. In neither case should the government feel that there is anything especially good or bad about this result; it should merely concentrate on keeping the total rate of spending neither too small nor too great, in this way preventing both unemployment and inflation.

An interesting, and to many a shocking, corollary is that taxing is *never* to be undertaken merely because the government needs to make money payments. According to the principles of Functional Finance, taxation must be judged only by its effects. Its main effects are two: the taxpayer has less money left to spend and the government has more money. The second effect can be brought about so much more easily by printing the money that only the first effect is significant. Taxation should therefore be imposed only when it is desirable that the taxpayers shall have less money to spend, for example, when they would otherwise spend enough to bring about inflation.

The second law of Functional Finance is that the government should borrow money only if it is desirable that the public should have less money and more government bonds, for these are the *effects* of government borrowing. This might be desirable if otherwise the rate of interest would be reduced too low (by attempts on the part of the holders of the cash to lend it out) and induce too much investment, thus bringing about inflation. Conversely, the government should lend money (or repay some of its debt) only if it is desirable to increase the money or to reduce the quantity of government bonds in the hands of the public. When taxing, spending, borrowing and lending (or repaying loans) are governed by the principles of Functional Finance, any excess of money outlays over money revenues, if it cannot be met out of money hoards, must be met by printing new money, and any excess of revenues over outlays can be destroyed or used to replenish hoards.

The almost instinctive revulsion that we have to the idea of printing money, and the tendency to identify it with inflation, can be overcome if we calm ourselves and take note that this printing does not affect the amount of money *spent*. That is regulated by the first law of Functional Finance, which refers especially to inflation and unemployment. The printing of money takes place only when it is needed to implement Functional Finance in spending or lending (or repayment of government debt).[1]

In brief, Functional Finance rejects completely the traditional doctrines of "sound finance" and the principle of trying to balance the budget over a solar year or any other arbitrary period. In their place it prescribes: first, the adjustment of total spending (by everybody in the economy, including the government) in order to eliminate both unemployment and inflation, using government spending when total spending is too low and taxation when total spending is too high; second, the adjustment of public holdings of money and of government bonds, by government borrowing or debt repayment, in order to achieve the rate of interest which results in the most desirable level of investment; and, third, the printing, hoarding or destruction of money as needed for carrying out the first two parts of the program.

II.

In judging the formulations of economists on this subject it is difficult to distinguish between tact in smoothing over the more staggering statements of Functional Finance and insufficient clarity on the part of those who do not fully realize the extremes that are implied in their relatively orthodox formulations. First there were the pump-primers, whose argument was that the government merely had to get things going and then the economy could go on by itself. There are very few pump-primers left now. A formula similar in some ways to pump-priming was developed by Scandinavian economists in terms of a series of cyclical, capital and other special budgets which had to be balanced not annually but over longer periods. Like the pump-priming formula it fails because there is no reason for supposing that the spending and taxation policy which maintains full employment and prevents inflation must necessarily balance the budget over a decade any more than during a year or at the end of each fortnight.

As soon as this was seen—the lack of any guarantee that the maintenance of prosperity would permit the budget to be balanced even over longer periods—it had to be recognized that the result might be a continually increasing national debt (if the additional spending were provided by the government's borrowing of the money and not by printing the excess of its spending over its tax revenues). At this point two things should have been made clear: first, that this possibility presented no danger to society, no matter what unimagined heights the national debt might reach, so long as Functional Finance maintained the proper level of total demand for current output; and second (though this is much less important), that there is an automatic tendency for the budget to be balanced in the long run as a *result* of the application of Functional Finance, even if there is no place for the *principle* of balancing the budget. No matter how much interest has to be paid on the debt, taxation must not be applied unless it is necessary to keep spending down to prevent inflation. The interest can be paid by borrowing still more.

As long as the public is willing to keep on lending to the government there is no difficulty, no matter how many zeros are added to the national debt. If the public becomes reluctant to keep on lending, it must either hoard the money or spend it. If the public hoards, the government can print the money to meet its interest and other obligations, and the only effect is that the public holds government currency instead of government bonds and the government is saved the trouble of making interest payments. If the public spends, this will increase the rate of total spending so that it will not be necessary for the government to borrow for this purpose; and if the rate of spending becomes too great, *then* is the time to tax to prevent inflation. The proceeds can then be used to pay interest and repay government debt. In every case Functional Finance provides a simple, quasi-automatic response.

But either this was not seen clearly or it was considered too shocking or too logical to be told to the public. Instead it was argued, for example by Alvin Hansen, that as long as there is a reasonable ratio between national income and debt, the interest payment on the national debt can easily come from taxes paid out of the increased national income created by the deficit financing.

This unnecessary "appeasement" opened the way to an extremely effective opposition to Functional Finance. Even men who have a clear understanding of the mechanism whereby government spending in times of depression can increase the national income by several times the amount laid out by the government, and who understand perfectly well that the national debt, when it is not owed to other nations, is not a burden on the nation in the same way as an individual's debt to other individuals is a burden on the individual, have come out strongly against "deficit spending."[2] It has been argued that "it would be impossible to devise a program better adapted to the systematic undermining of the private-enterprise system and the hastening of the final catastrophe than 'deficit spending.' "[3]

These objections are based on the recognition that although every dollar spent by the government may create several dollars of income in the course of the next year or two, the effects then disappear. From this it follows that if the national income is to be maintained at a high level the government has to keep up its contribution to spending for as long as private spending is insufficient by itself to provide full employment. This might mean an indefinite continuation of government support to spending (though not necessarily at an increasing rate); and if, as the "appeasement" formulation suggests, all this spending comes out of borrowing, the debt will keep on growing until it is no longer in a "reasonable" ratio to income.

This leads to the crux of the argument. If the interest on the debt must be raised out of taxes (again an assumption that is unchallenged by the "appeasement" formulation) it will in time constitute an important fraction of the national income. The very high income tax necessary to collect this amount of money and pay it to the holders of government bonds will discourage risky private investment, by so reducing the net return on it that the investor is not compensated for the risk of losing his capital. This will make it necessary for the government to undertake still more deficit financing to keep up the level of income and employment. Still heavier taxation will then be necessary to pay the interest on the growing debt—until the burden of taxation is so crushing that private investment becomes unprofitable, and the private enterprise economy collapses. Private firms and corporations will all be bankrupted by the taxes, and the government will have to take over all industry.

This argument is not new. The identical calamities, although they are now receiving much more attention than usual, were promised when the first income tax law of one penny in the pound was proposed. All this only makes it more important to evaluate the significance of the argument.

III.

There are four major errors in the argument against deficit spending, four reasons why its apparent conclusiveness is only illusory.

In the first place, the same high income tax that reduces the return on the investment is deductible for the loss that is incurred if the investment turns out a failure. As a result of this the *net* return on the risk of loss is unaffected by the income tax rate, no matter how high that may be. Consider an investor in the $50,000-a-year income class who has accumulated $10,000 to invest. At 6 percent this would yield $600, but after paying income tax on this addition to his income at 60 cents in the dollar he would have only $240 left. It is argued, therefore, that he would not invest because this is insufficient compensation for the risk of losing $10,000. This argument forgets that if the $10,000 is all lost, the net loss to the investor, after he has deducted his income tax allowance, will be only $4,000, and the rate of return on the amount he actually risks is still exactly 6 percent; $240 is 6 percent of $4,000. The effect of the income tax is to make the rich man act as a kind of agent working for society on commission. He receives only a part of the return on the investment, but he loses only a part of the money that is invested. Any investment that was worth undertaking in the absence of the income tax is still worth undertaking.

Of course, this correction of the argument is strictly true only where 100 percent of the loss is deductible from taxable income, where relief from taxation occurs at the same rate as the tax on returns. There is a good case against certain limitations on permissible deduction from the income tax base for losses incurred, but that is another story. Something of the argument remains, too, if the loss would put the taxpayer into a lower income tax bracket, where the rebate (and the tax) is at a lower rate. There would then be some reduction in the net return as compared with the potential net loss. But this would apply only to such investments as are large enough to threaten to impoverish the investor if they fail. It was for the express purpose of dealing with this problem that the corporation was devised, making it possible for many individuals to combine and undertake risky enterprises without any one person having to risk all his fortune on one venture. But quite apart from corporate investment, this problem would be met almost entirely if the maximum rate of income tax were reached at a relatively low level, say at $25,000 a year (low, that is, from the point of view of the rich men who are the supposed source of risk capital). Even if all income in excess of $25,000 were taxed at 90 percent there would be no discouragement in the investment of any part of income over this level. True, the net return, after payment of tax, would be only one-tenth of the nominal interest payments, but the amount risked by the investors would also be only ten percent of the actual capital invested, and therefore the net return on the capital actually risked by the investor would be unaffected.

In the second place, this argument against deficit spending in time of depression would be indefensible even if the harm done by debt were as great as has been suggested. It must be remembered that spending by the government increases the *real* national income of goods and services by several times the amount spent by the government, and that the burden is measured not by the amount of the interest payments but only by the inconveniences involved in the process of transferring the money from the taxpayers to the bondholders. Therefore objecting to deficit spending is like arguing that if you are offered a job when out of work on the condition that you promise to pay your wife interest on a part of the money earned (or that your wife pay it to you) it would be wiser to continue to be unemployed, because in time you will be owing your wife a great deal of money (or she will be owing it to you), and this might cause matrimonial difficulties in the future. Even if the interest payments were really lost to society, instead of being merely transferred within the society, they would come to much less than the loss through permitting unemployment to continue. That loss would be several times as great as the *capital* on which these interest payments have to be made.

In the third place, there is no good reason for supposing that the government would have to raise all the interest on the national debt by current taxes. We have seen that Functional Finance permits taxation only when the *direct* effect of the tax is in the social interest, as when it prevents excessive spending or excessive investment which would bring about inflation. If taxes imposed to prevent inflation do not result in sufficient proceeds, the interest on the debt can be met by borrowing or printing the money. There is no risk of inflation from this, because if there were such a risk a greater amount would have to be collected in taxes.

This means that the absolute size of the national debt does not matter at all, and that however large the interest payments that have to be made, these do not constitute any burden upon society as a whole. A completely fantastic exaggeration may illustrate the point. Suppose the national debt reaches the stupendous total of ten thousand billion dollars (that is, ten trillion, $10,000,000,000,000), so that the interest on it is 300 billion a year. Suppose the real national income of goods and services which can be produced by the economy when fully employed is 150 billion. The interest alone, therefore, comes to twice the real national income. There is no doubt that a debt of this size would be called "unreasonable." But even in this fantastic case the payment of the interest constitutes no burden on society. Although the real income is only 150 billion dollars the money income is 450 billion—150 billion in income from the production of goods and services and 300 billion in income from ownership of the government bonds which constitute the national debt. Of this money income of 450 billion, 300 billion has to be collected in taxes by the government for interest payments (if 10 trillion is the legal debt limit), but after payment of these taxes there remains 150 billion dollars in the hands of the taxpayers, and this is enough to pay for all the goods and services that the economy can produce. Indeed it would do the public no good to have any more money left after tax payments, because if it spent more than 150 billion dollars it would merely be raising the prices of the goods bought. It would not be able to obtain more goods to consume than the country is able to produce.

Of course this illustration must not be taken to imply that a debt of this size is at all likely to come about as a result of the application of Functional Finance. As will be shown below, there is a natural tendency for the national debt to stop growing long before it comes anywhere near the astronomical figures that we have been playing with.

The unfounded assumption that current interest on the debt must be collected in taxes springs from the idea that the debt must be kept in a "reasonable" or "manageable" ratio to income (whatever that may be). If this restriction is accepted, *borrowing* to pay the interest is eliminated as soon as the limit of "reasonableness" is reached, and if we further rule out, as an indecent thought, the possibility of *printing* the money, there remains only the possibility of raising the interest payments by taxes. Fortunately there is no need to assume these limitations so long as Functional Finance is on guard against inflation, for it is the fear of inflation which is the only rational basis for suspicion of the printing of money.

Finally, there is no reason for assuming that, as a result of the continued application of Functional Finance to maintain full employment, the government must always be borrowing more money and increasing the national debt. There are a number of reasons for this.

First, full employment *can* be maintained by printing the money needed for it, and this does not increase the debt at all. It is probably advisable, however, to allow debt and money to increase together in a certain balance, as long as one or the other has to increase.

Second, since one of the greatest deterrents to private investment is the fear that the depression will come before the investment has paid for itself, the guarantee of permanent full employment will make private investment much more attractive, once investors have got over their suspicions of the new procedure. The greater private investment will diminish the need for deficit spending.

Third, as the national debt increases, and with it the sum of private wealth, there will be an increasing yield from taxes on higher incomes and inheritances, even if the tax rates are unchanged. These higher tax payments do not represent reductions of spending by the taxpayers. Therefore the government does not have to use these proceeds to maintain the requisite rate of spending, and it can devote them to paying the interest on the national debt.

Fourth, as the national debt increases it acts as a self-equilibrating force, gradually diminishing the further need for its growth and finally reaching an equilibrium level where its tendency to grow comes completely to an end. The greater the national debt the greater is the quantity of private wealth. The reason for this is simply that for every dollar of debt owed by the government there is a private creditor who owns the government obligations (possibly through a corporation in which he has shares), and who regards these obligations as part of his private fortune. The greater the private fortunes the less is the incentive to add to them by saving out of current income. As current saving is thus discouraged by the great accumulation of past savings, spending out of current income increases (since spending is the only alternative to saving income). This increase in private spending makes it less necessary for the government to undertake deficit financing to keep total spending at the level which provides full employment. When the government debt has become so great that private spending is enough to provide the total spending needed for full employment, there is no need for any deficit financing by the government, the budget is balanced and the national debt automatically stops growing. The size of this equilibrium level of debt depends on many things. It can only be guessed at, and in the very roughest manner. My guess is that it is between 100 and 300 billion dollars. Since the level is a result and not a principle of Functional Finance the latitude of such a guess does not matter; it is not needed for the application of the laws of Functional Finance.

Fifth, if for any reason the government does not wish to see private property grow too much (whether in the form of government bonds or otherwise) it can check this by taxing the rich instead of borrowing from them, in its program of financing government spending to maintain full employment. The rich will not reduce their spending significantly, and thus the effects on the economy, apart from the smaller debt, will be the same as if the money had been borrowed from them. By this means the debt can be reduced to any desired level and kept there.

The answers to the argument against deficit spending may thus be summarized as follows:

> The national debt does not have to keep on increasing;
>
> Even if the national debt does grow, the interest on it does not have to
> be raised out of current taxes;

Even if the interest on the debt is raised out of current taxes, these taxes constitute only the interest on only a fraction of the benefit enjoyed from the government spending, and are not lost to the nation but are merely transferred from taxpayers to bondholders;

High income taxes need not discourage investment, because appropriate deductions for losses can diminish the capital actually risked by the investor in the same proportion as his net income from the investment is reduced.

IV.

If the propositions of Functional Finance were put forward without fear of appearing too logical, criticisms like those discussed above would not be as popular as they now are, and it would not be necessary to defend Functional Finance from its friends. An especially embarrassing task arises from the claim that Functional Finance (or deficit financing, as it is frequently but unsatisfactorily called) is primarily a defense of private enterprise. In the attempt to gain popularity for Functional Finance, it has been given other names and declared to be essentially directed toward saving private enterprise. I myself have sinned similarly in previous writings in identifying it with democracy,[4] thus joining the army of salesmen who wrap up their wares in the flag and tie anything they have to sell to victory or morale.

Functional Finance is not especially related to democracy or to private enterprise. It is applicable to a communist society just as well as to a fascist society or a democratic society. It is applicable to any society in which money is used as an important element in the economic mechanism. It consists of the simple principle of giving up our preconceptions of what is proper or sound or traditional, of what "is done," and instead considering the *functions* performed in the economy by government taxing and spending and borrowing and lending. It means using these instruments simply as instruments, and not as magic charms that will cause mysterious hurt if they are manipulated by the wrong people or without due reverence for tradition. Like any other mechanism, Functional Finance will work no matter who pulls the levers. Its relationship to democracy and free enterprise consists simply in the fact that if the people who believe in these things will not use Functional Finance, they will stand no chance in the long run against others who will.

Notes

1. Borrowing money from the banks, on conditions which permit the banks to issue new credit money based on their additional holdings of government securities, must be considered for our purpose as printing money. In effect the banks are acting as agents for the government in issuing credit or bank money.

2. An excellent example of this is the persuasive article by John T. Flynn in *Harper's Magazine* for July 1942.

3. Flynn, *ibid.*

4. In "Total Democracy and Full Employment," *Social Change* (May 1941).

Mises suggests that Keynes's rhetorical ability, rather than the brilliance of his economic theory, was one of the main reasons for the triumph of Keynesian economics. The idea behind stabilization policy, that government can spend its way out of a depression, is neither new nor true. Deficit spending leads either to massive tax burdens or inflation by way of monetization of the debt.

STONES INTO BREAD:
THE KEYNESIAN MIRACLE

Ludwig von Mises

I

The stock-in-trade of all Socialist authors is the idea that there is potential plenty and that the substitution of socialism for capitalism would make it possible to give to everybody "according to his needs." Other authors want to bring about this paradise by a reform of the monetary and credit system. As they see it, all that is lacking is more money and credit. They consider that the rate of interest is a phenomenon artificially created by the man-made scarcity of the "means of payment." In hundreds, even thousands, of books and pamphlets they passionately blame the "orthodox" economists for their reluctance to admit that inflationist and expansionist doctrines are sound. All evils, they repeat again and again, are caused by the erroneous teachings of the "dismal science" of economics and the "credit monopoly" of the bankers and usurers. To unchain money from the fetters of "restrictionism," to create free money (*Freigeld*, in the terminology of Silvio Gesell) and to grant cheap or even gratuitous credit, is the main plank in their political platform.

Such ideas appeal to the uninformed masses. And they are very popular with governments committed to a policy of increasing the quantity both of money in circulation and of deposits subject to check. However, the inflationist governments and parties have not been ready to admit openly their endorsement of the tenets of the inflationists. While most countries embarked upon inflation and on a policy of easy money, the literary champions of inflationism were still spurned as "monetary cranks." Their doctrines were not taught at the universities.

"Stones into Bread: The Keynesian Miracle" has been reprinted from *Planning for Freedom*, fourth edition, by Ludwig von Mises with permission from Libertarian Press, Inc., Spring Mills, PA 16875.

John Maynard Keynes, late economic advisor to the British Government, is the new prophet of inflationism. The "Keynesian Revolution" consisted in the fact that he openly espoused the doctrines of Silvio Gesell. As the foremost of the British Gesellians, Lord Keynes adopted also the peculiar messianic jargon of inflationist literature and introduced it into official documents. Credit expansion, says the *Paper of the British Experts* of April 8, 1943, performs the "miracle . . . of turning a stone into bread." The author of this document was, of course, Keynes. Great Britain has indeed traveled a long way to this statement from Hume's and Mill's views on miracles.

II

Keynes entered the political scene in 1920 with his book, *The Economic Consequences of the Peace*. He tried to prove that the sums demanded for reparations were far in excess of what Germany could afford to pay and to "transfer." The success of the book was overwhelming. The propaganda machine of the German nationalists, well-entrenched in every country, was busily representing Keynes as the world's most eminent economist and Great Britain's wisest statesman.

Yet it would be a mistake to blame Keynes for the suicidal foreign policy that Great Britain followed in the interwar period. Other forces, especially the adoption of the Marxian doctrine of imperialism and "capitalist warmongering," were of incomparably greater importance in the rise of appeasement. With the exception of a small number of keen-sighted men, all Britons supported the policy which finally made it possible for the Nazis to start the second World War.

A highly gifted French economist, Etienne Mantoux, has analyzed Keynes' famous book point for point. The result of his very careful and conscientious study is devastating for Keynes the economist and statistician, as well as Keynes the statesman. The friends of Keynes are at a loss to find any substantial rejoinder. The only argument that his friend and biographer, Professor E. A. G. Robinson, could advance is that this powerful indictment of Keynes' position came "as might have been expected, from a Frenchman." (*Economic Journal,* Vol. LVII, p. 23). As if the disastrous effects of appeasement and defeatism had not affected Great Britain also!

Etienne Mantoux, son of the famous historian, Paul Mantoux, was the most distinguished of the younger French economists. He had already made valuable contributions to economic theory—among them a keen critique of Keynes' *General Theory,* published in 1937 in the *Revue d'Economie Politique*—before he began his *The Carthaginian Peace or the Economic Consequences of Mr. Keynes* (Oxford University Press, 1946). He did not live to see his book published. As an officer in the French forces he was killed on active service during the last days of the war. His premature death was a heavy blow to France, which is today badly in need of sound and courageous economists.

III

It would be a mistake, also, to blame Keynes for the faults and failures of contemporary British economic and financial policies. When he began to write,

Britain had long since abandoned the principle of *laissez-faire*. That was the achievement of such men as Thomas Carlyle and John Ruskin and, especially, of the Fabians. Those born in the eighties of the ninteenth century and later were merely epigones of the university and parlor Socialists of the late Victorian period. They were no critics of the ruling system, as their predecessors had been, but apologists of government and pressure group policies whose inadequacy, futility and perniciousness became more and more evident.

Professor Seymour E. Harris has just published a stout volume of collected essays by various academic and bureaucratic authors dealing with Keynes' doctrines as developed in his *General Theory of Employment, Interest and Money,* published in 1936. The title of the volume is *The New Economics, Keynes' Influence on Theory and Public Policy* (Alfred A. Knopf, New York, 1947). Whether Keynesianism has a fair claim to the appellation "new economics" or whether it is not, rather, a rehash of often-refuted Mercantilist fallacies, and of the syllogisms of the innumerable authors who wanted to make everybody prosperous by fiat money, is unimportant. What matters is not whether a doctrine is new, but whether it is sound.

The remarkable thing about this symposium is that it does not even attempt to refute the *substantiated* objections raised against Keynes by serious economists. The editor seems to be unable to conceive that any honest and uncorrupted man could disagree with Keynes. As he sees it, opposition to Keynes comes from "the vested interests of scholars in the older theory" and "the preponderant influence of press, radio, finance and subsidized research." In his eyes, non-Keynesians are just a bunch of bribed sycophants, unworthy of attention. Professor Harris thus adopts the methods of the Marxians and the Nazis, who preferred to smear their critics and to question their motives instead of refuting their theses.

A few of the contributions are written in dignified language and are reserved, even critical, in their appraisal of Keynes' achievements. Others are simply dithyrambic outbursts. Thus Professor Paul E. Samuelson tells us: "To have been born as an economist before 1936 was a boon—yes. But not to have been born too long before!" And he proceeds to quote Wordsworth:

> "Bliss was it in that dawn to be alive,
> But to be young was very heaven!"

Descending from the lofty heights of Parnassus into the prosaic valleys of quantitative science, Professor Samuelson provides us with exact information about the susceptibility of economists to the Keynesian gospel of 1936. Those under the age of 35 fully grasped its meaning after some time; those beyond 50 turned out to be quite immune, while economists in-between were divided. After thus serving us a warmed-over version of Mussolini's *giovanezza* theme, he offers more of the outworn slogans of fascism, e.g., the "wave of the future." However, on this point another contributor, Mr. Paul M. Sweezy, disagrees. In his eyes Keynes, tainted by "the shortcomings of bourgeois thought" as he was, is not the savior of mankind, but only the forerunner whose historical mission it is to prepare the British mind for the acceptance of pure Marxism and to make Great Britain ideologically ripe for full socialism.

IV

In resorting to the method of innuendo and trying to make their adversaries suspect by referring to them in ambiguous terms allowing of various interpretations, the camp-followers of Lord Keynes are imitating their idol's own procedures. For what many people have admiringly called Keynes' "brilliance of style" and "mastery of language" were, in fact, cheap rhetorical tricks.

Ricardo, says Keynes, "conquered England as completely as the Holy Inquisition conquered Spain." This is as vicious as any comparison could be. The Inquisition, aided by armed constables and executioners, beat the Spanish people into submission. Ricardo's theories were accepted as correct by British intellectuals without any pressure or compulsion being exercised in their favor. But in comparing the two entirely different things, Keynes obliquely hints that there was something shameful in the success of Ricardo's teachings and that those who disapprove of them are as heroic, noble and fearless champions of freedom as were those who fought the horrors of the Inquisition.

The most famous of Keynes' *apercus* is: "Two pyramids, two masses for the dead, are twice as good as one; but not so two railways from London to York." It is obvious that this sally, worthy of a character in a play by Oscar Wilde or Bernard Shaw, does not in any way prove the thesis that digging holes in the ground and paying for them out of savings "will increase the real national dividend of useful goods and services." But it puts the adversary in the awkward position of either leaving an apparent argument unanswered or of employing the tools of logic and discursive reasoning against sparkling wit.

Another instance of Keynes' technique is provided by his malicious description of the Paris Peace Conference. Keynes disagreed with Clemenceau's ideas. Thus, he tried to ridicule his adversary by broadly expatiating upon his clothing and appearance which, it seems, did not meet with the standard set by London outfitters. It is hard to discover any connection with the German reparations problem in the fact that Clemenceau's boots "were of thick black leather, very good, but of a country style, and sometimes fastened in front, curiously, by a buckle instead of laces." After 15 million human beings had perished in the war, the foremost statesmen of the world were assembled to give mankind a new international order and lasting peace . . . and the British Empire's financial expert was amused by the rustic style of the French Prime Minister's footwear.

Fourteen years later there was another international conference. This time Keynes was not a subordinate adviser, as in 1919, but one of the main figures. Concerning this London World Economic Conference of 1933, Professor Robinson observes: "Many economists the world over will remember . . . the performance in 1933 at Covent Garden in honour of the Delegates of the World Economic Conference, which owned its conception and organization very much to Maynard Keynes."

Those economists who were not in the service of one of the lamentably inept governments of 1933 and therefore were not Delegates and did not attend the delightful ballet evening, will remember the London Conference for other reasons. It marked the most spectacular failure in the history of international affairs of those policies of neo-Mercantilism which Keynes backed. Compared with this fiasco of 1933, the Paris Conference of 1919 appears to have been a highly successful affair. But Keynes did not publish any sarcastic comments on the coats, boots and gloves of the Delegates of 1933.

V

Although Keynes looked upon "the strange, unduly neglected prophet Silvio Gesell" as a forerunner, his own teachings differ considerably from those of Gesell. What Keynes borrowed from Gesell as well as from the host of other pro-inflation propagandists was not the content of their doctrine, but their practical conclusions and the tactics they applied to undermine their opponents' prestige. These stratagems are:

(a) All adversaries, that is, all those who do not consider credit expansion as the panacea, are lumped together and called orthodox. It is implied that there are no differences between them.

(b) It is assumed that the evolution of economic science culminated in Alfred Marshall and ended with him. The findings of modern subjective economics are disregarded.

(c) All that economists from David Hume on down to our time have done to clarify the results of changes in the quantity of money and money-substitutes is simply ignored. Keynes never embarked upon the hopeless task of refuting these teachings by ratiocination.

In all these respects the contributors to the symposium adopt their master's technique. Their critique aims at a body of doctrine created by their own illusions, which has no resemblance to the theories expounded by serious economists. They pass over in silence all that economists have said about the inevitable outcome of credit expansion. It seems as if they have never heard anything about the monetary theory of the trade cycle.

For a correct appraisal of the success which Keynes' *General Theory* found in academic circles, one must consider the conditions prevailing in university economics during the period between the two world wars.

Among the men who occupied chairs of economics in the last few decades, there have been only a few genuine economists, i.e., men fully conversant with the theories developed by modern subjective economics. The ideas of the old classical economists, as well as those of the modern economists, were caricatured in the textbooks and in the classrooms; they were called such names as old-fashioned, orthodox, reactionary, bourgeois or Wall Street economics. The teachers prided themselves on having refuted for all time the abstract doctrines of Manchesterism and *laissez-faire*.

The antagonism between the two schools of thought had its practical focus in the treatment of the labor union problem. Those economists disparaged as orthodox taught that a permanent rise in wage rates for all people eager to earn wages is possible only to the extent that the per capita quota of capital invested and the productivity of labor increases. If—whether by government decree or by labor union pressure—minimum wage rates are fixed at a higher level than that at which the unhampered market would have fixed them, unemployment results as a permanent mass phenomenon.

Almost all professors of the fashionable universities sharply attacked this theory. As these self-styled "unorthodox" doctrinaires interpreted the economic history of the last two hundred years, the unprecedented rise in real wage rates and standards of living was caused by labor unionism and government pro-labor legislation. Labor unionism was, in their opinion, highly beneficial to the true interests of all wage-earners and of the whole nation. Only dishonest apologists of the manifestly unfair interests of callous exploiters could find fault with the violent acts of the unions, they maintained. The foremost concern of popular government, they said, should be to encourage the unions as much as possible and to give them all the assistance they needed to combat the intrigues of the employers and to fix wage rates higher and higher.

But as soon as the governments and legislatures had vested the unions with all the powers they needed to enforce their minimum wage rates, the consequences appeared which the "orthodox" economists had predicted; unemployment of a considerable part of the potential labor force was prolonged year after year.

The "unorthodox" doctrinaires were perplexed. The only argument they had advanced against the "orthodox" theory was the appeal to their own fallacious interpretation of experience. But now events developed precisely as the "abstract school" had predicted. There was confusion among the "unorthodox."

It was at this moment that Keynes published his *General Theory*. What a comfort for the embarrassed "progressives"! Here, at last, they had something to oppose to the "orthodox" view. The cause of unemployment was not the inappropriate labor policies, but the shortcomings of the monetary and credit system. No need to worry any longer about the insufficiency of savings and capital accumulation and about deficits in the public household. On the contrary. The only method to do away with unemployment was to increase "effective demand" through public spending financed by credit expansion and inflation.

The policies which the *General Theory* recommended were precisely those which the "monetary cranks" had advanced long before and which most governments had espoused in the depression of 1929 and the following years. Some people believe that Keynes' earlier writings played an important part in the process which converted the world's most powerful governments to the doctrines of reckless spending, credit expansion and inflation. We may leave this minor issue undecided. At any rate it cannot be denied that the governments and peoples did not wait for the *General Theory* to embark upon these "Keynesian"—or more correctly, Gesellian, policies.

VI

Keynes' *General Theory* by 1936 did not inaugurate a new age of economic policies; rather it marked the end of a period. The policies which Keynes recommended were already then very close to the time when their inevitable consequences would be apparent and their continuation would be impossible. Even the most fanatical Keynesians do not dare to say that present-day England's distress is an effect of too much saving and insufficient spending. The essence of the much glorified "progressive" economic policies of the last decades was to expropriate ever-increasing parts of the higher incomes and to employ the funds thus raised for financing public waste and for subsidizing the members of the most powerful pressure groups. In the eyes of the "unorthodox," every kind of policy, however manifest its inadequacy may have been, was justified as a means of bringing about more equality. Now this process has reached its end. With the present tax rates and the methods applied in the control of prices, profits and interest rates, the system has liquidated itself. Even the confiscation of every penny earned above 1,000 pounds a year will not provide any perceptible increase to Great Britain's public revenue. The most bigoted Fabians cannot fail to realize that henceforth funds for public spending must be taken from the same people who are supposed to profit from it. Great Britain has reached the limit both of monetary expansionism and of spending.

Conditions in this country are not essentially different. The Keynesian recipe to make wage rates soar no longer works. Credit expansion, on an unprecedented scale engineered by the New Deal, for a short time delayed the consequences of inappropriate labor policies. During this interval the Administration and the union bosses could boast of the "social gains" they had secured for the "common man." But now the inevitable consequences of the increase in the quantity of money and deposits has become visible; prices are rising higher and higher. What is going on today in the United States is the final failure of Keynesianism.

There is no doubt that the American public is moving away from the Keynesian notions and slogans. Their prestige is dwindling. Only a few years ago politicians were naively discussing the extent of national income in dollars without taking into account the changes which government-made inflation had brought about in the dollar's purchasing power. Demagogues specified the level to which they wanted to bring the national (dollar) income. Today this form of reasoning is no longer popular. At last the "common man" has learned that increasing the quantity of dollars does not make America richer. Professor Harris still praises the Roosevelt Administration for having raised dollar incomes. But such Keynesian consistency is found today only in classrooms.

There are still teachers who tell their students that "an economy can lift itself by its own bootstraps" and that "we can spend our way into prosperity."[1] But the Keynesian miracle fails to materialize; the stones do not turn into bread. The panegyrics of the learned authors who cooperated in the production of the present volume merely confirm the editor's introductory statement that "Keynes could awaken in his disciples an almost religious fervor for his economics, which could be effectively harnessed for the dissemination of the new economics." And Professor Harris goes on to say, "Keynes indeed had the Revelation."

There is no use in arguing with people who are driven by "an almost religious fervor" and believe that their master "had the Revelation." It is one of the tasks of economics to analyze carefully each of the inflationist plans, those of Keynes and

Gesell no less than those of their innumerable predecessors from John Law down
to Major Douglas. Yet, no one should expect that any logical argument or any
experience could ever shake the almost religious fervor of those who believe in
salvation through spending and credit expansion.

Notes

1. Cf. Lorie Tarshis, *The Elements of Economics,* New York 1947, p. 565.

Chapter 3: MODERN CONTROVERSIES

Tobin claims that the 1980–81 recession was a direct result of the Federal Reserve System's anti-inflation policies. He concludes that what is needed is a new mix of tighter fiscal policy and looser monetary policy.

A KEYNESIAN VIEW OF THE BUDGET DEFICIT

James Tobin

The two instruments of macroeconomic management available to the government are fiscal policy and monetary policy. Together they determine the total dose of demand stimulus or restraint administered to the economy. In principle there are numerous mixtures of the two medicines which yield the same net stimulus or restraint of aggregate demand for goods and services. These various policy mixtures can differ significantly in their side effects. A tight budget, whose effects on aggregate demand are offset by an appropriately easy monetary policy, will bring lower interest rates than the opposite combination. Consequently, it will channel more of the nation's resources into domestic and foreign investment and relatively less into private and public consumption. The two issues—direction and size of total dose, and mix of the dose—are separable. Both are important issues today.

What I shall argue here is that much the greater current question is the adequacy of the net stimulus to demand from fiscal and monetary policies together. I shall advocate a bigger total dose and contend that its only feasible source is easier monetary policy. This will contribute to a desirable change in the fiscal-monetary mix later in this decade, if and when more expansionary policy in the immediate future restores prosperity. At that time, tightening the budget, lowering the deficit, would achieve a policy mix more favorable to capital formation and long-run growth. It would be desirable, though politically difficult, to plan and announce now a future correction of the policy mix of this kind, because the anticipations of such a plan would assist recovery in the interim.

The Case for Greater Demand Stimulus for Recovery

Do we want recovery now? I do, I think most people do. But anyone who thinks recovery now is premature could argue his case from the logic of the policy that brought the recession—along with George Stigler, I am inclined to call it a depression. Make no mistake about it, the recession was the deliberate conse-

---

quence of monetary policy. It was neither an accident nor the result of some inexorable cyclical rhythm in our capitalist system. It was the result of Federal Reserve policies adopted and announced in October 1979 when inflation, for the second time in the 1970s, was touching double digits.

The Fed announced that they would reduce the rate of monetary growth year after year until inflation was conquered. The conquest of inflation became not just the primary goal but the sole objective, regardless of consequences for interest rates, unemployment, and real GNP. This stance was indeed assumed by the central banks of all major countries in unanimous agreement.

In the battle against inflation, the policy has succeeded in considerable measure, but its triumph is not yet complete. Inflation has subsided; in the United States recent monthly statistics place it well below 5% annual rate. But many of the sources of statistical improvement are transient. They would be reversed during recovery. For example, flexible commodity prices in world markets have actually fallen; they will have to rise once recovery gets under way. A better measure of permanent inflation reduction is given by what is called the "core" inflation rate, closely related to labor costs. This has declined from 9–10% per year to 5–6%, judging from the decline in wage inflation, and perhaps further with allowance for some revival of productivity growth.

Though the gains against inflation are impressive, a true crusader could say the war is not yet won, it's too early to take off the pressure, we need two more years and another three or four points of disinflation before proclaiming V-I (Victory over Inflation) Day. The sentiment is understandable, though it does not accord with my priorities or with those of most citizens. The country is hungry for recovery.

Paul Volcker, perhaps partly because he sensed the national mood, relaxed Fed policy in August 1982. He looked out the window beyond the Potomac and saw the damage his single-minded anti-inflationary policy was inflicting on the real economy—lost production, unemployment, low investment, business losses, bankruptcies, financial insolvencies. He looked overseas and saw the world-wide damage inflicted by the concerted anti-inflationary policies of the leading developed economies, especially to a Third World heavily in debt.

The original policy had carried a threat: "We won't relent, we will keep the counter-inflationary pressure on, whatever its consequences." Otherwise, he and his counterparts in Europe and Japan believed, workers, their unions, and businessmen would not take them seriously and would persist in inflationary wage- and price-setting in the belief that central banks would once again rescue them from irresponsible behavior. The idea, supported by new theories of influential economists, was that a credibly relentless monetary disinflation would succeed sooner and with much less real damage than the "stop-go" policies of previous business cycles. But, as Volcker came to realize, the 1979 policy stance produced no miracle of costless disinflation, and was much more damaging to the domestic and world economies than the Fed had expected. Volcker's August 1982 suspension of monetarist targets averted a truly disastrous collapse, turned the American economy around the following winter, and so far allowed a vigorous beginning of recovery. But neither the Fed nor any other major central bank has abandoned the war on inflation. Unless and until the central bankers see further progress in that war, they will not wish to accommodate a rapid or a full recovery.

The costs of disinflation have been substantial. Unemployment reached 10½% and remains above 9% of the labor force; only in 1975 did any business cycle after World War II generate an unemployment rate above 8%. Besides the 10–11 million people unemployed, there are some 3 million employed part-time though they would like to be working full time. There are another 1.7 million "discouraged workers," not counted as unemployed though they would look for work if they thought any jobs were available. These days some commentators say that mass unemployment is no longer a social problem because unemployment compensation and other safety nets overcome the personal costs to the unemployed worker. Compared to the 1930s, it is true, we treat laid-off workers generously. But in this depression only 40% of the unemployed in a given month are receiving any unemployment compensation. New workers do not qualify, many others are ineligible, and many exhaust benefits in a prolonged slump.

Even if it were true, as it is not, that unemployment is no great personal hardship, either financial or psychological, on workers and their families, a mammoth social loss remains. The difference between 6% and 10% unemployment corresponds roughly to 10% of Gross National Product. Currently, 10% of GNP equals $300 billion a year. That is the annual output we are losing by running our economy at low speed, with a degree of slack of which the unemployment statistics are just one symptom. Another is the under-utilization of capacity in industry. The rate of utilization fell as low as 68% last year, and even after some recovery in 1983 is still below 75%; a prosperity norm is 88–90%. If we knew of any other way the country could raise its GNP for a few years by hundreds of billions of dollars, we would surely seize it.

A large part of the extra $300 billion would be capital investment. Our low rate of capital formation has been widely recognized as a major problem, a failure to provide adequately for the well-being of Americans in the future. The motivation of the Economic Recovery Tax Act of 1981 was largely to improve dramatically the incentives for saving and investment. Yet the percentage of GNP devoted to gross business capital formation has declined from 11-1/2% in 1978 to nearly 9% at present, while GNP itself has fallen far below its potential trend. The new tax incentives have been swamped by the negative effects of high interest rates, recession, excess capacity, and pessimism regarding recovery and growth.

Not only business investment but other provisions for our economic future have suffered. Public capital facilities are deteriorating because of the fiscal binds on state and local governments. Human capital is damaged by prolonged unemployment and by shrinking of educational budgets. No tax incentives, no financial gimmicks could possibly do as much for the accumulation of capital in its several forms by business, governments, and households as a general recovery of GNP to its full employment potential.

The International Dimension

The depression is an international one. The losses and wastes due to unemployment and excess capacity are worldwide. Indeed other countries are as yet far behind the United States in recovery. Unemployment is still rising in Europe. Japan and the major nations of Europe are still pursuing restrictive monetary and fiscal policies.

The economic plight of the Third World is prominent in the news because of the inability of Mexico, Brazil, Argentina, and other countries to meet their debt obligations. The debt crisis is also a product of the depression. As each country gets in trouble, its particular difficulties are attributed to its imprudent and over-extended borrowing, and to the thoughtless rapacity of the lending banks in this country and Europe. But the problems arise largely from the depression, which has deprived the debtor countries of their export markets in developed economies, and to the high interest rates imposed by the major central banks. The International Monetary Fund goes round the world telling the debtors to pull up their socks and tighten their belts. Perhaps austerity is the requirement the IMF, representing lenders, must inevitably impose on each country individually. But collectively the austerity programs are counter-productive. Every country cuts back its demands for the others' products, intensifying the slump in world trade and production. If the leaders of the seven principal economic powers, those who feasted at the Williamsburg summit, were truly concerned with the economic and financial difficulties of the Third World, they would engineer a world-wide recovery by following expansionary monetary and fiscal policies in their own countries.

Protectionism is on the march in all countries, advanced or less developed, on all continents. The Williamsburg summit leaders were quite properly alarmed. Clearly the political drive for protectionist policies receives powerful impetus in hard times, when international competition is a visible proximate scapegoat for layoffs, losses, and bankruptcies. Sermons about the abstract virtues of free trade are likely to fall on deaf ears. What is required is an alternative program for restoring health to the economies of the world.

The Federal Budget and Recovery

To judge from the preoccupations of the Congress, the press, the financial community, and some Administration spokesmen, the most serious problem before the United States is the deficit in the federal budget—not recovery, not unemployment—the deficit. It's such an obligatory cliché these days to say that the deficit is going to "choke off" the recovery that I hesitate to question that proposition in respectable company. Yet that is precisely what I shall do.

Large federal deficits are accused of commandeering so much national saving that business investors and other prospective borrowers are crowded out of the financial markets. It takes high interest rates to crowd them out, so the deficits are the culprits for the high interest rates and for their deterrence of recovery.

To think straight about this matter, it is essential to distinguish deficits in the current state of the economy from deficits in hypothetical conditions of full prosperity in, say, 1987 or 1988. At present federal budget deficits are not crowding out anything. What is there to crowd out? Investment demand has already been crowded out by high interest rates generated not by fiscal policy but by monetary policies adopted long before the present Administration's tax and spending initiatives. The deep depression produced by the monetary policies further reduced investment demands on national saving and generated most of the rising deficits of the past two years. Deficit outcomes are extremely sensitive to the state of the economy. A rule of thumb is $25 –30 billion, about 0.8% of GNP, extra deficit for each point of unemployment. If the unemployment rate were this fiscal year 6% instead of 10%, the deficit would be $100–120 billion smaller than the $180 billion officially forecast.

The conventional formulation thus reverses the true causation. The deficit is mostly result, not cause, of recent and current high interest rates and the depression caused by those rates, themselves the consequences of monetary policy.

In every macro-econometric model, as in every textbook of macroeconomics, additional government spending and reduced taxation have *positive* effects on aggregate demand for goods and services, assuming monetary policies remain unchanged. Those positive effects may be welcome, when they put idle labor and capacity to work, or unwelcome, when they simply raise prices. Today there are ample idle resources, and those effects should be welcome. Every forecaster and student of the economic outlook knows that the favorable factors in this year's recovery have been and will continue to be the expansion of defense spending and the rise in consumer spending supported by tax cuts.

Anyone who tells you that it would help the recovery if either the Pentagon cut back spending or taxes were now increased for 1984 is talking nonsense. The first order effects are obvious. You don't increase spending by cutting it down; less is not more. The second order effects of measures of fiscal austerity would be, it is true, a fall in interest rates. The government will borrow less. The private sector might then borrow more and spend more, but not enough to make up for the negative first order effects. For if the private sector borrowed and spent no less than the decline in the government's borrowing requirement, interest rates could not have fallen. But if interest rates are the same as they were before the deficit-reducing measures were adopted, or higher, private agents have no incentive to borrow and spend any more at all. The contradiction in the argument exposes its fallacy. I do not understand fashions in popular media macro-economics, but they defy logic.

Things would be different if the Federal Reserve would offset the effects of fiscal austerity on aggregate demand by simultaneously easing its monetary policy, and still better if the Fed would ease enough to raise the total dose of demand stimulus. But there is no indication that the Fed would act in this manner. Paul Volcker has condemned deficits and urged fiscal austerity. He has also said that the adoption of a "responsible" fiscal policy by the Congress is no reason he should adopt an "irresponsible" monetary policy.

Long-run Fiscal Stability

In a hypothetical situation dated 1987 or 1988, where the economy is prosperous and close to high employment (say 6% unemployment) and to normal capacity utilization, the crowding out story makes sense. The Administration and the Congressional Budget Office now project $200 billion deficits for those years in those circumstances. Without idle resources which could be put to use, such claims on national saving would compete with those of business, households, and state and local governments. In the interests of long run growth, it would be desirable to alter the policy mix to avoid such crowding out. Higher taxes to restrain consumption would do the trick, together with a monetary policy that would bring low enough interest rates to insure that the national saving released by the federal government is used elsewhere in the economy, not wasted in unemployment. It would be desirable to plan now a future budget correction of this kind, together with the accompanying monetary policy. Anticipation of an improved fiscal-monetary mix in those future years of full recovery would have a salutary effect on long-term interest rates today, and thus on current investment. At the same time, there is no case for reducing fiscal stimulus for the next two fiscal years, while the economy is still slack.

Why are those "out-year" high-employment deficits—now the preferred term is "structural deficits"—so high? They far exceed the hypothetical structural deficit for 6% unemployment for fiscal year 1983—they even exceed the actual deficit. One big reason is the slowness of the recovery projected by the Administration and the Congressional Budget Office. Cyclical deficits pile up, and so does the national debt. By 1987 and 1988, even if recovery is then fully achieved, the Treasury faces a huge outlay of interest payments. Cyclical deficits are transformed into structural deficits by slow recovery and high interest rates.

Even so, the structural deficits are overstated. The federal government does not use inflation accounting. The full dollar outlays for interest are counted in the calculation of the deficit, even though they contain an inflation premium which is really repayment of principal. This is a substantial overstatement, even with the lower inflation rates now projected. Were this correction made, the 1986 structural deficit, estimated officially to be 5-1/2% of GNP, would be 3.7%. This is still large, and as I stated above should be eventually corrected by tax increases. But it is considerably lower than the numbers usually cited.

There are two other ways to improve the long-run deficit outlook. One is to speed up the recovery, suffering fewer and smaller cyclical deficits during the transition to prosperity. The other is to engineer lower interest rates, lower than those now projected for the transition and for the years of full prosperity. Both these ways require the active cooperation of the monetary authorities on Constitution Avenue. Lower interest rates are to be desired for promoting recovery, and I now argue that they are also important, one might say essential, for fiscal stability in the long run.

At the end of World War II, federal debt exceeded one year's national income; it was 120% of GNP. By the early 1970s it was 25% of GNP, a quarter-year's production. In the interim GNP grew faster than the debt. Over the intervening years, contrary to popular belief and endless propaganda, the government followed a fairly conservative fiscal policy. Only recently, in this decade, the ratio began to rise. It is now around 30%. According to official budget and economic projections, it will rise to 50% by the end of this decade. That is not a colossal disaster. After all, the economy managed to survive, prosper, and grow with debt/GNP ratios 50% or higher in the 1950s. The problem is to keep the ratio from rising indefinitely.

It will be much easier to do that if the interest cost of the debt is kept lower than the growth rate of the economy. Consider the difference between budget outlays and revenues, excluding those connected with debt service. I call that difference the "primary deficit." Suppose it were zero, but the government's interest rate (net of federal taxes that return to the Treasury part of its interest outlays) was 4% while the economy was growing at only 2-1/2%. Clearly the debt/GNP ratio is going to rise, and even faster if the primary deficit is positive. The only way to stabilize the ratio, under the assumed conditions, is to run a primary surplus— not a very realistic objective at the moment.

Throughout the postwar period, anyway until very recently, the Treasury's net interest rate has been lower than the GNP growth rate—I refer to averages over business cycles, not literally to every fiscal year. Most of the time the relevant real interest rate on government debt has been 0% or 1%, while the economy has grown at 2-1/2 or 3%. The primary deficit has been less than 1% of GNP. As I previously recalled to you, the debt has fallen relative to GNP. To preserve that situation in the long run, we need a policy mix that keeps the real rate on government debt below the economy's growth rate, as well as a reduction in the structural primary deficit later in this decade.

Concluding Remarks: For Easier Monetary Policy

I have argued that monetary policy bears the responsibility for recovery, now and in the years immediately ahead, and half the responsibility for an improved policy mix in the long run. The improved mix—a tighter fiscal policy along with an easier monetary policy—will better the prospects for long-run economic growth and for fiscal stability. Anticipation of an improved mix will help the recovery now by lowering long-term interest rates without raising fears that the recovery will be aborted or reversed.

Of course, monetary policy was eased in 1982, and that change in policy, together with our inadvertent but timely expansionary fiscal policy, started our economy on the road to recovery. Monetary growth rates, especially for M-1, have been pretty high for several quarters. Interest rates, both long and short, declined under the new Fed policy, and then stabilized. So what am I complaining about? Current interest rates are still unprecedentedly high compared to inflation rates, especially for this phase of a business cycle. It is hard to see how the incipient recovery can be sustained with real rates three to four points higher than in previous recoveries and prosperities. The high rates of monetary growth in recent months did little more than offset the fall in the growth of velocity of M-1 due to the regulatory changes which, by allowing payment of high market interest rates on deposits counted in money stock, have increased the demand for money. It is fortunate that the Federal Reserve decided belatedly to offset the negative shocks to velocity, but that does not make its policy truly expansionary. The recovery still has a long way to go, and the Fed, in my view, should push real interest rates down a few more points.

Roberts cites empirical work in support of his claim that budget deficits are causally related to neither inflation nor high interest rates. High interest rates, he asserts, are the result of slow money growth combined with expanding business demand for loans.

WHY THE DEFICIT HYSTERIA IS UNJUSTIFIED

Paul Craig Roberts

According to traditional conventional wisdom, budget deficits are a necessary ingredient of a pro-growth economic policy, particularly in the aftermath of recession. Keynesian economists argue that by adding to aggregate demand, deficits in effect "crowd in" business profits, raising investment and the growth of gross national product. During the past three years, however, a new logic has replaced the old wisdom: Deficits must either "crowd out" investment by raising interest rates or be monetized by the Federal Reserve Board, adding to inflation and leading ultimately to higher interest rates. By this logic, raising taxes to reduce the deficit would spur rather than retard economic growth in the U.S. and worldwide.

This new conventional wisdom is widely trumpeted by both the press and top government policymakers. It is astonishing, therefore, that economists have not been able to find a scrap of evidence to justify this overriding concern with budget deficits that has kept President Reagan on the defensive despite the economic recovery.

In recent years economists have begun to search for empirical evidence that deficits cause inflation and higher interest rates. So far they have not been able to find any. In 1978, William A. Niskanen, now a member of President Reagan's Council of Economic Advisers, published his findings that the rate of inflation was determined by the rate of money growth and that "federal deficits do not have any significant effects on the inflation rate operating either through or independent of the rate of money growth."

At least a dozen studies by able economists on the effects of deficits on the economy have appeared recently. Here are summaries of the findings of some of them:

Reprinted from the December 5, 1983 issue of *Business Week* by special permission. Copyright © 1983 by McGraw-Hill, Inc.

- At Stanford University, Paul D. Evans examined the empirical evidence to test the proposition that large deficits produce high interest rates. He found that the proposition "is not supported by the facts. In over a century of U.S. history (including three periods during which the federal deficit exceeded 10% of national income) large deficits have never been associated with high interest rates. Moreover, postwar data offer little or no support for a positive relationship between deficits and interest rates. Indeed, the evidence more strongly supports a negative association than a positive one"—that is, large deficits correspond with low interest rates.
- Richard W. Kopcke, vice-president and economist at the Federal Reserve Bank of Boston, concluded that "the deficit itself is a harmful guide for policy, a misleading nuisance statistic that deflects budget debate from the important issues." Raising taxes to balance the budget may cause rather than prevent crowding out. "In the long run a reliance on taxes could diminish the growth of living standards—a more subtle version of crowding out—if tax rules needlessly distort investment incentives or households' choice between labor and leisure." Kopcke believes that "tax hikes are a bad bet," because higher taxes would lower interest rates by reducing investment and GNP growth, results that are inconsistent with their purpose.
- Ali Reza, manager of economic analysis for Gulf Oil Corp., found that federal deficits do not affect real output or the rate of interest and "do not crowd out private investment." For the 1968–82 period he found that "the federal deficit has depressed interest rates," not raised them. Numerous recent studies, including a three-year effort by the Treasury Dept., have come to similar conclusions.
- Research by David Meiselman, a Virginia Polytechnic Institute professor, shows that deficits have no meaningful relationship to interest rates, inflation, or the course of monetary policy.
- At Northwestern University, Professor Robert Eisner concludes that "federal budget deficits are not the general cause of inflation," and Yale University Nobelist James Tobin finds the consternation over the deficit unwarranted.
- University of Rochester Professor Charles Plosser concluded that interest rates "are unrelated to how the government finances its expenditures." He found instead that "higher interest rates are associated with increases in government purchases."

This is a common finding of many of the empirical studies. Plosser, Reza, and Evans all found that increased government spending—whether financed by taxes or borrowing—raises interest rates. Since, experience has shown, tax increases lead to higher spending, the effect of a tax increase would be to raise, not lower, interest rates.

In short, allegations by top government officials and legislators that budget deficits cause interest rates to rise fly in the face of overwhelming evidence. They make up what University of Washington Professor Dudley Johnson calls "the mythology of the deficit."

In this context, the wide attention paid by businessmen and the press to the views of CEA Chairman Martin Feldstein on the deficit requires a response. In a paper published 13 years ago, Feldstein purported to find that a 10% increase in public debt raises the corporate bond rate by about one-quarter of a point. But when Treasury Dept. staff economists carefully duplicated Feldstein's work, they found the opposite result. Even staff economists at the CEA itself have recently expressed puzzlement at the "vehemence" with which Feldstein espouses his deficit views, without empirical support.

Reza has also attacked Feldstein's work for being "deficient or inadequate in several respects." It fails, for instance, to adjust the rate of interest "for changes in the marginal tax rate on interest earnings in order to accurately measure the impact federal deficits have on interest rates."

If federal budget deficits are not the cause of high real interest rates, what is? The empirical evidence shows that monetary policy is to blame. In a 1982 study, Everson Hull, then a specialist in macroeconomics for the Congressional Research Service of the Library of Congress, could not find any evidence to support the theory that blames high interest rates on the deficit and on a lack of confidence by financial institutions in Reagan's economic program.

Concludes Hull: "There is a more plausible and basic reason for the high rates of interest experienced during most of 1980 and 1981. In the absence of institutionally imposed ceilings, the price of any specific commodity including money has always increased when there is excess demand for that commodity. . . .While money-supply growth decelerated sharply during most of 1981, continued strong business-loan expansion through the first three quarters of the year helped sustain the commercial paper rate at high levels." Whenever monetary policy reduces inflation too rapidly, especially if the reduction is unexpected, the probable result is higher short-term interest rates. James Tobin agrees that when the Fed fails to respond to the "needs of trade," an insufficient supply of money pushes up interest rates.

VOLATILITY. David Meiselman also finds the Fed's conduct of monetary policy responsible for high interest rates. The volatile movements in money supply growth make prediction of the direction of monetary policy impossible and create doubts in the financial markets about the Fed's willingness or ability to meet its targets. During 1981–82, short-term interest rates were kept high during months when money supply growth was too slow to meet the needs of trade and inflation expectations revived during months when money supply growth exploded, adding inflation premiums to interest rates.

Kopcke argues that not only is monetary policy responsible for high interest rates but it is also responsible for the budget deficit: "In fact, a monetary policy that restricts the growth of investment and GNP also increases the government's deficit: The slower growth of national income depresses tax revenues; these larger deficits then build up the public debt faster, increasing future net interest expenses; and the monetary restraint may increase real interest rates, contributing further to net interest expenses."

Recent economic research has reached another interesting conclusion: that the Fed, and not Reagan's tax cut, is responsible for the recession. Everson Hull's statistical comparisons show that the 1981–82 deceleration in monetary growth is "of sharper magnitude and of longer duration than that of any comparable period during the last 20 years." With the tax cuts delayed, there was no appropriate fiscal policy in place to offset the adverse effects of extraordinarily tight money on the economy. The tax cuts were "not initiated early enough to moderate the effects of restraint in money-supply growth." Recession and large budget deficits were inevitable.

MISPERCEPTIONS. Robert Eisner states that "the grievous economic losses" of the recent recession "may be traced in part to the active support by some and undue tolerance by others of an excessively tight monetary policy in the mistaken view that it was necessary to correct a federal budget incorrectly perceived as overly stimulative. It is important for current and future economic analysis and policy that we avoid such misperceptions." Despite Eisner's warning, backed up by extensive empirical research representing a wide spectrum of economic views, the Reagan Administration (except for the Treasury Dept.), the Fed, Congress, and most of the press have learned nothing.

Money supply growth continues to be extremely volatile. From August, 1982, to May, 1983, the supply grew at unprecedented annual rates. In May, the Fed again changed course, collapsing the growth of the monetary base from 15% in April to 6% at the beginning of November (compounded annual rates measured over 13-week periods). The deceleration in base growth has resulted in a sharp deceleration in M1 growth from a 16% annual rate in July to 1.3% as of Nov. 9. Further, the current 6% growth in the monetary base is due entirely to currency growth. For the last two months the growth of reserves on a 13-week basis has been negative. Unborrowed reserves have been growing but not fast enough to offset a decline in borrowed reserves, a sign that open-market operations are propping up the federal-funds rate, keeping interest rates high.

The Treasury is concerned about the sharp deceleration in money growth caused by Federal Reserve Chairman Paul A. Volcker's propping up interest rates. Hull and other researchers have found that "there is a very significant and close relationship which suggests that the probability of recession increases significantly with the degree of monetary deceleration." The Treasury believes that every week of continued tight money raises the probability of a recession in 1984.

Recently, even monetarists have expressed concern that the Fed is not supplying enough money. Nobel Laureate Milton Friedman has predicted renewed recession some time in the first half of 1984 if the current slow rate of monetary growth continues. Economists who are expecting a sharp rebound in velocity to compensate for monetary tightness may be disappointed. Velocity, when calculated using final sales rather than GNP, has continued to decline.

The recent success of conservative Republican senators in delaying the increase in the government's borrowing authority may result in artificially higher money growth numbers that could hide a policy of continuing tightening by the Fed. The delay of the debt ceiling bill forced the Treasury to draw down its cash balances, which then end up in various money supply measures. Unless the Fed succeeds in smoothing out the effects, some analysts think that weeks of abnormally high money supply could be reported even while the monetary authorities remain on a tight course.

If overly restrictive monetary policy does indeed cause the economy to turn down, the deficit will become even larger. Ironically, Volcker's view that the combination of strong economic growth and large deficits will force up interest rates and abort the recovery is leading him to keep interest rates up in order to slow the economy's growth. More and more economists seem to feel that Volcker should deal with the deficit by letting the economy grow and not base his policy on unsubstantiated fears of crowding out.

The authors suggest that the manner in which the federal deficit and debt are calculated may mislead observers into thinking that there is a deficit when in reality there is a surplus. Deficits do matter, they say, but public debt was declining until a few years ago and official deficits were really surpluses. These surpluses have contributed to economic stagnation in the past decade.

HOW TO MAKE SENSE OF THE DEFICIT

Robert Eisner and Paul J. Pieper

Debt and deficits are like sin. To most of the public they are morally wrong, difficult to avoid, and not easy to keep track of. To some, the sheer magnitude of the federal debt, surpassing $1.6 trillion this year, suggests the danger of some kind of national bankruptcy. To others, the large and growing budget deficits, which have recently reached 6 percent of gross national product, are a harbinger of a new acceleration of inflation.

There has always been a certain amount of hysteria surrounding the federal debt and deficits. If we look into how they are calculated, though, we find that they are not always what they seem. And that has some important implications for past mistakes in economic policy—and potential future disasters.

First, some considerations, elementary to economists, if not widely understood by the public, as to how the debt and deficits are supposed to affect the economy. Government debt held within the nation is, to begin with, not a burden in the conventional sense of the private debt that individuals or business have to pay to outsiders. While the public, if it stops to think about it, is responsible for paying off the debt—if it is ever paid off, a rather big if—and is responsible for the interest payments on the debt, it is also the public itself which would be paid off and which receives the interest payments. In some sense, then, this can be considered a "wash," and one current neo-Ricardian view (associated more properly with the name of Robert Barro of the University of Rochester) suggests that the debt and increases in the debt really do not make any difference.

The still-dominant view, and we believe the correct one, is that the debt and changes in the debt do matter, because they affect private perceptions of wealth and hence affect private spending. Put simply, if we own government savings bonds, Treasury bills, or notes we feel richer. We value our holdings of govern-

Reprinted with permission of the authors from *The Public Interest*, No. 78, Winter 1985, pp. 101–118.

ment debt more highly than the "present value" we attach to the uncertain future tax burden which may be associated with them, and the wealthier we feel—either through our direct holdings of government debt, through the money backed by Federal Reserve holdings of the debt, or through expected pension or insurance payments from funds holding the debt—the more we feel free to spend. To the extent that more spending is desirable, because we are in a recession, more government debt is actually beneficial, however paradoxical it may seem. To the extent, however, that we are in an inflationary boom brought on by a surfeit of aggregate demand and spending, a high or greater government debt only adds to the problem.

It is in this context that we may appropriately view federal budget deficits. Essentially, while government expenditures in excess of revenues add to private incomes, the deficits add to private holding of government debt. This increased wealth in government debt induces more consumption spending, which will be realized in actual production of consumer goods, *if there is slack in the economy.* But it will engender only higher prices and inflation and higher interest rates if there is full employment.

But what does this presumed role of debt and deficits have to do with the debt and deficits of common parlance? By official measures, except for 1969, when we recorded a modest surplus of $3 billion, the government has run a deficit every year since 1960. Yet, until 1980, *real*, net federal debt (after adjustment for inflation and government financial assets) generally declined. And for those concerned not with the arguments just presented about the impact of government debt and deficits on private spending, but rather with a more elemental notion of potential government financial insolvency, it should be noted that, by 1980, the government's total assets far outweighed its debts, and its positive net worth was growing.

How indeed could the government balance sheet move more and more into the black while it ran yearly deficits? The problem lies in the oddities of accounting, and federal government accounting in particular.

For one thing, the federal government does not have a separate capital budget. As a result, all federal expenditures for such things as public buildings, roads, harbors, post offices, trucks, and computers become a part of the deficit, as if they were government consumption rather than investment in hard assets. Similarly, unlike private business, the government charges to current expense and the deficit the acquisition of materials for future use.

Under private accounting practices, the government's 1980 budget deficit of $61 billion would have been cut by a third, and the 1981 deficit of $62 billion by $27 billion. The corrections for 1982 and 1983 would have been even larger—$43 billion and $31 billion. But the official deficits then were also much larger—$112 billion and $186 billion.

But there is much more that distorts measures of government debt and deficits and their applications for the economy. A lot of this has to do with the tricks played by inflation. Let us begin to unravel some of those tricks and other distortions.

The debt: from par to market, from gross to net

First, government debt figures usually reflect the par or face value of government obligations. If the debt were overwhelmingly in very short-term securities or if interest rates did not change much over the life of securities, the difference between par and market values would be small. But in recent years neither of these conditions was met. A substantial amount of government obligations are medium and long-term. And with varying combinations of tight money and inflation, interest rates have generally soared and have varied substantially.

As is well known to investors, higher interest rates mean lower prices for outstanding debt securities. An originally-issued 10 percent bond, for example, promising to pay $100 per year, will no longer sell at or be worth its original $1,000 if interest rates have risen to 14 percent. Since anyone who lends $1,000 when the rate of interest is 14 percent can receive $140 per year, no one will be willing to pay $1,000 for a bond paying only $100 per year. Hence, the market price of the $1,000 face-value, 10 percent bond must fall until the $100 per year return on that *market* price is equivalent to the 14 percent rate on new securities and in the market generally.

As a first step, therefore, one may construct market-to-par indices for major financial components of government balance sheets. We find then that, with par equal to 100, the market index for the composite of all U.S. government securities had fallen by the end of 1980 to 92.86 (as shown in Table I).

Table I. Market-to-Par Indices (100 = Par), Selected Years[a]

	U.S. Government Securities			
	Total	Bills	Notes	Notes; Bonds
1946	102.71	99.95	100.47	103.58
1959	94.07	98.80	98.00	91.73
1969	92.04	97.69	94.99	89.23
1976	101.15	98.68	103.42	102.72
1977	98.31	98.10	99.64	98.43
1978	95.30	97.15	95.80	94.38
1979	94.44	96.64	95.47	93.38
1980	92.86	96.00	94.34	91.29

[a]Complete tables corresponding to this table and to Tables III, IV, and V, with data for all of the years from 1946 to 1980, are available from the authors on request. The sources for this table and those that follow are given in the authors' March 1984 *American Economic Review* article.

A second step is to recognize that the gross public debt is a correct measure of neither the total liabilities (interest-bearing and non-interest-bearing) of the

federal government (including its associated credit agencies and the Federal
Reserve) nor of the net debt, that is, the difference between total liabilities and
total financial assets. We find, as indicated in Table II, that total liabilities associated with the U.S. government came, at the end of 1980, to $1,220 billion at par.
The par value of financial assets amounted to $592 billion. Par value of net
government debt was thus only $628 billion.

Table II. The Budget Deficit, Gross Public Debt, and Market Value of Net Debt, 1980
(Billions of Dollars)

A. *Reconciliation of Gross Public Debt and Market Value of Net Debt*

Gross Public Debt	930.2
+ Other Liabilities of Federal Government	120.1
+ Liabilities of Credit Agencies	188.2
+ Liabilities of Federal Reserve	173.8
− Debt held by Federal Government	− 192.46
Total U.S. Government Liabilities at Par	1,220.0
+ Par-to-Market Conversion	− 65.7
Total U.S. Government Liabilities at Market	1,154.3
Federal Government Financial Assets	225.3
+ Credit Agency Assets	192.54
+ Federal Reserve Assets[a]	173.8
Total U.S. Government Liabilities at Par[a]	591.7
+ Par-to-Market Conversion	115.0
On Gold	141.1
On Other Assets	− 26.1
Total U.S. Government Financial Assets at Market	706.7
U.S. Government Net Debt	447.5

B. *Reconciliation of Budget Deficit and Changes in Gross Public Debt*

Budget Deficit on National Income Account	61.2
+ Insurance Credits to Households	+ 8.8
+ Change in U.S. Financial Assets	+ 26.0
+ Change in Treasury Debt Held by U.S. Government	+ 7.4
− Change in other U.S. Liabilities	− 11.0
− Mineral Rights Sales	− 6.5
− Statistical Discrepancy (Flow of Funds)	− 0.8
Change in Gross Public Debt	85.1

[a] Includes small amount of tangible Federal Reserve assets.

But the *market* value of total U.S. government liabilities was $1,154 billion, $66
billion less than its par value. The market value of U.S. government financial
assets was $707 billion, or $115 billion more than par, reflecting a market value of
gold $141 billion greater than the statutory figure which is based on the $42 per
ounce at which gold is held in Treasury account books. Thus, the market value of
U.S. government net debt in 1980 was $448 billion, a considerable cry from the
original "gross public debt" figure of $930 billion.

Like any business, the federal government also has some tangible assets. These include reproducible assets in the form of residential structures, equipment, and inventories, which by BEA estimates at the end of 1980 had a net replacement cost, which we will take as market value, of $608 billion. We estimate land owned by the federal government at $119 billion. Total tangible assets at the end of 1980 were thus $727 billion.

We add $707 billion of financial assets to reach a total assets figure at the end of 1980 of $1,434 billion. We subtract liabilities of $1,154 billion. The result, shown in Table III, is a positive net worth of $279 billion.

Table III. Federal Government Net Debt and Net Worth
(Billions of Dollars)

	1946	1950	1960	1970	1980
Assets					
Tangible	170.1	112.2	207.3	301.0	727.0
Reproducible Assets	162.6	102.6	188.9	264.6	607.6
Residential Structures	2.6	2.2	3.2	5.7	20.6
Nonresidential Structures	33.1	39.1	60.8	100.2	251.6
Equipment	75.4	34.4	65.6	95.3	202.4
Inventories	51.6	26.9	59.2	63.4	132.9
Land	7.5	9.5	18.4	36.4	119.5
Financial	74.2	93.9	117.8	218.0	706.7
Currency, Demand + Time					
Deposits	8.8	9.7	12.8	18.0	33.9
Gold	20.7	22.8	17.8	12.0	152.3
U.S. Government Securities	24.3	21.3	28.5	63.6	123.4
Treasury Issues	24.3	21.3	28.5	63.4	114.2
Agency Issues	0.0	0.0	0.0	0.2	9.2
Mortgages	2.1	2.8	10.9	31.5	126.2
Other Loans	8.1	16.0	25.0	64.8	199.7
Taxes Receivable	8.2	16.5	12.7	5.7	9.3
Miscellaneous Assets	2.0	4.7	10.0	22.2	62.0
TOTAL ASSETS	244.3	206.0	325.1	519.0	1,433.7
Liabilities					
Treasury Currency + SDR Cer-					
tificates	2.4	2.4	2.7	6.0	13.6
Demand Deposits + Currency	30.4	28.2	30.6	52.0	121.5
Bank Reserves + Vault Cash	18.2	19.9	20.4	31.2	47.3
Credit Market Instruments	234.3	219.5	240.2	324.9	834.6
Savings Bonds	44.4	50.0	46.5	53.1	68.4
Other Treasury Issues	188.8	168.1	185.9	232.4	617.8
Agency Issues	1.2	1.8	7.8	39.3	148.4
Insurance, Retirement Reserves	8.0	12.7	20.5	34.9	85.5
Miscellaneous Liabilities	6.8	7.4	10.9	21.8	51.9
TOTAL LIABILITIES	300.1	290.0	325.2	407.7	1,154.3
Net Debt[a]	225.9	196.2	207.4	252.7	447.5
Net Worth	−55.9	−84.0	−0.1	48.3	279.4

[a]Total liabilities minus financial assets.

The contrasting results for the series of gross Treasury debt and total liabilities on the one hand, and net debt and net worth on the other, are striking. Gross Treasury debt of $259 billion in 1946 had risen only to $321 billion by 1965, but then increased at an accelerating rate to $930 billion by the end of 1980 (and now of course to over $1.6 trillion). Net debt as late as 1966 was, at $223 billion, still below the 1946 high point of $226 billion. Net debt climbed thereafter to a total of $448 billion by the end of 1980.

Looking at what would for a private business be the bottom line, the net worth figures tell a different story, although a story that would hardly be unfamiliar to any successful large corporation. For all the while that gross Treasury debt, or even the difference between total liabilities and total financial assets which we have been calling net debt, was growing, so was net worth. By our measures, net worth was a negative $56 billion at the end of 1946, as shown in Table III. It became even more negative, finally reaching a lower bound of minus $92 billion at the end of 1949. But, by the end of 1956, the federal government was at least briefly in the black, with a net worth of $8 billion. Net worth was then trivially negative, hovering around zero, for the years 1960–62, before it again began to rise. It dipped in the 1974–75 recession and its wake, but came up very sharply in the next five years, when gross Treasury debt was soaring dramatically. We measure federal net worth at the end of 1980 at $279 billion. Our federal government, like many individuals and businesses that borrowed heavily in an inflationary period, came out pretty well with its investments in tangible assets—and in gold!

We may be reminded, however, that there are further complications. At the end of the 1982 fiscal year, for example, the Treasury listed "liabilities" accountable to the public of $1,085 billion, but it also reported obligations for "undelivered orders" (mainly of the Departments of Defense and Housing and Urban Development) of $475 billion and, dwarfing both, "contingency" obligations which summed to $6,982 billion.

These last comprised $347 billion in loan and credit guarantees and $2,080 billion in insurance commitments, largely for the Federal Deposit Insurance Corporation and the Federal Savings and Loan Investment Corporation, and "annuity programs," which totalled $4,474 billion. Of these, $836 billion were for retirement pay, chiefly for the armed forces and the civil service, and, as actuarial values of net obligations for the three Social Security Trust Funds, $578 billion for hospital insurance, $2,298 billion for old age and survivors insurance, and $656 billion in net assets for disability insurance. Adding together all the figures (which the Treasury does not do), we come to a total of $8,542 billion.

Such vast government obligations may well have a substantial impact on the economy. They are clearly, however, in varying ways different in character and implication from the formal, current debt. As the U.S. Treasury pointed out: "Clearly, there is a vast difference between items . . . where the liability is certain and relatively precise . . . and . . . where the possible future liability is highly speculative and may never arise . . . The [latter] amounts, if they can be projected at all, are stated . . . without regard to probability of occurrence and without deduction for existing and contingent assets which would be available. . . ."

It is clear that construction of relevant measures of government commitments that go beyond net current liabilities would take us far afield. It would also be subject to huge uncertainty regarding the anticipated tax receipts which may eventually be generated to meet the commitments. In any event, in our analysis here we shall take the narrower, Treasury measure of federal liabilities and exclude the present value of government personnel retirement provisions, the projected Social Security commitments under current law, and other "contingent" obligations.

Deficits and real changes in net debt

Common sense suggests that when a person, business, or government runs a deficit, that is, spends more than it takes in, it must finance that deficit by increasing its debt. Thus, if the government had a debt of, say, $1,300 billion at the end of the 1983 fiscal year, and ran a deficit of $200 billion during the 1984 fiscal year, its debt at the end of the 1984 fiscal year would be $1,500 billion.

But, in fact, while the federal government reported budget deficits totaling $336 billion from 1947 to 1980, the market value of net federal debt grew by only $222 billion from the end of 1946 to the end of 1980 (Table III). And over that period, the *real* market value of that debt (in constant 1972 dollars) *declined* by $231 billion (Table IV). Even the usual measure of Treasury debt known as the gross public debt was no larger in 1980, in real terms, than in 1946. In fact, it declined (in 1972 dollars) from $539 billion to $496 billion. This reduction in real gross debt reflects large negative net revaluations, that is, changes in value of outstanding debt, net of changes in the price level. Higher interest rates lowering the market value of debt, higher prices of gold increasing the value of that government asset, and, particularly, general inflation, combined further to cut the real market value of the *net* debt virtually in half since the end of World War II.

Table IV. The Real Value of Federal Debt

	Billions of 1972 Dollars					1972 Dollars	
	Gross Public Debt	Net Debt	Budget Surplus (Deficit −)	Net Revaluation of Net Debt	Change in Net Debt	Net Debt per Capita	Change in Net Debt per Capita
1946	539.2	470.1	8.0	−83.6	—	3,384	—
1950	459.1	350.8	17.2	−31.8	44.0	2,326	−338
1960	421.4	299.1	4.4	8.7	5.8	1,679	6
1970	415.3	269.9	−15.3	1.7	15.4	1,338	60
1975	445.9	278.9	−55.2	− 2.2	57.3	1,320	259
1976	481.3	318.2	−40.2	− 4.2	39.3	1,482	162
1977	498.6	320.5	−33.2	−37.9	2.3	1,482	0
1978	503.4	296.7	−19.5	−51.1	−23.8	1,364	−118
1979	496.6	244.8	− 9.1	−71.4	−51.9	1,120	−244
1980	495.9	238.6	−34.5	−42.9	− 6.2	1,078	− 42

This suggests that our conventional measure of the budget deficit is particularly misleading in periods of significant inflation and high and fluctuating nominal interest rates. Federal government net interest payments of $53 billion in 1980 were only modestly less than the $61 billion deficit (on National Income Accounts). With interest rates on Treasury securities rising from about 11.5 percent to over 14 percent, net interest payments in 1981 came to $72 billion, well exceeding a $60 billion reported deficit. (For 1982, however, while net interest payments rose to $85 billion, the deficit on national income account soared to $150 billion.) But measures of real interest, taking into account inflation and changes in the real market value of the federal debt, would have been small fractions of nominal payments, or actually negative. *Substitution of real for nominal interest costs in budget expenditures would indicate that the budget was close to balanced in 1980*, a result consistent with the changes in the real value of the debt (Table V).

Table V. Reconciliation of Federal Budget Surplus (Deficit) and Change in Real Net Debt

(1)	Surplus (Deficit −) on National Income Accounts (2)	Interest Rate Effects (Par-to-Market Adjustment) (3)	Price Effects (Nominal to Real Adjustment) (4)	Adjusted Surplus (Deficit −) (5)	Off-Budget Items[a] (6)	Net Revaluation on Gold (7)	Decrease (Increase −) In Real Net Debt in Current Dollars (8)
1976	− 53.1	− 12.5	21.2	− 44.5	− 4.2	− 3.3	− 52.0
1977	− 46.4	16.9	29.3	− .2	− 9.0	6.0	− 3.3
1978	− 29.2	18.6	43.3	32.7	− 8.7	11.8	35.7
1979	− 14.8	1.7	44.1	31.0	− 9.8	63.6	84.9
1980	− 61.2	12.6	55.9	7.3	− 2.1	6.0	11.2

Note: Column (5) is total of cols. (2), (3), and (4); Column (8) is total of cols. (5), (6), and (7).

[a]This is the sum of insurance credits to households, federal mineral sales, credit agency surplus, net revaluations on foreign exchange and miscellaneous assets, and the Flow of Funds statistical discrepancy.

Of course, the population has been growing over the last 35 years. Our ultimate measure of the trend in debt then may well be the real net debt per capita. This figure declined (in 1972 dollars) from $3,384 at the end of 1946 to $1,078 at the end of 1980, as also shown in Table IV. Real debt per capita was thus, at the end of 1980, less than one-third of what it was at the end of 1946.

From the standpoint of fundamental and meaningful economic analysis, a proper measure of the government deficit is the increase in real value of government net debt. If the net debt is declining, whether because the government is taking in larger tax revenues than it is spending, or because of the effects of inflation, we should consider the government budget in surplus. The budget deficit is the amount that expenditures must be reduced to keep real net debt unchanged. If there were no net revaluations of existing financial assets and liabilities, this definition would correspond to conventional measures of the deficit. Net revaluations have in fact generally been considerable, however, as we have just noted, and all the more so in periods of significant inflation and high and fluctuating nominal interest rates.

As with the debt, therefore, we make two adjustments to the deficit, a par-to-market adjustment and a nominal-to-real adjustment. The first of these is the change in net debt due to changing market rates of interest, which we term the interest effect. With generally rising interest rates, this effect has been, on balance, positive in the postwar era, thus reducing the adjusted deficit.

The second and usually larger adjustment, incorporating what we denote as the price effect, is the change in the real value of the net debt due to changes in the price level. It has of course become of major importance with the higher inflation of the 1970s. By reducing our measure of the deficit by the amount of decrease in the real value of existing net government debt, we are in effect including the so-called "inflation tax" in budget revenues. Since inflation (and expected inflation) forces borrowers to offer higher nominal interest rates to compensate for the inflation tax on holders of securities, the price-effect adjustment may alternatively be viewed as a conversion of interest expenditures from nominal to real.

In Table V we show the interest and price effects to present an adjusted measure of the federal budget surplus or deficit. The conventional and the adjusted budgets prove quite different. The officially reported deficit of $61 billion in 1980, for example, is converted to a $7 billion surplus when price and interest effects are considered! And the adjustments have not been constant in amount; in earlier years, when inflation was lower, they were decidedly smaller.[1]

Adjusting the high-employment budget

What difference does all of this make? Can we say that the government has not really been spending too much or is taxing too little? Correctly evaluated, can past government fiscal policy really be considered too tight, causing recessions, rather than too expansive, causing inflation?

To get at this question we must add a new measure, well known to economists, to avoid an all too frequent public confusion between causes and effects with regard to budget deficits, inflation, and recession. While, as we have pointed out earlier, a bigger budget deficit, other things equal, will tend to increase spending and hence be expansionary, a recession will itself produce a bigger budget deficit. For with a recession, tax payments, largely geared to income and profits, will be less, and government expenditures for welfare and unemployment benefits, in particular, will be larger. On the other hand, with inflation, higher incomes and prices have meant higher government tax revenues and hence a lower deficit or a surplus.

So, to measure *the effect of the budget on the economy* rather than *the effect of the economy on the budget,* we want to look at what the budget would be at some fixed level of economic activity or, more precisely, at some fixed level of employment or unemployment. Economists have therefore developed a cyclically-adjusted or "high-employment budget" surplus or deficit as a measure of the impact of the budget on the economy, separate from the reverse effect of the economy on the budget. It should be recognized that it does not really matter at what level of unemployment this hypothetical budget is estimated. The important thing is that the employment level used for the calculations reflects an essentially constant level of economic activity.

The high-employment budget, currently calculated for an unemployment level of 5.1 percent, is thus generally understood to provide a first-order measure of the thrust of federal fiscal policy on aggregate demand. Increases in the high-employment budget surplus, or decreases in the deficit, are viewed as contractionary.

But even looking at the official high-employment budget, we find a striking move toward deficit in recent years, in contrast to years before 1966. This has contributed to the view that, despite generally increasing inflation, which might have called for lower deficits and greater surpluses to slow the economy, the federal budget has been, perversely, expansionary. The depth and severity of the recession of 1981–82 have then been attributed to the great potency of a tight and tough monetary policy which has overbalanced an easy fiscal policy.

But for the high-employment budget to measure correctly the thrust of federal fiscal policy, it must also be corrected for the effects of inflation on the real value of net debt of the government, and hence the public's perceived net wealth, which affects its spending. *A deficit that does not increase the net debt of the government does not increase the correctly-measured net income or net worth of the private sector,* and hence does not *per se* have an expansionary effect on aggregate demand.

Perception of the gap in the relation between measured deficits and changes in net debt of the government, or net worth of the private sector, points to the major effect of inflation on a relevant high-employment budget. For inflation and changing rates of inflation break whatever links have existed between budget deficits and real income or changes in net worth of the private sector.

A measure of the real, actual surplus or deficit may be viewed as essentially the sum of three components: 1) the nominal surplus or deficit as currently measured; 2) an adjustment for changes in market value of government financial assets and liabilities due to changing market rates of interest; and 3) changes in the real value of net debt due to changing general price levels incident to inflation. An identical or analogous set of adjustments is appropriate for the high-employment budget surplus or deficit.

We have hence undertaken to calculate a high-employment budget that, by correcting for these inflation effects, comes closer to measuring the real surplus or deficit, and the consequent thrust of fiscal policy on aggregate demand. Applying our calculations of net revaluations on actual net federal debt, we have adjusted the official high-employment budget surplus series for the years 1955 through 1981. The results, shown in Table VI, are dramatic. Inflation and rates of interest were low and relatively steady in the early years of the period prior to

Table VI. High-Employment Budget Surplus (Deficit) as Percent of GNP, Official and Adjusted

| | *High-Employment Budget Surplus (Deficit −)* | | |
	Official	*Adjusted for Price Effects*	*Adjusted for Price and Interest Effects*
1955	1.30	2.81	3.71
1956	1.87	3.83	4.63
1957	1.37	2.47	1.26
1958	0	.93	2.21
1959	1.11	2.09	2.90
1960	2.39	2.84	.98
1961	1.35	1.99	2.44
1962	.53	1.29	.91
1963	1.24	1.79	2.26
1964	.17	.78	.73
1965	.13	.98	1.42
1966	− .74	.34	.09
1967	− 1.89	− .89	− .38
1968	− 1.26	.06	.20
1969	.52	1.95	2.68
1970	− .46	.77	− .64
1971	− 1.05	.12	− .21
1972	− 1.02	.02	.42
1973	− .72	.89	1.13
1974	− .02	2.16	1.97
1975	− 1.88	− .37	− .55
1976	− 1.01	.22	− .52
1977	− 1.13	.39	1.27
1978	− .70	1.30	2.16
1979	− .09	1.74	1.81
1980	− .81	1.31	1.63
1981	.15	1.92	1.97

escalation of our military involvement in Vietnam. Corrections to the high-employment budget surplus are hence small in those early years. In the years from our heavy Vietnam involvement on, however, when the high-employment budget as well as the actual budget moved substantially to deficit, the corrections are striking. *The entire perceived trend in the direction of fiscal ease or expansion is eliminated or reversed.* The fully adjusted high-employment budget surplus, as a percent of GNP, for every year from 1977 through 1981, was higher than the surplus of any single year going back to 1965, except for the tax-surcharge year of 1969 and the oil-price-shock year of 1974. With similar exceptions, the surplus adjusted only for price (and not interest) effects was higher in every year from 1978 to 1981 than that of any single year back to 1963.

This suggests a need for some significant rewriting of recent economic history. Inflation can hardly be ascribed to excess demand associated with increasing fiscal ease and stimulus if, at least by the high-employment budget measure, appropriately defined, there was no such movement to fiscal ease. Some explanation of sluggishness in the economy in the last several years, climaxed by the recent recession, may then be found in a relatively tight fiscal policy, as measured by the adjusted high-employment budget surplus, as well as in the widely perceived role of monetary policy.

The impact on the economy

Movements in real economic activity in the United States have in fact been negatively related to the high-employment budget surplus. Essentially, the greater the high-employment budget deficit, the greater were the real rate of growth of GNP and the increase in employment the following year.

Precise statistical analysis of the relations (to be found in our March, 1984 *American Economic Review* article) reveals some striking facts about what has happened to the deficit and its impact, as inflation took hold of the economy. Up to 1966, when inflation was relatively minor, and little in the way of our inflation correction was necessary, budget deficits were really budget deficits. In that earlier period, therefore, even a balanced official high-employment budget tended to be associated with a healthy 5.7 percent growth in real GNP and an annual decline of 0.9 percentage points in unemployment.

In the period from 1967 on, however, when inflation became substantial, the officially balanced budget turned into one of surplus when inflation corrections were made. A balanced official high-employment budget in the later period, therefore, tended to produce a real rate of annual growth of GNP of only 0.5 percent. This in turn was associated with a 1.3 percent per year increase in the rate of unemployment. In that later period, the official high-employment budget would have had to be in deficit by some 1.77 percent of GNP in order to compensate for the inflation-erosion of the real value of the debt. Only if it had been in deficit by that amount could we have expected the increases in real GNP of some 5.7 percent and declines in unemployment of 0.9 percentage points per year associated with a balanced high-employment budget in the earlier, relatively inflation-free period.

After 1967, a balanced *inflation-adjusted,* high-employment budget would have been substantially expansionary, producing high rates of growth of GNP and declines in unemployment. But in fact, as late as 1981 we had a roughly balanced official high-employment budget, as shown in Table VI, while that budget, adjusted for inflation effects, was substantially in surplus, by about 2 percent of GNP. And each percentage point of surplus in the inflation-adjusted high-employment budget was associated with about 2.4 percentage points *reduction* in the rate of growth of real GNP and .95 percentage points *increase* in unemployment. It is these inflation-adjusted surpluses, the statistical relation indicates strongly, that largely accounted for the 1981–82 recession.

All of this suggests two important correctives to widespread views of fiscal and monetary policy. First, the 1981–82 recession cannot properly be interpreted as the triumph of all-powerful monetary constraints over relatively ineffective fiscal ease. Without denying the significant effects of a tight money policy in depressing the economy, it is necessary to point out that the verdict is not in on what might have happened if tight money had been pitted against *real* fiscal stimulus.

Second, the absence of real fiscal stimulus—and indeed the presence of some measure of fiscal tightness—makes clear the extent of the overkill of monetary restraint which contributed to the highest unemployment levels in almost two generations. Those who acquiesced in tight money as "the only game in town" to slow a presumably overheated, inflationary economy were wrong on two counts. The absence of increasing fiscal thrust reinforces the inference that inflation had come from supply shocks rather than excess demand. And the strong-willed rejection of accommodative monetary policy, rather than balancing budget excesses, offered a near lethal combination of monetary and fiscal contraction.

We have extended this analysis to consider the debt and budget deficit in six other developed, industrial economies—Canada, France, West Germany, Italy, Japan and the United Kingdom. We find some confirmation there of the relations imputed to the United States. For the countries outside of the United States, their own cyclically-adjusted budget deficits, when adjusted for inflation, do show some positive relation with subsequent change in real gross domestic product. There is also evidence that where countries, price-adjusted, cyclically-adjusted deficits were greater than such deficits in other countries, their growth in real product the next year was greater.

Indeed, the inflation adjustments resolve certain paradoxes and challenge some conventional notions. The case of West Germany has traditionally been cited as one of rapid growth with relatively little budget deficits and that of the United Kingdom and Italy as nations with very poor and moderate performance, respectively, with very large budget deficits. But when the inflation adjustments are applied, it turns out that West Germany, along with Japan—nations with relatively rapid rates of growth—had relatively expansionary budgets; Japan was most significantly in deficit. The United Kingdom, with its chronic stagnation, actually had a substantial surplus when inflation adjustments were included!

But the most striking note in our preliminary international analysis was that the inflation-adjusted high-employment deficit of the United States showed a very sharp, indeed dominant, positive relation with subsequent growth in real gross domestic product of the other nations. Whatever effect each country's budget posture had on its rate of growth, that paled before the effects on its own economy of the budget surplus or deficit of the United States!

The implications of the inflation adjustments go beyond economic policy to fundamental issues of economic theory. As must be well known to laymen as well as professional economists, the Keynesian model of the economy, which came to dominate macroeconomic theory by the 1960s, came under major challenge in the 1970s. The motivation and foundation for the challenge, as indicated by leaders of the neoclassical and rational expectations counterrevolutions such as Milton Friedman and Robert Lucas of the University of Chicago, was that the policies generated by Keynesian theory were not working. A major specific charge was that Keynesians expected increases in budget deficits—aside from those brought on by recessions—to prove expansionary. Yet, the years of increasing high-employment budget deficits from the end of the Vietnam War on were associated with slower rates of growth and increasing unemployment. The Keynesian theory, it was then argued, was fundamentally flawed and new ideas—or the refurbishing of old ones—were in order.

Application of the inflation adjustments suggests sharply that this line of attack on the Keynesian revolution of a half century ago is unjustified. Budget surpluses do slow down the economy, and budget deficits, correctly measured, do prove expansionary. The Keynesian paragon, at this level of discourse at least, lives on. A successful challenge will have to look for other grounds.

What really matters, now and in the future?

With massive tax cuts and increases in military spending dwarfing reductions in non-military government outlay, fiscal policy took a sharp turn towards stimulus in 1982. This was measured in the official high-employment budget, which moved from a surplus equal to 0.15 percent of GNP in 1981 to a deficit of 1.08 percent of GNP in 1982. With the sharp decline in inflation and interest rates in 1982, the high-employment budget (adjusted for price and interest effects) moved from a surplus equal to 1.97 percent of GNP in the previous year to a deficit equal to 1.77 percent of GNP, as shown in Table VII—the greatest such swing to expansion on record. Our estimated relations between budget deficits and GNP and unemployment predicted a major swing to economic recovery and lower unemployment in 1983 and on into 1984, and that is of course precisely what occurred.

Table VII. Projected High-Employment Budget Surplus or Deficit as Percent of GNP, Official and Adjusted

	High-Employment Budget Surplus (Deficit −)		
Year	Official[a]	Adjusted for Price Effects	Adjusted for Price and Interest Effects
1981	0.15	1.92	1.97
1982	−1.08	.01	−1.77
1983	−2.04	− .93	− .87
1984	−2.59	− .92	− .50
1985	−3.06	−1.45	−1.27
1986	−3.38	−1.70	−2.25
1987	−3.92	−2.16	−2.60
1988	−4.38	−2.52	−2.23

[a] Years from 1982 to 1988 calculated from Congressional Budget Office figures furnished by Frank Russek.

Congressional Budget Office estimates have indicated very large and increasing official high-employment budget deficits in the years ahead to 1988. It is not clear as yet that there have been substantial changes in projected expenditures or in the tax structure that will alter that picture. What is particularly significant, though, is that current and projected rates of inflation do not now indicate that inflation adjustments to these official high-employment budget deficit projections will come anywhere close to wiping them out. Our equations would then predict, if we stayed on our current budget course, an amount of stimulus which would push real rates of growth to from 6 to 8 percent per year over the next half decade. One set of projections would bring the 1988 unemployment rate to an obviously impossible minus 0.8 percent!

This clearly indicates a collision course between the projected budget deficits and interest and inflation rates on the one hand, and the capacity of the economy on the other. If government expenditures are not significantly cut or taxes raised, the inevitable economic forces of supply and demand will solve the problem and force the adjustments. For inflation will then rekindle and interest rates will rise, the latter all the more so if the Federal Reserve, as expected, moves to try to curb the inflation by ever tighter monetary policy. But, as we have seen, rising interest rates and inflation mean declines in the real value of outstanding government debt. Hence the real, adjusted deficits will be eliminated by the very inflation and high interest rates which the deficits bring on.

The real story then is that debt and deficits do matter, but we must measure them correctly. When we do, we find that the debt had been declining substantially until a few years ago and the official deficits were really surpluses. These surpluses contributed greatly to the increasing stagnation of the economy in the last decade and to the major 1981–1982 recession.

Despite their loud rejections—and ignorance—of the "old" Keynesian theory and policies, the Reagan administration's massive move to budget deficits, reinforced by lower rates of inflation, contributed significantly to the sharp recovery of 1983–84.

Continued ignorance and rejection of this analysis and the policies it implies can only lead to new economic trauma in the future.

Notes

1. The adjusted surplus, it will be noted, differs from the real change of government net debt, expressed in current dollars, by the amounts of the off-budget items and net revaluations of gold. We have excluded net revaluations on gold from the adjusted surplus on the principle that an increase in the value of government gold holdings, unlike an increase in the value of government holdings of private debt, does not decrease private net worth. It may indeed be argued, rather, that an increase in the value of gold will be perceived by the private sector as increased backing for government debt and thus as increased private wealth. Similar considerations apply to the off-budget items.

In this article, the founder of the "public choice" school of economics traces the breakdown of fiscal responsibility in government back to Keynes and the Keynesian revolution. A balanced budget amendment, he says, is one of the deliberately contrived constitutional constraints which must now take the place of the unwritten "fiscal constitution" which Keynes and his followers destroyed.

THE MORAL DIMENSION OF DEBT FINANCING

James M. Buchanan

I. Introduction

Economists have almost totally neglected moral or ethical elements of the behavior that has generated the observed modern regime of continuing and accelerating government budget deficits. To the extent that moral principles affect choice constraints, such neglect is inexcusable. It is incumbent on us, as economic analysts, to understand how morals impinge upon choice, and especially how an erosion of moral precepts can modify the established functioning of economic and political institutions. A positive, empirical theory of the operation of moral rules is in order even if we want to leave the preaching to the moralists.

An understanding of how moral constraints affect patterns of political outcomes need not require comparable understanding of the origins of moral rules themselves. Indeed, one of the arguments I want to develop depends critically on the "non-rational" attributes of such moral rules. The effects of moral constraints are, of course, fully symmetrical. If moral rules constrain choices, that is, if there exists what we may call a moral feasibility frontier, then it is the case that an erosion or destruction of moral norms relaxes the constraints and thereby shifts the frontier locus "outward," with consequences that we, as economists, can analyze.

I shall argue that the explosive increase in debt or deficit financing of public consumption outlays can be explained, at least in part, by an erosion of previously-existing moral constraints. The political decision makers did not "discover" a new technology of debt financing midway through this century. Their rational self-interest has always dictated resort to nontax sources of public revenues. What happened in this century was that debt financing ceased to be immoral. We have

Reprinted with permission of the author from *Economic Inquiry*, Vol. 13, no. 1, January 1985, pp. 1–6. Also reprinted in *Liberty, Market, and the State*. Brighton, England: Wheatsheaf Press, and New York: New York University Press, 1985, pp. 189–94.

here an almost perfect example of the harm that "rationalist constructivism" (to use this term pejoratively in the Hayekian sense) can produce. The attempt to impose "rational choice" behavior on those who were constrained by previously-existing and culturally-evolved moral rules has, in fact, allowed a reversion to the more primitive instincts that previously were held in check.

This moral dimension of the modern fiscal dilemma must be appreciated if there is to be any hope of escape. Abstract rules that have evolved unconsciously cannot themselves be rationally restored. However, rationally-chosen constraints can be introduced to serve, in part, as substitutes for the eroded moral rules. Balanced budgets formerly dictated by moral standards, were never explicitly mentioned in formal constitutional documents. Without such standards, however, balanced budget constraints must be explicitly chosen, imposed, and enforced.

II. The Tribal Heritage

I am neither ethnologist nor anthropologist, and I make no claim to more than minimal lay knowledge of such areas of inquiry. Hence, my remarks should be treated as conjectural rather than as recorded history. With this disclaimer made, let me suggest that there is nothing in our genetic or biological "nature" which dictates an abiding interest in the abstract future of the human species, or even in the future of the arbitrary collectives which include large populations and claim dominion over large territories. Biologically, we remain tribal animals, and our natural instincts have not evolved beyond those which emerged in very small human communities. Precepts for behavior which we call moral often reflect merely our communitarian sense of loyalty to fellow members of the tribe.

The evolution of post-Enlightenment attitudes toward the formation, accumulation, and maintenance of capital (stored up capacity to satisfy wants) reflected a continuing perception of the extended family as the relevant tribal unit. Through the process of group selection, those families whose members exhibited financial prudence survived and prospered. Generalized norms for human behavior with regard to the accumulation and maintenance of wealth and property were unconsciously directed toward family interests, not primarily those of individuals and not at all to the interests of political entities akin to modern nation-states.

III. From Moral Community to Moral Order

I have found it useful to employ the terms "moral community" and "moral order" to distinguish between the two sets of human interaction relevant for the discussion here (See Buchanan 1981). Persons belong to a moral community if they share loyalties to the group, as such. They participate in a "moral order" if they share commonly accepted codes of conduct that enable productive interaction to take place between persons of differing moral communities. Norms for fiscal prudence on the part of persons who act on behalf of political entities are norms for a "moral order" rather than norms for a "moral community." In a very real sense, these norms for collective fiscal prudence run counter to basic genetic drives. As Hayek in particular has emphasized, especially in his more recent writings, the norms for "moral order" have emerged in a long process of cultural rather than biological evolution (See Hayek 1979).

Modern man gradually came to adopt modes of behavior that enabled him to escape the limits imposed by his tribal heritage; he learned to behave in accordance with moral norms that are not of genetic origin, but which, nonetheless, are not learned consciously or rationally. As he did so, he was able to develop what Hayek has called "the great society," which is equivalent to what I have called "moral order." Man came to behave *vis-à-vis* persons who were not members of his own tribe in such fashion that reciprocal dealings became possible. In this way, ownership rights came to be mutually respected, even between members of wholly separate tribes. Trade and exchange as we know it in all its forms, from the simplest to the most complex, emerged; the specialization of labor was extended, and the miracle of coordination of modern markets was achieved.

My purpose here is neither to criticize nor to elaborate the Hayekian story. My purpose is the more limited one of suggesting that we can see an example of a move from moral community to moral order in the shift in the norms for fiscal prudence on the part of those who make decisions for the relevant polities. There is nothing in our tribal heritage that compels respect for our "national capital stock," any more than there is that compels respect for the lives and property of persons whom we do not include and have never included in our moral community. Individual behavior that evinces respect for the capital stock of the nation, as a unit, is (or was) a product of cultural evolution, not an outgrowth of any genetic heritage. The fiscal norms of the Victorians, which we may now view as praiseworthy, were culturally derived norms. The shift from a prudent attitude toward family capital, which may be at least partly of biological origin, to a comparable attitude toward national capital was a shift resulting from cultural evolution. It is of considerable interest that this shift was well under way when Adam Smith decided upon the very title of his book.

IV. Keynes as a Moral Revolutionary

The Victorian fiscal morality, a set of behavioral precepts which dictated adherence to strict budget balance, to a limited absolute level of taxation, and to a self-enforcing monetary regime, was neither rationally nor biologically derived. It was an outgrowth of a cultural evolutionary process which was not understood by those who shared the morality. It existed in continual tension with the tribal morality which remained essentially indifferent to the Victorian rules for fiscal behavior; indeed allegedly rational arguments for fiscal-monetary debauchery were introduced on occasion.

On the moral dimension that is my emphasis here, Keynes may be viewed as a successful revolutionary who destroyed the Victorian precepts. He did so for rationally-based reasons, and he sought to replace the strong but essentially unconscious adherence to long-standing rules by what seemed at the time to be a well-reasoned "logic of policy." However, Keynes totally failed to recognize that the long-standing rules for fiscal-monetary prudence were required to hold the tribal instincts in check, and that, once the Victorian precepts were eroded, the tribal instincts would emerge with force sufficient to overwhelm all rationally-derived argument.

The debt-finance we observe today we might have predicted from the simple public-choice analysis of political behavior. Constituents enjoy receiving the benefits of public outlays, and they deplore paying taxes. Elected politicians attempt to satisfy constituents. There is little need here to elaborate on this simple model of public choice, which now seems so straightforward. As you know, I have discussed this model in the book I wrote with Richard Wagner several years ago (Buchanan and Wagner 1977). This paper goes beyond the model in that book by offering an explanation as to why the natural proclivities of citizens and politicians alike emerged only in the post-Keynesian era. I have previously referred to the fact that the Keynesian theory of economic policy essentially repealed the implicit fiscal and monetary constitution evident in the Victorian era.

V. The Vulnerability of Culturally Evolved Norms

Why did these implicit rules exist and why were they so vulnerable? It is useful to consider here the Hayekian distinction between culturally evolved codes of conduct and biologically driven instincts. The human animal, in modern political structures, has chosen to "eat up" the capital stock of his nation. (For let us make no mistake about it: this is precisely what the debt financing of public consumption is, an "eating up" of national capital.) This choice has been taken because of the shift in moral standards that the Keynesian revolution embodied. It is no longer immoral to mortgage the future flow of the national income, at best an abstraction which commands little moral assent.

The erosion of the standards of fiscal morality applied to political units has exerted predictable spillover influences on the standards of morality applied to family and personal portfolios. There remains, nonetheless, a major difference in the vulnerability of the two sets of standards. To some extent at least, the immorality of destroying family or personal capital stems from biological origins. Public profligacy now seems almost unlimited because of the destruction of moral standards that were clearly produced in a cultural evolutionary process. Private profligacy continues to be held in check by moral standards that are only in part culturally determined.

From the perspective taken here, it is interesting to observe that attempts by modern economists to de-emphasize the consequences of our changed behavior with respect to public debt issues have included the revival of the Ricardian equivalence theorem, which involves the conversion of public debt into its private debt equivalents. To the extent that such conversion does, in fact, take place, individual standards of morality for the consumption of family or private capital stocks are implicitly extended to the aggregate national capital stock. These models are deficient, however, in precisely the same sense as the simple public choice models. They provide no explanation at all for the explosion in public debt financing of ordinary public outlays during middle decades of this century. If, indeed, individuals act in a supra-rational Ricardo-Barro manner, why did the financing mix between taxation and debt shift so dramatically in the post-Keynesian era?

VI. Culturally Evolved Norms as Public Capital

If my basic diagnosis is correct, that we have lived through a period in which culturally evolved rules of fiscal prudence as applied to the behavior of public choosers (in all capacities) have lost their previously-existing moral force, it is necessary to acknowledge that we have destroyed a valuable portion of our public capital stock. The metaphor is useful in that it suggests that there is a quasi-permanency involved here, even if it were possible to "reconstruct" that which has been destroyed. If moral rules must evolve slowly and without deliberate construction, then there is little hope for any attempt at restoration. We can take a somewhat more optimistic view, however, if we recognize that there is always some substitutability between rules for behavior which reflect moral norms and those which are explicitly chosen as constraints.

If this substitutability is accepted, then an observed erosion in constraining moral norms can be offset, at least in part, by deliberate adoption and enforcement of behavioral constraints. If, in our varying capacities as public choosers (as voters, as members of benefit-receiving special interest groups, as taxpayers, as members of political parties, as elected politicians, as bureaucrats), we are not constrained by moral sanctions against the accelerating destruction of our national capital stock through the deficit financing of public consumption, we must look to the more formal rules of the political institutions within which we make public decisions. It is not at all contradictory or inconsistent to recognize that the rules under which we choose may be non-optimal while at the same time we behave within those existing rules in accordance with rational utility-maximizing norms. Given the absence of moral constraints and given the observed open-ended rules for fiscal decisions, rational behavior on the part of public choosers insures the regime of continuing and accelerating budget deficits.[1] In view of the difficulty if not the impossibility of any deliberative restoration of moral precepts, we must indeed look to explicit rules if reform in the pattern of results is to be expected.

I think that the discussion on the constitutional amendment to require government budget balance offers the most constructive advance in policy reform in several decades. Having lived through the destruction of fiscal morality by the Keynesian mind-set, we must make every effort to replace this morality with deliberatively-chosen constraints which will produce substantially the pre-Keynesian pattern of results. Economists, in particular, need to bring their own thinking up to date on all such matters and to rid themselves, once and for all, of the notion that they need only proffer advice to a benevolent government which eagerly pays heed.

Notes

1. There are, of course, limits to deficit financing. Continued increase in debt service charges cannot be characteristic of economic or political equilibrium. Explicit default, or default through inflation, will, of course, impose such limits. Even fear of such default may, however, be sufficient to generate the requisite political support for *temporary* reductions in deficit size. But there is nothing in modern democracies to generate permanent changes in the pattern of results.

References

Buchanan, James M., "Moral Community, Moral Order, or Moral Anarchy," Abbott Memorial Lecture No. 17, in *The Colorado College Studies*, The Colorado College, Colorado Springs, 1981.

_____ and Wagner, Richard, *Democracy in Deficit*, Academic Press, New York, 1977.

Hayek, F.A., *Law, Legislation, and Liberty: The Political Order of a Free People*, Vol. III, University of Chicago Press, Chicago, 1979.

West summarizes public debt controversies among academic economists from the mid-1940s to the mid-1960s. These debates generated a great deal of confusion, and West maintains that they can be made sense of by defining the public debt burden in opportunity cost terms. What emerges is a classification of various uses of the term "debt burden" into the categories of individual and aggregate, on the one hand, and gross and net, on the other.

PUBLIC DEBT BURDEN AND COST THEORY

E. G. West

After the "great public debt debate" we need a new taxonomy of debt "burdens." One is constructed here, beginning with the definition of "burdens" as opportunity costs. On this view, the difference between internal and external and also between public and private debt burdens—the central features of the great debate—are shown to disappear. The intense debate that occurred between 1958 and 1964 on the subject of the national debt centered upon three basic questions: 1) whether the analogy between private (individual) debt and public debt was fallacious in all essential respects; 2) whether there was a sharp and important distinction between an internal and external debt; and 3) whether public debt involves any transfer of the primary burden to future generations. Initiating the debate James M. Buchanan (1958) challenged what he described as the "new orthodoxy" (started by Alfred Pigou) that was answering these questions in the positive.

The basic view in this article is that the debt burden debate was, in retrospect, largely based on an elementary confusion. Much of the controversy can be resolved when each aspect of the debate is placed in its appropriate category of "cost." Part I examines the first of the three questions in terms of a new taxonomy. Part II offers a corrective to the (still customary) argument that external debt is different from internal debt. Part III, which relates mainly to the third question, reviews the notion that has come to be called "the Ricardo-Pigou burden." Part IV develops the distinction between gross and net burdens. Finally, in Part V, the concept of debt burden as cost is related to tax incidence.

I. A Taxonomy of Debt Burdens

One feature of the controversy was the objection that the terminology of "burdens" was too emotive. Several writers urged that "burdens" be translated into the

Reprinted with permission of the author from *Economic Inquiry*, Vol. 13, no. 2, June 1975, pp. 179–90.

more neutral framework of "costs"—namely "opportunity costs."[1] Accordingly, the opportunity cost concept of debt burden will be used hereafter.

As Robbins (1934) emphasized many years ago, the concept of costs is not only one of displaced alternatives but is also inextricably linked with the process of choice. The idea that cost might be avoided by not making a choice, goes back to Wieser, Wicksteed, Knight, and the London School, and has been further developed by J.M. Buchanan (1969, 1973). Buchanan has emphasized that there is a distinction between the Austrian (=London) notion of opportunity cost, and cost in the sense of money actually paid out. The latter can be variously described as "historical," "objective," or "ex post" cost. I shall also use the term "outlay."

In retrospect Buchanan's position in the debt controversy would have been considerably clarified had he used his most recent separation of subjective cost into "choice influencing" and "choice-influenced" cost (Buchanan 1969). Both of these costs are subjective in that they must each be reckoned in a utility dimension. This of course is in contrast to objective or historical costs (outlays), which are reckoned in a commodity dimension. "Choice influencing cost," Buchanan explains, has three features. First, it must be borne exclusively by the decision maker. Second, it cannot be shifted to others. Third, it is dated at the moment of decision or choice. "Choice-influenced" cost differs mainly in that it is extended into the future (when taxes are paid). The essence of the subjective utility loss in choice-influenced cost is that present day decision-makers experience "regrets" in the future when the consequences of their decisions are realized and taxes have to be paid. "The coward dies a thousand deaths."

As used in the controversy, the word "burden" has had more (implied) meanings than subjective (opportunity) and objective (outlay) cost. A fuller taxonomy of debt is presented in Table 1. Gross debt burdens (GDB) occupy the left column and net debt burdens (NDB) the right column. NDB represents the residual burden (positive or negative) after the benefits have been taken into account. Note the distinctions between the stock concept of debt (rows 2 and 5) and the flow concept (rows 1 and 4). Also, the distinction between individual and aggregate (national) burden is shown in sections A and B. The cost of the debt instrument to the bond purchaser is a separate meaning of "burden" and is shown in the third row; it will receive special attention in Part IV. Opportunity costs are the (a) items and objective costs are the (b) items in the first column. Although the classification could easily be extended beyond our ten cases, these will be sufficient for present purposes.

Since opportunity costs are subjective in nature, it is more convenient to deal with the individual rather than with an abstract "aggregation." In addition, we will be initially concerned with the allocation of the costs of the project (not the costs of the bond). Thus we focus upon the first two rows of Table 1. Moreover, since we are concerned with costs as foregone alternatives, we shall concentrate on gross burdens in the first column. Being left with GDB 1(a) and GDB 2(a) we shall select the former as the clearest benchmark case of "burden" as an opportunity cost. GDB 2(a) will be the subject of further discussion in Part III. The senses in

Table 1
A Classification of Debt Burdens

A. Individual Burdens

GDB 1 The future *flow* of an individual's payments in sharing the costs of the project
(a) expected (opportunity cost)
(b) realized (actual outlay)

NDB 1 The future residential burden to the individual (positive or negative) after the deduction of benefits from GDB 1

GDB 2 The stock decrease in the individual's net worth after capitalization of future taxes associated with the project
(a) expected (opportunity cost)
(b) realized (actual outlay)

NDB 2 The change in the individual's net worth after capitalization of his future taxes (GDB 2) *and* benefits

GDB 3 The burden (cost) of purchasing the debt instruments (securities)
(a) expected (opportunity cost)
(b) realized (actual outlay)

NDB 3 The residual burden to the bond purchaser (usually negative) defined as the difference between the benefits and the cost GDB 3

B. Aggregate Burdens

GDB 4 The future aggregate cost of the project in flow terms, i.e., the periodic debt servicing and amortization payments by the nation to foreign countries
(a) expected (opportunity cost)
(b) realized (actual outlay)

NDB 4 The aggregate cost (GDB 4) to the *nation* less the aggregate value of the flow of public benefits from projects purchased with external loans

GDB 5 The once-for-all capitalized cost of domestic resources foregone by the *nation* at the time of the building of the public project
(a) expected (opportunity cost)
(b) realized (actual outlay)

NDB 5 The aggregate cost (GDB 5) to the nation less the aggregate capitalized value of the future expected services to the *nation* from newly acquired public assets

which "aggregate burdens" can also be translated into terms of opportunity costs will be examined in Parts IV and V. One should not draw the implication here that objective costs are irrelevant; indeed they are necessary in any empirical application of economics. The immediate point in the selection of GDB 1(a) as the benchmark is to bring into perspective the contrasting nature of "burdens."

II. The External versus the Internal Debt

The National Case

The argument of A. P. Lerner, (1948), is that internal debt amounts to mere transfers from one set of people in the country to another; it is self cancelling because "we owe it to ourselves." In Table 1 this argument refers to category GDB 5. Public debt, the argument goes, is distinct from private debt in this sense. Imagine, however, an American population of Smiths and Joneses. Assume that the Joneses are the debt holders. As taxpayers called upon to service the debt, each Smith family is inescapably burdened in the sense of GDB 1. To be told that this burden will be less because each Mr. Jones is "one of ourselves" is of no consolation. The Smiths have to service the debt just as if they had borrowed from a Canadian or Australian Mr. Jones. Any creditor to whom he owes money is external to Mr. Smith; and this is the case whether the debt is public or private.

Foreign debt, just like domestic debt, involves a "choice-influencing" opportunity cost immediately before the decision is made. The opportunity cost associated with domestic debt has no connection with the fact that resources are used up in the initial period—a connection that is implied in the Lerner-Pigou reasoning. The cost arises simply because the decision is made; foregone opportunities are experienced. Both domestic and foreign debt involve such present costs (opportunity costs). Future settlements (outlays) are of course associated in all cases; and these are made by future taxpayers to bond holders (domestic or foreign) in final payment for the project; but these future settlements are not choice-influencing opportunity costs.

It is probable that participants in the debate would acknowledge that opportunity costs are involved with an *internal* debt. For a given expenditure, the "internal" opportunity cost of increasing public expenditures on roads is, say, a reduction in expenditure on public housing programs. The argument that external debt is "different" seems to be that when funds are imported the earlier opportunity cost of roads versus houses is avoided; expenditure on houses is now not curtailed when road spending is increased. However, one elementary item is overlooked in this argument; *the increased expenditure expands the total budget.* Consequently new opportunity costs in terms of expected future utility losses due to extra budgeted taxes for serving and repayment are involved, costs that cannot be postponed. Whether the source of funds is external or internal does not affect this conclusion. In fact, with free capital markets and at the appropriate price (interest rate), the extra borrowing *can* take place from within. If rates of interest are equal everywhere and transfer problems are negligible the geographic origin of the loan funds is irrelevant. If there are transfer problems and interest rate differences these are probably second order problems. Moreover, the fact that the investment may produce benefits that are more than sufficient to cover the costs does not deny that present opportunity costs exist immediately preceding the decision. *Those who have argued that external debt is different because it allows costs to be postponed have thus been in error if by costs they mean opportunity costs.* The choice of external debt involves a present cost of decision making. In this sense the burden of external debt like that of internal debt is *always* in the present; and, moreover, this is so whether the debt is seen as an individual or an aggregate burden.

The Municipal Case

These same points can, of course, be applied to issues in local government finance. It has been suggested (Musgrave 1959) that the cost of current local projects such as municipal playgrounds or local highways can be shifted to future generations only because the debt that is used is external (to the municipal boundary). Again if "cost" means opportunity cost, as reflected in category GDB 1, this is incorrect.[2]

Examine now the capitalization of future debt in terms of a decrease in overlife net-worth, GDB 2. The argument in the municipal finance literature is that the taxpayer-voter-beneficiary can correctly calculate his future net-worth at the beginning of every new local government project. On this reasoning, which originated with Ricardo (1951 ed., pp. 244–245), there is no fundamental economic difference between taxes and debts. Note also that the debt burden is experienced in the present.[3]

Municipal debt that is serviced and amortized by taxes on privately owned property such as houses offers a clear example of this process. Developing an argument of Vickrey (1961), Daly (1969) stresses that the reduction in an individual taxpayer's net worth is done for him automatically and with great accuracy by the property market. The debt burden thus falls entirely and unambiguously upon the present generation. Again there is no theoretical objection to the use of this version of burden, which fits clearly into one of our classifications (GBD 2) in Table 1.

However, some special dangers of confusion should be avoided. Consider the argument by Daly (1969) that because property markets adjust downwards the present owners of property are "trapped" and cannot transfer any of the burden to people who move into an area at future times. Immigrants, knowing that they will be obliged to pay taxes "attached to" the property, are not really "burdened" because they move voluntarily and thereby move to a preferred position.[4] This way of describing the situation can be misleading. The market price of house property is affected by benefits as well as the costs of the public project. Residents will certainly enjoy the benefits independently of the means used to finance them. Property values, however, will differ with debt compared to tax finance.

Assume that A has an income of $10,000 and a house worth $50,000. Assume perfect certainty and perfect capital markets. A public project is introduced that will cost Mr. A $5,000 if presented as a once for all charge. Assume the public project generates proportional benefits that accrue exclusively to residents. On completion of the project, A's house value will rise immediately to $55,000. Compare now public debt financing. At the introduction of the project Mr. A's income will remain at $10,000, and the market value of his house will also remain unaffected. The reason is that although the public project benefits of $5,000 still "go with" the house, so do the future taxes that service the debt. When fully capitalized these future tax obligations exactly offset the public project benefits. The market value of the house thus remains at $50,000.

In this example potential future immigrants can *not* avoid their appropriate share of the debt burden. If immigrant B wishes to move into A's house immediately after the project is initiated, he will not escape the debt burden by virtue of a lower house price. He will have to pay $50,000 as before. If B does consider purchasing from A at this figure, he is faced with an opportunity cost (a choice-influenced cost) in the shape of a decision to be subjected to future taxes to service the public debt. There is, in other words, a system of linked exchanges. The exchange of a residence amounts to a kind of joint sale; the public project is tied in. The assumption of perfect certainty is of course a strong one. The model nevertheless helps clarify the basic issues and illustrates the potential analytical pitfalls.

III. The Ricardo-Pigou Burden

The focus has so far been upon item GDB 1(a) in Table 1, since it offers a clear case of opportunity cost. It relates to identifiable individuals, it is anticipatory (ex ante), and it is a gross burden (cost). We will have cause to discuss further the relation of this item to the others in Table 1. First we examine GDB 2(a)—its closest neighbor. GDB 2(a), which we touched upon in the municipal debt discussion, is reflected in David Ricardo's *Principles of Political Economy and Taxation*. The well-known "Ricardian equivalence theorem" appears in Chapter XVII.

> "When for the expenses of a year's war, twenty millions are raised by means of a loan, it is the twenty millions which are withdrawn from the productive capital of the nation . . . Government might at once have required the twenty millions in the shape of taxes; in which case it would not have been necessary to raise annual taxes to the amount of a million. This, however, would not have changed the nature of the transaction. An individual instead of being called upon to pay £100 per annum, might have been obliged to pay £2000 once and for all."

> (Ricardo 1951, pp. 244–45)

On Ricardo's reasoning, loans and taxes are thus equivalent instruments. The argument appears to imply perfect capital markets. If, assuming an interest rate of 5 percent, the individual is called upon to pay the £100 per annum in perpetuity for his contribution to public debt charges, he will reduce the capitalized values of his future income streams by £2000. This "burden" of reduction is our item GDB 2, and it implies a simple capitalization of the flow terms of GDB 1. Like us, Ricardo sees the "key" burden as resting upon individual taxpayers and not upon bond purchasers; in terms of Table 1, Ricardo selects GDB 1 and GDB 2, not GDB 3.

Consider then Ricardo's conclusion that, under the special assumptions involved, the present day taxpayer bears the burden whether the government employs loans or extraordinary taxes. On our reasoning those in the present generation clearly do bear the main burden if by that we mean the opportunity cost. This is because opportunity costs, GDB 1(a) and GDB 2(a), rest with the decision makers who, by definition, operate in the present. But *can* the second generation be burdened by the choice of public debt over taxes in a different sense? It has been argued that a significant assumption is that taxation results in reduced present consumption whereas borrowing leads to reductions in private capital formation. Thus, if generation 1 uses loans instead of taxes, generation 2 suffers a "burden" in the shape of reduced inheritance. It is this real "burden" that has come to be known as the "Ricardo-Pigou burden" (Shoup 1962).

This discussion route takes us away from individuals, into aggregates such as "generations." Moreover, the linkage with individual choice is obscured; individuals are assumed in advance to respond in a deterministic way to given stimuli. It is not at all clear, however, that the reduction in the inheritance of the second generation is inevitably dependent upon the choice of debt. If the first generation is informed of the consequences of their actions, there is no reason why they should not be equally disposed to use the tax alternative and reduce their private savings (or use the loan alternative and reduce consumption). The decision makers are able to make identical adjustments in their consumption in the case of a loan as with a tax; thus they will leave the same real inheritance to their heirs. The choice of a loan over a tax is not a resource allocation decision or a decision about future "burden" but merely a financial decision.[5]

To clarify this, return to our example of a community of Smiths and Joneses. Assume again that the Joneses are the purchasers of bonds, but initially these are all private. The national income is $100,000 and private annual savings investment is 10 percent or $10,000. The government now finances a war and sells bonds; to service them calls for another $10,000 per year. Suppose the Joneses purchased the government bonds entirely out of reduced consumption. Annual private capital formation is unaffected at $10,000. In this situation there is no burden of the debt to future generations in terms of the Ricardo-Pigou effect since there is no reduction in capital formation and the inheritance potential remains constant. In cost terms, however, the burden does remain. The Smiths still have to make future net transfers to the Joneses for their purchase of the public "project." Each individual Jones is an "external" lender to each Smith. Each transfer is an objective cost (outlay) that is paid in the future by the Smiths or by future generations of taxpayers. And immediately prior to the decision on the project the future anticipated utility loss to future Smiths is an obstacle to choice—an opportunity cost. Thus although there is no Ricardo-Pigou burden there is still a burden in terms of GDB 1(a) and GDB 1(b).

The Ricardo-Pigou effect is then revealed as an *aggregate* effect upon an *aggregate* entity. It relates to the net "global" result after all the various pluses and minuses have been considered. This cannot be shown in Table 1. Burden viewed as a cost on the other hand is strictly related to affected *individuals* and to the *purchase of particular projects*. Suppose in our example that the government spent the proceeds of public debt, not upon an (undesirable) war but upon (desirable) durable social capital such as roads. The net result could be an *increase* in total (public plus private) capital formation. The Ricardo-Pigou "burden" would then be *negative*. This "burden" therefore refers to the effect of a chain of possible events upon the national accounts. Compare this with the notion of burden as cost which refers to utility losses of identifiable individuals in their tax "purchase" of given projects. If, in our example of debt financed war, government bonds were purchased at the expense of private bonds causing capital formation to fall to zero, the Ricardo-Pigou burden is still different from burden as cost even though both are now positive. The objective cost on individuals of future tax obligations remains, as before, the result of a single event—the decision to undertake the project. The Ricardo-Pigou burden, in contrast, relates (a) not to identifiable individuals but to aggregate entities like "nations," (b) not to one event but to the algebraic sum of two—the first being the gains from the project itself, the second being the decision of bondholders to purchase bonds by running down either their consumption or their saving.

IV. Gross and Net Benefits and Movements to Preferred Positions

It is understandable that participants in the debt burden debate wanted to neutralize the word "burden" and substitute the word "cost." As illustrated in the previous section, the interests of clarity also demand that "costs" should be clearly separated from "benefits." Consider Mishan's observation: "If, for instance, the government invested the funds in productive assets whose service could be sold profitably to the public, it would have no need to raise taxes on future generations to service the debt" (Mishan 1963, p. 533). This proposition of course is correct, but throws attention away from the opportunity cost aspects of debt financing as illustrated on the left of Table 1 and on to "net burdens" which are shown on the right. If we wish to substitute opportunity cost for burden (as Mishan recommended), the productivity or unproductivity (net benefit) of the public expenditure is irrelevant. An "opportunity cost" is always there whether the public project be productive or wasteful.

The practice of seeing the burden in terms of net outcome can be traced to Ricardo. To him the real burden of the public debt was the destruction of capital caused by the "profuse expenditure of government." The burden rested with the generation living in the initial period for *this* reason. Ricardo's example is the converse of Mishan's since it focuses on unproductive as distinct from productive government investment. In both cases the burden referred to is a *net* burden (NDB in Table 1).

The phrase, "moving to a preferred position," also refers to a net outcome. It is frequently argued for instance that issuance of government debt, as distinct from the taxes levied to service it, imposes no burden on anyone because although the bond purchasers certainly supply the resources, "they move to a preferred position" in their portfolio.[6] There may be a special sense in which bond purchasers don't bear a burden, but it is never adequately specified.

Assume the debt financing is tied to a particular project. It is necessary to distinguish (see Table 1) between the cost of the debt instrument *per se* (GDB3) and the ultimate cost of the public project (GDB1). The two exchanges that are involved are (a) the sale of the bond, (b) the purchase of the project. *Any exchange involves opportunity costs.* Hence there is a valid sense in which the bond purchaser is burdened, but he is burdened only by the purchase of *the debt instrument*. The statement that the issue of debt, as distinct from a tax, imposes no burden on anyone must mean therefore that the burden is not *directly* associated with the purchase *of the project*.

It must be recognized, however, that public projects are provided through sets of linked exchanges; and since there is a sequence of exchanges there is a corresponding sequence of (both objective and opportunity) costs. Opportunity costs are experienced immediately by the citizen purchasers of the project (or their representatives) and by the bond purchaser; but the citizen's opportunity costs are related to the project while the bond purchaser's are related to the bond. The bond purchaser experiences an objective cost (outlay) almost simultaneously with the opportunity cost. He makes the decision which involves opportunity cost and almost immediately makes the actual payment—which involves objective cost. The objective cost (outlay) of taxpayers, on the other hand, is experienced in the future. Complete analysis of the effects of debt financing calls for the recognition of all the four types of cost: GDB 3(a) and (b) and GDB 1(a) and (b). Without such specification the statement that the bond purchaser does not bear a burden because "he moves to a preferred position" can be misleading. There may be a temptation to extend the proposition and argue that the taxpayer "buys" a public project he also bears no burden because he too "moves to a preferred position." For the unsophisticated the next step could be for the phenomenon of "burden" (cost) to be conjured away altogether.

V. Tax Incidence and the Opportunity Cost Theory of Debt

Since the "great debt controversy" (1958–64) some writers have attempted to integrate the concept of debt burden with the traditional public finance theory of tax incidence (Shoup 1969, Head 1967). It is equally important to link "incidence" theory with the economic theory of cost.

To some theorists the term "incidence" applies exclusively to taxation. They would thus not use "price incidence" to describe the "burden" of private market purchasers; indeed the analogy between taxes and prices is often played down. But if "incidence" loses all connection with "price" it loses all connection too with cost. Similarly the connection between incidence and decision-making will become blurred. This final section is confined to a brief clarification of the issues.

Consider again the argument (Shoup 1969, Head 1967) that, unlike current taxation, public debt enables an individual to leave a reduced estate. When the second generation is bequeathed a tax liability (to service a debt) but not the bonds, and *when there are no offsetting increases in private capital bequests,* the older generation is enabled to leave not just a reduced inheritance but even a *negative* estate.

In what sense can we translate such choices of debt into terms of cost? Ideally the present opportunity cost associated with such choice of debt to finance a given public project is experienced by public decision makers who, as representatives, gauge utility losses of their constituents. Assuming the well-being of generation II is an argument in the welfare function of generation I, the expected "negative estate" is an opportunity cost to the latter. The average public decision maker is not likely to make very sensitive judgments, however. Meanwhile individuals can, within limits, make their own adjustments. Positive analysis of the events, therefore, must proceed in two stages. Governments sell bonds and private individuals buy them. The choices and motivation of the latter, including their private arrangements for future individual bequests to their heirs, should then be distinguished from the choices and motivations of governments as bond sellers (Buchanan 1969, p. 65). Whether debt compared with tax finance will in fact reduce capital formation is an open question. The two alternatives may lead to identical changes in savings. These are matters of individual choice that are difficult to predict in advance.

The traditional incidence theory seems to have always confused two things: the location of the costs of the government spending project that is financed by the tax in question, and the total effects of the tax on distribution, which involves net pluses and minuses over and above the costs of the project. Cost theory is mainly concerned with Allocation rather than Distribution. Incidence theory can, of course, continue to study questions of total effect on distribution; it should, however, also extend into cost theory as a conscious and clearly separate exercise.[7]

VI. Conclusions

The main conclusions can now be summarized.

(a) Individual (private) burdens need to be carefully distinguished from aggregate burdens. In terms of the opportunity cost of tax burdens on individuals, the distinction between internal and external debt disappears; and this applies also to municipal finance.

(b) The Ricardo-Pigou version of the debt burden is distinct from the cost version in that it relates to several events, not one; it is expressed as an algebraic sum of these events, and it is primarily concerned with aggregates.

(c) Bond purchasing is an exchange transaction and since all exchanges involve costs (burdens), the bond purchaser also experiences a gross cost (burden) even though the benefits outweigh them and he moves to a preferred position. This cost, however, is in exchange for the paper-asset only. The postponed cost of the public project is made via two separate but linked exchanges. The final one is the exchange between the sellers and the final purchasers of the public project and is settled by payments from future taxpayers.

(d) Traditional incidence theory has become somewhat separate from cost theory because it has been predominantly occupied not with exchange relationship of "tax-priced" public projects but with the effects on general income distribution. Incidence theory now needs supplementing by an extension into cost theory; for the direct effect of tax *per se* is that of both opportunity, and objective, cost.

Notes

1. See J.M. Buchanan (1958), E. Mishan (1963), J. Wiseman (1961).
2. Consider the following comment by Musgrave (1959, p. 575) which is made in context of municipal finance: "The crucial difference between internal and external finance is that the latter permits an import of real resources, thereby enabling the (local) government to provide additional facilities without an immediate reduction to the other uses of resources, whether for consumption or capital formation. That is, the realization of opportunity cost is postponed until later, when the debt is serviced and repaid, thus giving rise to an outflow of resources at the time."

3. To be consistent, the same individual would also have to write down his net worth every time he undertook a private purchase on the installment system.
4. The whole concept of "movements to preferred positions" and their relationship to debt-burden receives special attention in Part IV.
5. In the absence of perfect certainty and perfect capital markets, however, a Ricardo-Pigou effect can emerge "by accident" so that loan finance turns out to have "less favourable" effects for the second generation's inheritance than would extraordinary tax finance. The precise analysis of these possibilities was the chief concern of some of the most distinguished papers in the controversy of the 1960's. It is not possible in one article to present a full review of these contributions. In any case that was competently done by Ferguson (1964). The present essay is concerned with clarifying and developing the argument with reference to post-1964 discussion and to the opportunity cost concept in particular.
6. This point was stressed early in the debate by Buchanan (1958). It has since been repeated often by others. See Shoup (1969), Daly (1969).
7. Hitherto discussion and analysis have been hindered because some participants have been at cross-purposes by implicit use of these two separate approaches. It is this state of affairs which seem to have prompted James Tobin (1965) to claim that "Buchanan's simplistic view of burden throws away the whole 'incidence and effects' literature of public finance," and to have prompted Buchanan (1966) into reporting that "no statement could be more in error."

References

Buchanan, James M., *Public Principles of Public Debt*, Homewood, Illinois, 1958.
────── , "The Icons of Public Debt," *Journal of Finance* 21, 1966.
────── , *Cost and Choice*, Chicago, 1969.
────── and S.F. Thirlby (eds.), *L.S.E. Essays on Cost*, London, 1973.
Daly, George D., "The Burden of the Debt and Future Generations," *Southern Economic Journal*, 1969.
Ferguson, James M., ed., *Public Debt and Future Generations*, Chapel Hill, 1964.
Head, John G., "The Theory of Debt Incidence," *Rivista Li Dioritto Finanzario e delle Finanze*, June, 1967.
Lerner, Abba P., "The Burden of the National Debt" in *Income Equipment and National Policy*, New York, 1948.
Meade, J.E., "Is the National Debt a Burden?" *Oxford Economic Papers*, 10 June, 1958.
Mishan, Edward J., "How to Make a Burden of the Public Debt," *J.P.E.*, 71, Dec., 1963.
Modigliani, Franco, "Long-Run Implications of Alternative Fiscal Policies and the Burden of the National Debt," *The Economic Journal* 71, Dec., 1961.
Musgrave, Richard A., *The Theory of Public Finance*, New York: McGraw Hill, 1959.
Ricardo, David, "Principles of Political Economy and Taxation," *Works and Correspondence*, Vol. 1, Cambridge, 1951.
Robbins, Lionel, "Remarks Upon Certain Aspects of the Theory of Costs" *Economic Journal*, March, 1934.
Shoup, Carl S., *Public Finance*, London, 1969, p. 444.
────── , "Debt Financing and Future Generations," *Economic Journal*, 72, Dec., 1962.
Tobin, James, "The Burden of Public Debt: A Review Article," *Journal of Finance*, 20, Dec., 1965.
Wiseman, Jack, "The Logic of National Debt Policy," *Westminster Bank Review*, Aug., 1961.
Vickrey, William, "The Burden of the Public Debt: Comment," *American Economic Review*, March, 1961.

Deficit finance is just as much of a burden on citizens as direct taxation, the Friedmans maintain, because it just as surely drains resources out of the private sector. Growing budget deficits, moreover, are the result of an explosion in government spending. President Reagan partially succeeded in his goal of lowering some tax rates, but he has been largely unable to get a grip on spending. Both spending and deficits have continued to rise as a fraction of income.

THE FACTS: GOVERNMENT SPENDING, TAXES, AND DEFICITS

Milton and Rose Friedman

We must keep the rate of growth of government spending at reasonable and prudent levels.
We must balance the budget, reduce tax rates, and restore our defenses.
—Ronald Reagan, September 9, 1980

We suggest that you conduct a simple personal experiment. Add up the taxes that you are reasonably aware of having paid in 1982: personal income taxes— state, federal, and local—and the Social Security tax that are deducted from your paycheck, the property tax on gasoline, the taxes on your telephone bill, and any other assorted taxes that you pay directly. If you are an average, representative taxpayer of the United States, that total will come to more than $2,500 for each person in your household—or more than $10,000 for the typical four-person family of husband, wife, and two children.

That sum only begins to measure how much government is costing you. In the first place, those taxes finance less than 60 percent of total government spending at all levels. Governments get the rest of their money from three sources: (1) taxes that most individuals are not aware of—taxes paid by corporations, customs duties, and a good many other miscellaneous imposts; (2) creating money out of worthless paper; (3) borrowing from the public in a wide variety of forms.

But do not be fooled. These "other" taxes are also laid on you! We always bear the cost. Businesses, whether incorporated or not, do not pay taxes. They simply serve as unappointed tax collectors. The taxes they transmit to the government can come only from their customers or their workers or their owners or their

Reprinted with permission of the publisher from *Tyranny of the Status Quo*. New York: Harcourt Brace Jovanovich, 1984, pp. 11–34.

shareholders. And that is true whether the tax is called a corporate income tax or a windfall profits tax or a tariff or an excise tax—or by any other name.

Similarly, what is called a deficit is an even more subtle hidden tax, whether it is financed by pieces of paper or bookkeeping entries called money or by pieces of paper or bookkeeping entries called notes or bills or bonds. During the year ended September 30, 1982, the federal government spent $746 billion and took in $618 billion in what were called budget receipts. Who do you suppose paid the $128 billion difference, labeled a "deficit"? There is no Dutch uncle—not even an Uncle Sam—to pay it. We all pay, one way or the other.

Deficit financing also has a major political cost. It enables our legislative representatives to vote for expenditures that their constituents want without having to vote for the taxes to pay for them. "Who benefits" is something that legislators are delighted to stress. "Who pays" is something they prefer not to have to talk about. If Congress were required to balance the budget, this shell game would end.

If the government finances its deficit by creating money, it imposes a hidden tax of inflation—each dollar you have will buy less. In addition, inflation raises the amount that government collects through open taxes. Income taxes go up more than in proportion to inflation because increases in income that just match inflation push the taxpayer into higher income tax brackets subject to higher tax rates—the phenomenon that has been termed bracket creep. Excise and sales taxes go up roughly in proportion to inflation. The net result is that government gets additional funds without any new taxes having to be legislated.

If the government finances its deficit by borrowing, it gets funds that would otherwise be available for building houses or factories or machines. In the process, it assumes a heavier burden of interest payments, so that we can confidently look forward to higher taxes—both open and hidden—in the future.

However the government gets the money it spends, the goods and services that it buys, or that are bought by the people to whom it transfers money, are thereby not available for other use. *Those goods and services—not the pieces of paper that pay for them—are the real cost of government to the taxpayers.*

Even these goods and services do not measure in full what our government really costs us. Many costs that we bear as a result of government action are not recorded in the books of government as either spending or taxing. An obvious example is the time that we spend preparing our personal income tax returns or the money that we spend to hire others to do so. That surely is a cost of government that we pay even though it never enters the government's books.

In a 1970 Newsweek column, one of us estimated that

> the total time [spent on preparing personal income tax returns] amounted to the horrendous total of 300 million man hours, or the equivalent of 150,000 men working 40 hours a week for 50 weeks a year—and this does not include the time spent by employees of business enterprises in withholding taxes and preparing W-2s, or by high-priced lawyers and accountants advising clients on tax matters, or by the government employees on the other side of the Internal Revenue desk.

> As I struggled with my own income-tax return, visions kept going through my head of all the useful things that this hypothetical army could accomplish—the rows on rows of new houses, schools, churches, factories, autos, that they might be producing instead of rows on rows of numbers and of uneasy consciences.[1]

More recently, "The Treasury Department estimated that the public spent 613 million hours in 1977 filling out some 260 different tax forms."[2] That is roughly double the estimate we made in 1970—or more than 300,000 people working forty hours a week for fifty weeks a year. Yet even that is clearly a gross understatement.

A different kind of hidden cost arises when government acts through regulation. By means of regulation, legislators can spend our money without *either* the expenditure *or* the tax appearing in the government ledgers. For example, government regulations requiring antipollution equipment for automobiles impose a hidden tax of several hundred dollars on each purchaser of an automobile and a hidden expenditure by the government of that sum on the antipollution equipment. The significant difference from an open tax plus direct government expenditure is that neither the legislator nor the voter nor the automobile owner evaluates the expenditure properly—or even knows how large it is. Such antipollution requirements may or may not be desirable; they may or may not be worth their cost. Whether desirable or not, their cost is part of the total cost that we impose on ourselves through government.

Costs of this kind are so numerous and widespread, so interwoven with other costs, that there exists no satisfactory estimate of how much they amount to. What is clear is that they are substantial.

We propose in this chapter to present the background facts on how government spending grew to its present size, what the taxpayers' money is spent on, how it is raised and what the outstanding governmental obligations amount to, and finally, what has occurred in all these areas since President Reagan was inaugurated.

How Government Spending Grew

At the turn of the twentieth century, total spending by government amounted to less than 10 percent of the national income (Table 1). Equally important, two thirds of that total was spent by state and local governments. The largest item of expenditure was education, followed closely by highway construction and maintenance. More than half of all state and local expenditures was on education, highways, and local police, fire, and sanitation.

Only about 3 percent of national income, one third of total government spending, was spent by the federal government—and more than half of that was for defense and veterans benefits. Expenditures on the items that bulk so large in today's federal budget—"health, education, and welfare," as the most expensive department in the current U.S. government used to be named—amounted to only $10 million out of a total federal budget of less than $600 million. That was less than 2 percent of the federal budget and only six one-hundredths of 1 percent of the national income—2 percent of 3 percent. Today, federal expenditures on health, education, and welfare total more than 14 percent of national income, *or 233 times as much as in 1902.*

**Table 1: Government Spending as a Percentage
of National Income in Selected Years**

Year	Federal	State and Local	Total
1902	3.2	6.1	9.3
1913	3.0	7.0	10.0
1922	6.3	9.2	15.5
1930	3.7	11.3	15.0
1940	12.5	10.8	23.3
1950	17.2	8.5	25.7
1960	22.4	10.4	32.8
1970	25.2	13.5	38.7
1980	28.4	12.7	41.1

Moreover, total federal government spending as a share of the national income was not very different in 1900 from what it had been throughout the previous century, or what it continued to be over the next three decades until the Great Depression, except only that it increased sharply with each major war—the War of 1812, the Civil War, and World War I. Each time, as peace returned, federal spending tended to drift back to roughly 3 percent of national income.

For close to 150 years, spending by Washington showed no tendency to rise as a fraction of national income except when it was performing what was regarded as its major function—defending the nation. Its share stayed about 3 percent while the population of the United States swelled from 5 million persons hugging a narrow strip along the Atlantic coast to 125 million spread across a vast continent, while the United States changed from an overwhelmingly agricultural to a predominantly industrial country and became the driving force of the industrial revolution that transformed the world in the nineteenth and twentieth centuries, while the United States moved from a minor country of only peripheral interest to the Great Powers, to the Greatest Power of them all. *This remarkable fact should destroy once and for all the contention that economic growth and development require big government and especially centralized government.* It is a fact that should be taken to heart by the international planners of all those countries of the world that are euphemistically designated "the developing countries" but which for the most part are not developing but rather regressing under the iron hand of strong centralized governments.

During the early twentieth century, government spending did grow as a share of income, but entirely at the state and local level. As Table 1 and Figure 1 show, the state and local share rose fairly steadily from 1902—the first date for which we have comprehensive estimates—to 1930, nearly doubling by that year. At the same time, the federal share first went up, during and after World War I, and then declined. As a result, by 1930, state and local spending amounted to more than three times federal spending. Education and highways remained the largest items, and indeed, rose as a fraction of the total, accounting between them for well over half of total state and local spending.

FIGURE 1: Federal, State and Local, and Total Government Spending as Percentage of National Income, for Selected Years, 1902–1980

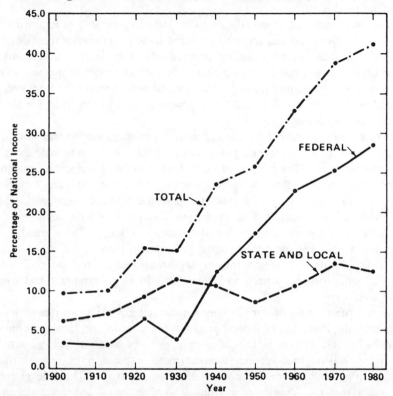

The general picture is clear. Until the 1930s, the United States remained largely as its founders had envisaged it, a decentralized society in which the state and local governments were the primary governmental entities, with the federal government serving to defend the nation, administer a common commercial policy for the several states, adjudicate disputes arising among them, and provide a common framework of law—as an umpire and defender, not as a participant in the day-to-day lives of its citizens.

On the state and local level, as income and wealth increased, the citizens were willing to spend a larger fraction of their income on the services that they had decided to acquire through government, in particular education and highways. In addition, the shift of power from local communities to the states tended to increase total state and local spending for the same reasons—though on a smaller scale—as the subsequent shift of power from states to the federal government tended to increase total spending.

Competition disciplined the provision of these services as it did the provision of services produced through private markets, though less promptly and less effectively. Freedom to move meant that people who were dissatisfied with the services provided by their local or state government could vote not only at the ballot box but also with their feet—though voting with their feet was less effective at the state than at the local level.

The situation changed drastically after the Great Depression, as Figure 1 makes very clear. Funds raised and spent by state and local governments went down and then back up, but federal spending zoomed—from 3 percent of the national income to 30 percent, raising total government spending from 15 percent to more than 40 percent. Spending financed by the federal government rose from one third of spending financed by state and local governments to more than double such state and local spending.

In the *Federalist Papers,* James Madison went out of his way to reassure citizens who were fearful that the federal government would come to dominate the states. He pointed out that, "The number of individuals employed under the Constitution will be much smaller than the number employed under the particular States. There will consequently . . . be less of a personal influence on the side of the former than of the latter."[3] This prediction about the relative number of employees has been remarkably accurate. It remains true today. There are still many more direct employees of state and local government than of the federal government. In 1981, the federal government employed about 3 million civilians and about 1.5 million military personnel. State and local governments had over 13 million employees.

However, the framers of our Constitution did not envisage two recent developments: first, the invention of federal grants-in-aid to state and local governments, so that the funds to pay the salaries of many persons in state and local governments come from Washington; second, the enormous expansion of federal transfer payments to individuals who are not classified as employees. These developments have meant that the number of persons who directly or indirectly depend on spending financed by the federal government for their livelihood vastly exceeds the number who depend on spending financed by state and local governments.

Figure 1 conceals one important detail. During World War II, federal spending soared, reaching a peak of nearly half the national income at the height of the war in 1944. It then declined sharply as it had after earlier wars. The difference from earlier episodes is that, instead of declining to its prewar level, federal spending resumed the rapid rise that the New Deal had set in train.

This brief survey makes clear that the current problem of excessive government spending is primarily at the federal level. Indeed, many problems faced by states and localities derive from programs mandated by the federal government. Accordingly we turn to a more detailed examination of spending at the federal level, with special attention to what our money is being spent on.

Federal Government Spending

Trying to find out what our money is spent on is easier promised than done. The 1984 budget documents submitted by the President in January 1983, for example, consist of four items: *The United States Budget in Brief, Fiscal Year 1984,* a summary of eighty-six pages intended for wide circulation; *The Budget of the*

United States Government, Fiscal Year 1984, a hefty volume of 615 pages which contains "the Budget Message of the President and presents an overview of the President's budget proposals"; *Budget of the United States Government, 1984— Appendix,* an even more massive volume of 1,025 extra large pages which contains "detailed information on the various appropriations and funds that comprise the budget"; and finally *Special Analyses, Budget of the United States Government, 1984,* one volume of 363 pages containing "analyses that are designed to highlight specified program areas or provide other significant presentations of Federal budget data"—a grand total of 2,089 pages.

The several volumes are for sale to the public by the Government Printing Office at prices of $5.00, $7.50, $15.00, and $6.50 respectively—a total package price of $34.00. And that, no doubt, is a subsidized price financed out of the Government Printing Office's 1983 budget appropriation of over $120 million.

It is a major detective job to ferret out from these massive volumes how much the government spends on a particular program or category of programs. It is easy enough to find out that the Government Printing Office spent $91,237,000 in fiscal year 1982 (i.e., the twelve months ending September 30, 1982)—that is to be found in part 8, page 12, of the general budget document. It would be far more difficult to find out how much it cost to print the various budget documents just referred to. No doubt, a week's research in Washington could yield an estimate, but it would be imprecise. How much of the overhead, of the cost of equipment, etc., should be attributed to that one project? And how about figures for earlier years? And for a *calendar* year, rather than fiscal year?

How much it cost to print the budget documents is of no great importance, but it illustrates the extent to which the federal government has grown into an organization that is wholly beyond the comprehension of any single individual, literally uncontrollable by the collection of individuals whom we elect to Congress and to the presidency, feeding on itself—and us—and getting larger and larger like some enormous tumor.

Deliberate obfuscation renders the situation even more incomprehensible. Every program enacted to benefit a specific interest, even if the program is a price knowingly paid for gaining political support and campaign funds, is described as promoting the general welfare. Worse, if at all possible, the cost is buried in a total in order to disguise a sop to a special interest. Consider one particularly transparent case. "Conservation of agricultural resources" seems an appropriate object for governmental concern—until you realize that it is a euphemism for a program to subsidize farmers to keep land out of cultivation in order to keep up the price of farm products and the income of farmers. Or, take another example: the 1984 budget includes a proposed appropriation of $50 million to help finance the Summer Olympics. Where do you suppose that item is included? In the Department of Defense budget, under Operation and Maintenance, where another item is the more than $1,500 million budgeted for "Wildlife Conservation, Military Reservations."

Under the circumstances, we are forced to rely on the excellent summaries prepared by the Bureau of Economic Analysis of the Department of Commerce—

financed out of the $50 million spent in (fiscal) 1982 by that department on "Economic and Statistical Analyses." In preparing the summaries, the Bureau of Economic Analysis drew on the data generated by the Bureau of the Census ($156 million) and the statistical divisions of the Department of Agriculture ($54 million) and the Department of Labor ($110 million), plus data generated by a score of other agencies, the expenditures of some of which, like the Federal Reserve System, are not recorded in any form in the mammoth budget volumes. As economic statisticians, we are delighted to have this plethora of data. As taxpayers, we are appalled at the cost.

Table 2 classifies total federal spending in three broad categories: (a) defense plus veterans benefits; (b) income support, Social Security, and welfare; and (c) all other. In view of what we have already said, we need hardly note that we offer no guarantees that the labels accurately describe the contents. To achieve comparability over time, we have expressed spending as a percentage of national income. The table gives estimates for each tenth year from 1930 to 1980. Figure 2 presents these decennial figures plus annual data from 1952 on. We start the annual data with 1952 because these are available in a convenient form only for that period. For earlier years, the estimates were built up by us from a number of bits and pieces.

Table 2: Federal Government Spending on Defense, Income Support, and Other as Percentage of National Income, for Selected Years, 1930–1980

Year	Defense plus Veterans' Benefits	Income Support, Social Security, and Welfare	Other	Total
1930	2.4	0.2	1.2	3.8
1940	3.6	1.6	7.3	12.5
1950	9.9	2.2	5.1	17.2
1960	12.1	4.8	5.5	22.4
1970	10.3	7.9	7.0	25.2
1980	7.3	12.6	8.5	28.4

In 1930, before the major shift in the role of government embodied in the New Deal, total federal spending amounted to less than 4 percent of the national income, and nearly two thirds of that went to defend the nation or to compensate the veterans of earlier wars. Of the rest, only a trivial amount—about 7 percent of the federal budget or one quarter of 1 percent of the national income—was in the category that by 1980 accounted for more than 40 percent of the budget and nearly one eighth of the national income: income support, Social Security, and welfare. The 1.2 percent of the national income spent in 1930 on "other" paid for interest on the federal debt, for the cost of running the executive, legislative, and judiciary branches of the government, for agricultural research and extensions, for maintaining airfields, and other activities.

FIGURE 2: Federal Spending as Percentage of National Income

Percent of National Income

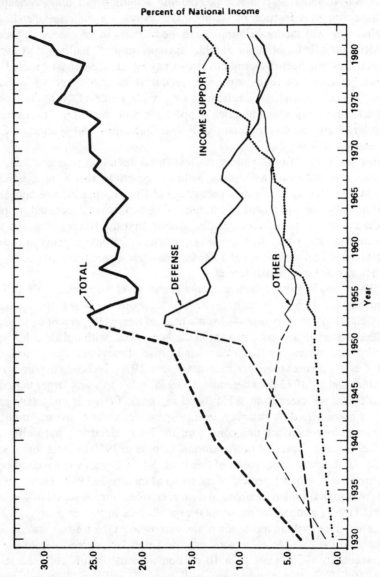

By 1940, total spending had soared to one-eighth of the national income. With World War II under way in Europe, defense spending had understandably risen by 50 percent as a fraction of income. The increase in defense spending, large though it was, was moderate compared to the increase in the other categories, both of which multiplied more than sixfold. "Income support" ballooned as the recently enacted Social Security program began paying out benefits to retired persons and the "emergency" relief legislation produced substantial grants-in-aid to the states. "Other" expenditures ballooned as a wide range of New Deal programs gathered steam—agricultural price supports, public housing, Tennessee Valley Authority, National Labor Relations Board, Securities and Exchange Commission, and on and on.

The post-World War II pattern is clear: total spending rose and fell, but the increases and decreases took place within a generally rising trend which more than doubled total spending as a percentage of the national income between 1940 and 1980. The ups and downs within this rising trend were accounted for partly by the ups and downs in military spending during first the Korean War and then the Vietnam War, and partly by the ups and downs in income support in response to successive cyclical recessions and expansions—each recession producing a sharp up, each expansion a partial retreat.

Military spending throughout was on a higher level than before World War II in response to the changed status of the United States in the world. But the trend was clearly and fairly sharply down—from a peak of nearly 18 percent in 1952, during the Korean War, to around 7 percent in the late 1970s, with only a mild rise since. All other categories, on the other hand, rose throughout the period, income support even more explosively than other. By 1970, income support was larger than other and by 1972 than defense. By 1976, other too was larger than defense.

Two things are clear from Table 2 and Figure 2: first, our budgetary problems have *not* been caused by runaway defense spending; second, the major culprit has been the explosive growth in income support, Social Security, and welfare, which went from around 2 percent of the national income in 1950 to more than 13 percent in 1982. Of the three components of this total, Social Security is the chief culprit. It accounted for less than 1 percent of the national income in 1952. Thirty years later, its share had multiplied tenfold, and it accounted for more than 8 percent of national income and two thirds of total expenditures in this category.

An even more striking indication of the explosion of the welfare state is what has happened to the number of persons receiving transfer payments from the federal government. In 1950, more than 10 million persons already received such payments. By 1980, that number was well over 50 million. Although per capita income nearly doubled from 1950 to 1980 (after allowing for inflation), more persons received payments in 1980 under the Aid to Families with Dependent Children program alone than received payments in 1950 under all the programs then in existence.

The growth in other seems moderate only by comparison with the growth in income support. It went from 5 percent of the national income in 1950 to twice that by 1982. Interest payments tripled, from 2 percent of the national income in 1950 to 6 percent in 1982. But some individual items—especially those encompassed by the Johnson Great Society programs—grew even more spectacularly. For example, expenditures on higher education went from $1 million (yes, million, *not* billion) in 1952 to $300 million in 1962 to nearly $9 billion in 1981, almost all of it in the form of aid (i.e., subsidies) to students.

Agriculture is another example. The number of persons employed on farms (including self-employed) declined from 6 million in 1952 to fewer than 3 million in 1982, yet total federal expenditures on agriculture rose from $1.25 billion in 1952 to close to $16 billion in 1982—from $210 per person employed on farms to over $6,000 per person. Apparently, the fewer the number of farmers, the greater their political clout. Both in 1952 and in 1982, most of the money went to support the price of farm crops: we paid farmers to keep output down; we bought some of the output and put it in storage; we subsidized the export of farm products. The intended result was to raise the price of farm products—that is, to make us pay more at the grocery counter for our food—and thereby transfer still more money from taxpayers to farmers. Nineteen eighty-three is scheduled to be another record year, with expenditures expected to zoom to more than $25 billion.

During the sixties and early seventies, the decline in spending on defense counterbalanced much of the increase in other spending. Nonetheless, total spending continued to rise. When the decline in defense spending tapered off and after 1979 was replaced by a rise, the full force of the increase in other categories of spending was reflected in total spending. As a result, from about 1973 or 1974 onward, total spending—if you average out peaks and troughs—rose without checks, and it precipitated the current budget crisis.

To summarize: the growth in total government spending from 15 percent of the national income in 1930 to over 45 percent today, and in spending by the federal government from less than 4 percent of the national income in 1930 to over 30 percent today, occurred only in small part because national defense (including veterans benefits) became more expensive. Defense accounted for less than 6 percentage points of the 26 percentage-point increase in the federal government's share of national income. Where did the rest of the money go? It went to finance *new* functions the government undertook. It went to transfer income from persons currently in the labor force to those who are retired, from persons who are employed to the unemployed. It went to pay for medical costs and costs of education that never before were a federal responsibility. It went to guide and direct our lives in a myriad of other ways.

States and localities have little choice about how to finance their spending. Most are required by their constitutions to balance their budgets. Even those that are not required to balance their budgets lack one alternative open to the federal government—creating money out of worthless paper or by accounting entries. States and cities must borrow on the open market, and that market imposes its own stringent discipline. But state and local governments do have a source of funds not available to the federal government, which is to say the federal government itself. During the past thirty years federal grants-in-aid to states grew from 12 percent of total state spending in 1950 to 21 percent in 1980. Because of their own constitutional and practical restraints, and aided by grants from Uncle Sam, state and local governments have run surpluses rather more frequently than deficits. During the 1970s, indeed, they recorded a surplus every year—again with the indirect help of the federal government. Inflation generated by the federal government tended to raise state revenues faster than state expenses, especially in states that had graduated income taxes. Bracket creep was just as effective in raising state taxes without legislation as it was in raising federal taxes. The growth of deficits as of government spending is a problem that must be attacked primarily at the federal level.

Deficits

The daily or weekly news media and the TV nightly news give the false impression that the major problems with the federal budget are, first, the size of the deficit and, second, the mounting public debt. It's not so. It would be hard to be further from the truth, as Table 3 makes clear. Taxes and spending are the real culprits, not deficits and debt.

Table 3: Federal Spending, Tax Receipts, Deficit, and Outstanding Debt as Percentage of National Income, for Selected Years, 1930–1980

Year	Spending	Tax Receipts	Deficit	Outstanding Debt
1930	3.7	4.1	−0.4	21.1
1940	12.5	10.8	1.7	45.4
1950	17.2	21.1	−3.9	84.1
1960	22.4	23.1	−0.7	50.5
1970	25.2	23.7	1.5	26.8
1980	28.4	25.5	2.9	27.8

Tax receipts have risen on average only slightly less rapidly than spending. Between 1950 and 1970, some years had a surplus, some a deficit. The net deficit averaged only about one tenth of 1 percent of the national income per year. From 1970 on, the situation changed. Every year has seen a deficit. The deficits for the thirteen years from 1970 to 1982 averaged 2.5 percent of the national income. Even so, the deficit has not shown a consistent tendency to increase; it has gone up and down. It was 2.5 percent in 1971 and 2.6 percent in 1981; it was 5.6 percent in 1975 and 6.1 percent in 1982. The real problem is not the bookkeeping deficit; it is the consistent growth in both spending and taxes. *The federal budget would have been roughly balanced, or gained a surplus in 1980, 1981, and 1982, had total spending been held down to the same percentage of the national income as in 1979.*

Like the concern with the deficit, the wailing and gnashing of teeth over the supposedly trillion-dollar public debt is a false emotion. In the first place, the figures cited for the public debt owned by private citizens are almost invariably overstated because they include the debt owned by the Federal Reserve System—$130 billion at the end of 1982. But the Federal Reserve is "private" only through misleading packaging and labeling. In every relevant respect, the Fed is part of the government. In the second place, while the dollar total of the debt has quadrupled since the end of World War II—from around $200 billion then to $800 billion at the end of 1982—prices have more than quadrupled, *so the debt adjusted for inflation has actually fallen.* Moreover, our economy has grown, so, as Table 3 shows, the debt has fallen even more sharply when it is expressed as a percentage of national income. Just after World War II, the national debt amounted to roughly one year's national income. By 1980, it had fallen to a little over a quarter of a year's national income.

What explains this paradox? Deficits occur year after year, yet debt declines both in real terms and as a fraction of national income. The answer is clear. By paying the debt off in cheaper and cheaper dollars, we have in fact defaulted on much of it. Or, to use polite language, we have imposed a hidden tax on many holders of the public debt—particularly those who were persuaded to buy the debt, particularly savings bonds, by eloquent appeals to their patriotism. The deficit recorded on the books is highly misleading. It should be reduced by the inflation tax imposed on each person who patriotically purchased government bonds.

But that is cold comfort. We have a debt problem many times more serious that is not recorded on the books. The debt that is recorded on the books is only the tip of the iceberg. We are committed to pay future benefits to retired persons under Social Security, federal employee and railroad retirement programs, and future medical costs under Medicare. Future receipts from the taxes now on the books to meet these costs are far from adequate. TV trumpeted the news that the presidential commission had "saved Social Security." But the system was not saved. Band-Aids may hide the bleeding, but they don't cure the wound. Estimates of the unfunded debt vary, yet even the most conservative one sets it at currently more than $6 trillion—yes, trillion, not billion—and more pessimistic estimates go as high as $10 trillion, which is more than seven times as large as the official public debt.

The Record since 1980

With this background, it is time to zero in on what has happened since Ronald Reagan was elected President. The data in Table 4 are comparable to those given in earlier tables. However, the "year" in Table 4 is the government's fiscal year ending September 30, instead of the calendar year ending December 31, as in the earlier tables. Here we use the fiscal year to enable us to make better use of the figures in the government's budget documents, all of which are on a fiscal year basis.

Ronald Reagan was elected President in 1980, but he did not assume office until January 1981, by which time four months of the 1981 fiscal year had already passed and the pipeline was pretty well full for the rest of that fiscal year. So, the first fiscal year on which he could have any significant impact was 1982, beginning in October 1981.

At first glance, the impression is one of business pretty much as usual: total spending continued its sharp climb, because of rises in income support and

Table 4: Federal Government Expenditures on Defense, Income Support, and Other; Total Expenditures; Receipts; and Deficit as Percentage of National Income, fiscal years 1980–83

Year (ending Sept.)	Expenditures on				Total Receipts	Deficit
	Defense plus Veterans' Benefits	Income Support, Social Security, and Welfare	Other	Total		
1980	7.6	12.0	8.2	27.8	25.3	2.5
1981	8.0	12.7	8.3	29.0	26.7	2.3
1982	8.7	13.4	8.5	30.6	25.6	5.0
1983 (est.)	9.2	13.9	8.5	31.6	24.5	7.1

defense. The only apparent changes are these: first, the other category stabilized from 1982 to 1983; and, second, receipts fell from 1981 to 1983. Both changes are partly attributable to Reagan's policies. He persuaded Congress in 1981 to cut some categories of spending—or, rather, to cut the increases in some categories of spending. He also persuaded Congress to cut tax rates in that same year. True, for 1981 and 1982, those tax cuts were largely offset by increases in Social Security taxes that had been legislated earlier, as well as by bracket creep. However, if the tax-rate cuts had not occurred, the higher Social Security taxes and bracket creep would not have been offset at all.

As it was, the main reason why receipts declined as a fraction of income in 1982 and 1983, rather than remaining stable, was *not* the Reagan tax program. Rather, it was the effect of the long and severe recession from mid-1981 up to the very end of 1982. That recession, too, was responsible for some part of the increase in spending, particularly through benefits paid to the unemployed.

Four categories of spending increased consistently and markedly from 1980 to 1983. Look at Table 5.

Spending on defense increased the most—carrying out President Reagan's campaign commitment to strengthen the national defense.

The second largest increase was in a class of programs that together can accurately be described as middle-class or, indeed, upper-class welfare: Social Security and other government administered retirement and disability programs, plus Medicare.

The long and sharp recession increased both unemployment compensation and subsidies to agriculture. This third category accounted for between a quarter and a third of the total net increase.

The fourth item showing a large increase was net interest, an item that is grossly overstated because it does not allow for the simultaneous effect of inflation in reducing the public debt as a fraction of income.

Together, these four categories rose nearly one-third more than the total net increase in expenditures.

Table 5: Change in Expenditures on Budget Items as Percentage of National Income, 1980–1983, 1981–1983

Items	Change in Percentage of National Income	
	1980–1983	*1981–1983*
Major Increases		
Defense plus Veterans Benefits	+ 1.61	+ 1.24
Middle-Class Welfare (retirement, disability, Medicare)	− 1.44	+ 0.90
Recession-induced (unemployment insurance and agricultural subsidies)	+ 1.02	+ 0.95
Net Interest	+ 0.88	+ 0.42
Total of Major Increases	+ 4.95	+ 3.51
Major Decreases		
Natural Resources, Energy, Transportation, Community, and Regional Development	− 0.63	− 0.49
Education, Training, and Employment	− 0.44	− 0.38
Revenue Sharing	− 0.17	− 0.06
Total of Major Decreases	− 1.24	− 0.93
All Other	+ 0.04	+ 0.02
Total Net Change	+ 3.75	+ 2.60

The offsetting reductions are spread throughout the budget. The largest reduction is in a category of programs that can perhaps be described as expenditures on things: spending on natural resources, energy, transportation, community and regional development. A second category showing a net reduction consists of a variety of programs directed at elementary, secondary, vocational, and higher education, and at job training and direct employment. These are hard to characterize simply. Most are directed at benefiting relatively low-income persons—notably the training and employment programs, and education programs for the disadvantaged and handicapped, which together account for more than half of total spending in this category. But they also include expenditures on higher education, which mostly affect middle- or upper-income persons. A major reduction was the elimination of the CETA program, which was castigated widely as a boondoggle.

A third category showing a reduction consists of grants of funds by the federal government to state and local governments not for specific programs but for use as the recipient government units see fit.

A fascinating aspect of this list of reductions is that it does not include any of the welfare programs for the poor—it does *not* include Aid to Families with Dependent Children, *not* SSI (Supplementary Security Income), *not* food stamps, *not* housing subsidies, *not* Medicaid, *not* social services. Some of these items went down, some went up, but both the increases and decreases were slight. Taken as a whole, the best description is that *welfare programs for the poor were held constant as a fraction of income.*

These facts paint a very different picture from that drawn by either President Reagan's supporters or his opponents. Welfare for the poor has not been cut. To that extent, the charge that President Reagan has destroyed the safety net for the poor is not correct. Welfare for the middle class and upper-income class went up sharply. To that extent, the charge that changes in spending were biased against the poor is correct. However, the blame, or credit, for this development can hardly be assigned to President Reagan. He proposed in 1981 and again in 1982 major changes in the Social Security programs that were designed to hold down their cost. Not surprisingly, these changes, which would have introduced greater even-handedness, were denounced and ridiculed by the very legislators who complained loudest about the supposed "unfairness" of the President's proposed cuts in the budget.

The only substantial decreases in spending were in programs largely administered by states and localities, whether federal programs in education, training and employment, transportation, community and regional development, or state programs financed by revenue sharing. These programs are so diverse that it is literally impossible to judge how cuts in them affected different income classes. Partly these reductions reflect the President's commitment to federalization—to returning powers and responsibility to the states and to local communities. Mostly, the cuts came here because both the President and the Congress were under pressure to hold down spending, and state and local governments offered less resistance to cuts than other pressure groups. Expediency, not principle, ruled.

On the side of taxes, President Reagan's opponents attacked his proposed cuts as favoring the rich. Here again the situation is more complex. The increase in Social Security taxes did raise the taxes imposed on lower-income groups—but those increases were legislated during Carter's term, not Reagan's. Bracket creep because of inflation does affect low-income and middle-income groups—but again, inflation was an inheritance from the Carter years, and it has come down sharply since the 1980 election. The first two installments of the across-the-board cuts in tax rates—those that took effect in 1981 and 1982—roughly offset bracket creep. The final installment, which took effect on July 1, 1983, more than offset bracket creep. Thus, it is the first *real* cut in tax rates. Further, the provision for indexing the tax rates for inflation assures that bracket creep will not rear its ugly head in the future. These changes were evenhanded or, if anything, biased toward low-income and middle-income groups, not toward the rich. The one tax change that can be said to favor the rich was the reduction in the top rate on "unearned" income from 70 to 50 percent, which took effect in 1981. But that change was not recommended by President Reagan. It was added in the course of the legislative process in the House of Representatives by the Democrat-controlled Committee on Ways and Means. Moreover, it has produced higher not lower revenue.

The Reagan years have seen a start toward achieving President Reagan's objective of cutting tax rates. They have seen no progress toward his parallel objectives of cutting government spending and balancing the budget. Even after the fullest possible allowance for the effect of the recession on government spending and the deficit, both spending and the deficit have continued to rise as a fraction of income. Progress on these objectives will have to wait for President Reagan's second term.

Notes

1. Milton Friedman, "Tax Follies of 1970," *Newsweek*, April 27, 1970.
2. From Robert E. Hall and Alvin Rabushka, *Low Tax, Simple Tax, Flat Tax* (New York: McGraw-Hill, 1983), p. 3.
3. Alexander Hamilton, James Madison, and John Jay, *The Federalist Papers* (1788), ed. Clinton Rossiter (New York: New American Library, 1961), no. 45, p. 291.

Galbraith admits that the budget deficit poses a serious threat to the economy, especially when combined with the Fed's tight money policy. He does not believe that the part of the budget devoted to social programs should be cut. Instead, he calls for a freeze in military spending and increased taxes.

THE BUDGET AND THE BUST

John Kenneth Galbraith

On the consequences of President Reagan's budget I find myself in harmony with the great majority of other economists and the instincts of the American people at large. Indeed, for the first time in my professional life, stretching now over half a century, there is a broad unity of view extending from Wall Street and the conservative economists of the American Enterprise Institute to my liberal co-religionists. All manifest a concerned opposition to the economic design being offered for the years 1983 and thereafter.

The surface concern is with the deficits that are being projected: $91.5 billion in 1983, similarly massive figures for the years following. This concern has been deepened by the imaginative fudging of the figures to get the deficit down to the stated levels. It is likely that the gap between revenues and real expenditures will be much greater; indeed, the reliance on monetary policy to curb inflation ensures it. The sound instinct of the American people is that deficits of this magnitude are unwise and dangerous. Nor do I believe that people accept as a defense that all budget problems—indeed, all economic problems—are the inheritance of previous Administrations. This, the archaeological alibi, must never be taken seriously. All Administrations, of whatever political color, must be held firmly responsible for what happens in their own time. Otherwise, one day, some imaginative economist will attribute his failures to the erroneous economic framework established by Alexander Hamilton.

The problem of the deficit lies deeper than in the fact that more money is spent than received. It lies in the constraints and contradictions that this imposes on other economic policy.

Specifically, in an economy with a strong tendency to inflation, there are only three countering lines of policy. One is direct restraint on wages and prices in the highly organized sector of the economy. This the Administration eschews. The second is restraint on inflation through the budget. This the prospective deficit

Reprinted with permission of the author from *The New Republic*, March 17, 1982, p. 9.

denies; as one cannot sink and swim at the same time, so one cannot have a large budget deficit and fiscal restraint at the same time.

There remains only monetary policy as an agent against inflation. Prayer aside, it is the only recourse. That a flaccid fiscal policy places the burden on monetary policy the Administration does not deny. It so affirms. This year's *Economic Report of the President* says flatly that a "deficit financed by money creation will have persistent inflationary consequences." These inflationary consequences, it follows, can only be avoided by a firm refusal of the Federal Reserve to allow such money creation: in short, by rigorously stern monetary policy.

Here we encounter the first of the contradictions. Control of the money supply, the essence of monetary policy, is far more difficult than once imagined by its advocates. But if the effort is sufficiently pressed, it will work. It is working now. The question is the cost. There is no mystery in how monetary policy works against inflation. It works by restraining bank lending and the subsequent bank deposit and other money creation, and the spending therefrom. It does this primarily through high interest rates; these put the price of credit beyond the reach of would-be borrowers. From the constraint imposed on lending comes reduced spending for capital and consumer goods, a recession in economic activity, and, if not lower prices, at least a lessened rate of inflation. That has been the effect of the policy in these last months. The recession we now experience was not an adventitious or accidental thing. It was the scheduled result of the policy we are now using against inflation, for it is through a recession such as we are now experiencing that monetary policy works.

A further contradiction in the budget prospect will now be obvious. The budget deficit, as currently projected, assumes an expansion in real output in calendar year 1983 of 5.8 percent. But if inflation is to be controlled, the monetary policy will have to be sufficiently restrictive so as to deny any considerable expansion in output. Perhaps, as in these last months, it will require a contraction in output. (Inflation is not a one-time thing that, once extruded from the system, is like some poison gone for good.) The effect of the restrictive money policy that the deficit requires will, in turn, cut down on tax revenues and increase payments under the various entitlement programs—and thus increase the deficit. There is nothing hypothetical about this prospect. It is precisely what has happened in Britain as the British government has followed similar budget policies with a similar reliance on monetary policy. Economics is not a compassionate thing. It does not deal gently with those who pursue such basically contradictory policies.

A recession has a restraining effect on spending in general and thus on prices. But monetary policy also has a more specific effect on those industries that are particularly dependent on borrowed money—what are coming to be called the credit-sensitive industries. Thus it works generally on the auto industry by causing fewer people to buy cars. But it has a more specific effect by cutting back, through high interest rates, on lending for the purchase of cars. It also raises the cost of credit to dealers and thus the cost of carrying inventory, with the further effect of putting some out of business. These effects we shall continue to have so long as we are forced by deficit financing to rely on monetary policy to dampen inflation—for that, to repeat, is the way it works.

There is a similar selective effect on the other credit-sensitive industries. Reduced demand from the recession acts against farm prices in general, with ancillary and highly visible effects on the farm equipment industry. The policy similarly singles out the housing, construction, and real estate industries, and small business in general, where the failure rate last year reached the highest level, one year excepted, since the Great Depression. This is the way monetary policy is working and is meant to work. These are the consequences we must expect if budget deficits require a continued reliance on monetary policy as the alternative to severe inflation.

We have heard much from liberals and the trade unions of the effect of monetary policy on employment—of the social cruelty of a policy that works by making unemployment the restraining influence on wages, and that, at the most optimistic, promises unemployment in the range of 8 percent of the labor force. (It would be much less painful to have a direct restraint on wages rather than the sanguinary, indirect restraint of the present monetary policy.) But the cruelty of the policy extends also to car dealers, home builders, construction firms, merchants, and farmers. This is small business; most small-business people are Republicans; they have often been called the backbone of the party. No one can accuse this Administration of sparing its own.

This is the policy and punishment that, in the absence of any fiscal restraint, will have to be continued and intensified in the months ahead—the policy that is made necessary, always assuming that inflation is to be contained, by the deficits.

There are three further consequences of the present policy. First, it is from borrowing for investment that we get improvement in productivity. High interest rates squelch such investment, especially by smaller enterprises. The recession by which monetary policy suppresses inflation also has an adverse effect on productivity. There is no mystery as to why this should be so. It is when business is expanding and firms are operating at or near capacity that new plant is wanted and new investment made. New plant is almost always more efficient than old. The years of high interest rates have, in virtually all countries, been years of low productivity gains.

A continuation of the monetary policy that the prospective large deficits will require will also have a deeply damaging effect on the international financial system. The high interest rates here draw funds from the other industrial countries. In defense, they are forced to raise *their* interest rates. In such fashion we export our economic policy—including the associated unemployment and recession—to our friends abroad. This is no hypothetical prospect: in recent weeks, the British Chancellor of the Exchequer, the German Chancellor, the head of the Bundesbank in Germany, the President of France, the Belgian Prime Minister, and the Prime Minister of Canada have all expressed deep concern, verging on anguish, over our policy. Rarely have we promoted such unity. If our policy continues, the European countries, acting through European monetary arrangements now in place, will be strongly tempted to control capital outflows, therewith to lower their interest rates and thus get control over their own policy. Few European leaders wish to see the world economic system broken in two; but many would accept it as an alternative to the disastrous policies that Washington's fiscal policy is otherwise forcing upon them.

Finally, the deficits now in prospect and the countering monetary action make nonsense of the talk of a supply-side economics—of a vigorous expansion in the economy unleashed by the tax cuts. This was always an exceptionally dubious design. But not even the most ardent advocates, men who have shown that they will believe anything, can suppose that there can be a vigorous supply-side expansion in combination with tight monetary restraint to control inflation. Those who so suggest, were they doctors, would tell an obese patient with a large appetite that he had only to eat a great deal more in order to grow thin. This is an economics guided not by what is right, but by what people looking for a painless life prefer to hear.

Let it be noted that it is no case for the present budget that governments in the past deliberately resorted to deficit-financing. The deficit-financing of the Depression era was undertaken when prices were falling and interest rates at all-but-nominal levels. The massive deflationary tendencies of the time allowed, indeed required, both an easier monetary policy and an expansive fiscal policy. The case of the Kennedy-Johnson tax reductions is also cited. That too was a time of nearly stable prices and of low interest rates; and with the tax reduction of that time also went pressure on the Federal Reserve to lower interest rates. No lessons from these periods are applicable to a time when inflation is a central concern and when fiscal irresponsibility enhances the emphasis on monetary policy.

Let me now turn to remedies—to what needs to be done. I shall pass over the proposed cuts in social and other civilian expenditures. Much has been said about this and about the consequences. This expenditure, much of it on behalf of the poorest of our people, is not wasteful, dishonest, or out of control. Rather, it is the expression of compassion and concern that all modern industrial states have manifested for the least protected of their citizens. Our expenditures for this purpose have not, in relative terms, been high; in relation to gross national product they have been lower than those of the other major industrial countries with the exception of Japan. It is such expenditure that has tempered the rough edges of the economic system and helped ensure its survival. Social tranquility is not less important for conservatives than for liberals. It serves all.

The military budget does call for comment and action. All know of the factors that determine its scale; some of them have nothing to do with defense. To the calculation of military need is added what serves bureaucratic interest, what serves the competition between the services, and what serves, often at military cost, the technical dynamic of gadgetry—the belief that whatever is technically more arcane is always better. To this is added the large influence, which no one denies, of the weapons firms. Finally there is the protection that comes from political fear. In this day and age motherhood can be criticized; but mention Russia and the bravest men, politically speaking, take to the hills.

There is a question as to whether military expenditures at their present and projected levels add to our national strength. The history on this matter is persuasive. During the 1970s we spent, in round figures, a hundred billion dollars annually on the defense establishment, for a total for the decade of roughly a thousand billion (in constant 1976 dollars). Capital in this magnitude could be used for arms; it could be used for private capital investment; it could not be used for both. If an appreciable part of this outlay had gone into the improvement of our industrial plant—as it would have, had it not been requisitioned by the government—no one can doubt that the American economy would be stronger today. And from this stronger economic position would have come, in turn, the economic primacy and political prestige that were enjoyed in the early years following World War II. It was economic, not military, strength on which the American world position then depended.

There is striking empirical evidence of the industrial effect of the arms race, as I have argued recently in the *Bulletin of Atomic Scientists*. In modern times the American competitive position has declined, specifically in relation to that of Germany and Japan. We are not, it is generally believed, less intelligent than the Germans or Japanese. The American raw material and energy base is not less good—indeed, it is far better. Germany spends more per capita on social services than does the United States; Japan does not spend greatly less. The difference is that the Germans and Japanese have been using their capital to replace old civilian plant and build new and better plant. The United States has been using much more of its capital for industrially limited or sterile military purposes.

Through the 1970s the United States used from 5 to 8 percent of its gross national product for military purposes. The Germans during this decade used between 3 and 4 percent—in most years relatively about half as much. The Japanese in these ten years devoted less than 1 percent of their gross national product annually to military use. In 1977, a fairly typical year, American military spending was $441 per capita; that of Germany was $252 per capita; that of Japan a mere $47 per capita.

It was from the capital so saved and invested that a substantial share of the civilian investment came which brought these countries to the industrial eminence that now so successfully challenges our own. Again the figures are striking. Through the 1970s our investment in fixed nonmilitary and nonresidential investment ranged from 16.9 percent of gross national product to 19 percent. That of Germany began where ours reached its peak; it ranged upward from 20.6 to 26.7 percent of gross national product. The Japanese range in these years was even greater—from 31 percent to a towering 36.6 percent. The investment in improvement of civilian plant was broadly the reciprocal of what went for weapons. No one looking at these figures can doubt that our military spending has been at cost to our industrial eminence and to the prestige and influence that go therewith. Certainly no one looking at these figures from the past can view the projected increases in the military budget with equanimity. The Administration itself affirms in the *Economic Report of the President* that these increases will be at cost to private capital formation. Is it really sensible to sacrifice our industrial eminence to a military budget that comprises so many elements so slightly related to any valid national concept of security? Lurking at the back of much past defense calculation has been the notion that we could somehow spend the Soviet Union into submission. It is a thought we can no longer tolerate, if, indeed, we ever could.

So, by all means, let us freeze the military budget along the lines proposed by Senator Ernest Hollings. Let us then have a serious look for savings—a look at the rehabilitation of those two old battleships, museum pieces both; at the B-1 bomber with its four or five years of useful survival; at aircraft carriers that in modern conflict would have to be rushed to the nearest harbor and might not make it; at the massive overkill in the strategic forces. And let there be serious pressure for an arms control agreement. (The issues here, needless to say, go beyond economics to survival.) The military budget has a highly leveraged relationship to the civilian budget. A modest reduction in marginal military gadgetry frees a large number of dollars for civilian need or for covering the deficit. We would be wise to use this leverage to the full.

However vigorous and sustained the movement on the military budget, the deficit, or some of it, will remain. That means taxes must be raised. Let there be no flinching at this prospect; and let there be no doubt on one basic and indispensable point. Higher taxes are far better for the economy than higher interest rates. Investment, productivity, and economic growth are consistent, or can be made consistent, with higher taxes. They cannot be reconciled with the high interest rates which are the alternative.

There should be prompt repeal of the corporate tax concessions, including the transfer of tax credits. I would also make a strong case for the windfall tax on gains from oil and gas deregulation. But the obvious and practical action is to defer the tax reductions scheduled for this coming summer and for a year hence. Nothing would have a more immediate and positive effect. There would be a prompt rally in the stock market; interest rates would fall and bond prices would rise; economic activity in the credit-sensitive industries would respond. I am never sanguine about economic predictions, including, and perhaps especially, my own. This one I make with a confidence that would be widely shared.

I urge two final points. Let us be very careful about any action, however disguised by rhetoric, which praises local responsibility or a new federalism and which transfers costs to state and especially to local governments. All public action must take account of one of the major features, one can say flaws, of the American fiscal system. The government of the United States, with its access to diverse tax sources and the tendency of its revenue sources to keep abreast of inflation, is by nature one of the best-financed units of government anywhere in the world. And, over the last half-century, nothing has been so persistently evident and so grievously underestimated as the costs of operating the modern large city at any tolerable level of safety, decency, and compassion. When people live in close juxtaposition, the costs of government go up exponentially. And they go up on a tax base that, unlike the taxable resources of the federal government, is circumscribed. We have already had, in the last budget, a major shift in fiscal responsibility from the best-financed unit of our system of government to the ones in the greatest inherent difficulty. It is a path on which we should proceed no farther. So to proceed will not strengthen local governments; it will weaken them. The new federalism, there is little doubt, is a singularly transparent device for shifting public costs away from the personal and corporate income tax bases of the federal government, with the particular incidence on the affluent, to the more regressive sales and property tax bases of states and localities.

Mr. David Stockman, with admirable candor, said last year that the concept of supply-side economics and its associated rhetoric were a cover for the reduction of income taxes in the upper brackets. That conservatives should seek a reduction in the upper-income tax brackets is not remarkable; no less than liberals, conservatives have their constituency. What is not forgivable is that conservatives should disguise their purposes behind supply-side or new federalist rhetoric. Plain speech is proper to people of all political faiths.

Conservatives especially should not accept the deficit in its prospective magnitude. There is room for ideological difference on how public services should be financed. There is no room for difference on the question of whether or not they should be financed. Deficits on the scale now projected effectively remove all freedom of economic action and commit the government to a monetary policy that we are learning—as the British have learned—is painfully repressive and potentially disastrous.

Hayek analyzes the Western world's recent bout with "stagflation" (high unemployment and high inflation) from the perspective of Austrian business cycle theory. Stagflation is the result of Keynesian policies which aim to achieve full employment through monetization of government deficits. Monetary expansion, however, can only temporarily reduce unemployment. The jobs which it "creates" are not permanent because the influx of money distorts relative prices, making some lines of business appear profitable even though they cannot be permanently sustained without ever-increasing injections of money. A stable monetary system, Hayek argues, can protect the economy from both inflation and unemployment in the future.

INFLATION, MISDIRECTION OF LABOR, AND UNEMPLOYMENT

Friedrich von Hayek

1. Inflation and Unemployment

After a unique quarter-century of great prosperity, the economy of the Western world has arrived at a critical point. I expect that the period will enter history under the name of the Great Prosperity, just as the 1930s are known as the Great Depression.

By eliminating the automatic brakes that operated in the past (namely, the gold standard and fixed rates of exchange), we have indeed succeeded in maintaining the full employment—and even overemployment—created by an expansion of credit and ultimately prolonged by open inflation. We have, in fact, succeeded in maintaining this for a much longer time than I should have thought possible. But the inevitable end is now near, or perhaps it has already arrived.

I find myself in an unpleasant situation. I had preached for forty years that the time to prevent the coming of a depression is during the boom. During the boom nobody listened to me. Now people again turn to me and ask how we can avoid the consequences of a policy about which I had constantly warned. I must witness the heads of the governments of all the Western industrial countries promising their people that they will stop the inflation *and* preserve full employment. But I know that they cannot do this. I even fear that attempts to postpone the inevitable crisis by a new inflationary push may temporarily succeed and make the eventual breakdown even worse.

Reprinted with permission of the publisher from *Unemployment and Monetary Policy*. Washington, D.C.: Cato Institute, 1979, pp. 3–19.

Three choices in policy

The disquieting but unalterable truth is that a false monetary and credit policy, pursued through almost the entire post-World War II period, has placed the economic systems of all the Western industrial countries in a highly unstable position—one in which anything we do will produce most unpleasant consequences. We have only three choices:

> 1. To allow a rapidly accelerating open inflation to continue until it has brought about a complete disorganization of all economic activity.
> 2. To impose controls of wages and prices that would for a time conceal the effects of a continued inflation but would inevitably lead to a centrally directed, totalitarian economic system.
> 3. To terminate resolutely the increase in the quantity of money—a step that would soon, through the appearance of substantial unemployment, make manifest all the misdirections of labor that the inflation of the past years has caused and that the other two procedures would further increase.

Lessons of the Great Inflation

To understand why the whole Western world allowed itself to be led into this frightful dilemma, it is necessary to glance back briefly at two events that occurred soon after World War I and that largely determined the views governing the policy of the post-World War II years. First I want to recall an experience that has unfortunately been largely forgotten. In Austria and Germany the Great Inflation had directed our attention to the connection between changes in the quantity of money and changes in the degree of employment. It especially showed us that the employment created by inflation diminished as soon as the inflation slowed down, and that the termination of the inflation always produced what came to be called a "stabilization crisis," with substantial unemployment. It was the insight into this connection that made me and some of my contemporaries reject and oppose from the outset the kind of full employment policy propagated by Lord Keynes and his followers.

To this recollection of the Great Inflation I must add an acknowledgment of how much I learned, not only from personal observation, but also from being taught to see—mostly by my teacher, the late Ludwig von Mises—the utter stupidity of the arguments then propounded, especially in Germany, to explain and justify the increases in the quantity of money. Most of these arguments I am now encountering again in the countries, not the least Great Britain and the United States, that then seemed better trained in economics and whose economists rather looked down at the foolishness of their German colleagues. None of these apologists for the inflationary policy was able to propose or apply measures to terminate the inflation, which was finally ended by Hjalmar Schacht, a man who firmly believed in a crude and primitive version of the quantity theory.

The policy of the recent decades, or the theory that underlies it, had its origin, however, in the specific experiences of Great Britain during the 1920s and 1930s. After what now seems the very modest inflation of the First World War, Great Britain returned to the gold standard in 1925; in my opinion very sensibly and honestly, but unfortunately and unwisely at the former parity. This had in no way been required by classical doctrine: David Ricardo wrote to a friend in 1821, "I never should advise a government to restore a currency, which was depreciated 30 per cent, to par."[1] I often ask myself how different the economic history of the world might have been if, in the discussion during the years preceding 1925, just one English economist had remembered and pointed out this passage from Ricardo.

In any event, the unfortunate decision taken in 1925 made a prolonged process of deflation inevitable. This process might have been successful in maintaining the gold standard if it had been continued until a large part of the wages had been reduced. I believe this attempt was near success when, in the world crisis of 1931, Britain abandoned it along with the gold standard, which was thereby greatly discredited.

2. Keynes's Political "Cure" for Unemployment

Development of Keynesian ideas

It was during the period of extensive unemployment in Great Britain preceding the worldwide economic crisis of 1929–1931 that John Maynard Keynes developed his basic ideas. It is important to note that this development of his economic thought took place while his country was in a very exceptional and almost unique position: As a result of the big appreciation in the international value of the pound sterling, the real wages of practically all British workers had increased substantially compared with real wages in the rest of the world, and Britain had in consequence become unable to compete successfully with other countries. In order to give employment to the unemployed, it would have been necessary either to reduce practically all wages or to raise the sterling prices of most commodities.

It is possible to distinguish three distinct phases in the development of Keynes's thought. First, he began with the recognition that it was necessary to reduce real wages. Second, he arrived at the conclusion that this was politically impossible. Third, he convinced himself that it would be useless and even harmful. The Keynes of 1919 still understood that

> there is no subtler, no surer means of overturning the existing basis of society than to debauch the currency. The process engages all the hidden forces of economic law on the side of destruction, and does it in a manner which not one man in a million is able to diagnose.[2]

His political judgment made him the inflationist, or at least avid antideflationist, of the 1930s. I have, however, good reason to believe that he would have disapproved of what his followers did in the postwar period. If he had not died so soon, he would have become one of the leaders in the fight against inflation.

The "fatal idea"

It was in that unfortunate episode of English monetary history in which he became the intellectual leader that Keynes gained acceptance for the fatal idea, namely, that unemployment is predominantly due to an insufficiency of aggregate demand when compared with the total of wages that would have to be paid if all workers were employed at current rates.

This formula of employment as a direct function of total demand proved so extraordinarily effective because it seemed to be confirmed in some degree by the results of quantitative empirical data. In contrast, the alternative explanations of unemployment, which I regard as correct, could make no such claims. The dangerous effects that the "scientistic" prejudice has had in this diagnosis is the subject of my Nobel lecture at Stockholm (Part II). Briefly, we find the curious situation that the Keynesian theory, which is confirmed by statistics because it happens to be the only one that can be tested quantitatively, is nevertheless false. Yet it is widely accepted only because the explanation earlier regarded as true, and which I still regard as true, cannot *by its very nature* be tested by statistics.

3. The True Theory of Unemployment

The true, though untestable, explanation for extensive unemployment ascribes it to a discrepancy between the distribution of labor (and the other factors of production) among industries (and localities) and the distribution of demand among their products. This discrepancy is caused by a distortion of the system of *relative* prices and wages. And it can be corrected only by a change in these relations, that is, by establishing in each sector of the economy those prices and wages at which supply will equal demand.

The cause of unemployment, in other words, is a deviation from the equilibrium prices and wages that would establish themselves given a free market and stable money. But we can never know beforehand at what structure of relative prices and wages such an equilibrium would establish itself. We are therefore unable to measure the deviation of current prices from the equilibrium prices which makes it impossible to sell part of the labor supply. We are therefore also unable to demonstrate a statistical correlation between the distortion of relative prices and the volume of unemployment. Yet, although not measurable, causes may be very effective. The current superstition that only the measurable can be important has done much to mislead economists and the world in general.

Keynes's theory—a temptation to politicians

The fact that Keynesian theory provided the politicians with tempting opportunities was probably even more important than the fashionable prejudices concerning scientific method that made it attractive to professional economists. It offered not only a cheap and quick method of removing a major source of real human suffering, but also a release from the most confining restrictions that had impeded their striving for popularity. Spending money and having budget deficits were suddenly represented as virtues. It was even argued persuasively that increased government expenditure was wholly meritorious, since it led to the utilization of hitherto unused resources, thus costing the community nothing and bringing it a net gain.

These beliefs led in particular to the gradual removal of all effective barriers to an increase in the quantity of money by the monetary authorities. The Bretton

Woods agreement had tried to place the burden of international adjustment exclusively on the surplus countries, that is, to require them to expand but not to require the deficit countries to contract. It thus laid the foundation for a world inflation. But this was at least done in the laudable endeavor to secure fixed rates of exchange. Yet when the criticism of the inflation-minded majority of economists succeeded in removing this last obstacle to national inflation, no effective brake remained, as the experience of Britain since the late 1960s illustrates.

Floating exchanges, full employment, and stable currency

It is, I believe, undeniable that the demand for flexible rates of exchange originated wholly from countries such as Great Britain, some of whose economists wanted a wider margin for inflationary expansion (called "full employment policy"). They later received support, unfortunately, from other economists who were not inspired by the desire for inflation, but who seem to have overlooked the strongest argument in favor of fixed rates of exchange, namely, that they constitute the practically irreplaceable curb we need to compel the politicians, and the monetary authorities responsible to them, to maintain a stable currency.

The maintenance of the value of money and the avoidance of inflation constantly demand from the politicians highly unpopular measures. Only by showing that government is compelled to take these measures can the politicians justify them to people adversely affected. So long as the preservation of the external value of the national currency is regarded as an indisputable necessity, as it is with fixed exchange rates, politicians can resist the constant demands for cheaper credits, for avoidance of a rise in interest rates, for more expenditure on "public works," and so on. With fixed exchanges, a fall in the foreign value of the currency, or an outflow of gold or foreign exchange reserves, acts as a signal requiring prompt government action. With flexible exchange rates, the effect of an increase in the quantity of money on the internal price level is much too slow to be generally apparent or to be charged to those ultimately responsible for it. Moreover, the inflation of prices is usually preceded by a welcome increase in employment; it may therefore even be welcomed because its harmful effects are not visible until later.

It is therefore easy to understand why, in the hope of restraining countries all too inclined toward inflation, other nations like Germany, itself noticeably suffering from imported inflation, hesitated in the postwar period to destroy altogether the system of fixed rates of exchange. For a time that seemed likely to restrain the temptation to further speed up inflation. But now that the system of fixed rates of exchange appears to have totally collapsed and scarcely any hope remains that self-discipline might induce some countries to restrain themselves, there is little reason to adhere to a system that is no longer effective. In retrospect one may even ask whether, out of a mistaken hope, the German Bundesbank or the Swiss National Bank waited too long, and then raised the value of their currency too little. But in the long run I do not believe we shall regain a system of international stability without returning to a system of fixed exchange rates, which imposes upon the national central banks the restraint essential for successfully resisting the pressure of the advocates of inflation in their countries—usually including ministers of finance.

4. Inflation Ultimately Increases Unemployment

But why all this fear of inflation? Should we not try to learn to live with it, as some South American states seem to have done, particularly if, as some believe, this is necessary to secure full employment? If this were true and the harm done by inflation were only that which many people emphasize, we would have to consider this possibility seriously.

Why we cannot live with inflation

The answer, however, is twofold. First, such inflation, in order to achieve the goal aimed at, would have to *accelerate* constantly, and accelerating inflation would sooner or later reach a degree that makes all effective order of a market economy impossible. Second, and more important, in the long run such inflation inevitably creates much *more* unemployment than the amount it was originally designed to prevent.

The argument is often advanced that inflation merely produces a *redistribution* of the social product, while unemployment reduces it and therefore represents a worse evil. This argument is false, because *inflation becomes the cause of increased unemployment*.

Harmful effects of inflation

I certainly do not wish to underestimate the other harmful effects of inflation. They are much worse than anyone can conceive who has not lived through a great inflation: During my first eight months in a job, my salary rose to 200 times the initial amount. I am indeed convinced that such a mismanagement of the currency is tolerated only because nobody has the time or energy during an inflation to organize a popular rebellion.

I want to stress that even the effects every citizen experiences are not the worst consequences of inflation; this is usually not understood because *it becomes visible only when the inflation is past*. This must particularly be said to economists, politicians, or others who like to point to the South American countries that have had inflations lasting through several generations and seem to have learned to live with them. In these predominantly agrarian countries, the effects of inflation are chiefly limited to those mentioned. The most serious effects that inflation produces in the labor markets of industrial countries are of minor importance in South America.

The attempts made in some of these countries, Brazil in particular, to deal with the problems of inflation by some method of indexing can, at best, remedy some of the consequences but certainly not the chief causes or the most harmful effects. They cannot prevent the worst damage that inflation causes—the misdirection of labor, a subject I must now consider more fully.

The misdirection of labor

Inflation makes certain jobs *temporarily* attractive. These jobs will disappear when inflation stops, or even when it ceases to accelerate fast enough. This result follows because inflation (a) changes the distribution of the money stream between the various sectors and stages of the process of production, and (b) creates expectation of a further rise in prices.

The defenders of a monetary full-employment policy often represent the position as if a *single* increase of total demand were sufficient to secure full employment for an indefinite but fairly long period. This argument overlooks the inevitable effects of such a policy, both on the distribution of labor among industries and on the wage policy of the trade unions.

As soon as government assumes the responsibility for maintaining full employment at whatever wages the trade unions succeed in obtaining, the latter no longer have any reason to take into account the unemployment their wage demands might have caused. In this situation every rise of wages that exceeds the increase in productivity will make necessary an increase in total demand if unemployment is not to ensue. The increase in the quantity of money made necessary by the upward movement of wages thus released becomes a *continuous* process requiring a constant influx of additional quantities of money.

The additional money supply must lead to changes in the relative strength of demand for various kinds of goods and services. And these changes in relative demand must lead to further changes in relative prices and consequent changes in the direction of production and the allocation of the factors of production, including labor. I must leave aside here all the other reasons why the prices of different goods—and the quantities produced—will react differently to changes in the demand (such as elasticities—the speed with which supply can respond to demand).

The chief conclusion I want to demonstrate is that the longer the inflation lasts, the larger will be the number of workers whose jobs depend on a *continuation* of the inflation, often even on a continuing *acceleration* of the rate of inflation—not because they would not have found employment without the inflation, but because they were drawn by the inflation into *temporarily* attractive jobs, which after a slowing down or cessation of the inflation, will again disappear.

The consequences are unavoidable

We ought to have no illusion that we can escape the consequences of the mistakes we have made. Any attempt to preserve the jobs made profitable by inflation would lead to a complete destruction of the market order. We have once again in the postwar period missed the opportunity to forestall a depression while there was still time to do so. We have in fact used our emancipation from institutional restraints—the gold standard and fixed exchange rates—to act more stupidly than ever before.

But if we cannot escape the reappearance of substantial unemployment, this is not the effect of a failure of "capitalism" or the market economy, but the exclusive consequence of our own errors—errors that past experience and available knowledge ought to have enabled us to avoid. It is unfortunately only too true that the disappointment of expectations they have created may lead to serious social unrest. But this does not mean that we can avoid it. The most serious danger now is that attempts, so attractive for the politicians, to postpone the evil day and thereby make things even worse in the long run, may still succeed. I must confess I have been wishing for some time that the inescapable crisis would come soon. And I hope now that any attempts made to promptly restart the process of monetary expansion will not succeed and that we are forced to choose a new policy.

Temporary, not mass, unemployment

Let me emphasize, however, that although I regard a period of some months, perhaps even more than a year, of considerable unemployment as unavoidable, this does not mean that we must expect another long period of mass unemployment comparable to the Great Depression of the 1930s—provided we do not commit very bad mistakes in policy. Such a development can be prevented by a sensible policy that does not repeat the errors responsible for the duration of the Great Depression.

Before I turn to what our future policy ought to be, I want to reject emphatically a misrepresentation of my point of view. I certainly do not recommend unemployment as a *means* to combat inflation. But my advice is being given at a time when the choice open to us is solely between some unemployment in the near future and more unemployment at a later date. What I fear above all is the *après moi le déluge* attitude of the politicians, who in their concern about the next elections, are likely to opt for more unemployment later. Unfortunately even some commentators, such as the writers of *The Economist,* argue in a similar manner and have called for "reflation" when the increase in the quantity of money is still continuing.

5. What Can Be Done Now?

The first step

The first necessity now is to stop the increase in the quantity of money—or at least to reduce it to the rate of the real growth of production—and this cannot happen soon enough. Moreover, I can see no advantage in a gradual deceleration, although for purely technical reasons, it may be all we can achieve.

It does not follow that we should not endeavor to stop a real deflation when it threatens to set in. Although I do not regard deflation as the original cause of a decline in business activity, a disappointment of expectations unquestionably tends to induce a process of deflation—what more than forty years ago I called a "secondary deflation."[3] Its effect may be worse (and in the 1930s certainly was worse) than warranted by the original cause of the reaction; moreover, it performs no steering function.

I must confess that forty years ago I argued differently. I have since altered my opinion—not about the theoretical explanation of the events, but about the practical possibility of removing the obstacles to the functioning of the system by allowing deflation to proceed for a while.

I then believed that a short period of deflation might modify the rigidity of money wages (what economists have since come to call their "rigidity downwards"), or the resistance to the reduction of some particular money wages, and that in this way we could restore relative wages determined by the market. This still seems an indispensable condition if the market mechanism is to function satisfactorily. But I no longer believe it is possible to achieve it in this manner. I probably should have seen then that the last chance was lost when the British government in 1931 abandoned the attempt to bring costs down by deflation just when it seemed near success.

Prevent recession from degenerating into depression

If I were today responsible for the monetary policy of a country, I would certainly try to prevent an impending deflation (that is, an absolute decrease of the stream of incomes) by all suitable means, and would announce that I intended to do so. This alone would probably be sufficient to prevent a degeneration of the recession into a long-lasting depression.

The reestablishment of a properly functioning market would, however, still require a restructuring of the whole system of relative prices and wages, and a readjustment to the expectation of stable prices, which presupposes a much greater flexibility of wages than now exists. What chance we have to achieve such a determination of relative wage-rates by the market and how long it may take, I dare not predict. But although I recognize that a *general* reduction of money wages is politically unachievable, I am still convinced that the required adjustment of the structure of *relative* wages can be achieved without inflation only through the reduction of the money wages of some groups of workers, and therefore must be thus achieved.

From a longer point of view, it is obvious that once we have got over the immediate difficulties, we must not again avail ourselves of the seemingly cheap and easy method of achieving full employment by aiming at the maximum of employment that can in the short run be achieved by monetary pressure.

The Keynesian dream

The Keynesian dream is gone, even though its ghost will continue to plague politics for decades. It is to be wished, although this is clearly too much to hope for, that the term "full employment" itself, which has become so closely associated with the inflationist policy, could be abandoned—or that we should at least remember that it was the aim of classical economists long before Keynes. John Stuart Mill reports in his autobiography how "full employment with high wages" appeared to him in his youth as the chief *desideratum* of economic policy.[4]

Primary aim: stable money, not unstable "full employment"

What we must now be clear about is that our aim must be, not the maximum of employment that can be achieved in the short run, but a "high and stable [i.e., *continuing*] level of employment," as one of the wartime British White Papers on employment policy phrased it.[5] We can achieve this, however, only through the reestablishment of a properly functioning market which, by the free play of prices and wages, establishes the correspondence of supply and demand for each sector.

Though monetary policy must prevent wide fluctuations in the quantity of money or in the volume of the income stream, the effect on employment must not be its dominating consideration. *The primary aim must again become the stability of the value of money.* The currency authorities must again be effectively protected against the political pressure that today forces them so often to take measures that are politically advantageous in the short run but harmful to the community in the long run.

Disciplining the monetary authorities

I wish I could share the confidence of my friend Milton Friedman, who thinks that in order to prevent the abuse of their powers for political purposes, one could deprive the monetary authorities of all discretionary powers by prescribing the amount of money they may and should add to circulation in any one year. Perhaps he regards this as practicable because, for statistical purposes, he has become accustomed to drawing a sharp distinction between what is to be regarded as money and what is not. This distinction does not exist in the real world.

I believe that to ensure the convertibility of all kinds of near-money into real money, which is necessary if we are to avoid severe liquidity crises or panics, the monetary authorities must be given some discretion. But I agree with Friedman that we will have to try to get back to a more or less automatic system for regulating the quantity of money in ordinary times. His principle is one that monetary authorities ought to aim at, not one to which they ought to be tied by law. The necessity of "suspending" Sir Robert Peel's Bank Act of 1844 three times within twenty-five years after it was passed ought to have taught us this once and for all.

And although I am not as optimistic as the editor of the London *Times*, Mr. William Rees-Mogg, who in a sensational article[6] (and now in a book[7]) has proposed the return to the gold standard, it does make me feel somewhat more optimistic when I see such a proposal coming from so influential a source. I would even agree that among the feasible monetary systems, the international gold standard is the best, if I could believe that the most important countries could be trusted to obey the rules of the game necessary for its preservation. But this seems exceedingly unlikely, and no single country can, on its own, have an effective gold standard. By its nature the gold standard is an international system and can function only as an international system.

It is, however, a big step in the direction of a return to reason when, at the end of his book, Mr. Rees-Mogg argues that

> we should be tearing up the full employment commitment of the 1944 White Paper, a great political and economic revolution.
>
> This would until very recently have seemed a high price to pay; now it is no great price at all. There is little or no prospect of maintaining full employment with the present inflation, in Britain or in the world. The full employment standard became a commitment to inflation, but the inflation has now accelerated past the point at which it is compatible with full employment.[8]

Equally encouraging is a statement of the British Chancellor of the Exchequer, Mr. Denis Healey, who is reported to have said:

> It is far better that more people should be in work, *even if that means accepting lower wages on average*, than that those lucky enough to keep their jobs should scoop the pool while millions are living on the dole.[9] (Italics added.)

It would almost seem as if in Britain, the country in which the harmful doctrines originated, a reversal of opinion were now under way. Let us hope it will rapidly spread over the world.

Notes

1. Ricardo to Wheatley, 18 September 1821, reprinted in *The Works of David Ricardo*, ed. Piero Sraffa, vol. 9 (Cambridge: At the University Press, 1952), p. 73.
2. "The Economic Consequences of the Peace," in *The Collected Writings of John Maynard Keynes,* vol. 2 (London: Macmillan for the Royal Economic Society, 1971), p. 149.
3. Defined and discussed in Part III, p. 40. I recall that the phrase was frequently used in the London School of Economics Seminar in the 1930s.
4. J.S. Mill, *Autobiography and Other Writings,* ed. J. Stillinger (Boston: Houghton Mifflin, 1969).
5. *Employment Policy,* Cmd. 6527 (London: HMSO, May 1944), Foreword.
6. "Crisis of Paper Currencies: Has the Time Come for Britain to Return to the Gold Standard?" *Times* (London), 1 May 1974.
7. William Rees-Mogg, *The Reigning Error: The Crisis of World Inflation* (London: Hamish Hamilton, 1974).
8. Ibid., p. 112.
9. Speech at East Leeds Labour Club, reported in the *Times* (London), 11 January 1975.

Chapter 4: INTERNATIONAL CONSEQUENCES

Volcker argues that the United States just might be at the threshold of a new era of productivity growth, but possible future prosperity is threatened by record budget and trade deficits. The budget deficit's crowding-out effect on private investment has been mitigated only by the willingness of foreigners to invest in this country. If overseas events cut off the flow of foreign capital, American investment in industrial plant and housing will suffer greatly.

FACING UP TO THE TWIN DEFICITS

Paul A. Volcker

A year ago, in appearing before the House Banking Committee to discuss the Federal Reserve's monetary policy for the year ahead, I emphasized that, after too many years of pain and instability, we had an enormous opportunity to sustain growth for years to come in an environment of much greater price stability. Today, after a year of strong recovery, that sense of the opportunities before us has only been reinforced.

The simple fact is that the economy moved ahead faster, and unemployment dropped more sharply, than we or most others thought at all probable. At the same time, the inflation rate dropped further, to the point that producer prices were almost unchanged over the year as a whole and consumer prices rose by less than at any time over the past decade. The fact that we were able to combine strong growth with good price performance is what is so encouraging. It is the key to lasting success.

With job opportunities, real incomes, and profits all rising, so has the sense of optimism among both families and businesses. That widely shared impression is confirmed statistically in the results of "attitudinal" indices that attempt to measure confidence, expectations, and buying plans—they are mostly at the highest, or near the highest, levels in many years.

I realize that improvement must be measured from where we started. There was a lot of room to grow, and the early stages of recovery typically see rapid growth and less price pressure. Any satisfaction with what has been happening has to be tempered by the knowledge that there is still a considerable way to go to reach satisfactory levels of employment and before we can claim to have restored reasonable price stability. In particular, should inflationary trends and fears again take hold, prospects for the lower interest rates and orderly credit markets

Reprinted with permission of M.E. Sharpe, Inc., Publisher, Armonk, NY 10504, from the March/April 1984 issue of *Challenge*.

we need to support investment and productivity growth would be shattered.

I hardly need to remind you that inflation has tended to worsen during periods of cyclical expansion. But that need not be inevitable. Out of hard experience, I believe we can shape disciplined policies—indeed, we have already gone a long way toward shaping policies and attitudes—to deal with the threat.

What we have not done in this past year is face up to other hazards to our prosperity and to our stability, hazards that are new to our actual experience but which have been long identified. I am referring, of course, to our twin deficits: the structural deficit in our federal budget and the deficit in our external accounts, both at unprecedented levels and getting worse. Both of these deficits carry implications for the prospects of reducing our still historically high levels of interest rates.

So far, the strains have been masked by other factors of strength and by the rapidity of growth from the depths of recession. But with the passage of time and with full recovery, the predictable effects have become more obvious. They pose a clear and present danger to the sustainability of growth and the stability of markets, domestic and international. We still have time to act—but in my judgment, not much time.

Sources of strength

I can summarize briefly why I think the developments of the past year are, in key respects, so promising—why, potentially, what has been going on can be not "just another" cyclical recovery, but the start of a long process of growth and renewed stability.

Looking back, it is now apparent that the trend of productivity growth had practically stopped in the late 1970s. But productivity began to increase again during the recession and rose rapidly during most of last year. One or two years do not make a new trend, and relatively good productivity growth is typical of the early stages of recovery. But the evidence, quantitative and qualitative, suggests that something more than cyclical forces are at work in important areas of the economy. Under the pressure of adversity—and with the seemingly "easy pickings" of speculative and inflationary gains diminishing—management and labor alike have turned their efforts and their imagination toward ways to increase efficiency and curtail overhead.

That, together with growing markets, accounted for the speed of the rebound in total profits and improvement in profit margins last year from long-depressed levels, even as prices for many goods and services tended to stabilize. The cash flow of businesses has been further reinforced by the liberal treatment of depreciation and other tax changes enacted in recent years, and after-tax economic profits, only a year after recession, are approaching the highest levels of the 1970s relative to GNP. Strong expansion in some types of investment during 1983—particularly electronic equipment, where technological change has been so rapid—carries promise for future productivity.

We should not claim too much. Profits remain well below rates typical of the prosperous 1960s. Recent employment increases, while highly welcome in themselves, have been so large relative to output growth that they raise some questions about whether rapid productivity growth is being maintained. Long-lived investment—new plant for expansion of capacity—still lags. High interest rates, the uncertainty bred by years of disappointment, and strong competition from abroad have all restrained heavy investment. Already, a few industries are close to, or even at, sustainable capacity. But, on balance, the evidence and the omens are more favorable than for several years.

That is certainly true of the longer-term outlook for costs and prices. I am well aware that slack markets and excessive unemployment, the appreciating dollar together with the ready availability of goods from abroad, and the decline in world oil prices all helped account for the rapidity of the drop in the general inflation rate and the degree to which cost pressures have subsided. To that extent, progress toward stability has had a sizable "one-time," or cyclical, component. But we also now have a clear opportunity to "build in" that improvement—the best opportunity in many years.

As the increase in average wages and salaries, which account for some two-thirds of all costs, has declined in nominal terms, the *real* income of the average worker has increased. That reverses the pattern as inflation accelerated during much of the 1970s, when escalating wages often lagged behind more rapidly rising prices. The more favorable pattern should be assisted by greater stability in energy prices, where the outlook (barring political turmoil) appears favorable, and by stronger productivity growth. With real wages again rising on average and with prices more stable, the logic points toward much more moderate new wage contracts than became the norm in the inflationary 1970s. The competitive pressures associated with the process of deregulation in some important industries have also been a factor working to contain costs and prices, and, happily, we can begin to see some signs of more restrained cost increases in areas, such as medical care and education, that have been slow to reflect the disinflationary process.

To the extent that we can build confidence in the outlook for more stable prices, the process could, potentially, feed on itself. Incentives for speculation in commodities, and for speculative excesses, would be greatly reduced and possibilities for another burst in oil prices diminished. It could provide the best possible environment for declines in nominal and real interest rates over time, and interest rates are themselves an element of costs. Lower interest rates could, in turn, be a powerful factor supporting and encouraging housing and the business investment that we need to maintain economic momentum and to support productivity growth.

The twin deficits

Nonetheless, as I suggested earlier, the prospects for sustained growth and stability must remain conditional. There is another, and bleaker, reality. We are faced with two deficits—in our budget and in our international accounts—unprecedented in magnitude. Those twin deficits have multiple causes, but they are not unrelated. Left untended, each, rather than improving, will tend to cumulate on itself, until finally they will undercut all that has been achieved with so much effort and so much pain.

Looking back, the rising budget deficit provided a large and growing stimulus to purchasing power as we emerged from recession. It helped account for the vigor of consumption in the face of historically high interest rates. The other side of the coin is that financing the deficit last year amounted to three-quarters of our net new domestic savings. That was tolerable—we obviously have tolerated it—for a limited period of time when other demands on those savings were limited. Business inventories actually declined on balance last year, and housing and business investment were recovering from recession lows.

Even then, deficits were a factor keeping interest rates higher than otherwise, and the implications become much more serious as the economy grows closer to its potential. The hard fact is that for many years we have succeeded in saving (net of depreciation) only some 7 to 9 percent of our GNP. Despite the efforts to raise it, the domestic savings rate remains within that range now and foreseeably. If the budgetary deficit absorbs amounts equal to 5 percent or more of the GNP as the economy grows—and that is the present prospect for the "current services" or "base line" budget—not much of our domestic savings will be left over for the investment we need.

Over the past year, our needs have been increasingly met by savings from abroad in the form of a net capital inflow. That money has come easily; amid world economic and political uncertainty, the United States has been a highly attractive place to invest. But part of the attraction for investment in dollars has been relatively high interest rates. In effect, the growing capital inflow has, directly and indirectly, helped to finance the internal budget, by the same token helping to moderate the pressures of the budget deficit on the domestic financial markets. At the same time, the flow of funds into our capital and money markets pushed the dollar higher in the exchange markets even in the face of a growing trade and current account deficit—and the dollar appreciation in turn undercut our worldwide trading position further.

We simply can't have it both ways—on the one hand, look abroad for increasing help in financing the credits related to our budget deficit, our housing, and our investment, and on the other hand, expect to narrow the growing gap in our trade accounts. At the end of the day, the counterpart of a net capital inflow is a net deficit on our current account—trade and services—with other countries.

Most forecasts suggest that we, as a nation, will have to borrow abroad (net) about 2 percent or more of our GNP this year to meet projected domestic needs. That pace does not appear sustainable over a long period. Faced at some point with a reduction in the net flow of capital from abroad, the burden of financing the budget deficit would then be thrown back more fully on domestic sources of savings. If our federal financing needs remain so high, housing and investment will be squeezed harder.

The largest international debtor?

I must also point out that, in the same way that the interest costs of this year's deficit add to next year's requirements—and compound over many years thereafter—the interest and dividend payments related to the net capital inflow build up future charges against the current account of the balance of payments. Skepticism about our ability to account accurately and fully for all the flows of funds into or out of the country is justified; it is nonetheless ominous that the recorded net investment position of the United States overseas, built up gradually over the entire postwar period, will in the space of only three years—1983, 1984, and 1985—be reversed. If the data at all reflect reality, the largest and richest economy in the world is on the verge of becoming a net debtor internationally, and will soon become the largest.

Looking at the same development from another angle, it is the exporter and those competing directly with imports that have not shared at all proportionately in the recovery. Developments in the fourth quarter illustrate the point. There has been much comment about the slowing in the rate of GNP growth to a rate of about 4.5 percent. But, judging from the preliminary figures, domestic demands were quite well maintained, increasing at a rate of almost 7 percent. Much of that increased demand flowed abroad, adding to income and production elsewhere. It was domestic production, not demand, that grew appreciably more slowly.

For a time, as with the budget deficit, that kind of discrepancy is tolerable. Indeed, from one point of view, it has provided a welcome impetus toward stimulating the growth process in other countries of the industrialized world, and the strength of our markets assisted the external adjustments necessary in the developing world. We can also take pride in the fact that others find the United States an attractive place to invest; good performance and policies can help sustain those flows.

But we simply can't afford to become addicted to drawing on increasing amounts of foreign savings to help finance our internal economy. Part of our domestic industry—that part dependent on exports or competing with imports—would be sacrificed. The stability of the dollar and our domestic financial markets would become hostage to events abroad. If recovery is to proceed elsewhere, as we want, other countries will increasingly need their own savings. While we don't know when, at some point the process would break down.

The implications for monetary policy

In the abstract, the ultimate objective of monetary policy is simple to state and widely agreed: to provide just enough money to finance sustainable growth—and not so much as to feed inflation. Toward that end, the Federal Open Market Committee (FOMC) in February essentially reaffirmed the ranges for money and credit growth tentatively established in July of last year. The target ranges for M3 and for nonfinancial debt were lowered by 0.5 percent from the 1983 ranges to 6 to 9 and 8 to 11 percent, respectively, as tentatively set in July. The M2 range was reduced by 1 percent from the 1983 range, to 6 to 9 percent. That is 0.5 percent lower than anticipated in July, reflecting in part technical considerations bearing on the appropriate relationships among the broader aggregates. The M1 range was set at 4 to 8 percent, 1 percent lower than during the second half of 1983, as had been anticipated.

In the concrete, issues abound. Some of them are more or less technical: how we define and measure money and its relationship to the nominal GNP. These questions are dealt with in our formal report describing our decisions on the targets. I want to concentrate here on some broader implications of the current situation for the conduct of monetary policy.

There is no instrument of monetary policy that, in any direct or immediate sense, can earmark money only for expansion and not for inflation, or vice versa. The distribution of any given nominal growth of the GNP between real growth and inflation is a product of many factors—the flexibility and competitiveness of product and labor markets, the exchange rate, and internal or external shocks (such as the oil crises of the 1970s). Expectations and attitudes developed out of past experience are critically important.

In that respect we have not inherited a sense of stability. Quite to the contrary, the legacy of the 1970s was deeply ingrained patterns of behavior—in pricing, in wage bargaining, in interest rates, and in financial practices generally—built on the assumption of continuing, and accelerating, inflation. Starving an inflation of the money needed to sustain it is a difficult process in the best of circumstances; it was doubly so when the continuing inflationary momentum was so strong.

Now, after a great deal of pain and dislocation, attitudes have changed. There is a sense of greater restraint in pricing and wage behavior, a greater recognition of the need to improve efficiency, less alarm (at least for the short run) over the outlook for prices, and relative confidence by others in the outlook for the United States. In this setting, we can assume that, within limits, more of any given growth in the money supply will finance real activity and less rising prices than would have been the case when the inflationary momentum was high.

But we also recognize that the battle against inflation has not yet been won—that skepticism about our ability, as a nation, to maintain progress toward stability is still evident. That is one of the reasons why longer-term interest rates have lingered so far above current inflation levels. After so many false starts in the past, the skepticism is likely to remain until we can demonstrate that, in fact, the recent improvement is not simply a temporary matter—that the Federal Reserve is not prepared to accommodate a new inflationary surge as the economy grows. The doubts are reinforced by concerns that the pressures of the huge budget deficit on financial markets may, willy-nilly, push us in that direction, as has happened in so many countries.

The wrong way to lower interest rates

The desire to see interest rates lower, or to avoid increases, is natural. But attempts to accomplish that desirable end by excessive monetary growth would soon be counterproductive. By feeding concerns about inflation, the implications for interest rates themselves would in the end be perverse—and likely sooner rather than later. As things stand, credit markets are already faced with potential demands far in excess of our capacity to save domestically; to add renewed fears of inflation to the outlook would only be to reduce the willingness to commit funds for long periods of time and for productive investment. Inflationary policies would also discourage the continuing flow of funds from abroad, upon which, for the time being, we are dependent. In the last analysis, willingness to provide those funds freely at current or lower interest rates is dependent on confidence in our stability and in our economic management. Depreciation of the dollar externally as a result of inflationary policies will not, in the end, help our exporters, or those competing with imports, because that depreciation would be accompanied by inflated domestic costs.

In a real sense, the greatest contribution that the Federal Reserve itself can make to our lasting prosperity is to foster the expectation—and the reality—that we can sustain the hard-won gains against inflation and build upon them.

In my judgment, against a background of more stable prices, interest rates are indeed too high for the long-term health of the United States or the world economy. I have repeatedly expressed the view that, as we maintain the progress against inflation, interest rates should decline—and they should stay lower.

Much is at stake. We will need more industrial capacity, and relatively soon. Even after the sharp declines in interest rates from earlier peaks, many thrift institutions and businesses remain in marginal profit positions and with weakened financial structures; lower rates would bring much faster progress in repairing the damage. The cooperative efforts of borrowers, banks, and the governments and central banks of the industrialized world have managed to contain the strains on the international financial system, but the pressures are still strongly evident. Both economic growth and lower interest rates are needed as part of more fundamental solutions.

But wish and desire are not the same thing as reality; we have to deal with the situation as it is. In setting the targets for the various monetary and credit aggregates for 1984 as a whole, the FOMC has to remain alert to the danger of renewed inflation as well as to the need for growth. It also decided that, operationally, it would for the time being be appropriate to maintain essentially the same degree of restraint on the reserve positions of depository institutions that has prevailed since last autumn. That judgment reflects the fact that growth in the various measures of money and credit now appears broadly consistent with objectives, that the momentum of economic expansion remains strong, and inflationary tendencies contained. That operational judgment will, of course, be reviewed constantly in the weeks and months ahead.

Those decisions will reflect continuing appraisals of the rate of growth of money and credit, interpreted in the light of all the evidence about economic activity, prices, domestic and international financial markets, and other relevant considerations. All those factors will, in turn, be affected by other public and private policies. In that context, it is the strength of economic activity, the demand pressures on the credit markets, and the willingness of others to invest in the United States that will influence the course of interest rates.

In approaching our own operational decisions, the actual and prospective size of the budget deficit inevitably complicates the environment within which we work. By feeding consumer purchasing power, by heightening skepticism about our ability to control the money supply and contain inflation, by claiming a disproportionate share of available funds, and by increasing our dependence on foreign capital, monetary policy must carry more of the burden of maintaining stability, and its flexibility, to some degree, is constrained.

Toward a positive solution

Monetary policy is only one part of an economic program. It is an essential part, but success is dependent on a coherent whole.

If a sense of discipline is to be maintained, those of us responsible for public policy must be able to demonstrate that inflation will not again get the upper hand; that productivity and restraint will be rewarded, not penalized in favor of those seeking inflationary or speculative gain.

The contribution that monetary and other policies make to that environment is critical. As the expansion proceeds, and as some of the temporary factors restraining prices recede, we as a nation simply cannot afford to permit inflation to attain a new momentum. Our monetary policies are, and in my judgment must continue to be, geared to avoid that danger.

But for all the progress and promise, something is out of kilter.

Our common sense tells us that enormous and potentially rising budget deficits, and the high and rising deficits in our trade accounts, are wrong—they can not be indefinitely prolonged. We can, of course, sit back and wait a while longer, hoping for the best.

I certainly have some understanding of the difficulties of achieving a consensus on difficult budgetary choices when a sense of immediate crisis is lacking—when for the moment things seem to be going so well. But I also know that to wait too long would be to take risks with the American economy.

It is already late. The stakes are large. Markets have a mind of their own; they have never waited on the convenience of kings or Congressmen—or elections.

The time to take the initiative is now, when we can influence markets constructively—when we can demonstrate that we are in control of our own financial destiny. Real progress toward reducing the budget deficit is needed to clear away the dangers.

I sense a fresh opportunity in the proposals of the President for a joint effort to attack the deficit—for a sizable "down payment" on what is ultimately needed.

Certainly, that kind of demonstration that we are beginning to face up to our budgetary problem would make it easier for monetary policy to do its necessary work. And, in the larger scene, it would be tangible evidence to our own people that we can do what is necessary to seize the bright opportunities before us.

Humbert questions the conventional wisdom that budget deficits, by raising interest rates, cause trade deficits. Current U.S. trade deficits are due to the fact that the U.S. economic recovery has proceeded faster than that of the rest of the world; consequently, Americans' demand for foreign goods has risen faster than foreigners' demand for American goods. Increases in foreign lending to this country, he believes, are the result of low U.S. inflation and expanding investment opportunities.

UNDERSTANDING THE FEDERAL DEFICIT: PUTATIVE IMPACT ON TRADE

Thomas M. Humbert

Introduction

One of the most serious—yet unsubstantiated—charges hurled in the current budget debate is that the federal deficit is the cause of the "overvalued" dollar and the deepening U.S. merchandise and current account deficits. Government deficits, the argument goes, have intensified the demand for credit and pushed up real U.S. interest rates. These comparatively high U.S. rates, in turn, encourage foreigners to buy dollars and invest in the United States. The result: a soaring U.S. dollar.

The rising U.S. dollar, continues the theory, increases the price of U.S. exports and drives down the price of imports, creating the massive trade deficit. The moral: budget deficits severely harm exporting industries (such as farming and aircraft manufacturing), those sectors competing with imports (such as the U.S. automobile industry), and interest-sensitive industries (such as housing). Some prominent economists claim that the U.S. trade deficit may have cut the nation's Gross National Product (GNP) by 2 percentage points, destroyed up to 3 million jobs, jeopardized the economic recovery and eroded America's industrial base.[1]

On the face of it, the theory seems plausible. The robust U.S. dollar has been accompanied by a deep fall in U.S. exports. The U.S. merchandise trade deficit reached $42.7 billion in 1982, soared to $69.4 billion in 1983, and is forecast to be $110 billion in 1984.[2]

Yet the theory that budget deficits are the major force pushing up the dollar, widely accepted in the press and Congress, has little basis in fact. It involves a

Reprinted with permission of the publisher. Originally published as Heritage Foundation *Backgrounder*, no. 331, January 27, 1984.

serious mistake of analysis which could lead to disastrous policy initiatives that could cause U.S. international competitiveness to deteriorate, rather than improve.

Much research sheds considerable doubt on the link between budget deficits and the international trade balance, interest rates, and capital flows. Policymakers should ponder this research carefully before taking impulsive action.

1. Historical evidence and scholarly research have not found a strong link between U.S. interest rates and the level of the federal deficit. U.S. real and nominal interest rates have fallen substantially in recent years, while the budget deficit has soared.

2. Even if budget deficits did raise interest rates, the strong dollar probably is not caused by the current level of U.S. interest rates. Since the summer of 1982, both real and nominal interest rates have moved opposite from the direction moved by the value of the dollar. Interest rate differentials between the U.S. and most of the world have narrowed, yet the dollar has soared.

3. Capital flows show no clear relationship to U.S. budget deficits. While capital inflows undoubtedly will increase in the years ahead, the reason seems to have little to do with U.S. budget deficits.

4. Foreign ownership of the U.S. national debt actually has decreased since 1978, even though the U.S. budget deficit has grown. There is no indication that foreign capital is financing an unusually high proportion of the U.S. federal debt.

5. Budget deficits in various countries have existed alongside both strong and weak currencies. The budget deficit, by itself, is not the major factor determining the value of the dollar. Monetary policy is much more important.

6. Low budget deficits by themselves do not spur exports, nor do high budget deficits necessarily depress exports.

If the burgeoning budget deficit is not to blame, what is causing the widening of the current account deficit? A number of influences are to blame—factors that are more a sign of U.S. economic strength than weakness:

—The recovery is much more robust in the U.S. than in most other countries, so the world demand for U.S. exports is lagging behind the U.S. demand for imports.

—Many less-developed countries are reducing imports and increasing their exports to pay the interest charges on their enormous foreign debts.

—Capital flowing to the U.S. from abroad is attracted by business opportunities and the stable political environment.

—U.S. inflation has fallen, compared with the rest of the world, bolstering the value of the dollar relative to other currencies.

It is also a mistake to believe that a strong dollar and international current account deficit threaten the U.S. economy. Since each dollar a foreign company receives for products imported by Americans can only be used to buy American goods or invest in the U.S., every trade and services deficit is matched by a capital account surplus. So any loss of jobs or growth due to low U.S. exports is offset by investment and jobs resulting from capital inflows. A trade deficit does not destroy jobs, it only rearranges them throughout the economy. Many commentators also overlook the point that the availability of cheaper foreign imports in the U.S. enhances consumers' spending power and choice. Foreign imports also impose competitive discipline on U.S. business, encouraging improved productivity.

A trade deficit, in short, does not signal the loss of U.S. international competitiveness, a migration of jobs overseas, or a present threat to the recovery. Thriving countries such as South Korea, Taiwan, Singapore, and other rapidly expanding nations have continually run current account deficits. They, along with the U.S., have experienced large capital inflows as a means to finance the more rapid development of their economies.

Some would retort that foreign capital inflows give foreigners, not Americans, claims on U.S. assets. Yet foreigners can only use the dollars they earn from their investments and exports to buy U.S. products, or sell the dollars to others who wish to buy American exports. Seen from this perspective, the current account deficit is a sign that foreigners have confidence in U.S. products, services, and investments. The strong dollar, in other words, symbolizes the strength of the recovery and the resurgence of the American economy.

Background

Most news reports focus almost exclusively on the trade deficit when describing the export-import situation. A more complete picture of the U.S. trade position, however, would include the U.S. trade in services, investment income, government grants, remittances, pensions and transfers. Exports of services are just as important to national income as exports of goods (and may be even more important in the future) and should be included in trade calculations. The U.S. service surplus, in fact, widened from $13.8 billion in 1975 to $33.2 billion in 1982. And America has traditionally enjoyed large and growing surpluses in the service account, offsetting a large part of the trade deficits.

Chart 1 shows the current account balance for the first three quarters of 1983. While the merchandise deficit was a record $41.6 billion, it was offset by a surplus of services, amounting to $21.8 billion. The near record service surplus kept the three quarter 1983 current account deficit to $25.5 billion.

U.S. Budget Deficits: Do They Undermine U.S. Competitiveness?

A number of economists claim that the U.S. budget deficit is the principal cause of high U.S. interest rates and hence the high-priced dollar, and this threatens to choke off the recovery by devastating vital export industries. An examination of the elements of this theory, however, reveals little evidence to support its major contentions.

(1) *The federal budget deficit and real interest rates*

Many economists and legislators claim that current and anticipated budget deficits are causing real U.S. interest rates to remain high. This unfounded claim

Chart 1

U.S. Current Account Balance for the First Three Quarters of 1983

		Billions of dollars
Merchandise	− $41.6	
Other goods and services	+ 21.8	
Trade (total goods and services)		− $19.8
Remittances, pensions, and transfers		− 5.5
Total current account balance		− $25.3

Source: Department of Commerce

has been dealt with at length in an earlier paper in this series.[3] The analysis shows that interest rates and budget deficits have, in fact, been moving in opposite directions in recent years. And rather than intensifying credit demand and raising interest rates, government borrowing has simply replaced depressed sector borrowing in most instances.

(2) *Interest rates and the U.S. dollar*

Even if budget deficits could be shown to raise interest rates, it does not necessarily follow that interest rates are the primary cause of the strong dollar. In fact, the value of the dollar and interest rates have been moving in opposite directions. Real and nominal interest rates in the U.S. fell rapidly after August 1982, virtually eliminating the differential between the U.S. and its major trading partners (see Figure 1). Yet the dollar continued climbing. And from early July 1982 to early June 1983, short term U.S. interest rates declined by 6 percentage points. Despite this, the dollar did not fall in value.[4] Those who claim that high real U.S. interest rates are the cause of the high value of the dollar are directly contradicted by the historical evidence.

(3) *Budget deficits and capital flows*

Net capital flows show no simple or automatic relationship with federal deficits. Yet capital inflows in 1982 have been estimated by the Department of Commerce at $11 billion. Estimates for 1983 range as high as $30 billion.

These estimates of capital inflows, however, are likely to be exaggerated, because they assume that the entire $40 billion statistical discrepancy in the trade accounts consists entirely of unreported capital inflows. This discrepancy arises because all the elements of the trade and capital accounts are measured separately, yet the totals must balance. The discrepancy is the sum of the errors in each calculation.

The government admits, however, that it really does not know what makes up the statistical discrepancy. At least one respected analyst believes that $20 billion of the discrepancy can be traced to unreported service and trade exports, not unreported capital inflows.[5] Restatement of the figures in this way would bring the 1982 current account into surplus and the capital account that year would

Figure 1
U.S. EXCHANGE RATES AND INTEREST RATE DIFFERENTIALS

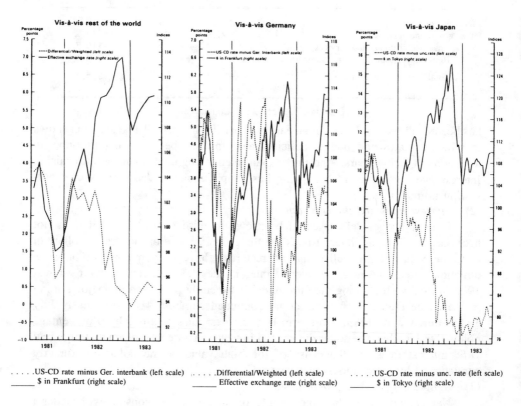

.....US-CD rate minus Ger. interbank (left scale)   .....Differential/Weighted (left scale)   .....US-CD rate minus unc. rate (left scale)
_____ $ in Frankfurt (right scale)   _____ Effective exchange rate (right scale) _____ $ in Tokyo (right scale)

Source: OECD, July 1983.

show a net outflow. This would substantially alter the complexion of the so-called balance of payments problem.

Even if all the statistical discrepancy occurs in the capital account (a very unlikely assumption), there still is no clear correlation between deficits and capital inflows (see Chart 2). The U.S. budget deficit in 1975 and 1976, for example, amounted to nearly 4 percent of GNP, then the largest peacetime level in history. If budget deficits lure foreign capital into the U.S., these should have been bumper years for capital inflows. Yet the U.S. actually registered large capital outflows in both years—the 1975 capital outflow was the largest in recent U.S. history.

The U.S. budget deficit was much smaller in 1977–1979, in GNP terms. Capital inflows should have been narrowed if smaller deficits mean less capital from abroad. In fact, capital inflows increased. Such patterns shed doubt on the

Chart 2

*Budget Deficits and Capital Flows**

	Capital Outflows (inflows −) in billions of dollars	Federal Budget Deficit (percentage of GNP)
1971	− 1.433	2.2
1972	− 5.795	2.1
1973	7.140	1.2
1974	1.962	0.3
1975	18.136	3.1
1976	4.207	4.0
1977	− 14.511	2.4
1978	− 15.446	2.3
1979	− 0.964	1.2
1980	0.421	2.3
1981	4.592	2.0
1982	− 11.211	3.6
1983 (estimate)	− 32.700	6.1
1984 (estimate)	− 50.400	5.2

* Assumes all statistical discrepancies can be attributed to unreported capital inflows.
Source: Department of Commerce, Bureau of Economic Analysis

simplistic view that budget deficits are the major determinate of capital flows into the U.S.

(4) *Budget deficits and the dollar*

High budget deficits have been associated with both a weak and a strong U.S. dollar, as have small budget deficits. If high budget deficits automatically produce a strong dollar, the dollar should have been extremely robust in 1975, given that year's huge deficit. The value of the dollar, however, was appreciably lower that year than during the 1960s and early 1970s, when budget deficits were much smaller.

The foreign experience also exhibits no clear relationship between budget deficits and the strength of their currencies. The Japanese budget deficit throughout the 1970s, as a proportion of GNP, was higher than that of the U.S., and Japan enjoyed a strong currency. But Italy, which ran deficits over twice the share of GNP experienced in the U.S., suffered from a weak currency. The United Kingdom ran up large budget deficits from 1975 to 1977, but the pound fell in value. There are many other examples of budget deficits coexisting with both strong and weak currencies. Clearly budget deficits do not provide an adequate explanation for the relative value of world currencies.

(5) *Budget deficits and world trade*

Budget deficits do not always mean a loss of competitive advantage. Japan's export trade expanded almost sevenfold during the 1970s, despite large deficits.[6] And Italy, which ran budget deficits in the range of 10 to 15 percent of its GNP throughout the 1970s, experienced nearly a sixfold expansion of exports.

U.S. merchandise exports did drop by about 10 percent in 1982, as the deficit increased, and by another 5.5 percent in 1983. But then so did the trade volume of almost every U.S. trading partner, including Canada, Japan, France, West Germany, and the United Kingdom. This reduction in trade did not result from the U.S. budget deficit, but from the worldwide recession. During other recessions, world trade also shrank.

Causes of the Current Account Deficit

If the budget deficit is not closely linked to the trade situation, then what are the causes of America's enormous current account deficits? While there is no consensus, there appear to be a number of factors causing American exports to decline, imports to grow, and capital to be attracted to the U.S.:

(1) *The robust U.S. recovery*

Trade deficits normally accompany strong economic expansions. In the current U.S. recovery, the phenomenon is compounded by the slower rate of recovery in the rest of the world. In 1983, the U.S. economy grew 3.8 percent faster than a weighted average of the rest of the world, and it is expected to continue growing at a much faster pace than in the rest of the industrial world during 1984. Many foreign countries are still just turning the economic corner. While U.S. consumers are buying more imports, therefore, America's trading partners have not increased their imports as rapidly. This component of the current account deficit, however, is primarily a cyclical phenomenon. As foreign economies catch up to U.S. rates of growth, the trade deficit should shrink to more typical levels.

(2) *The problems of less developed countries*

U.S. exports to less developed countries and financially weak countries have fallen sharply because many of these countries are struggling to cut imports and expand exports to pay interest charges on their huge foreign debts. U.S. exports to less developed nations declined by over $100 billion between 1981 and 1983. Moreover, the OPEC countries no longer have huge oil surpluses to buy Western goods and technology.

(3) *Capital flows to the U.S. from abroad*

The Department of Commerce attributes billions of dollars in errors and omissions in the trade balance sheet to unrecorded capital inflows. This is an unsupported assumption. If only half of these errors were actually in the service account, the current account in 1982 would have shown a surplus, and the U.S. capital accounts would have shown a net capital outflow.

Even if there is, in fact, a net capital inflow into the U.S., federal budget deficits are probably not to blame. Funds also are attracted because the U.S. economy is much more safe and stable than that of very many other countries. The U.S. is experiencing greater productivity and higher real rates of return on investments, and holds the promise of continuing low rates of inflation.

Do Deficits and the Strong Dollar Endanger the Recovery?

The current account deficit, therefore, results from a strong U.S. economy, not a weak one. But does the current account deficit jeopardize the U.S. economic recovery by destroying American jobs and signalling a loss of U.S. international competitiveness?

The answer is no. One cannot even speak of an "overvalued" dollar in a strict sense—any more than one can speak of an overvalued stock, bond, or house. The market determines the value of currency in response to supply and demand pressures, just as it does with any other asset. If an individual believes that the market price of the dollar is too high, he will sell the currency and eventually make a profit. Just as it does with an overvalued stock, the market will soon respond to an overvalued currency.

While reports focus on the loss of jobs due to falling exports and increasing imports, very little attention is paid to the offsetting benefits. Consumers save money by buying lower-priced imports, for instance. This raises the U.S. living standard and frees money for consumers to spend on other products, most of which are produced domestically—meaning more jobs. Moreover, capital inflows—the flip-side of current account deficits—are very beneficial to the recovery. Foreign capital provides funds for new investment, reducing the pressure on the capital markets and interest rates. Foreign capital inflows are likely to reach about $80 billion in 1984, or 2 percent of GNP.

Some economists complain that a strong dollar costs jobs in exporting industries. But this is only part of the story. The costs of a strong dollar can be measured only against the benefits.[7] One of the most important benefits is lower domestic inflation. According to most estimates, inflation drops 0.1 to 0.2 percent for every 1 percent increase in exchange rate. Using this rule, the U.S. inflation rate has probably fallen between 2 and 2-1/2 percentage points because of the strong dollar. Added to the extra consumer purchasing resulting from lower cost imports, this means higher real living standards and a stimulus to industries catering for the domestic market.

A strong currency, moreover, does not necessarily harm export competitiveness. For example, the Japanese yen increased by almost 40 percent against the dollar in the 1970s; Japanese exports did not suffer. The French franc, by comparison, plunged over 50 percent in value against the dollar between 1980 and 1983; this anemic franc did not spur France's exports, which fell sharply.

In short, a strong U.S. dollar does not automatically doom the U.S. to a permanent loss of international competitiveness—if its value reflects a strong U.S. economic recovery and lower inflation. Similarly, a weaker dollar would not guarantee more U.S. exports, if the dollar's declining value simply reflects an inflationary increase in the supply of money in an effort to depress interest rates.

Conclusion

Many factors bolster the U.S. dollar. Fundamentally, investors hold dollars for the same reasons they hold any asset: they believe dollars will yield a greater return than other available assets. The price of currency, like stock prices, responds to news concerning that return. And currency prices, like stock prices, may change without any substantial change in the volume of trade, simply because the market changes its view about future returns.

The expectations that the U.S. inflation rate will continue to remain low, and economic growth strong, compared with that of other countries, are probably the most important causes of the dollar's increased value. It is the political stability of the U.S., the promise of economic vitality, improving productivity, and other such factors that encourage foreigners to buy dollars—not the federal deficit.

While government budget and trade deficits are not necessarily debilitating, the deficit could have an enormous—and very damaging—impact on domestic and international trade if it prompts dangerous economic "remedies" in Congress. Many of the initiatives offered to reduce deficits could harm gravely the U.S. economy and international trade:

1. *Tax increases.* Higher taxes on savings, investment, and corporations, designed to reduce the budget deficit, would shrink capital formation and undermine U.S. international competitiveness.

2. *Rapid expansion of the money supply.* Excessive expansion of the money supply, to generate a short term acceleration of economic growth and temporarily reduce interest rates, would merely ignite inflation and lead to stagnation in both export and domestic industries.

3. *Tariffs and quotas.* Tariffs and quotas would trigger trade wars and reduce U.S. living standards by raising the cost of imported products. Moreover, tariffs only shield inefficient firms from lower-priced foreign competition, and therefore reduce long-term competitiveness.

Congress can increase U.S. exports and domestic production by reducing government spending, lowering tax rates to encourage investment, and eliminating burdensome regulation. This would release resources to the private sector for investment, research, and spending. Money growth should be held stable and predictable, creating a climate for price stability and economic expansion. And policymakers should emphatically reject protectionism. Taking these steps, rather than flirting with trade barriers and tax increases, would assure continued growth and prosperity.

Notes

1. See, for example, Statement by C. Fred Bergsten, Director of the Institute for International Economics, "Economists See Shortfall in '84 of $100 Billion," *The Washington Post*, January 28, 1984. See also, David Ernst, Evans Economics, and Malcolm Baldrige, Commerce Secretary, reported in "1983 Trade Deficit Hit $69.4 Billion," *The New York Times*, January 28, 1984.
2. "1983 Trade Deficit Hit $69.4 Billion," *The New York Times*, January 28, 1984.
3. Thomas M. Humbert, "Understanding the Federal Deficit, Part 3: The Unproven Impact," Heritage Foundation *Backgrounder* No. 330, January 27, 1984.
4. *OECD Economic Outlook*, Organization for Economic Cooperation and Development, July 1983, p. 74.
5. "World Financial Markets," Morgan Guaranty Trust Company of New York, May 1983.
6. *The Economic Report of the President,* Council of Economic Advisers, February 1983, p. 282.
7. See Robert J. Samuelson, "Trade Deficit Offers Danger, Opportunity," *The Washington Post*, January 24, 1984.

Fieleke finds that the U.S. current accounts deficit is in part attributable to federal budget deficits. To the extent that American borrowing from foreigners is used for investment, it generates a return which can ultimately be used to pay back foreign debts. To the extent that it is used for consumption, though, loans from foreigners can be paid back only by restricting consumption in the future.

THE BUDGET DEFICIT: ARE THE INTERNATIONAL CONSEQUENCES UNFAVORABLE?

Norman S. Fieleke

A large deficit in the federal budget or in the international balance of payments has always provoked concern within the United States, and the conjuncture of unprecedented deficits in both the budget and the balance of payments has aroused strong foreboding. Is there any relationship between the two deficits? In particular, do large budget deficits lead, as some have argued, to large deficits in our current account transactions with other nations? What are the consequences of large deficits in our international transactions? Although there are no simple *and* correct answers to these questions, it is possible in a brief article to shed some light on the underlying issues.

The Link between the Deficits

To begin with, there is an accounting relationship between the total governmental (federal, state, and local) deficit and the deficit in the current account of the balance of payments. For one thing, both the governmental surplus or deficit and the current account surplus or deficit are linked to private domestic investment. Other things equal, a government surplus (net government saving) adds to the flow of saving from which private investment can be financed, while a government deficit (government dissaving) diminishes that flow. By contrast, a current account deficit in international transactions—that is, a shortfall of export receipts below payments for imports of goods and services (and unilateral transfers)— means that foreigners are lending this nation the shortfall, or adding to the flow of saving from which private domestic investment can be financed; by the same token a current account surplus diminishes that flow.

Reprinted with permission of the Federal Reserve Bank of Boston from *New England Economic Review*, May/June 1984, pp. 5–10.

Norman S. Fieleke

The relative magnitudes involved in this accounting relationship for the United States in recent years are shown in Table 1, where private domestic investment in the fourth column is equal to the sum of its sources of financing itemized in the first three columns (private saving, government saving, and lending or investment by foreigners). A negative number in one of the first three columns means that saving is being absorbed, on balance, rather than being made available for private domestic investment; thus, in 1975 foreigners borrowed from current U.S. saving, rather than lending out of their own saving, and government in the United States also borrowed to finance a deficit, so that out of private saving amounting to 18.2 percent of GNP only 13.3 percent was left for private investment within the United States (after adjustment for problems of measurement, represented by the statistical discrepancy).

Table 1
Major Categories of Saving and Investment as Percent of
GNP for the United States, 1970–83

Year	Gross private saving (1)	Government saving (2)	Net invest-ment (lending) by foreigners (3)	Gross private domestic investment (4)	Statistical discrepancy (5)
1970	16.0	−1.1	−0.3	14.5	−0.2
1971	16.7	−1.8	0.1	15.4	0.4
1972	16.0	−0.3	0.4	16.4	0.3
1973	17.2	0.6	−0.5	17.3	0.1
1974	16.4	−0.3	−0.2	15.9	0.3
1975	18.2	−4.1	−1.2	13.3	0.4
1976	17.1	−2.1	−0.3	15.0	0.3
1977	17.0	−0.9	0.7	16.9	0.1
1978	17.3	0.0	0.7	17.9	−0.1
1979	16.8	0.6	0.1	17.5	−0.1
1980	16.5	−1.2	−0.2	15.3	0.1
1981	17.3	−0.9	−0.1	16.1	−0.2
1982	17.0	−3.8	0.3	13.5	0.0
1983	17.2	−4.0	1.0	14.2	0.0

Source: *Economic Report of the President*, February 1984, pp. 220 and 250, and Commerce Department Staff.

The pattern displayed by these data since 1981 has aroused concern that government borrowing not only is diverting funds from ("crowding out") private investors, but is relying on net foreign lending with the associated current account deficit for this country. Thus, while the great bulk of federal borrowing is from U.S. residents, federal debt held by foreigners has been rising and increased by $19.5 billion in 1983 (Chart 1). Since other sectors of the economy also borrowed

Chart I
Both Domestic and Foreign Holdings
of the Federal Debt Have Been Rising

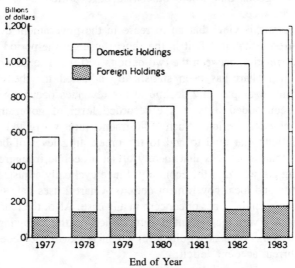

Source: *Treasury Bulletin* and U.S. Treasury Department staff.

from foreigners in 1983, net foreign lending to this country—roughly the current account deficit—amounted to some $32 billion. Correspondingly, as shown by Table 1, as the government deficit has risen over the last two years without any increase in private saving (as a percent of GNP), the accompanying decline in funding for private domestic investment has been mitigated by greater borrowing from abroad.

Although the government deficit and the current account deficit are components of a related set of accounts, the sizes of the two deficits could still vary independently of each other. On occasion, independent variation does seem to occur. For example, from 1971 to 1972 the government deficit declined while borrowing from foreigners (the current account deficit) increased (Table 1). Nonetheless, economic theory suggests that there is a mechanism linking the two deficits such that an increase in the government deficit tends to increase the current account deficit.

While there are differing views regarding the short-run impact of government deficits, the dominant theory is that an increase in government borrowing in a country will, other things equal, put upward pressure on interest rates (adjusted for expected inflation) in that country, thereby attracting foreign investment. As foreign investors acquire the country's currency in order to invest there, they bid up the price of that currency in the foreign exchange markets. The higher price of the country's currency will discourage foreigners from purchasing its goods but will encourage residents of the country to use their now more valuable currency to

purchase foreign goods, so that the country's current account will move toward
a deficit (or toward a larger deficit). In addition, any increase in the country's total
spending resulting from the enlarged government deficit will go partly for imports
and for domestic goods that would otherwise be exported, also worsening the
current account balance.

Chart 2 supports this view that an increase in the government deficit tends to
increase the current account deficit in the short run; over the period 1973–83 the
coefficient of correlation between the two deficits is 0.92. The government deficit
represented in this chart has been statistically adjusted for the effects of the
business cycle; for example, any decline in tax revenues occurring because of a
recession has been added back to the recorded level of government receipts,
reducing the recorded deficit. Such adjustments are warranted because our
interest is in deficits that tend to add to the preexisting level of borrowing and
spending rather than in deficits that merely offset a decline in aggregate borrowing and spending elsewhere in the economy. Since cyclically adjusted data are not
available for state and local government deficits, Chart 2 uses data for the federal
deficit, which has been the focus of concern in any case. Also, the federal deficit for
each year is matched with the current account deficit for the following year, on the
assumption that some time is required for an increase in the federal deficit to
influence the current account deficit.

Chart 2
The Current Account Deficit is Correlated
with the Federal Budget Deficit

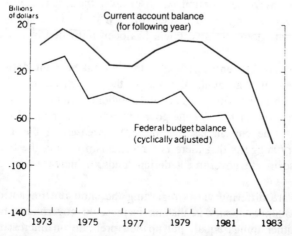

Source: Budget data are from *Survey of Current Business,* December, 1983, p. 32
and from Commerce Department staff; current account data are from *Economic
Report of the President,* 1984, p. 250 (net foreign investment) and Commerce
Department staff, except for 1984, which is a forecast.

As noted above, a change in the federal deficit is presumed to affect the current account deficit partly through its impact on the dollar price of foreign exchange. Chart 3 suggests that the hypothesized relationship between the government deficit and the exchange rate does indeed exist; the coefficient of correlation between the two variables over the years 1973–83 is 0.85. In this case, the government deficit for each year is paired with the exchange rate for the same year, with no lag, on the common assumption that exchange rates react promptly to stimuli (but then affect the current account with a lag). The dollar price index of foreign exchange used in the chart is roughly adjusted for differing inflation rates between the United States and other countries; thus, the index indicates whether prices of foreign goods change after taking exchange rates into account.[1] Accordingly, the marked decline in the index after 1979 can be interpreted as a decline in the relative price of foreign goods, or as a decline in the price competitiveness of the United States.

Chart 3
Changes in the Real Exchange Rate
Roughly Parallel Changes
in the Federal Budget Deficit

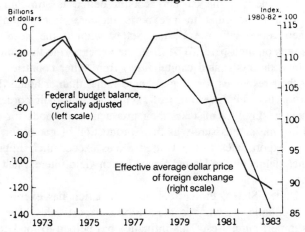

Source: For budget data, see Chart 2; exchange rate data are from Morgan Guaranty Trust Company.

Although Charts 2 and 3 are suggestive, strong conclusions should not be drawn from them alone. To begin with, the exchange rate and the current account are influenced not just by the government deficit but by other factors as well.[2] In this connection, it should be noted that the closeness of the correlations in the charts arises largely from the experience of 1982 and 1983. If those years are excluded, the correlations are appreciably lower (0.55 for Chart 2 and 0.36 for Chart 3), so the extremely high correlations for the entire period may be somewhat fortuitous, representing the influence in 1982 and 1983 of some factor not explicitly recognized by the charts. In addition, a troublesome measurement problem plagues Chart 2 and the related correlation; although there is no doubt that the current account deficit has increased substantially, there is evidence that it has been overstated recently because of difficulties of measurement.

While such qualifications should be borne in mind, Charts 2 and 3 still provide support for the theory that an increase in the government deficit (cyclically adjusted) tends to produce an increase in the current account deficit of the balance of payments. Again, this result comes about partly through the deficit's upward pressure on interest rates and thus on the foreign exchange value of the dollar.[3]

The Consequences of Large Current Account Deficits

If big government deficits contribute to big current account deficits, is that more reason to worry about the government deficit? The answer depends on the circumstances.

Consider first the impact of the U.S. current account deficit on the rest of the world, in the near term. The rise in (inflation-adjusted) interest rates that accompanied the emergence of the large U.S. government and current account deficits has clearly been adverse for the debtor nations, particularly the less developed ones, which must pay the higher rates. The impact of the current account deficit is another matter. Insofar as the U.S. current account deficit arises from the nation's government deficit, the current account deficit is stimulative to foreign economies, for it means that their exports increase more rapidly than their imports in their trade with the United States without the need for demand-reducing measures on their part. To be sure, the net export to this country of goods and services (and the associated capital flow) from other countries represents an investment of their resources, or savings, here rather than at home. However, the frequent assertion that this investment of savings beyond their borders is contractionary for them is simply a mistake; their production of goods for export generates jobs and income just as surely as their production of goods for use at home, and when their export sales to the United States exceed their import purchases they acquire net claims on the United States which yield interest just as do investments at home.

As for the United States, the current account deficit has exerted a restraining influence on economic activity, as the nation's export sales have fallen off in relation to its import purchases. This influence has helped to moderate the recent strong expansion, inhibiting the development of a boom and the associated excesses. In light of the 8.8 percent rate of growth estimated for U.S. GNP in the first quarter, it would be hard to make the case that the restraining influence of the current account deficit has been too severe.

Nonetheless, it is often argued that the large trade deficit underlying the U.S. current account deficit signifies an alarming loss of U.S. competitiveness in world markets, a phenomenon which will generate rising pressure for protection from foreign competition. In the first quarter of this year, U.S. merchandise imports amounted to $105 billion more than U.S. merchandise exports, at an annual rate. Does this imbalance demonstrate a sharp deterioration in U.S. competitive prowess?

Not really. To be sure, the U.S. competitive position would be stronger if the foreign exchange value of the dollar had not risen and the trade deficit were smaller, other things being equal. However, the trade balance by itself is not a valid indicator of competitiveness. Other more comprehensive measures suggest that the United States remains a powerful competitor.

For example, between 1982 and 1983 U.S. total output grew more than twice as fast as the total output of the 23 other advanced countries belonging to the Organization for Economic Cooperation and Development, and for 1984 a similar outcome is widely expected.[4] Since the U.S. share of world output is rising in this fashion, U.S. producers are more than holding their own in the world economy. From this perspective, the trade deficit arose largely because U.S. demand has been climbing even faster than U.S. output (so that the gap has been filled by net imports), not because U.S. firms collectively have lost competitiveness in any damaging sense.

Because goods are generally more transportable than services, firms which produce goods are subject to potentially more foreign competition than are firms which produce services, other things being equal. According to Table 2, the production of U.S. goods has been growing faster than U.S. GNP or the production of U.S. services since the last recession, and the growth of goods production compares favorably with that during previous recent recoveries. Therefore, U.S. firms are holding their own against foreign competition by this standard also.

Table 2
Percentage Changes in Real Output during Recession and the Following First Four Quarters of Recovery

Period (year and quarter)	Percentage Change			
	Goods	*Services*	*Structures*	*Total GNP*
1969:4 to 1970:4 (recession)	− 3.0	2.5	1.8	− 0.1
1970:4 to 1971:4 (recovery)	4.6	3.5	9.8	4.7
1973:4 to 1975:1 (recession)	− 8.9	3.3	− 21.1	− 4.9
1975:1 to 1976:1 (recovery)	9.7	3.2	10.4	6.7
1980:1 to 1980:3 (recession)	− 3.9	1.0	− 10.1	− 2.2
1980:3 to 1981:2 (recovery)*	5.1	1.3	4.8	3.3
1981:3 to 1982:4 (recession)	− 7.3	1.4	− 3.1	− 3.0
1982:4 to 1983:4 (recovery)	9.1	2.4	12.4	6.2

*This period includes only three quarters because the recovery lasted only that long.
Source: DRI

Another measure of U.S. competitiveness is the Commerce Department's series on the U.S. share of world exports of manufactured goods. The latest available data, for the third quarter of 1983, reveal this share to be about 20 percent, which is somewhat below the recent peak attained in 1981 but is above the average for the past five years.[5] Finally, the ratio of U.S. gross merchandise imports to U.S. GNP declined in each of the past three years.

In sum, whatever else the large U.S. current account deficit may signify, it does not signify any loss in the U.S. share of world output, compared with past levels, nor does it demonstrate any injurious loss of competitiveness for the aggregate of U.S. firms which compete in world markets. Such losses may well eventuate— especially if the budget deficit and foreign exchange value of the dollar remain so high—but the current account deficit by itself would not be a reliable measure of them.

Longer Term Considerations

For many years the United States has been a net creditor, as its residents have held claims on foreigners in excess of their liabilities to foreigners. This excess amounted to nearly $169 billion at the end of 1982, the latest date for which data have been published. Continuing current account deficits of the magnitude envisioned for 1984—some $80 billion—would soon convert the nation into a net debtor.

As common sense would suggest, history shows that nations do not incur debt without regard to ability to repay. Data relevant to this question for 14 industrial countries for the period 1952–1980 are presented in Table 3. The first column shows the accumulated net current account deficit (-) or surplus for each country over the 29-year span, while the second column shows the ratio of that accumulated deficit or surplus to the gross saving done by the nation during 1980. The ratios do not seem large. The largest negative ratio is only -1.6, signifying that the nations with this ratio, Denmark and Ireland, could pay back with approximately 1-1/2 years' savings their net foreign debt incurred on current account over a period of 29 years. Even if a nation were inclined to borrow without limit, others would not lend to it beyond its perceived capacity to service its debt. These considerations suggest that the United States will not continue to incur large current account deficits in the long run, even if the government deficit remains large.

The prospect that some sort of adjustment process will eventually shrink the U.S. current account deficit is scarcely a reason for complacency. Adjustment can be gradual and painless; or it can be abrupt and stressful, as demonstrated by the current experience of some indebted less developed countries.

On the face of it, there are grounds for concern if a surge in borrowing from foreigners goes to finance consumption rather than investment, because sound investment, unlike consumption, generates a return with which to repay the foreign borrowing. In face, as Table 1 indicates, gross private domestic investment as a percent of GNP has declined notably in the United States from the level recorded in 1981, the year before the big increase in the government deficit and the shift into deficit by the current account. A continuation of this configuration would almost certainly imply a more difficult eventual adjustment—specifically, a cutback in consumption—than would be required if the rise in borrowing from abroad were associated with a rise in domestic investment.

Table 3
Cumulative Current Account Balances for 14 OECD
Countries, for 1952–1980

Country	*Cumulative current-account balance (in billions of U.S. dollars)* (1)	*Col. (1) divided by 1980 gross national saving* (2)
Austria	−13.2	−0.6
Canada	−41.4	−0.8
Denmark	−15.4	−1.6
Finland	−7.5	−0.6
Germany	30.0	0.2
Ireland	−6.5	−1.6
Italy	8.5	0.1
Japan	24.9	0.1
Netherlands	5.3	0.2
Norway	−16.1	−0.9
Sweden	−11.7	−0.6
Switzerland	18.4	0.7
United Kingdom	−5.8	−0.1
United States	41.9	0.1

Source: International Monetary Fund, *Balance of Payments Yearbook*, various issues, and *International Financial Statistics Supplement on Exchange Rates*, 1981; Organization for Economic Cooperation and Development, *National Accounts, Vol. 1, 1951–1980*, 1982.

Another factor that could add pain to the reduction of the current account deficit would be abruptness of the adjustment process. A sudden inclination by foreign residents to stop lending, net, to the United States, that is, to stop acquiring net claims on the United States, would tend to produce both higher interest rates in the United States and a sharp fall in the foreign exchange value of the dollar. The rise in interest rates would discourage private investment, and the reduced purchasing power of the dollar over foreign goods would translate into more inflation. The more abrupt these developments were, the more likely a recession would be. While forecasts of foreign exchange rates are no more reliable than forecasts of the stock market, under present tendencies a sharp, severe depreciation of the dollar seems less likely than a slow decline, as foreigners gradually reduce the rate at which they have been accumulating U.S. dollar assets in order to avoid putting too many eggs into that particular basket. Whether gradual or rapid, the likely depreciation of the dollar would help to reduce the current account deficit.

Of course, the mere fact that the dollar may have to depreciate in the future does not, in and of itself, prove that the dollar is too highly valued ("overvalued") for current conditions. Like other prices, the foreign exchange value of the dollar can be expected to change as the underlying circumstances change.

Conclusion

The record current account deficit in the U.S. balance of payments is partly attributable to the record deficit in the federal budget. The budget-induced rise in the current account deficit has stimulated foreign economic activity while moderating the U.S. expansion. Contrary to frequent assertions, the current account deficit does not yet signify a severe decline in the international competitiveness of U.S. producers.

Over the longer term the current account deficit will have to be reduced. Most likely, this adjustment will be promoted by a gradual depreciation of the dollar's foreign exchange value; but the adjustment would be less painful if the borrowing from abroad associated with the current account deficit were used to finance investment rather than, as has been the case, to finance consumption.

Notes

1. If the government deficit, too, is corrected for inflation, i.e., is converted into 1972 dollars by use of the GNP deflator, the correlation between the (inflation-corrected) deficit and the exchange rate is 0.79.
2. Among these factors are resource discoveries, changes in tastes and technology, and differences in national growth rates. However, changes in tastes and in technology, as well as growth differentials, generally exert their influence gradually over long periods, and major resource discoveries are rare. From year to year, movements in the real exchange rate and the current account are more powerfully influenced by business cycle fluctuations, by government controls, and by government monetary and fiscal policy, including changes in the government deficit such as those depicted in Charts 2 and 3.
3. For amplification of the view that the larger government deficit has boosted real interest rates and the real exchange value of the dollar, see *Economic Report of the President,* February 1984, pp. 52–55.
4. Last December, for example, the Organization for Economic Cooperation and Development forecasted that U.S. GNP would grow by 5 percent in 1984, twice the rate expected for the rest of the OECD.
5. Actually, the share is of exports by 15 major industrial countries to the world excluding shipments to the United States, and is based on exports valued at current exchange rates; see *Business America,* April 16, 1984, p. 17. Because the U.S. share valued at current exchange rates has remained fairly stable while the foreign exchange value of the dollar has risen, it follows that the U.S. share, if valued at constant exchange rates, would have recorded a decline.

Chapter 5: CONSTITUTIONAL REFORM

Wagner and Tollison trace the history of economists' thinking on deficits from the balanced budget orthodoxy to the modern decline of the stabilization ideal. Fiscal policy destabilizes the economy, they maintain, and they advocate a balanced budget amendment to constrain government's tendency toward expansion.

BALANCED BUDGETS, FISCAL RESPONSIBILITY, AND THE CONSTITUTION

Richard E. Wagner and Robert D. Tollison

Preface

Thirty-one states have now called for a constitutional convention to consider an amendment that would require the federal government to balance its budget. This is only three states short of the number required by Article V of the U.S. Constitution to convene a convention. Besides this approval by 60 percent of the states, various polls have shown that between 70 and 80 percent of all Americans favor such an amendment. Only in the federal legislature—where the deficit spending originates—has the idea of a balanced budget amendment been received coolly. It is possible that Congress will not always be so reluctant. Between 1901 and 1911 thirty states called for a constitutional convention to consider the direct election of senators. Only one more state was needed at that time to convene a convention. Fearful of appearing not to be leading the nation, Congress responded in 1912 by proposing the seventeenth amendment, which was adopted in 1913. Congress may similarly overcome its reluctance to embrace the balanced budget. Whatever Congress does, however, we will surely be hearing a lot about balanced budgets in the coming months.

The balanced budget amendment raises an issue of economic principle. Some people suggest that a balanced budget amendment would be the height of fiscal folly, for it would hamstring the government's ability to use budgetary policy to promote prosperity. Others argue that a balanced budget is one necessary element in a program of fiscal responsibility, to which we must adhere if the budgetary affairs of the state are to be consistent with the promotion of our common prosperity. Besides examining this issue of economic principle, it is also important to explore some points of practice. Even though one might recognize

Reprinted with permission of the publisher from *Balanced Budgets, Fiscal Responsibility, and the Constitution*. Washington, D.C.: Cato Institute, 1982, pp. 1–56.

that a balanced budget is desirable in principle, one might be concerned about how this principle would be put into practice. After assessing the balanced budget amendment in terms of economic and fiscal principle, this monograph considers various issues of practice that would inform an actual balanced budget amendment.

I. From Fiscal Responsibility to Chronic Deficits

Surpluses, Deficits, and Our Changing Budgetary History

During the century and a half before the Great Depression, budget deficits were essentially limited to times of war and recession. Budget surpluses were typical in other periods, and they were used to reduce the national debt that had accumulated during the times of war and recession.[1] Between 1795 and 1811, our national debt was reduced by nearly half, from $83.8 million to $45.2 million. Moreover, budget surpluses tended to be quite large, for they averaged about $2.5 million annually in a budget in which total expenditures averaged only about $8 million.

The War of 1812 brought deficits once again. Between 1815 and 1836, eighteen surpluses in twenty-one years had reduced the national debt from $127 million to $337,000. We experienced a major depression during 1837–43 and then, four years later, the Mexican-American War. The 1850s saw eight years of surplus, but then came the Civil War. By the end of 1865, our national debt was $2.7 billion. By the end of 1893, twenty-eight consecutive years of budget surplus had reduced the national debt to $961 million. During this period, about 25 percent of all public expenditure was devoted to debt amortization.

After the Spanish-American War, the national debt was reduced—though slowly in comparison with our earlier experience—from $1.4 billion to $1.2 billion by 1917, when we got involved in World War I. The $25.5 billion of national debt in 1918 was reduced by eleven consecutive years of surplus to $16.2 billion by 1930. Then came sixteen years of deficits with the Great Depression and World War II, leaving a national debt of $169.4 billion in 1946.

While the Great Depression and World War II brought us a decade and a half of deficits, this pattern did not depart from our previous experience during recessions and wars. Between 1947 and 1960, there were seven years of surplus and seven years of deficit. With $32 billion of deficits and $31 billion of surpluses, the budget can be said to have been roughly balanced over this period. This period differed from similar periods earlier in our history in that no conscious effort was made to reduce the previously accumulated national debt, though it might also be noted that we fought a war in Korea during this time. Looking back, we can see the Truman and Eisenhower years as an interregnum that separated the former period of general opposition to budget deficits from the post-1960 period epitomized by budget deficits under all circumstances.

Since 1960, budget deficits have become a way of life. During this period we have had only one year of budget surplus, 1969, and this was only $3 billion. The remaining budgets during this two-decade period were all in deficit, and the total deficit accumulated during these two decades exceeds $400 billion. It appears that a watershed in our fiscal history was reached around 1960.

Constitutional Erosion and Chronic Budget Deficits

This shift from balanced budgets to chronic deficits occurred because of some fundamental changes in the constraints within which Congress makes its budgetary decisions. Some of these changes made money creation easier. Under the gold standard in operation before World War I, inflation would be offset by a drainage of gold that would reduce the stock of money. This would occur because prices in the inflating country would rise relative to those in other countries. Consumers would then find imports more attractive, and as they purchased more from abroad, a gold outflow would result. The pattern of U.S. monetary history after World War I was one of reducing the constraints on domestic monetary authorities. In 1933, for instance, the U.S. government prohibited American citizens from redeeming their currency for gold. The constraints on issuing paper money consequently become looser. The gold reserve standard of the postwar period did less to restrict the money-creating actions of government. However, this system was more restrictive than the purely fiduciary standard our government embraced in 1971 when President Nixon repudiated the gold convertibility of the dollar, thereby removing the last external constraint on money creation.[2] This pattern of development in our monetary order cannot be said to have directly caused our chronic deficits. However, by facilitating the creation of money, this development encouraged deficit finance, as will become clear later when we examine government borrowing and money creation.

This monetary development occurred along with an important change in the ethos within which budgetary policy had been made. For the first century and a half of our history, our budgetary policy was influenced by the prevailing belief that budget deficits were proper only during wars or recessions and that at other times some effort should be made to retire national debt through budget surpluses. This ethos can be said to have constituted an unwritten element of our Constitution.

It found widespread expression in intellectual discourse.[3] Many economists felt that budget deficits would erode a nation's capital stock, thereby reducing standards of living. They believed that in order to contribute to prosperity rather than to detract from it, government should promote the creation of capital and not its consumption. What was wise for an individual was wise for a nation as well. As Adam Smith put it in *The Wealth of Nations,* "What is prudence in the conduct of every private family, can scarce be folly in that of a great kingdom."

C.F. Bastable, one of the leading scholars of public finance during the late nineteenth and early twentieth centuries, typified this period's views on budget deficits:

> Under normal conditions, there ought to be a balance between these two sides [expenditure and revenue] of financial activity. Outlay should not exceed income, . . . tax revenue ought to be kept up to the amount required to defray expenses.[4]

Bastable went on to modify this statement slightly, though tellingly:

> This general principle must, however, admit of modifications. Temporary deficits and surpluses cannot be avoided. . . . All that can be claimed is a

substantial approach to a balance in the two sides of the account. The safest rule for practice is that which lays down the expedience of *estimating for a moderate surplus,* by which the possibility of a deficit will be reduced to a minimum.[5]

In other words, Bastable believed governments should aim for some budget surplus to provide a cushion for difficulties that might arise. This was the way of fiscal prudence and responsibility.

This effective "constitutional" opposition to budget deficits dissolved during the generation from President Roosevelt to President Kennedy. The old norms of responsible fiscal conduct and generally held perceptions of self-interest fell before the Keynesian onslaught that monopolized channels of public opinion during this period.[6] Budget deficits were no longer seen as a sign of irresponsible government action. Indeed, to an increasing degree, people believed that government could use deficit finance to improve the economy. Therefore, an avoidance of budget deficits, along with some effort to retire the national debt, ceased to be a *sine qua non* of fiscal conduct.

The Keynesian revolution in economic policy succeeded in creating a view that budgetary imbalance was consistent with, indeed was required for, "responsible" fiscal conduct. When unemployment became a problem, it was suggested that a budget deficit could be used to increase spending, which would stimulate employment. Similarly, if inflation became a problem, it was suggested that a budget surplus could be used to decrease spending, which would reduce the pressure on prices. The Keynesian platform for economic management replaced the old-fashioned belief in a balanced budget with what was viewed as a new and superior principle, that of using the budget—deficits *and* surpluses—to balance the economy. This sharp shift in norms for government conduct was expressed concisely by Hugh Dalton:

> The new approach to budgetary policy owes more to Keynes than to any other man. Thus it is just that we should speak to "the Keynesian revolution.". . . We may now free ourselves from the *old and narrow conception of balancing the budget,* no matter over what period, and move towards the *new and wider conception of the budget balancing the whole economy.*[7]

II. Budgetary Politics and Deficit Financing

The Keynesian precept of using the budget to balance the economy called for a symmetry in its application. Deficits would be created when unemployment threatened, but surpluses would be created when inflation threatened. However, over the past two decades our budget deficits have occurred in good economic periods as well as in bad, and they have occurred despite repeated statements that budget surpluses were just a year or two away. Aside from the recession of 1975, the 1970s were a period of economic expansion. Unemployment was a little higher than it was in earlier times, but the standard measures of industrial production showed a general rise throughout the decade. Yet, quite unlike our experience during similar times in the past, we are plagued by deficits. As noted above, this sharp contrast with our previous history resulted from a weakening in an ethos of strong opposition to deficit finance.

In a democracy, a political bias exists in favor of deficit finance.[8] This bias remained latent until the past two decades or so, when it emerged as a force in our budgetary politics. Periodically, politicians must face a test of their incumbency. Budgetary policies can enhance or retard the likelihood of their remaining in office. Tax reductions and increases in expenditure will both generally strengthen a politician's base of support. In contrast, tax increases and reductions in expenditure will tend to weaken that base. A politician interested in using budgetary policy to strengthen his electoral support will tend to favor policies that increase expenditures and reduce taxes. Policies that reduce expenditures and increase taxes will have the contrary effect of diminishing electoral support. As compared with a balanced budget, a budget surplus will require either higher taxes or lower expenditures, or a combination of the two. Therefore, a budget surplus will tend to command less political support than a balanced budget. A budget deficit, when compared with a balanced budget, will make it possible to offer some combination of lower taxes and higher expenditures. Therefore, a budget deficit will tend to command more support than a balanced budget and *ipso facto* more support than a budget surplus. A simple consideration of these pressures shows why democracies, which are based on electoral competition, possess a political bias in favor of deficit finance.

Until the 1960s, this political bias remained latent because our political process was constrained by the prevailing ethos, the belief that deficits were a sign of fiscal irresponsibility. This ethos, in effect, made a general prohibition of budget deficits an unwritten part of our Constitution and prevented resort to deficit finance under normal circumstances. As this ethos began to weaken as a result of the Keynesian-inspired shift in the understanding of what constituted irresponsible fiscal conduct, a fundamental asymmetry developed in budgetary politics. Deficit spending came to command increasing political support. The record of the past two decades is adequate testimony on this point.

III. Economic Disruption through Deficit Finance

Capital Consumption and Deficit Finance

The political bias toward deficit finance that has developed over the past two decades contributes to both capital consumption and inflation. Within our present monetary system, budget deficits may be financed either by borrowing or by creating money, and the manner in which the deficit is financed influences the relative importance of these two consequences of capital consumption and inflation. Basically, capital consumption results when budget deficits are financed by borrowing, while inflation results when deficits are financed by money creation.

In the absence of government borrowing and money creation, capital markets would reflect the actions of individual citizens who wished to borrow or lend. Borrowing is possible only to the extent that there are people who are willing to lend. Saving provides the resources for lending. People who save relinquish their control over these resources in exchange for repayment of principal and interest at some later time. Investors, on the other hand, put these savings to productive use, hoping to be able to amortize the debt from the yield on the investment. The rate of interest indicates the rate of return to savers from lending, while it is also the price of borrowing. Consequently, the higher the rate of interest, the more people will want to save, but the less they will want to borrow. As a starting point for the subsequent discussion, we might suppose that, in the absence of government borrowing and money creation, saving and investment would be equal to $100 billion annually, with an interest rate of 8 percent.

Government borrowing to finance a budget deficit adds a new dimension to the operation of capital markets. When a federal deficit is financed through the Treasury's borrowing from private citizens, the total amount desired for borrowing will increase. To illustrate, suppose the government runs a $40 billion deficit. In addition to the desires of private citizens to borrow $100 billion, government now wishes to borrow $40 billion to finance its deficit. Yet only $100 billion has been saved, so the amount desired for loans exceeds by $40 billion the amount that can be supplied. As in any such situation of excess demand, the price of borrowing will rise because of the competition among borrowers for funds. As the rate of interest rises above 8 percent, some potential borrowers will curtail their desire for funds. This process of reduction in the amount requested in loans must continue until the excess demand for loans disappears.

The rise in the rate of interest due to this competition among borrowers does two things. As borrowing becomes more expensive, potential borrowers will reduce the amounts they wish to borrow. Private citizens might wish to borrow $100 billion at an 8 percent rate of interest, but wish to borrow only $85 billion at 9 percent. Furthermore, the return to savings will increase with the rise in the rate of interest. At a 9 percent rate of interest, people might be willing to save $105 billion. The rate of interest will continue to rise until the amount demanded in loans equals the amount supplied. Suppose the rate of interest rises to 10 percent before this equality is attained. Further, suppose the amount of saving at this higher interest rate is $110 billion. With government requiring $40 billion to finance its deficit, there will be $70 billion remaining for private borrowers. The $40 billion budget deficit will have crowded out $30 billion of private investment. As a result of the $40 billion deficit financed by borrowing, private borrowing is reduced from $100 billion to $70 billion. Saving is also increased by $10 billion because of the rise in the rate of interest.

Crowding out private borrowing will, in turn, bring about a reduction in our standard of living. This reduction can be prevented only if government borrowing replaces the private investment that was crowded out and if it is as efficient as the private investment. Studies of the economic aspects of government in recent years indicate that the productivity of government investment will generally be considerably lower than that of private investment. Moreover, government borrowing does not typically replace the private investment that is crowded out. While some private borrowing is for consumption, most of it is for investment. And while some government borrowing is for investment, most of it is for consumption. This means that budget deficits replace the creation of capital goods with the subsidization of consumption. By crowding out investment for consumption, deficit finance results in capital consumption. Capital accumulation can still take place, of course, but the amount of accumulation will be less than it would have been in the absence of the budget deficit. Because of this reduction in our stock of capital, we become less prosperous than we would otherwise have been.

Inflation and Deficit Finance

Money creation is another way of financing a budget deficit. This is as true for private citizens as it is for governments, although governments typically look upon money creation by private citizens as a crime. That there are two distinct methods of financing a budget deficit is sometimes obscured by our monetary system, which confounds them. This confounding of borrowing and money creation takes place because both require the use of government debt. It is necessary to distinguish between two kinds of borrowing. The financing of budget deficits by borrowing from private citizens is truly borrowing, as was discussed above. This same transaction, however, can also result in money creation. Which of the two takes place depends upon the action taken by the Federal Reserve Board. If the Federal Reserve System increases its ownership of Treasury debt, money creation will occur. This process of money creation is referred to as *debt monetization*, for it describes the conversion of government debt into money through the mechanics of the Federal Reserve System. Its impact is the same as if the Treasury had simply printed money to finance its excess expenditures.

The impact of budget deficits on the stock of money will depend upon Federal Reserve Board actions in regard to its ownership of government debt. Even in the absence of a budget deficit, the Federal Reserve Board can increase its ownership of outstanding government debt, thereby expanding the stock of money. And in the presence of a budget deficit, the Federal Reserve Board can keep its ownership of government debt unchanged. There is no mechanical connection between budget deficits and the stock of money, but this does not imply the absence of an actual connection between budget deficits and money creation.

In the absence of any debt monetization, budget deficits will, as explained above, place an upward pressure on interest rates and, therefore, crowd out private investment. There will be political gains from some resistance to this crowding out. Congress will choose the budget deficit because a majority of its members will believe that, in comparison with the higher taxes or lower expenditures required to balance the budget, deficits will strengthen their bases of support. The political gains from deficit finance vary in direct proportion to the degree of diffusion of the costs of budget deficits among the population. A cost of $10 billion spread over one hundred million people will generally provoke less opposition than the same cost spread over only one million people. To the extent that budget deficits are financed by genuine government borrowing, the costs of deficit finance will be concentrated upon the investors who are crowded out. In contrast, money creation will diffuse the cost among the population. Therefore, since deficit finance accompanied by money creation will diffuse the cost more generally, it will evoke less opposition than deficit finance in the absence of money creation. To the extent that congressional interests are reflected in the actions of the Federal Reserve Board, budget deficits will result in monetary expansion.[9]

The Federal Reserve Board will also reflect the interests of the financial and banking community. With respect to the financing of budget deficits, there is a strong congruence of interests between Congress and the Federal Reserve Board. Both interests will be better served by a policy that allows some debt monetization than by one that permits the process of crowding out potential investors to operate to its fullest extent. In the absence of any debt monetization, the burden of deficit finance is borne by potential borrowers and the financial community through the rise in interest rates, which crowds out private borrowing. Debt monetization will offset this process.

With debt monetization, the supply of loanable funds is no longer limited to what people save. If $10 billion is created through debt monetization, the amount of lending, continuing the above illustration, can rise to $120 billion. If the government borrows $40 billion, $80 billion will now be available for private borrowing, and the rate of interest will be, say, 9 percent. As a result of debt monetization, the budget deficit will have crowded out only $20 billion of private investment. Debt monetization is able to reduce the extent of crowding out because inflation in the stock of money is used to provide the resources necessary to finance the additional $10 billion of investment. However, money creation reduces the real value of the existing stock of money, and it is this erosion in value that provides the means for reducing the extent of crowding out.

IV. Economic Instability and Fiscal Policy

Economic Instability through Inflation

Money creation through debt monetization will initially generate economic expansion. The creation of money increases the spending power of those who receive the newly created money. This increased spending will create an increased demand for the output of some producers. As inventories are drawn down and bottlenecks to expansion confronted, prices will also start to rise in those areas where the added spending takes place. The process of money expansion is one in which particular areas of the economy will be favored over others, and, in consequence, some prices will rise relative to others. Employment will expand principally in areas where the new money is spent, while prices will tend to rise in those areas of the economy as well.

To some extent, the newly created money will go to finance activities supported by the government deficit. To a larger extent, in our fractional reserve system of banking, the monetary expansion will take place through credit markets as banks expand their loans. Consequently, the newly created money will, to an important degree, be used to finance investment. There will be a relative expansion in the producer goods industries, as opposed to the consumer goods industries. Instead of bringing about a uniform economic expansion, monetary expansion will bring about some change in the structure of economic activity. Since money creation takes place at particular points in the economic process, the expansion will tend to be concentrated at these points. Total spending will increase, but it will increase particularly heavily in the producer goods industries.

While this money creation initially will quicken the pace of economic activity, it also will create the conditions for a subsequent recession.[10] The pace of economic activity quickens because monetary expansion alters people's anticipations of the relative profitability of different lines of business. Anticipations of profit rise in those lines into which the new money flows. For instance, the expansion in the volume of funds available for lending will lower the price of credit, which in turn will make some lines of investment now seem profitable where they did not seem so before.

There are two types of reasons for an increase in the anticipated profitability of lines of business. One type refers to changes in a variety of real economic circumstances. Consumer preferences may change, the availability of inputs of resources or labor may change, or new technologies may be developed. In consequence of changes in such real economic conditions, the pattern of economic activity will change. There is no reason why these real changes should reverse themselves, so the new pattern will generally be a stable one. The other type of reason is changes in the creation of money and the availability of credit. However, the changes these bring about in the pattern of economic activity cannot be sustained without a continuing and accelerating injection of money into the economy.

Without this acceleration of inflation, much of the increased investment will turn out to be unprofitable. As these investments are scrapped or put to different uses, economic contraction will result. Excess capacity will arise as capital becomes unemployed. But labor will become unemployed as well. Both types of unemployment will result from the previous inflation because the money expansion will have created an artificial economic high by leading people to make investments that they would not have made otherwise. In the absence of perfect foresight, some investments will always turn out to be unprofitable. What money creation does, however, is to increase the number of such mistaken investments. As people subsequently come to revise downward their estimates of profitability and to take corrective action, economic contraction will result as a necessary corrective to these previous mistakes. Thus the decision to have an inflation in the stock of money implies a simultaneous decision to have a subsequent recession.

What if the government attempts to counteract the economic contraction by further money creation? With a sufficiently strong injection of money, the contractionary forces can be offset, temporarily. But inflation cannot accelerate indefinitely. When inflation ceases, as it eventually must, contraction will result. The longer the inflation is allowed to accelerate before the recession is faced, the greater will be the distortion in prices and the pattern of investment in the economy. Consequently, the latent economic contraction will have increased. A dilemma results because attempts to resist the contraction increase the economic distortion. But resistance cannot continue indefinitely, and the longer the resistance before monetary expansion is brought under control—or even not allowed to accelerate further—the greater will be the subsequent economic contraction. Once we recognize that inflation breeds recession, we can see why it is possible to confront rising prices and unemployment at the same time. This situation, called stagflation, is a natural outgrowth of inflation; in particular, it results from attempts to resist or counteract by further monetary expansion the recession that was made necessary by the initial inflation.[11]

The Effect of Fiscal Policy

Many people have argued that requiring the government to balance its budget would interfere with the government's ability to stabilize the economy through fiscal policy. This line of argument reflects the Keynesian notion that the state can use its budget to promote economic stability, using deficits to offset unemployment and surpluses to counteract inflation. A balanced budget requirement would, it is argued, conflict with the needs of an activist fiscal policy, for such a policy can be implemented only if government is able to resort to budget imbalance.

This argument ignores the prodeficit bias in budgetary policy in a democracy. An activist fiscal policy pursued according to Keynesian principles requires a symmetrical application. However, the politics of fiscal policy operate asymmetrically. Even if we accept the argument that fiscal policy can be used to promote economic stability, fiscal policy would not tend to be used in this manner. Budget deficits would tend to be too large, thereby providing too much expansion. And budget surpluses, if they could be found at all, would tend to be too small, thereby providing too little restraint on inflation. In other words, unemployment would be contested too strongly, while inflation would be counteracted too weakly. As a result, actual fiscal policy would have a bias toward inflation and capital consumption.

This entire approach to budget policy is based on the presumption that there is a trade-off between inflation and unemployment. Within the Phillips curve framework, more inflation implies less unemployment and vice versa.[12] A nation is depicted as facing a choice between different rates of inflation and unemployment, and the problem of policy is to choose the desired combination of the two.[13] The political bias toward deficit finance would tilt the economy toward higher inflation and lower unemployment than would result from the symmetrical application of the Keynesian norms. It would not, however, change the basic existence of a trade-off or deny the need for policy makers to make some choice between inflation and unemployment.

Within the Keynesian framework, such circumstances as stagflation are a mystery. Inflation or unemployment could be troublesome, but according to the Keynesian system, it is impossible for an economy to be plagued by inflation, unemployment, and sluggish economic performance all at once. Therefore, the joint presence of substantial inflation and high unemployment is evidence that the Keynesian framework itself is inappropriate. The reason it is inappropriate is that it does not recognize the way inflation creates economic maladjustments that cannot be sustained without an accelerating inflation. In the absence of an accelerating inflation, recession must follow. Inflation and unemployment are *not* options, for a nation does not have the ability to choose one or the other at a particular time. Obviously, at any time there is both a rate of inflation and a rate of unemployment. These two variables are not independent of each other, as the

Phillips curve framework assumes they are. Instead, inflation and unemployment are linked as cause and effect. Unemployment today results from inflation yesterday, so to speak, and today's inflation will breed tomorrow's unemployment. A failure to accept the inexorability of this sequence or an attempt to avoid it, say by increasing the rate of money creation, results in stagflation, in which case economic sluggishness comes to exist along with inflation.

Fiscal policy is simply not a tool for creating economic stability. Budget deficits cannot be used to promote economic stability. Rather, budget deficits contribute to economic instability in the future. Economic instability can result in several ways. It suffices here to note that there is an important and enduring link between monetary instability and economic instability. And monetary instability seems inherent in our present institutional order, in which money is so tightly controlled by the government.[14] Our main problem is how monetary stability can be promoted in our present political system, where the pressures for budget deficits, capital consumption, inflation, and economic instability seem so remorseless.

V. Constitutional Principles, Balanced Budgets, and Fiscal Responsibility

A Constitutional Framework for Budgetary Policy

It seems clear that we would be better off with a government that balanced its budget than with one that had a budget chronically in deficit. Yet there is a strong political bias in democracies toward deficit finance. Thus there is a gulf between desirable and actual budgetary policy. The recognition of this gulf inspired the call for a balanced budget amendment to the Constitution.

Many people who agree with this diagnosis of budget deficits may nevertheless be reluctant to have a balanced budget be made a constitutional requirement. These people would prefer to rely upon Congress to return us to fiscal responsibility. This approach, they feel, would be better than imposing upon ourselves a constitutional straitjacket. Congress has been responsible for our deficits, so Congress has the ability to restore budget balance. But how reasonable is it to rely upon the normal processes of congressional decision-making? It is these very processes that have brought about our chronic deficits. The change in our monetary order from a commodity to a purely fiduciary standard, along with the deterioration of a longstanding ethos hostile to budget deficits, brought about a climate favorable to deficit finance. An ethos cannot be adopted or rejected at will, so we cannot look to some simple restoration of past attitudes. We must look toward the development of constitutional requirements to offset our chronic bouts with deficit finance.

Constitutional rules can serve an important function in preventing or curtailing outcomes that, while undesirable, might nonetheless tend to result from ordinary legislative processes. The Constitution provides the framework within which legislative action can take place. The importance of a constitutional framework can be seen by analogy with the rules of a game. In this analogy, the rules are analogous to the Constitution, the play of the game is analogous to the legislative process, and the outcome of the game is analogous to the budget that is enacted.

In a basketball game, a player on defense can improve his chances of success by holding his opponent. Yet, if all defenders played this way, the end result would be a less interesting game. All, or at least nearly all, players are worse off when holding occurs than they would be in the presence of a constitutional rule against holding. If one person holds, he can gain a relative advantage. If another person refrains from holding, he will be disadvantaged. Without a constitutional rule against holding, holding will become rampant once the players recognize its usefulness. Yet all players would be better off playing the game without holding. They cannot do so without a constitutional rule against holding.

In the theory of games, the situation in which such generally undesirable outcomes can emerge is referred to as a prisoner's dilemma. The basic idea behind the prisoner's dilemma is a simple one. It describes a situation in which each person's pursuit of his self-interest can produce an outcome that is undesirable from the perspective of all participants. The tendency to resort to deficit finance fits within this framework. A legislator will typically secure more political support through budgetary policy under deficit spending than under a balanced budget because deficit spending makes it possible to confer additional expenditure programs or tax reductions upon desired constituencies. Each legislator individually will be motivated to support deficit financing. If one legislator refrains, the deficit will not be affected, but the benefits to his particular constituents may be reduced.

Suppose a congressman voted against all spending proposals in excess of the balanced budget level. The congressman's impact on spending would be negligible, and his political support would have weakened because some of his negative votes would have been contrary to the preferences of some of his constituents. The situation is like the one that would result if one basketball player tried to refrain from holding. The overall incidence of holding would be only minutely affected, and the player's team would be disadvantaged. As with a rule against holding, the requirement of a balanced budget would redound to the benefit of all, or practically all, legislators and their constituents. A constitutional requirement of a balanced budget is one way to provide this rule.

Budget Balance and Fiscal Responsibility in a Democracy

There is a fundamental sense in which any budget must of necessity always be in balance. By the nature of double entry accounting, each debit must possess an equal credit, so that a balanced budget is a tautology. A person who earns $30,000 in one year, paying $10,000 in taxes and spending $15,000, has in this sense a balanced budget, not a budget surplus. This is because the $5,000 that is saved is as much a debit item as the amounts spent or lost in taxes. Likewise, a person who earns $30,000, pays $10,000 in taxes, and spends $25,000 also has a balanced budget. While his debits add up to $35,000, so do his credits. He has a $30,000 credit from income, but he must also have a $5,000 credit item as well, possibly from a bank loan, or perhaps from the liquidation of capital—the particular source is unimportant.

When people speak of budgetary imbalance, of surplus and deficit, they have in mind something different from this double entry tautology. Of the two situations described above, the first would be commonly considered one of budget surplus, while the second would be considered one of budget deficit. What this means is that imbalance becomes meaningful through the exclusion of certain items from consideration—like the saving and the borrowing in the above illustration. The reason for excluding certain items is largely normative. One use of a system of accounts is to provide an assessment of a set of transactions. There are three patterns of sets of transactions: one allows for reproduction over time, with neither gain nor loss; one allows for expansion; and one allows for contraction. A person who earns $30,000, pays $10,000 in taxes, and spends $20,000 would, by virtue of this set of transactions, have done nothing to influence, for good or for bad, future transactions. In contrast, when $5,000 is saved, future growth is made possible, so the saving is excluded from the budget, and the budget is considered to be in surplus. And when $5,000 is borrowed, a mortgage is placed on future transactions, so the borrowing is excluded as a normal credit item, and the budget is considered to be in deficit.

By extension of this reasoning, a government's budget must always be in balance. When we speak of surplus or deficit, we are excluding from consideration some of the credit or debit items that necessarily must be present in and implied by the set of transactions of which the budget is a description.[15] For instance, government debt or government revenues from money creation are as much a credit item as are tax revenues. Regardless of the method of finance, command over resources is transferred from private citizens to the government, and the budget is a reflection of this transfer. Expenditures indicate the amount of this transfer as reflected in the debit items on the government's account. The credit items must indicate the same amount, for they refer to the same transfer of resources. Whether expenditures are financed fully by taxation or whether to some extent they are financed by borrowing and money creation does not alter the fact that command over resources is transferred from citizens to government.

The fundamental distinction is really not so much one of balance or imbalance in the budget, but rather is one of whether the balance was achieved explicitly and openly or was achieved implicitly and secretively. Our present accounting convention, in which borrowing and money creation are treated as categorically distinct from taxes and fees, reflects the belief that taxes and fees are in some sense normal or proper, while borrowing and money creation are not. Borrowing and money creation are recognized as being expedient devices that cannot properly be looked upon as a normal part of the public finances of our nation.

There is much wisdom in the categorical difference in the treatment accorded to fees and taxes on the one hand and to borrowing and money creation on the other. While all these devices are means of transferring command over resources from citizens to government, they entail quite distinct ways of achieving this transfer. With fees and taxes, there is an explicit and open transfer of command over resources from citizens to government. It is impossible to increase the utilization of resources by government without reducing to the same extent the utilization of resources by citizens. Taxes and fees are methods of finance that openly acknowledge this necessarily balanced budget nature of government fiscal operations. With borrowing and money creation, no such openness exists. With genuine borrowing, resources appear to be transferred to government by those who buy the bonds. However, bondholders cannot be said to bear any burden, for they are lending to the government now in exchange for a greater return in the future. It is taxpayers who bear the burden, but this burden is not assigned at the time of borrowing. While the actual tax payments to amortize the debt will not be made until some time in the future, their necessity stems from the act of borrowing. Instead of this liability being made explicit at the time of borrowing, it is left as something to be worked out when the debt is amortized some time in the future.

It is the same with money creation. When government finances its activities by creating money, it erodes the real value of the money possessed by citizens. Money creation is equivalent to a tax on money, and it is a tax that operates by debasing the value of money. A doubling of the stock of money is essentially the same thing as taxing away one-half of the money possessed by each citizen. There is, however, a fundamental difference between creating money and taxing money holdings. In the latter case, government acts openly and aboveboard, but in the former case it does not. With money creation, the essential nature of its actions is hidden from view and is, to a large extent, obscure. The view, reflected in our accounting conventions, that money creation should not be regarded as a normal credit item in the government's account, though a tax on money holdings certainly would be so regarded, reflects ultimately the view that government should normally conduct its affairs in an open manner. An argument for a balanced budget is basically an argument for truth in packaging.

There is good reason for what might be called truth in packaging in government. It has long been recognized that the effective and responsive conduct of budgetary policy in a democracy requires that politicians bear the responsibility for their budgetary choices. It is indisputable that people will generally make better choices when they bear the responsibility for the consequences of those choices than if they are able to escape that responsibility. Tax finance forces legislators to take responsibility for their budgetary decisions; if they approve a greater utilization of resources through government, they must at the same time impose the higher taxes necessary to transfer command over the resources from taxpayers to government. Borrowing or money creation weakens this responsibility, for politicians need not face up openly to the transfer of resources implied by their budgetary decisions. A balanced budget requirement would promote responsibility or accountability in budgetary decision-making.

In 1896, Knut Wicksell articulated what is perhaps the essence of fiscal wisdom.[16] Wicksell set out not only to elaborate principles for effective budgetary decision-making but also to describe a set of constitutional rules that would implement such principles. Wicksell recognized that such a constitution would need to contain several elements. One exceedingly important element for fiscal responsibility, Wicksell recognized, was that proposals for expenditures must be coupled with proposals for covering the cost. If a legislator is able to propose expenditure programs without having to make an explicit proposal to cover the cost, fiscal irresponsibility will creep in because the legislator can get away with promising benefits without saying from whom the resources will be taken. Each budgetary debit necessarily has an equivalent credit that reflects that transfer of the command over resources from citizens to government. A rule that requires an open recognition of this inherently two-sided nature of government budgets promotes fiscal responsibility.

The balanced budget requirement is simply a requirement that government should make explicit the resource extractions promised by and implied in its expenditure promises. If a politician is to promise expenditure programs for his constituents, he should be asked to take responsibility for covering the cost of those programs as well. This simple point is the true meaning of the balanced budget amendment. What is wrong with requiring that people take responsibility for their actions? We expect it of ourselves—and of our children as they mature. Why should we not expect it of our politicians as well?

VI. Content of a Balanced Budget Amendment

A balanced budget is not some weird idea on the fringes of fiscal sanity. Quite the contrary, it is a practice that enhances sanity and responsibility in fiscal decision-making. While sound fiscal principle is on the side of a balanced budget, several aspects of a balanced budget amendment must be considered in any effort to make the transition from principle to practice. In particular, consideration must be given to the appropriate definition of the budget to be balanced, as well as to whether deficits will ever be allowed and what will be done about budget surpluses.

What "Budget" Should Be Balanced?

A balanced budget amendment would contain a clause stating something like "total outlays shall not exceed total receipts during any fiscal year." This statement seems clear enough, one might think. But there is no unambiguous meaning to the total outlays of government since there is much scope for sleight-of-hand maneuver in preparing a budget. The definition of a budget would have to address just what "budget" it is that is to be balanced.

The federal budget is a huge accounting document that details the various receipts and disbursements of the United States government. The receipts side of the federal budget is relatively simple. The biggest item is the individual income tax, a bite we all feel each month when it is withheld from our paychecks. Other federal receipts include corporation income taxes, excise taxes, social insurance taxes, and various other smaller sources of tax revenue. The expenditure side of the federal budget is quite complicated. The normal categories of expenditure go on and on, and include such well-known items as defense, transportation, health, agriculture, and research. For every gray brown building in Washington, there is an expenditure series. The magnitude of the funds involved in these expenditures is immense—on the order of $500 million in 1979. If spacemen could walk on dollar bills, they could easily visit the distant planets by walking on the dollars the federal government spends.

The figures in the budget mask a fairly involved budgetary process through which the numerous agencies of the government obtain their operating funds. This process runs through a cycle from budget preparation by the executive branch, to review and appropriations by Congress, to agency expenditure, and, finally, to an audit of agency operations to insure conformity with the law. The essence of this process, of course, consists of the negotiations between the executive branch, including its various agencies and bureaus, and the relevant committees in Congress for budgets to finance the myriad governmental activities that we see.

The sheer magnitude of the budget and of the process whereby it is evolved make the definition of what "budget" should be balanced a very important issue. In the face of the tremendous complexity of the budget and the budgetary process, one may reasonably wonder whether the balanced budget amendment is a *practical* proposal. While we feel that budget balance is a quite practical procedure for the government to follow, there are several aspects of a definition of the budget to be balanced that must be addressed in any effort to draft a balanced budget amendment.

There are some transactions that are never included in the government's budget, yet reflect government control over the allocation of resources. Similarly, there are some borrowing operations by government-linked agencies that do not enter into the totals for national debt. These various transactions are referred to as "off-budget" items. There are several ways of assessing the significance of these items. A deficit in the regular budget of $60 billion for 1979 would be increased to the vicinity of $100 billion by inclusion of the off-budget items. Put somewhat differently, the debt associated with such items would increase the amount of the federal debt by about 30 percent.

Many of these off-budget items relate to federal activities of an essentially commercial nature. The federal government operates a large number of quite substantial commercial enterprises. These include the Tennessee Valley Authority, the Federal Housing Administration, the Federal Deposit Insurance Corporation, the Commodity Credit Corporation, and the Postal Service. According to the way the government keeps its accounts, only the net income (positive or negative) plus the capital expenditures of these enterprises, rather than their gross expenditures and revenues, enter the budget.

While it is true that the receipts of such agencies as the Tennessee Valley Authority can be balanced against their expenses, it is nonetheless appropriate to treat the gross receipts and expenditures of these commercial operations as one would treat the receipts and expenditures of any other public program. For purposes of budgetary assessment and control, there is no particular substantive difference between the Tennessee Valley Authority and related ventures on the one hand, and the regular budgetary activities of government on the other. In both cases, resources are being directed through government action. It makes little difference whether the control over resources is attained through taxes or through prices. The extent of government's command over resources is not altered by changes in the way it gains that command. The present accounting treatment of the commercial activities of the federal government buries the total costs of such activities. The balanced budget amendment would need to come to terms with the treatment of such commercial activities. The reasonable course seems to be to include all the expenditures of the commercial agencies of government in the budget that is to be balanced.

Since the budget excludes many programs, it understates the fiscal impact of government. There are a number of loan and guaranty programs that are understated in either their budgetary magnitude or their implication for the amount of government debt. A partial listing of these agencies includes the Farm Credit Administration, the Federal National Mortgage Association, the Student Loan Marketing Association, the Rural Electrification Administration, and the Pension Benefit Guaranty Corporation. It is important that the budget come to include the money used to finance such activities and to cover their defaults so that it can reflect more accurately and adequately the government's claim on the allocation of resources.

There is an additional problem in defining the government's budget. Budgets refer to transactions that take place between two dates, typically one year apart. In many instances, legislation entails commitments in future years. For instance, social security legislation that increases benefits will increase expenditures in the future. Many of the financial problems of some of our large cities came about because public employee wage increases took the form of increases in pension benefits. A smaller immediate wage increase took place in exchange for a larger future payment. By doing this, city budgets appeared to be balanced because current revenues covered current expenditures. The explosion in future expenditure levels implied by the initial wage agreements was irrelevant to the requirement of a balanced budget. There apparently is always some way to fit within the requirements of a balanced budget today by promising even larger expenditures in the future. The only solution to this temptation is to institute a system of present value accounting in which the budget is balanced in present value terms. This would be exceedingly complex and extraordinarily arbitrary, and could in no sense be looked upon as a useful technique. All that can be said on this point is that the future obligations implied by present programs can be a source of budgetary growth, and it is important to be wary of these future items.

How Often Should the Budget Be Balanced?

We noted earlier that a balanced budget amendment would undoubtedly require a balanced budget each fiscal year. There is probably nothing essential about having the period over which balance is defined correspond to the time it takes for the earth to travel around the sun. One could easily propose shorter or longer periods, and one might reasonably wonder whether there is anything of particular importance about requiring a balanced budget on an annual basis. It could be argued that it makes little difference whether the budget is balanced over a one-year or a five-year period.

Nonetheless, we feel that such arguments ignore the basic reasons for the annual budgetary process that we presently have and to which the balanced budget amendment would apply. This process is designed to allow legislators to monitor and to control the activities of governmental agencies and their performance in carrying out the legislative mandates. Moreover, in a basic political sense, longer budgetary periods would insulate government programs from democratic controls. For example, a one-term president or a two-term member of the House of Representatives might find that he could have no impact on the budget if budgeting were done on a five-year cycle.

The reasons for annual budgeting are, therefore, related to the democratic control of the activities of governmental bureaucracies, and these reasons surely override any abstract case for budgeting over longer periods of time. Since the government conducts its business on an annual basis, this is the period of time that is pertinent to the balanced budget amendment. Moreover, the more frequently budgetary review takes place, the closer can be legislative scrutiny of bureaus and agencies. Thus annual budget balance makes both political and economic sense.

Should There Be a Separate Capital Budget?

A closely related criticism of the annual balanced budget approach concerns whether government should be allowed to issue debt in order to finance capital projects. These projects may take several years to complete and will generate output over a long period of time. Large expenditures are required to build a road in the present period, yet the benefits of the road will accrue to citizens in the indefinite future. Should not government, like a corporation, be allowed to issue debt to undertake such a project? Should not the annual budget balance rule be amended so as to separate current and capital account expenditures? It might seem as though only the current account budget should be required to be in balance. A separate capital budget could be created, with the current account budget reflecting only the amortization payments on the debt issued to finance the capital projects.

Despite the intuitive appeal this argument might have, a separate capital budget would not be a good idea. Among other things, a separate capital budget would render the political control of government spending even more difficult. This can be seen by comparing two different instances of political choice.

In the first instance, legislators vote on building a road system and in so doing, have the option of choosing to finance the capital outlays through debt issue. For these legislators there are no present tax costs of voting in favor of the project. The fiscal costs of the program lie in the future as the debt to finance the project is amortized and paid off. Moreover, these legislators are confronted with the extremely "lumpy" decision of whether or not to build the *entire* road system, and the consequences of this decision will fall on future legislators and taxpayers. There will most certainly be a bias toward voting for such projects and toward a not too careful evaluation of the relevant costs and benefits of such programs.

In the second instance, legislators must decide on the road project under a requirement of annual budget balance. Here, the development expenditures for the project must be pay-as-you-go, so to speak, in the budgetary periods in which they are incurred, and these expenses have to be paid from current tax revenues.

The bias is in the opposite direction from that in the first example. Legislators will have an incentive to scrutinize the costs and benefits of capital projects very carefully before casting their votes because present taxpayers will bear a large part of the cost of providing the road project. One might argue that such a situation would produce a bias against long-term capital projects by government. The issue would thus seem to boil down to the particular bias that one prefers—"too little" or "too much" public capital development.

However, the annual budget balance rule seems preferable because it gives political decision makers more incentive to evaluate carefully the pros and cons of public projects. Moreover, the presumption that current-period finance of capital projects would invoke a bias against such projects is not so certain as it might appear at first glance. For example, capital expenditures would be spread fairly evenly over the time that it takes to complete a project, and such projects usually take years (consider the Interstate Highway System). Each period's expenditures could be evaluated by each period's legislators. While some benefits to future taxpayers might still remain to be financed by present taxpayers, these might not be significant in practice. Indeed, a road system that is financed by current taxes over a series of years can be monitored for the feasibility of *marginal* additions more carefully than can a system financed entirely through debt issue.

Annual budget balance is, therefore, a good idea because it places useful and meaningful constraints on political choice. This is not to say that it is a *perfect* rule for the conduct of government, for there are no perfect rules for the conduct of something so massive as our government. The problem is to search for feasible, workable rules that encourage political decision makers to act as if they had good common sense. A rule of annual budget balance and careful up-front monitoring of the viability of long-term government projects seems to be the wisest course of action.

What Should Be Done with Government Surpluses?

In practice, the fiscal officers of the federal government cannot be expected to predict and plan an exactly balanced budget each year with pinpoint accuracy. To avoid deficits, then, each year's budget will probably have to aim at a small surplus. These surpluses raise several issues.

One use of budget surpluses would be to reduce the national debt. The Treasury could use its excess revenues to purchase government bonds from private citizens. If this were done, the surpluses would serve to reduce the interest-carrying cost of the debt over time. The surpluses will also make future taxpayers better off, for in the future there will be less public debt to be amortized and paid off.

A second use of budget surpluses would be to reduce taxes. While the debt retirement proposal would tend to favor future taxpayers, a tax reduction proposal would tend to favor present taxpayers. Of course, where the relevant surplus was small and resulted from planning to avoid deficits, the amount of the tax rebate would be small. Where the surplus evolved out of unusual growth in government tax revenues, the rebates would be more substantial, or, under the debt retirement proposal, more public debt could be liquidated.

There is no purely scientific way to resolve the choice between the alternative uses of government surpluses under a balanced budget regime. We tend to favor tax rebates because tax relief for the present generation of taxpayers is a paramount goal of virtually all fiscal reform groups. Indeed, since a balanced budget program that effectively constrains government would have very desirable consequences for future taxpayers in its own right, to couple such a proposal with debt retirement in effect gives a double subsidy to our children. Present tax relief for us and an effectively limited government for them seems to be a fair way to split the difference.

Could Government Ever Run a Deficit?

Surely no reasonable man would quarrel with the government's being allowed to resort to deficit finance in a period of emergency. However, some important qualifications must be attached. Since every politician tends to treat his pet issue as a national emergency, we must consider how "emergencies" will be defined for the purpose of allowing the government to issue debt.

A more restrictive voting rule would be the most effective means of defining emergencies for the purpose of making decisions about deficit finance. Under such a rule, after the president had declared an emergency, the Congress could authorize by a two-thirds vote in each house specified outlays in excess of the required budget limits. Emergencies, like treaties, would be defined by the number of votes required to authorize them. There would thus have to be a broad agreement among all legislators that a *bona fide* emergency existed before escape from a balanced budget amendment would be possible.

In this procedural approach to the definition of a state of emergency, the content of the emergency would not matter. An emergency would be whatever two-thirds of each house of Congress would declare it to be. An emergency could stem from a desire to fight a war; it could also stem from an unanticipated shortage of receipts. What matters is not the content but the procedure followed in circumventing the balanced budget requirement. It would also seem important to place some limit on the length of time that a declaration of emergency could remain in force. This period might be one year or two years, but it would hardly seem reasonable to have it extend for a longer period. And the time limit should be definite rather than indefinite or open-ended.

Although we can find nothing to complain about in the belief that it should take broad agreement to violate the balanced budget clause, we would, however, also make the point that in light of the size of Democratic majorities in the House and Senate in recent years, and in light of the fact that many politicians tend to view every issue as an emergency, some consideration ought to be given to a more inclusive voting rule for the definition of emergencies. The voting rule for legislative decisions has a profound impact on budgetary outcomes, and there is nothing sacred about the simple-majority rule. The primary effects of increasing the restrictiveness of the voting rule would be (1) to make legislators work harder to achieve a consensus for their proposals, and (2) to decrease the size of the minority that could be exploited (*e.g.*, taxed for someone else's benefit) by a collective decision. Neither effect presents a problem. Legislators are handsomely paid to legislate, and we should not avoid making their work more difficult. Making it more difficult for politicians to benefit some groups at the expense of others would also be beneficial. As we shall explain a bit more fully in our final chapter, there is nothing hallowed about the simple-majority rule in *any* collective decision. It is entirely conceivable that the overall quality of collective decision-making and of public economic policy would rise appreciably if the normal voting rule for *all* public business, not just for the declaration of states of emergency, were made more restrictive.

VII. Implementation of a Balanced Budget Amendment

It would not be too difficult to develop the specific content of a balanced budget amendment. Once this content was selected, it would still be necessary to implement the amendment. Several questions arise about making the transition from our present regime of chronic deficits to one guided by the constitutional requirement of a balanced budget. One relatively simple question is the length of time that would be allowed to elapse before the amendment would take effect. A one- or two-year period would seem sensible. However, a couple of other issues of implementation are more troublesome.

Budget Balance and State and Local Governments

Once it became clear that the forces in favor of budget balance were gathering significant political strength, various legislators at the federal level reacted by stating that the first objects of expenditure reduction would undoubtedly be federal grants to state and local governments, particularly units of government in states that were supporting the balanced budget movement. We can understand why federal politicians would issue such a thinly veiled threat. Budget balance carries many negative implications for their prerogatives of office. For example, many of their pet projects would disappear under a regime of budget balance. However, such threats illustrate the depraved level to which some federal politicians have fallen. Such threats seem equivalent to a small child's saying that he will not play with you anymore unless he can have his own way.

As a political tactic, however, the threat to cut off aid to state and local governments is probably an empty one. Above all else, Congress is a geographical battleground for public expenditures. Accordingly, the pattern of federal allocations among states results from a complicated process of vote trading among legislators, the plain talk version of which is "you scratch my back and I'll scratch yours." Within this system of allocating federal expenditures among states, it would be difficult for politicians to agree to cut off federal programs in only selected states. It would also probably be illegal. In practice, then, the threats of the federal politicians to punish states that go along with budget balance are not viable. And it is equally unlikely that the change to a balanced budget would be attained wholly by a reduction in federal payments to state and local governments.

In two senses, federal aid to state and local governments poses an interesting problem under a regime of budget balance. In one sense, the threats of the federal politicians to cut such aid may be an indication that expenditure in this area is of only marginal significance and can be easily pared back or stopped entirely. Maybe the federal legislators are right, and the best place to start reducing expenditures is in the area of federal aid to state and local governments. One suspects that this is not the case, or at least that politicians have not carefully thought through the matter of where to cut spending, so that such threats are just threats, pure and simple. But their comments do provide some food for thought about where to begin the process of reducing government.

The second sense in which federal aid to state and local governments poses an interesting issue concerns the appropriate form of federal-state economic relations under a regime of budget balance. Economists and other analysts have hashed over this issue for years, and there exists a variety of rationales for block grants, conditional grants, and so forth. We do not want to get into the issue of what form of federal assistance is the "best." Actually, Governor Reagan's statement that federal revenues returned to the states should never have been sent to Washington in the first place has much to recommend it as a program of intergovernmental aid. Under this scheme federal legislators could vote on aid allocation among the states, but as tax revenues came in, they would not be sent to Washington for the usual bureaucratic brokerage fee but could be retained and spent in the state in which they were collected. Whether this spending would be controlled by federal or state officials is an open question in this proposal, but the general drift of our argument, like Reagan's, would be to let states have full authority in the spending of these moneys.

The main point here, however, is not to advocate a specific program of intergovernmental relations but to suggest that the organization of these relations is a question of some importance that lies outside the realm of the balanced budget proposal. The primary thing to avoid in adopting a balanced budget requirement is any sort of silly, shortsighted, punitive action by federal politicians against states that seek this reform.

A final point about budget balance and intergovernmental relations is that the impulse of federal politicians to respond to budget balance by *mandating* expenditures by lower level governments must also be avoided. Mandating refers to federal agencies' practice of requiring of state and local governments certain expenditures, to be financed by state and local taxation. Mandating thus is a possible escape valve from the principle of budget balance, because federal politicians could cut back certain federal expenditures but require that they be undertaken by lower level governments. The net effect would be no change in public spending, but only a shifting of the locus of finance of these expenditures. Such escape routes must be closed off in a constitutional amendment.

The issues that some federal politicians have raised about what would happen to federal payments to state and local governments does point to a pertinent aspect of the implementation of a balanced budget amendment. Expenditures would have to be reduced relative to revenues. The strong and growing opposition to spending, on the average, more than 40 percent of one's working time to pay taxes suggests that some reduction in expenditures would be necessary. As with the two-thirds voting rule for escaping the balanced budget requirement in the case of a national emergency, the exact nature of expenditure reductions used to balance the budget is less important than the procedural constraint of budget balance that would require their reduction relative to revenues.

Budget Balance and Constitutional Choice

Many observers have expressed concern about calling a constitutional convention to consider a balanced budget amendment, and various arguments have been put forward against such an experiment in democratic decision-making. Two types of arguments have been advanced. One rests on the elitist premise that the "people" are not competent to take the processes of democracy into their own hands, even for a brief period. The other consists of fears about how such a convention might actually be conducted. Upon inspection, it becomes apparent that both types of argument rest on the flimsiest of foundations.

The concern of the elitists about a constitutional convention appears to have simple roots. In this view there are "leaders" and "followers." While it is fair game to disagree over which "leaders" should be in power at any particular time, heaven forbid that the "followers" should suddenly usurp the role of the "leaders." Only the special, hallowed few have the background and understanding that one must have to function as a productive participant in the legislative process. One form of this argument is that one must have certain special skills to be a good legislator. Legislators who are lawyers commonly think that these skills should include legal training. While there may be some merit in their position, we see many quite competent legislators who are not lawyers. It does not seem, therefore, that one would need to be a constitutional lawyer in order to be an effective legislator at a constitutional convention.

If background is not crucial, then, it would seem that the professed concerns of the elitists are simply a reflection of their fear of the consequences of a regime of budget balance. That is, they disagree with the idea of budget balance, and they endeavor to cast doubt on it by discrediting the view that a constitutional convention would be workable. Presumably, they are afraid—probably correctly so— that many of their prerogatives would vanish under a regime of budget balance. While it is normal and rational for existing politicians to try to protect their vested interests in big government, it is easy to see through such arguments, and they should be given no credibility whatsoever. It is thus easy to understand why most of the denizens of Washington do not want a constitutional convention to decide the question of budget balance. It has nothing to do with the competence of the people to legislate; it has to do with the protection of the prerogatives of those denizens.

At a substantive level, various types of consideration—fears, some might say—about a constitutional convention have been raised. A common concern is that we do not now have any Hamiltons or Madisons to guide our constitutional choices. The wisdom of 1789 appears to be lacking in 1979, and men of vision are extremely rare birds these days. But as a substantive criticism of a constitutional convention for the consideration of a balanced budget amendment, this is surely a trivial complaint. As we stressed above, one does not have to be a constitutional lawyer or scholar to appreciate the common sense of budget balance. Furthermore, expert advice is abundant, and one would think that it could be easily and amply supplied, if needed, to a present-day constitutional convention. Moreover, unlike the convention of 1789, the proposed constitutional convention for budget balance would not deal with a sweeping range of issues concerning the entire governmental process. It would focus only on budget and related reforms, rather than on a whole gamut of constitutional issues. A demand for wide-ranging expertise among the delegates to such a convention would, therefore, not be essential or crucial to the quality of the deliberations. Delegates would need only an understanding of the simple common sense basis of budget balance.

To go back to an issue raised above in a slightly different context, there may also be some genuine concern about the background of the delegates to a modern constitutional convention. These delegates would be drawn from the interested citizens of each state. In effect, they would represent a cross section of the country, and surely many state and local politicians would be elected as delegates and would play an important role. Many points of view would thus be brought to bear on the questions of fiscal reform, and, even more importantly, the level of disinterestedness among the delegates would be high. This latter condition is crucial to making long-run decisions about the health of the polity, since individuals must rise above their temporary stakes in an issue and choose a wise course of action for the future. This condition would be met at a once-and-for-all constitutional convention, since after the convention ended, the delegates would return to their normal pursuits. That is, they would have no short-run, vested interests in their decisions besides the *pro rata* benefits of controlling government through a constitutional amendment. In fact, this element of disinterestedness is a strong point in favor of fiscal reform via a constitutional convention rather than by the narrow, shortsighted, vested interests that inhabit the halls of Congress. Congress, for example, routinely repeals the legislative debt limitation each year to accommodate deficits. There is thus not much to fear from calling a constitutional convention to consider a balanced budget amendment; indeed, there is much to be gained.

The whole issue of a constitutional convention can be easily avoided. All that is necessary is for Congress to pass a balanced budget amendment for the consideration of the various state legislatures. If the present Washington politicians fear a more elemental exercise of democratic power, they can save us all time and trouble by proposing the amendment themselves. There are dangers in this route, however, dangers which make the route of a convention more reliable for achieving the desired reforms. For one thing, the present Congress might offer to balance the budget annually, thereby ostensibly obviating the need for a constitutional amendment. Such offers should be rejected, for they are binding only on the present generation of legislators. Moreover, as we mentioned previously, Congress might offer a balanced budget amendment with one hand and take it away with the other by threatening to withhold aid from the states that ultimately must decide whether to support it.

So while Congress could avoid the time and trouble of a constitutional convention by passing a budget balance proposal, our general view is that this is equivalent to putting the fox in charge of the henhouse. As a practical matter, a constitutional convention would be a viable enterprise. As an intellectual matter, it would be healthy for the people to go through the exercise of controlling the fiscal activities of government. In the process, many issues that trouble constitutional scholars—such as how a convention would be organized—could be settled, and guidelines for future constitutional revisions could be laid down. Who knows, if entrenched politicians continue on their merry ways, feathering their own nests and ignoring the more basic issues confronting us, constitutional conventions may become quite the rage. And, surely, the more practice we have at constitutional choices, the better at it we will become.

Alternative Strategies for Fiscal Reform

The balanced budget amendment, however, is only one of numerous proposals to place fiscal limitations on government in the United States. At the level of state government, state constitutions already impose numerous taxation and expenditure limitations, and numerous "sons of Proposition 13" have been proposed or are on the drawing boards of constitutional reformers. The various proposals for tax or expenditure limitation embody different *approaches* to the establishment of fiscal controls from those which we have examined here, but there is, nonetheless, a strong complementarity among the proposals since their *goal* is to control the growth of government.

The tax limitation amendment would limit *spending* by the federal government. As proposed by the National Tax Limitation Committee, a quantitative limit would be placed on the annual percentage increase in federal spending. This increase would be equal to the percentage increase in nominal gross national product during the last calendar year prior to the beginning of the same fiscal year. Moreover, if the inflation rate exceeds 3 percent for the last calendar year, the permitted percentage increase in federal spending during the subsequent fiscal year would have to be reduced by one-fourth of the percentage by which the inflation rate exceeds 3 percent.

In the absence of a balanced budget amendment, tax limitation would be likely to lead to even larger deficits and money creation in an effort to escape the tax limits. When combined with a balanced budget requirement, however, a greater measure of control over the size of government can be exercised. There is, it should be noted, one very important difference between the tax limitation approach and the balanced budget approach. The tax limitation approach makes no effort to deal with the reasons why government has become so wastefully large. It treats the symptoms rather than the cause of our troubles. It recognizes that the government is out of control but does not inquire into or attempt to correct the institutional defects that create this situation. The balanced budget approach, on the other hand, reflects an awareness that there are institutional defects that produce our difficulties with government and further reflects a desire to remedy these defects through modification of the institutional order within which budgetary decisions are made.

A balanced budget by itself is, of course, no panacea. However, the irresponsibility that is possible because the cost of government programs can be left implicit rather than made explicit is addressed and remedied by the balanced budget amendment. The balanced budget amendment represents a desirable first step in creating a set of fiscal institutions that will soften the conflict between democracy and prosperity—a conflict that has been developing over the past generation or so. We have nothing to lose by adopting the balanced budget amendment except the economic troubles that result from a set of political institutions that are not consistent with the essential requirements of fiscal and economic responsibility.

VIII. Institutional Requisites for a Prosperous Democracy: The Steps Remaining

Our economic performance in recent times can only be described as horrendous. Over the past decade real disposable income—allowing for inflation and taxes—has declined for about 20 percent of all American families.

This horrendous performance is due to defects in our present system for making budgetary choices. The ability to promise government expenditures without at the same time making commitments for financing them is one very substantial defect. The balanced budget amendment would address this defect. But there are also other defects in our constitutional framework for making budgetary choices.

Constitutional Reform beyond Budget Balance

One other major defect is the increasing ability of smaller and smaller subsets of the legislative assembly to implement budgetary decisions. It could be remedied by requiring that budgetary decisions be made, not by a simple majority of legislators, but by some qualified majority, comprising say three-fourths or more of the legislature. The reason for this proposal is to curtail further the scope for irresponsible fiscal action. As fewer legislators are required to approve budgetary actions, it becomes easier for special interest groups to impose the cost of their programs on those who do not benefit from the programs. The simple majority vote, for instance, makes it possible to enact expenditure programs that provide moderate benefits for 51 percent of the population while imposing substantial costs on the remaining 49 percent. As a consequence, many wasteful programs can be enacted, and government can become quite bloated. As voting rules become more restrictive, the opportunity for this type of fiscal irresponsibility diminishes. However, the trend in legislative assemblies has been in the opposite direction. With the development of a large legislative agenda, committee specialization increases. With much congressional decision-making delegated to such committees, decisions come to be made by less than a majority of participants.[17] Rule by minorities comes to occur, and it becomes possible to pass legislation that imposes more costs than benefits on most citizens.

There are other defects of existing budgetary processes that cannot be addressed in this monograph. With the growth of government, power has been shifting from the legislature to the bureaucracy. There has been a substantial increase in the relative importance of the bureaucracy, whether measured by the number of government agencies per legislator, by the number of government employees per legislator, or by some other indicator. This has led to an increase in the ability of various interests to enact budgets, leading to a further reduction in the consensus required before budgetary action can be taken. The Federal Reserve System of independent monetary control is yet another defect. And there are many more, which must be remedied by strategies other than a balanced budget if government is to be brought under control.

Appendix: Budgetary Equivalence of Government Regulation

The balanced budget amendment is designed to restrain the growth of public expenditures, and we have argued that budget balance is a useful first step in this regard. However, government affects our lives in many ways, not all of which can be summarized in the expenditures of the various agencies of the government. Government regulation is an example. The budgets of the various regulatory agencies of the government represent an extremely small proportion of federal expenditure. As direct expenditures for resources, these agencies do not "cost" taxpayers very much. As we shall see, however, the extent of their real impact on the economy far exceeds their budgetary cost to taxpayers.

In principle, anything that can be accomplished through the taxing and spending aspects of the budget can be accomplished instead through government regulation. A war can be fought by raising taxes and using the resources to hire the necessary labor, materials, and equipment. Alternatively, it could be fought by requiring that people simply make the needed labor and resources available. Education can likewise be provided by extracting taxes and using the proceeds to hire the necessary labor and facilities. It could also be provided without budgetary outlay simply by requiring parents to see that their children receive a stipulated education. Any adjustment in the allocation of resources that can be achieved through a budget can also be achieved through a program of government regulation.

The fundamental issue that we must confront in discussing government regulation is *why* government regulates the private economy. Modern economics has two theories of government regulation. An examination of these different theories will relate to and reinforce our earlier discussions about political processes and the constraining function of constitutions.

One theoretical approach stresses the reasons why the market economy fails to function properly in allocating resources, and proposes government intervention in the private economy to regulate and to "correct" such market failures. This approach rests on the value judgment that government *can* increase social welfare by intervening in the private sector. In this view the state is a *productive* entity that produces public goods, internalizes social costs and benefits, regulates natural monopolies effectively, redistributes income to obtain social justice, and in general is an all-around good guy.[18]

The second approach to understanding government regulation is based upon a recognition that in many instances there is a sizable gap between standard economic rationalizations for government intervention in the economy and the actual instances of state intervention. While the first approach might be termed the market-failure approach, the second approach to analyzing government regulation can be called the government-failure approach. This latter approach is based on the observed imperfections of governmental "solutions" to private "problems." The government-failure approach thus stresses that the market-failure approach is flawed by the unwarranted assumption that government can be called upon to correct imperfect markets in a costless and perfect manner. We hardly need demonstrate that the state is not a perfect instrument for doing anything.

What does this government-failure approach imply for government regulation? Primarily, it leads to a rejection of the market-failure approach to understanding why government regulates the private sector. While it is nice to think of governmental agents as selfless seekers after the public interest, this is not a very useful way to discuss government regulation. A public agent will no more pursue something called the public interest, as contrasted with pursuing his or her personal interest, than will a private agent. Public interest is an outcome of the pursuit of personal interest within a given institutional framework. Private firms in a competitive market adapt their production to the efficient satisfaction of consumer desires. They do this not from any self-effacing desire to sacrifice for consumer gain, but rather from a recognition that within a competitive institutional framework, this is the way in which they can best enhance their own prosperity. Likewise, the institutional framework of the public economy and the actions of self-interested agents in that setting serve as appropriate focal points for the analysis of government regulation.

In this analysis, what can be said about the origin of government regulation of the economy? Primarily, regulation comes about in this theory as the result of interest groups lobbying for protection from competition. The common line of analysis says that small groups of producers are able to effect a cartel through government regulation of entry and prices in their industry. This cartel operates at the expense of consumers and society generally. Producers are small enough in numbers to make the returns from lobbying exceed the costs, and despite the loss in real income that they suffer from monopoly-enhancing regulation, consumers will normally succumb to producer interests because consumers are a large and widely dispersed group that faces high costs of organizing to resist regulations in favor of producer monopoly. While this story fits some cases of government regulation (*e.g.*, the ICC), it is too monolithic to serve as a general theory of regulation. A more general theory would stress the configuration of costs and benefits that various interest groups face for seeking wealth transfers through the state and the fact that government regulation is not monolithically oriented to favor producer interests. Indeed, some of the most powerful and effective lobbying groups are large groups of laborers, *e.g.*, labor unions.[19]

However one chooses to do the analysis, the crux of this theory of government regulation is that the goal of groups who seek regulation is somehow to transfer wealth to themselves. Such activity is made possible by voter shirking. Voting is costly, and individuals will let their wealth be taken away from them so long as the costs of changing political decisions are greater than the amount of wealth taken away. Going back to our earlier discussion of voting rules and collective choice procedures, if collective decisions are easily influenced, only small amounts of wealth transfer will be allowed. As the costs of monitoring and sanctioning collective decisions rise, a larger quantity of wealth transfer via government regulation will take place.

We have now addressed the question of why government regulation exists; it exists as a means of wealth transfer to successful interest groups. These transfers are, in effect, a form of taxation. When they are combined with the associated economic costs of government regulation, their impact on the economy far exceeds the budgetary expenditures of the regulatory agencies. We turn now to a closer consideration of the nature of these costs of government regulation.

Essentially, there are two major types of cost of monopoly-inspired government regulation. The first is what conventional economics refers to as the welfare cost of monopoly. Government regulation typically restricts competition in an industry by banning both entry by outsiders and price competition by regulated producers (entry from within). These actions cause prices in the industry to rise toward a monopoly level. As prices rise above the competitive level, there are two effects in the market for the industry's output. First, some income is transferred from consumers to producers in the form of monopoly rents. This is an example of the wealth transfers that we discussed above, and we shall have more to say about it shortly. Second, as prices rise above the competitive level in the regulated industry, some consumers will refrain from purchasing the industry's product at higher prices. These consumers, who are priced out of the market, incur a loss that no one recoups. It is this loss that economists normally refer to as the welfare cost of monopoly.[20] The magnitude of this cost varies with the type and scope of government regulation of industry, and has been estimated to be in excess of $100 billion annually.

What about the other effect of higher prices due to government regulation—the transfer of income from consumers to producers? As we stressed above, producers will expand resources to lobby for these transfers. The fact that resources are employed to effect a pure transfer of wealth leads to a second cost of government regulation, which has been termed the rent-seeking cost of monopoly and regulation.

Rent-seeking may be explained by an example. An interest group hires a lawyer to represent to government officials its interest in higher prices. The worth of the higher prices to the interest group is represented by the monopoly rents inherent in the price increase. In general, then, the interest group will expend resources to capture these rents up to the value of the expected returns. However, these expenditures by the interest group to transfer income from consumers to themselves do not contribute to the real productive activity of the economy. They are merely expenditures designed to bring about a transfer of income. The cost to the economy of such rent-seeking expenditures is the value of the output that they could have produced had they been gainfully employed elsewhere. The lawyer, for example, could have been closing real estate transactions rather than seeking the transfer for the interest group. Any expenditures by an interest group to capture returns from government regulation are thus a waste from society's point of view, and represent an additional cost of monopoly and regulation to the economy.[21]

In both the case of the traditional cost of monopoly and the rent-seeking cost, then, government regulation imposes significant costs on the economy. The importance of these costs for the present study is twofold. First, and perhaps most important, the regulatory activities of government are normally cloaked in the rhetoric of public interest. Politicians claim that these agencies protect consumers from the power of big business. As we hope to have demonstrated, the basic function of these agencies is to protect us from *lower* prices and a *more efficient* economy.

Second, government regulation has a massive impact on the economy, the costs of which are *not* included in the expenditure totals for government. Control of the budget, therefore, will not control the real costs of government regulation. This is a battle in the fight to control governmental activity—a battle that must be fought *in addition to* the fight to control government expenditures. Moreover, there is no easy route to the deregulation of industry. One conceivable suggestion would be a sunset law, under which all government agencies, but in particular the regulatory agencies, periodically would have to justify their continued existence or otherwise face the prospect of being put out of business. Such a law would supersede the normal budgetary process, wherein all that is at stake in any given year is the increment to next year's budget. If the regulatory bodies had to defend their total operations every five years, there might be a far more reasonable prospect of reducing their impact on the economy. However, this is simply to suggest once again that the balanced budget amendment is only a first step in the process of reform to control government. Down the road surely lies a struggle to rid ourselves of the vast tax burden placed upon us through government regulation.

Notes

1. For a brief sketch of this history, see James M. Buchanan and Richard E. Wagner, *Democracy in Deficit: The Political Legacy of Lord Keynes* (New York: Academic Press, 1977), pp. 11–14.

2. See Benjamin Klein, "Our New Monetary Standard: The Measurement and Effects of Price Uncertainty, 1880–1973," *Economic Inquiry* 13 (December 1975): 461–84.

3. See William Breit, "Starving the Leviathan: Balanced Budget Prescriptions before Keynes," in *Fiscal Responsibility in Constitutional Democracy,* ed. James M. Buchanan and Richard E. Wagner (Leiden: Martinus Nijhoff, 1978), pp. 9–24.

4. C.F. Bastable, *Public Finance,* 3rd ed. (London: Macmillan, 1903), p. 611.

5. Ibid. (Italics added).

6. On this fundamental shift in the framework of budgetary policy, see Lawrence C. Pierce, *The Politics of Fiscal Policy Formation* (Pacific Palisades, Calif.: Goodyear, 1971).

7. Hugh Dalton, *Principles of Public Finance,* 4th ed. (London: Routledge and Kegan Paul, 1954), p. 221. (Italics added.)

8. For a conceptual examination of this point, see Buchanan and Wagner, *Democracy in Deficit.* This analysis is extended to the United Kingdom in James M. Buchanan, John Burton, and Richard E. Wagner, *The Consequences of Mr. Keynes* (London: Institute of Economic Affairs, 1978). Empirical support is developed in W. Mark Crain and Robert B. Ekelund, "Deficits and Democracy," *Southern Economic Journal* 44 (April 1978): 813–28.

9. On the relation between politics and the Federal Reserve Board, see Buchanan and Wagner, *Democracy in Deficit,* pp. 107–24.

10. A seminal exposition of this theme is Friedrich A. Hayek, *Prices and Production*, 2d ed. (London: Routledge and Kegan Paul, 1935). For an extensive survey of the foundations of these matters, see Gerald P. O'Driscoll, Jr., *Economics as a Coordination Problem: The Contributions of Friedrich A. Hayek* (Kansas City: Sheed Andrews and McMeel, 1977).

11. On stagflation, see Gerald P. O'Driscoll, Jr. and Sudha R. Shenoy, "Inflation, Recession, and Stagflation," in *The Foundations of Modern Austrian Economics*, ed. Edwin G. Dolan (Kansas City: Sheed and Ward, 1976), pp. 185–211.

12. The Phillips curve comes from A. W. Phillips, "The Relation between Unemployment and the Rate of Change in Money Wage Rates in the United Kingdom, 1869–1957," *Economica* 25 (November 1958): 283–99. A survey of different perspectives on the Phillips curve is presented in Thomas M. Humphrey, "Changing Views of the Phillips Curve," *Federal Reserve Bank of Richmond*, Monthly Review 59 (July 1973): 2–13.

13. See the development of this line of analysis in Paul A. Samuelson and Robert M. Solow, "Analytical Aspects of Anti-Inflation Policy," *American Economic Review* 50 (May 1960): 177–94.

14. On much of this, see Richard E. Wagner, *Politics, Business Cycles, and Economic Disruption* (New York: Center for Libertarian Studies, forthcoming).

15. On an application of this point to balance-of-payments accounting, see Fritz Machlup, "The Mysterious Numbers Game of Balance-of-Payments Statistics," in *International Payments, Debts, and Gold*, ed. Fritz Machlup (New York: Scribner, 1964), pp. 140–66.

16. Knut Wicksell, *Finanztheoretische Untersuchungen* (Jena: Gustav Fischer, 1896). A large part of this book is translated as "A New Principle of Just Taxation," in *Classics in the Theory of Public Finance*, ed. Richard A. Musgrave and Alan T. Peacock (London: Macmillan, 1958), pp. 72–118.

17. William A. Niskanen, "The Pathology of Politics," in *Capitalism and Freedom: Problems and Prospects*, ed. Richard T. Seldon (Charlottesville: University Press of Virginia, 1975), pp. 20–35.

18. A.C. Pigou is the modern grandfather of this approach. In particular, see his *The Economics of Welfare*, 4th ed. (London: Macmillan, 1932).

19. See George J. Stigler, "The Theory of Economic Regulation," *Bell Journal of Economics and Management Science* 2 (Spring 1971): 3–21; and Sam Peltzman, "Toward a More General Theory of Regulation," *Journal of Law and Economics* 2 (August 1976): 211–40, for two modern presentations of this theory of economic regulation.

20. See Arnold C. Harberger, "Monopoly and Resource Allocation," *American Economic Review* 44 (May 1954): 77–87.

21. For the basic papers on the rent-seeking costs of monopoly and regulation, see Gordon Tullock, "The Welfare Costs of Tariffs, Monopolies, and Theft," *Western Economic Journal* 5 (June 1967): 224–32; Anne O. Krueger, "Political Economy of the Rent-Seeking Society," *American Economic Review* 64 (June 1974): 291–303; and Richard A. Posner, "The Social Cost of Monopoly and Regulation," *Journal of Political Economy* 83 (August 1975): 807–27.

Rabushka sees federal spending as the root cause of federal deficits. However, he favors a constitutional amendment which will both balance the budget and limit taxation.

A COMPELLING CASE FOR A CONSTITUTIONAL AMENDMENT TO BALANCE THE BUDGET AND LIMIT TAXES

Alvin Rabushka

Preface

Throughout 1982 and early 1983, the U.S. economy underwent a severe recession, in the process bringing about a budget deficit of $110 billion in fiscal year 1983 and $195 billion in FY 1984. Throughout most of 1983, and early 1984, the economy briskly recovered, as would be expected in the upswing of a normal business cycle.

Recovery has brought improved productivity, higher real disposable income, and lower marginal tax rates for most taxpayers. However, economic recovery has not solved the budget problem. Government spending has risen to a peacetime record 25 percent of gross national product, while tax receipts remain at 19 percent, leaving a deficit equivalent to 6 percent of GNP, forcing the Treasury to borrow more than half of all personal savings to finance this deficit.

Many fear that a persistent regime of $200 billion and higher deficits threatens to make any recovery shortlived, and that such huge deficits will divert investment capital into consumption expenditure. Proposals to balance the budget are accompanied by recommendations to raise new taxes, thus institutionalizing a higher level of government spending. Until some effective constraint is imposed on the federal budget process, we face increasingly higher levels of spending, taxes, and interest charges to finance the national debt. Therefore, the arguments presented in this essay are as valid as ever and the need for a balanced budget-tax limitation amendment more compelling.

Originally published by the Taxpayers' Foundation, 325 Pennsylvania Ave., Washington, DC 20003. Copyright © 1982 by the Taxpayers' Foundation.

Introduction

On November 26, 1798, a decade after the U.S. Constitution was written, Thomas Jefferson wrote, "I wish it were possible to obtain a single amendment to our Constitution. I would be willing to depend on that alone for the reduction of the administration of our government to the genuine principles of its Constitution; I mean an additional article, taking from the federal government the power of borrowing."

Today, the need for such an amendment to the Constitution is greater than ever. Large and protracted federal deficits have brought havoc to today's economy. The nation's trillion dollar debt represents a true and onerous burden to the average American citizen. The carrying cost on the debt has skyrocketed. The bill we pay arrives in several forms: higher taxes, declining real income, higher interest rates and a recently ended recession.

Are deficits the only cause of our economic troubles? Of course not. Many of the undesirable consequences popularly attributed to deficits would have occurred if government spending and money creation had followed their historic path of the past twenty years even with the budget balanced. However, the burden of taxation on current and future generations would have been quantitatively different. Government debt would be lower, tax rates higher and inflation about the same. The disincentive effects of taxes on investment and employment would not have been avoided. Therefore, in order to preserve our economic and political freedom, it's necessary to both outlaw deficits and to place a cap on taxes such that the size of government, relative to the entire economy, does not increase.

Statutory Reform: Historically and Inherently Flawed

Reforming the federal budget process has been and remains a popular topic with politicians, scholars and taxpayers. Many of the reformers believe that statutory changes in the way Congress conducts its business can bring about a responsible federal budget without resort to a constitutional amendment. Proponents of this view claim that statutory reform would avoid the time-consuming and cumbersome process of amending the Constitution to achieve fiscal restraint. They believe that Congress is capable of drafting legislation that will put its fiscal house back in order. This view has repeatedly been proven false, however.

Concern over reforming the congressional budget process has been debated extensively since 1921. For example, the Revenue Act of 1964 stated:

> To further the objective of balanced budgets in the near future, Congress by this action recognizes the importance of taking all reasonable means to restrain government spending.

The Budget and Impoundment Control Act of 1974 enacted major reforms— the establishment of budget committees within each house, the creation of the Congressional Budget Office to supply timely information and analysis, and the development of a budgetary timetable—to enable Congress to consider individual spending measures in light of overall budget objectives. In the Humphrey-Hawkins Full Employment Act, a balanced budget was declared to be a national public policy priority. An amendment offered by Senator Charles Grassley and former Senator Harry Byrd, Jr. to an IMF loan program measure was enacted into law and requires that, beginning with FY 1981, total budget outlays of the federal government "shall not" exceed its receipts (P.L. 95–435). In 1979, a provision in a measure to increase the public debt limit stated that "Congress shall balance the federal budget" (P.L. 96–5), which required the congressional budget committees to propose balanced budgets for FY 1981 and subsequent years.

None of these measures has effectively constrained deficits. None has reduced the share of national income taxed or spent by government. The most obvious reason for this is that no Congress can bind a succeeding Congress by a simple statute. A balanced budget or tax limitation statute can itself be repealed by the simple expedient of adopting a new statute or new budget which is in conflict with the earlier measure. The Byrd-Grassley amendment, which required a balanced budget for FY 1981, provided no deterrent whatsoever to the adoption of a budget with a $50 billion deficit for that year.

Indeed, legislation passed by Congress has exacerbated the problem of runaway federal spending. A convincing case can be made that control over the budget has steadily declined since the 1974 Act. Despite congressional adherence to the budget timetable, deficits have assumed record proportions: seven deficits exceeded $40 billion in the 1970s, and a regime of $200 billion deficits appears likely during the 1980s. Control over off-budget outlays has eroded even more sharply: Off-budget outlays have increased from less than $1 billion in FY 1973 to surpass $20 billion in FY 1981. Finally, those items in the budget which are known as "uncontrollable" have increased from 71 percent in FY 1973 to 77 percent in the FY 1984 budget. (Technically defined, an uncontrollable is budget authority or an outlay which would require substantive legislation to cancel. These consist chiefly of open-ended entitlements such as Social Security and Medicare, open-ended programs such as interest payments on the national debt and farm price supports, and contracts and obligations entered upon in the past and payable in the present.) Congress has thus been wholly unable to impose its own priorities on the budget.

The source of this failure lies in the fact that there is a structural bias within our political system that causes higher levels of spending, taxing, and deficits than are desired by the people, even though most members of Congress believe that large deficits and excessive government spending damage the economy. This spending bias has yet to be corrected by internal reform, because none of these reforms allow members to cope with spending pressures. As will be demonstrated, the removal of prior constraints calls for the imposition of a new constraint. A constitutional amendment would reimpose those constraints that the framers of the Constitution originally imposed or assumed. It would go a long way to correcting the serious defects in the institutional setting within which Congress now operates.

Amending the Constitution

Article V of the Constitution provides two methods of proposing amendments. The first method, by which all 26 amendments have thus far been adopted, requires the proposal of an amendment by two-thirds of each House of Congress, and ratification by three-fourths of the states. The second method allows for an amendment drawn by a constitutional convention, which must be called by Congress in response to the application of two-thirds of the states. Whichever method is invoked, the proposed amendment must be approved by three-fourths of the states (38) before it becomes part of the Constitution.

Since 1975, the National Taxpayers Union has worked with the state legislatures to pass resolutions—of which thirty-two have thus far been approved—calling upon the Congress to invoke Article V of the Constitution and convene a constitutional convention for the purpose of writing a balanced budget amendment.

In early 1979, largely because of pressure being exerted by the states to convene a constitutional convention, the Senate Judiciary Subcommittee on the Constitution also began efforts to develop its own constitutional proposal to prohibit budget deficits. Senate Joint Resolution 58 (S.J. Res. 58), a combined balanced budget-tax limitation amendment, was reported out of the full Senate Committee on the Judiciary on May 19, 1981. Its companion in the House of Representatives is House Joint Resolution 350. The National Taxpayers Union is still actively working with several state legislatures—trying to bring the constitutional convention movement to a successful conclusion—in the belief that the continued pressure from the states will force the Congress to act. In 1982 such pressure resulted in the passage S. J. Res. 58 by the Senate, although the House rejected the companion bill, H.J. Res. 350.

A balanced budget amendment could overcome the inherent bias for increased federal spending by restoring the link between federal spending and taxing decisions. Under the terms of S.J. Res. 58, Congress could only adopt a planned budget deficit upon a three-fifths vote of the whole membership of both Houses. Moreover, unless Congress approved a bill by a majority vote of both Houses to increase taxes, federal revenues could not grow faster than the private economy; the amendment thus prohibits the federal government from consuming an ever-increasing share of our income.

Americans have come to the realization that the problem of deficits in this country is not one that can be resolved by any one individual or group of individuals. It is an institutional problem requiring a constitutional solution.

Many Americans believed that the election of fiscal conservatives would restore integrity to the conduct of the nation's fiscal business. They believed that a conservative President, Ronald Reagan, working with a conservative Congress would get control over the federal budget process. To their dismay, President Reagan has already abandoned his goal of a balanced budget by 1984. He has proposed future budgets with all-time record deficits, and he has even presided over an overall increase in government spending as a share of Gross National Product. The national debt, which surpassed $1 trillion in October 1981, is now forecast to grow by half-a-trillion dollars by 1985.

As a result of this abysmal failure to bring deficits under control, support for a balanced budget amendment now transcends both members of Congress and the state legislatures. Despairing of the federal government's ability to restrain spending and eliminate deficits, the American public has expressed its support for a constitutional amendment to require a balanced federal budget. According to Gallup, 80 percent of all Americans favor such an amendment.

Had the founding fathers not taken for granted the concepts of limited government, they might have incorporated a balanced budget amendment into the original constitution. Indeed, it was the sixteenth amendment, which authorized Congress to "lay and collect taxes on incomes," that is at the root of our present discontent with the budget process. Without a progressive income tax code, government spending might be substantially lower and the need for a restraining amendment correspondingly less.

175 Years of Fiscal Prudence

The founding fathers adopted two explicit constitutional provisions and assumed a third which served to restrain spending. One reserved powers not expressly delegated to the federal government to the states and to the people. The second provided for per capita distribution among the states of taxes on income. The third, implicit, assumed that federal spending would not exceed federal revenues except in times of war or recession. All three have been abrogated or eroded by time and events, especially by the adoption of the Sixteenth Amendment (income tax) in 1913. Indeed, it is the income tax amendment that lies at the roots of the current balanced budget amendment movement.

Someone born in the post-depression era would regard deficit financing as normal budget practice. Yet until the Great Depression, the balanced budget, save in wartime or recession, was considered part of our "unwritten constitution." Thomas Jefferson warned that "the public debt is the greatest of dangers to be feared by a republican government" and proposed the idea of a balanced budget amendment as early as September 6, 1789. Alexander Hamilton strongly urged the repayment of national debt. Presidents John Adams, James Madison, James Monroe, John Quincy Adams, and Andrew Jackson all urged avoiding public debt. A balanced budget was synonymous with sound political economy.

Until the Great Depression of the 1930s, budget deficits occurred only in times of war and recession. The budget surpluses generated in good times were invariably used to reduce the national debt these deficits produced. Historical deficits of large proportions arose during the Revolutionary War, the War of 1812, the Mexican War of 1846, and during brief recessions in the late 1830s and 1850s. In each instance, the debts were immediately reduced at the onset of peace or prosperity. Between 1795 and 1811, Congress cut the national debt nearly in half from $84 million to just over $45 million. After the War of 1812, 18 surpluses (of 21 budgets) between 1815 and 1836 virtually eliminated the national debt. A run of 28 consecutive surpluses following the Civil War lowered the national debt from $2.7 billion to $960 million. Finally, throughout the 1920s, consecutive surpluses reduced the national debt from $24 billion to $16 billion, at the very time that major tax rate reductions were approved.

Sustained deficits first arose during the depression years of the 1930s and the war years of the early 1940s, leaving in their wake a national debt of about $170 billion. These deficits were consistent with the national experience of wartime and recession. When peace returned, deficits again disappeared. Between 1947 and 1960, seven surpluses of $31 billion roughly offset seven deficits of $32 billion. However, for the first time in American history, no effort was made to reduce the national debt.

Why the Congress Can't and Won't Control Federal Spending and Deficits

Due to the operation of the unwritten norm of budget balance, the federal government was rarely troubled by budget deficits through almost 200 years of our history. Indeed, revenues and expenditures were not incorporated into an overall official budget until 1921.

But today federal budgets are wildly out of balance. Why?

The answer lies in the political reality that budget objectives and the budget process are in direct conflict. The Congress, as a whole, is concerned with stable prices, low interest rates, and full employment, which require some check on the scope of government spending. As individuals, however, each congressman confronts pressures to increase spending. The reality of our system has shown convincingly that the collective need to control spending is no match for the pressures each individual member faces to increase it.

The tendency for federal spending to grow is clearly highlighted in historical debates on congressional reform:

> The growth of the cost of government as expressed in the increase of Federal taxation has been astounding . . . Our failure to reduce that cost has called attention to our need of the adoption of a system which will prevent waste and extravagance with inevitable inefficiency in the various departments.

> Our present system cannot be conducive to economic administration, as it invited increased expenditures through the perfectly natural rivalry of numerous committees and the inevitable expansion of departments . . . Our present system is designed to increase expenditure rather than reduce it.

> Each committee in the House quite naturally is jealous of both its jurisdiction and success in legislation. It will therefore push to the limit its jurisdiction over legislation and its demand for appropriation that enlarges the function falling under its jurisdiction. Appropriations from the several committees become a race between or among rivals to secure funds from the Treasury rather than safeguard them . . . The pressure is for outlay.

These words stem from the various participants in the debate on the Budget and Accounting Act of 1921, not the 1974 Act! Yet they are the same misgivings articulated during the debate on the 1974 Act. And despite the 1974 Reform Act, the misgivings still remain.

The concerns they represent reflect the empirical fact that the American political process is biased toward higher levels of federal spending; levels which do not reflect the genuine will of the people on the overall size of the budget. Federal spending is skewed toward these artificially higher levels because members of Congress have powerful incentives to spend the taxpayers' money yet they face few offsetting incentives to watch out for the taxpayers' interests.

Spending Biases

This bias toward more spending is due, first, to what analysts of government call the phenomenon of "concentrated benefits versus dispersed costs." This describes the fact that the benefits of any given spending program normally are concentrated among a small number of persons, while the costs of such a program are dispersed throughout a much larger class, the general taxpayer.

The competition between tax-spenders and tax-payers is highly unequal: it is simply not as worthwhile for an individual taxpayer to spend much time and effort to save a few dollars in taxes as it is for the spending interests to secure millions or billions of dollars for themselves. The latter intensely focuses on those few spending measures from which they derive benefit, while the individual taxpayer, who might normally be concerned about the broader impact, is less likely to organize for the purpose of defeating a particular spending measure. Spending interests are able to reward or punish legislators with their organized electoral support or opposition. Taxpayers find it more difficult to perceive their self-interest in the context of isolated pieces of legislation. Thus, whenever government programs are considered one by one, as they are in our budgetary system, there is a bias toward government growth. The result has been annual budget growth in the neighborhood of $100 billion, with even larger deficits forecast.

The explosion in federal spending is not due to the failure to elect the "right" people, it is an institutional defect. The federal budget process is inherently biased toward deficits, higher taxes, and greater government spending. The trends toward bigger government and economic instability reflect the decisions of reasonable men and women in Congress who, as individuals, cannot successfully resist the pressures they face to increase spending.

A second source of bias toward greater spending is the separation of benefits, which are short-run, from costs which are typically more long-run. The benefits of spending programs are immediate, both to the recipients and the sitting congressmen who supported them. The costs of spending programs—in the form of potentially higher future taxes, higher future inflation, higher future unemployment or higher future interest rates—will be evident only at some future time, to be borne, perhaps, by future congressmen. Since the electoral time horizon of all House members and one-third of the senators is never more than a year or two away, short-term benefits invariably take precedence over potentially long-run adverse economic effects due to higher government spending.

A third bias arises within the structure of Congress itself. The committee system, whatever its original intentions, finds members of Congress gravitating to those specific committees that allow them to serve their geographic constituencies by bringing home their "fair share." Farm state members typically serve on the agricultural committees, Western legislators on interior policy committees, urban legislators on urban policy committees, and so on. Reelection rewards those congressmen who successfully serve their constituencies, at the same time the actions of Congress as a whole damage the growth rate of the economy. The driving elements in each congressman's calculation is protecting his turf, getting his share of the pork barrel, not transgressing his colleague's committee jurisdiction; in short, concerns about self come first. It is not in the interest of an individual congressman to give up those dollars that benefit his constituents, since that reduction will have only a modest or even insignificant effect on overall spending. The same situation fits all 535 members of Congress. Unless the entire membership can agree to limit spending, no one member or group of members dare risk their constituents' wrath by surrendering benefits that have no appreciable effect on the total size of government spending, while their colleagues, who do not forego spending, continue to earn the support of their respective constituents. The only viable solution to this dilemma is to alter the incentives which confront members of Congress. That is, we must change the rules under which congressmen operate.

Currently, there are two major gaps in these rules which nourish Congress' spending bias and flout widely recognized customs of fiscal prudence. First, members of Congress enjoy virtually unlimited access to deficit spending. As the "unwritten" rule of budget balance has been discarded, members of Congress can vote to increase spending without a concomitant vote to increase taxes. Spending decisions have become increasingly divorced from the availability of revenues. As a result, members of Congress can satisfy the demands of particular spending interests without either reducing spending for another interest or taking political heat for raising taxes. Rather than choose among alternative spending proposals, members jointly act to increase the deficit. The availability of deficit spending reduces the need for members to make hard political decisions by choosing among spending proposals.

A second element in the spending bias is that under our present tax system, members of Congress have access to annual, automatic tax increases. Our progressive tax code works to transfer more and more of our personal income to the government, because as individuals' income increase, they are taxed at progressively steeper rates. This rising share of national income paid in taxes is due to increases in real income or to inflation, a phenomenon known as "bracket creep," which has had the especially pernicious effects of raising tax burdens. In the last decade, government income tax collections have risen by about 16 percent for each 10 percent increase in personal income, largely as a result of inflation.

To the extent that government receipts outpace inflation, resources are shifted from private to public hands. The government gets richer but the typical wage earner falls behind. Moreover, funds that might have gone into investment are shifted to consumption, thus retarding future productivity gains and increases in the standard of living.

A progressive tax system allows Congress to raise taxes without having to vote an explicit increase either in tax rates or the size of the tax base. Federal income tax yields have grown about 75 percent faster than the GNP, which has allowed Congress to simultaneously collect a growing stream of revenues and enact a sequence of nominal tax cuts. Although Congress passed "tax-reform" measures in 1954, 1964, 1969, 1971, 1976, 1977, 1978, and 1981, taxes have not declined. It is only their rate of increase that has slowed. The accelerating frequency of congressional action reflects the higher rates of inflation throughout the 1970s. In each instance of tax reform, a rising trend of taxation was interrupted, but the long-run trend has been upwards.

Here again, individual congressmen confront strong incentives to do what is far from in the best interests of society. The benefits that they must deliver to retain their office prompts congressmen to support inflationary policies which net them greater spending authority, hence the ability to meet the demands of special interest groups.

Congress has finally voted to correct inflation-generated "bracket creep" by indexing tax rates to inflation, to take effect in 1985. In that event, the progressive tax code would only transfer a greater share of personal income to government when real growth occurs. But many economists and politicians have begun to suggest repeal or postponement of the indexing provision before 1985 to prevent "a drain" on Treasury revenues, thus maintaining the automatic increase mechanism.

The Fiscal Experience since 1960

Since 1960, these biases have yielded the current spending habits of the Congress; that is, deficits have become the accepted practice of federal budgeting. Apart from one modest surplus of $3 billion in 1969, the Congress has imposed a regime of persistent deficits. A national debt of $300 billion in fiscal year 1962 rose to $437 billion in fiscal 1972, surpassing $1 trillion in October 1981. Eight deficits in the 1970s were $40 billion or greater. Interest payments, which absorbed approximately six percent of the national budget twenty years ago, consumed about thirteen percent in FY 1984. It is a figure half as large as spending for national defense and one-third as large as spending for income security programs including Social Security. (Nor does this figure include the growing unfunded liability of social insurance programs and the implicit obligations of loan guarantees.)

The breakdown of the balanced budget norm fueled an explosive rise in federal spending. As recently as 1929, federal spending of $3 billion consumed only 3.1 percent of the gross national product (GNP). Since then, the federal sector has demonstrated a continuing propensity for growth, whatever the economic circumstances. In successive decades, federal spending grew to consume 10.0, 15.6, 18.5, 20.3, and 23.1 percent of GNP by 1980. In money terms, federal spending passed the $100 billion mark in 1962. A $200 billion budget was reached only 9 years later. In rapid-fire succession came $300 billion (1975), $400 billion (1977), $500 billion (1980), $600 billion (1981), $800 billion (1983), with estimates of $1.3 trillion by 1989.

A comprehensive picture of government spending must also include the spending totals of off-budget federal entities (e.g., Federal Financing Bank, Strategic Petroleum Reserve, Postal Service Fund, Rural Electrification and Telephone Revolving Fund, Rural Telephone Bank, U.S. Railways Association, and Synthetic Fuels Corporation). These have risen from $60 million in FY 1973 to $10 billion in FY 1978 to $21 billion in FY 1981. The Reagan administration, despite pledges to reduce off-budget outlays, even included the Strategic Petroleum Reserve as an off-budget item in its first year to lower the official budget deficit.

The growth of federal spending has carried with it an enormous increase in federal tax burdens, which have risen from 15 percent of GNP in 1949 to 25 percent today. Taxpayers also face much higher marginal rates on income as inflation has pushed them into higher tax brackets. Households in the 70th percentile of taxpayers have seen their average top marginal rate rise from 20 percent in 1966 to 28 percent by 1981; for those in the 95th percentile, from 25 to 46 percent. Per capita tax receipts have nearly doubled in the past five years alone. The number of individual taxpayers paying more than 20 percent of their income to the federal government has nearly tripled in the past 15 years. Rising tax burdens, especially high marginal rates faced by many taxpayers, have eroded the incentives to work, save and invest.

Thus in sharp contrast with historical experience, the federal budget process has failed to show restraint in the post-WW II era. For the better part of 200 years, Americans held to a limited role for the federal government. Save for periods of war or recession, revenues from customs and excises were sufficient to fund those activities widely regarded as "proper" federal function. This consensus has broken down in the last fifty years. The greater part of the current federal budget is devoted to activities not funded fifty years ago.

What It Means When Congress Orders a Deficit and the Effect It Has upon Our Lives

The federal government can finance its deficits in three ways. It can raise taxes. It can borrow in the capital markets. Or, it can print new money. By raising taxes, the government reduces the incentives of individuals and business to work, save and invest. By borrowing, the federal government competes with private borrowers, raises the rate of interest, and ultimately crowds out private borrowing. By printing money, the government fosters inflation which, in turn, reduces investment by increasing the risk-premium on long-term investment. In recent years tax burdens and high marginal rates have risen substantially. The 1981 tax rate cut attempts to correct this problem. Without new taxation, future deficits are likely to be financed largely by borrowing or new money creation. Let us examine the effects of these two methods.

Borrowing. When the government borrows to finance its budget deficit, it has an unfair advantage in its competition with private borrowers. Since government borrowing is backed up by the "full faith and credit" of the United States government, *viz.,* the power to tax, the government gets first call on the available supply of credit. Moreover, the government will pay whatever rate of interest is required to get the funds it needs to sustain government spending. Private borrowers are not so flexible.

The price of credit—the interest rate—is determined by the intersection of the supply of and demand for credit. In the past decade, the percentage of disposable personal income that was saved fell by about half, from nearly 8 percent in 1971 to about 4 percent in 1980. As a result, total real savings have fallen, reducing the supply of new credit. At the same time, the government has sharply increased its annual demand for new credit. Total federal and federally-related borrowings have risen from $33 billion in FY 1971 to $331 billion in FY 1984. The rate of increase in government demand for credit has outpaced new savings. As in any such situation of rising demand, the price of borrowing will rise because of the competition among borrowers for limited funds. But when interest rates rise, private citizens will borrow less. Thus private borrowing is crowded out.

Borrowing to finance large deficits need not crowd out private borrowers if the supply of new savings is large enough to satisfy both public and private demands for credit. In Germany and Japan, savings rates have been from three to five times as large as in the United States, which explains why the German and Japanese governments can run substantially larger deficits as a share of GNP than the United States government, without equally adverse economic effects. The conjunction of rising credit demands and lower savings rates in the United States has driven up real interest rates to levels higher than at any period in our nation's history. To the extent that deficit finance raises real rates of interest and reduces investment in plant and equipment, we have fewer tools or machines in our old age and leave fewer tools for our children. We consume relatively more today but we are poorer and have fewer goods available tomorrow.

It is important to note that private borrowing is used disproportionately more for investment than is government borrowing. Budget deficits that are financed by borrowing mean that funds which might be used for the creation of capital goods are instead used to subsidize consumption. Deficits thus crowd out some investment in favor of greater consumption. Although some capital investment will still take place, the amount is lower than it would have been in the absence of a budget deficit.

Money Supply Growth. The inflation which began in the late 1960s has been associated with large and continuing federal deficits. Apart from Treasury borrowing, the government can also finance deficits by printing new money. This result occurs when the Federal Reserve Board (the Fed) increases its ownership of Treasury debt, which, in turn, effectively increases the amount of money and credit in circulation. This process is referred to as monetizing debt, which is largely synonymous with printing money to finance deficits.

It is technically true that there is no necessary relationship between budget deficits and money creation. The Fed can keep its ownership of government debt unchanged despite deficits, or increase its ownership of outstanding government debt in the absence of a deficit. Assume it does the former. Persistently large deficits, coupled with inadequate savings, will place upward pressure on interest rates, thereby crowding out private investment. This, in turn, leads to recession and higher unemployment. To ease these effects, the Fed can increase its ownership of Treasury debt, thereby increasing the supply of money. As the supply of loanable funds expands, other things being equal, the rate of interest will fall and fewer private borrowers will be crowded out. However, money creation reduces the real value of the existing stock of money, thus contributing to inflation.

Persistently large deficits during a period of economic recovery foster long-run inflationary fears that the Fed might monetize some portion of this debt. In the past decade, purchase of government debt by the Fed has contributed to rising inflation. Inflation, in turn, disrupts savings, investment decisions, and the prospects for economic growth. Personal savings rates fell throughout the 1970s and the average service life of capital expenditures, so vital to future increases in production efficiency, began to shorten.

Inflation puts economic stability and growth at risk; it has undercut investment and employment by increasing uncertainty over the profitability of long-run investments. This uncertainty, which is embodied in investment calculations in the form of higher risk premiums, prevents a normal package of capital projects—especially those for which the profit expectations are skewed toward the later years of the investment, eight, ten, or fifteen years in the future—from meeting acceptable financial criteria.

Reflecting increased investment risk, price earnings ratios in the stock markets have fallen to their lowest levels in two decades, largely as a consequence of the increased discount rate imposed on expected earnings growth. An inflationary environment makes it more difficult and uncertain to calculate the rate of return on new investment. Inflation not only skews rate-of-return calculations, it also acts to shift the investment pattern toward shorter-lived projects in which the uncertainty is less.

High investment risk thus blunts capital formation and the level of economic activity. It replaces the creation of long-lived capital assets with undue focus on the short run. To restore long-term investment requires a high level of business confidence, which can only be obtained by a credible and sustained reduction in long-run expectations about inflation. This implies that budget deficits must be minimized, preferably eliminated, thereby removing the consequent pressures on the monetary system of large federal deficits.

Interest rates are high because the demand for credit is high, especially on the part of the federal government. Money supply growth in recent years has been excessive, in part, because the Fed feels compelled to suppress interest rates by at least partially accommodating the excess credit requirements. Thus the prospect of multi-hundred billion dollar deficits in the next few years implies (if savings do not increase dramatically) continued crowding out and high interest rates or purchase of additional debt and a renewed inflationary spiral, which was the cause of declining business investment in the first place.

In short, deficits matter!

In fact, deficits matter in ways other than those purely economic. Yet another effect of excessive government spending has been the erosion of public confidence in government. Surveys conducted by George Gallup, Louis Harris, the Institute of Social Research at the University of Michigan, and CBS/New York Times reveal major shifts in public opinion between 1957 and 1978. The percentage of respondents who said that government wastes money rose from 46 to 80. But the number of those who said they trust Washington to do what is right most of the time declined from 75 to 34 percent!

Americans have increasingly felt the effects of inflation. Between 1958 and 1973, for example, the number of Gallup's respondents naming inflation as the nation's most important problem was always less than 20 percent. Since 1974, the percentage has ranged from a low of 25 to a high of 79. Complaints about taxes and government waste have escalated as taxpayers endured rising rates of inflation and stagnant real income. Indeed, according to Gallup, 80 percent of the American people favor a constitutional amendment to require a balanced budget.

Senate Joint Resolution 58. A Balanced Budget-Tax Limitation Constitutional Amendment

Since 1979, members of the Senate Judiciary Subcommittee on the Constitution have sought to develop a "consensus" measure that would attract the support of as many proponents of a constitutional initiative as possible. Senate Joint Resolution 58, a combined balanced budget and tax limitation amendment, was passed by the Senate on August 4, 1982 by a vote of 69–31. The House considered the companion resolution, H.J. Res. 350 on October 1, defeating the proposed amendment by a vote of 236–187, thus failing to produce the two-thirds vote required for passage of a constitutional amendment. Nevertheless, the contents of that bill are very likely to be included in whatever amendment is finally sent to the states for ratification.

For this reason, it is worth examining each section of that proposed amendment to see how it would redress the present imbalance in our budgetary process.

Balanced Budget

> *Section 1.* Prior to each fiscal year, the Congress shall adopt a statement of receipts and outlays for that year in which total outlays are no greater than total receipts. The Congress may amend such statement provided revised outlays are no greater than revised receipts. Whenever three-fifths of the whole number of both Houses shall deem it necessary, Congress in such statement may provide for a specific excess of outlays over receipt by a vote directed solely to that subject. The Congress and the President shall ensure that actual outlays do not exceed the outlays set forth in such statement.

The purpose of Section 1 is two-fold. First, Congress would be required to plan to balance its budget every year. It would do so by adopting a "statement" or budget prior to the start of each fiscal year, in which planned outlays (spending) do not exceed planned receipts (revenue). Congress could violate this rule and plan for a deficit only by a three-fifths vote of the whole number of each House of Congress, not just three-fifths of those present and voting. In contrast, a simple majority could approve a budget surplus. Second, Section 1 also mandates that actual outlays do not exceed the spending levels set forth in the approved statement or budget.

It is important to point out that the amendment establishes the basis for a *planned* balanced budget. It does not require that the budget be in *actual* balance during the course of the fiscal year. In some circumstances, actual outlays may exceed actual receipts. For example, a recession might reduce actual receipts below the level of receipts set forth in the planned statement. This is permissible under the amendment, but actual outlays could not exceed statement outlays. Deficits caused by increased spending would also not be permitted.

If circumstances warrant, the Congress may adopt an amended statement of receipts and outlays for the fiscal year (provided again that outlays do not exceed receipts) at any time during the fiscal year. An amendment statement containing a deficit would require a three-fifths vote only if such deficit was greater than the deficit in the previous statement. Thus the budget would not be "locked in" and could be changed by an explicit vote of Congress in response to changing economic conditions.

An important feature of Section 1 is that it imposes upon the Congress and the President a mandate to prevent total actual outlays, which include both on- and off-budget items, from exceeding statement outlays. For example, should the economy perform below expectations, leading to increased spending on "entitlements" or on debt service due to higher interest rates, the Congress would be called upon *either* to increase statement outlays and approve a deficit (by a three-fifths vote), or to postpone spending programs and/or to reduce eligibility for "entitlements." To guard against the possibility that actual outlays might exceed statement outlays through unintentional and presumably modest error, an obvious remedy would be for Congress to plan a surplus of equivalent size for the next fiscal year.

The Congress is expected to adopt the most accurate estimates of receipts and outlays that it can in drafting its budget, but in all cases a congressional majority will be the final arbiter among the choice of estimates. As the fiscal year unfolds, actual receipts may or may not meet expectations. An unexpectedly more robust economy may yield receipts above statement receipts; an unexpectedly weaker economy may yield receipts below statement receipts. Either result is permissible. The amendment imposes no obligation upon the Congress to react to the flow of actual receipts during the fiscal year, only to the flow of actual outlays.

Recent years have witnessed congressional failure to adopt a budget by the October 1 date on which a new fiscal year begins. Congress has funded government operations in such instances by adopting continuing resolutions. Under the amendment, this practice would be banned. Failure to adopt a statement of receipts and outlays by the October 1 deadline would be construed as an implied adoption of a statement in which both receipts and outlays are zero. In that event, the Congress and the President would be mandated constitutionally to ensure that fiscal year outlays also would be zero. In short, the government would shut down on October 1 without prior passage by September 30.

Loans for which the federal government guarantees in whole or in part the repayment of principal and/or interest impose no funding obligation on the treasury unless and until such loans come into default and the treasury must discharge the guarantee obligation. Such a discharge is intended to be construed as an outlay in the fiscal year of discharge.

A large portion of federal spending is currently on automatic pilot. That is, spending for "entitlements" grows every year as a share of federal spending. An amendment prohibiting deficits would create a strong incentive to bring these "uncontrollables" under control, since they would compete directly with discretionary programs. At present, the automatic growth of spending on "uncontrollables" erodes the ability of Congress to impose its own priorities on the budget, which is tantamount to passing the congressional buck.

Section 1 proposes to overcome the spending bias of Congress by restoring the linkage between federal spending and taxing decisions. It does not propose to read any specific level of spending or taxing forever into the Constitution, nor does it intrude into the day-to-day decisions of the government as to how the federal dollar is allocated. It merely restores the balance between taxspenders by constraining spending totals to available revenues.

The amendment would compel public officials to determine first what resources are available to government (see Section 2 below) and, against that constraint, choose among the many competing claims on public spending.

Under the amendment, if politicians voted new spending programs, they would have to eliminate old programs or vote to raise additional taxes. Resistance to the elimination of existing programs or to tax increases would discourage many new spending proposals, thereby eliminating the current bias toward overspending. It would end future deficits and reduce the inflationary effect of new money creation, which has in past years both financed a portion of these deficits and raised taxes via bracket creep.

Political values and perceptions are important determinants of government action. For this reason, a balanced budget amendment is especially attractive. It is easy to understand—every household understands the need for living within its means. It is also widely supported.

Tax Limitation

> *Section 2.* Total receipts for any fiscal year set forth in the statement adopted pursuant to this article shall not increase by a rate greater than the rate of increase in national income in the last calendar year ending before such fiscal year, unless a majority of the whole number of both Houses of Congress shall have passed a bill directed solely to approving specific additional receipts and such bill has become law.

The purpose of Section 2 is to prevent tax receipts from growing more rapidly than the general economy, as occurs with our progressive tax code. Under the amendment, a "whole" majority of the membership of both Houses would have to vote to permit receipts to outpace general economic growth. In particular, Congress would be required to enact a bill expanding a specified tax base and/or increasing specified tax rates.

Put another way, Section 2 states that the balanced budget requirement in Section 1 should not occur at levels of receipts and outlays that consume an increasing proportion of the national economy. It attempts to achieve this result by limiting the increase in receipts for a new fiscal year to the percentage increase in the national income during the prior calendar year. If present tax laws are likely to yield revenues in excess of this limit, the Congress must modify the revenue laws to reduce anticipated receipts.

The relationship between the growth of national income during the prior calendar year and the growth of receipts during the following fiscal year provides the Congress with reasonably precise guideposts in its budgeting process. Quite accurate estimates of the growth in national income are available by mid-July prior to the beginning of the fiscal year.

Take fiscal year 1981, for example, which began October 1, 1980. The rate of increase in statement receipts for fiscal year 1981 would have been limited to the rate of increase of national income for calendar year 1979. Since national income rose 11.4 percent in 1979, statement receipts for fiscal 1981 could not have exceeded fiscal 1980 statement receipts by more than 11.4 percent. The planned increase for FY 1981 with no changes in the current tax law was set at 14.5 percent. Had the amendment been in effect, the tax law would not have produced this automatic tax increase. Taxes would have been about $16 billion or lower. To increase taxes, Congress would have had to explicitly vote for a tax increase for FY 1981.

Statement receipts may also rise by less than the proportionate increase in national income. In that event, the new lower level of receipts would then become the base for statement receipts in subsequent fiscal years, until the Congress voted a rise in allowable receipts.

Let's recapitulate how the budget process would work under the amendment. First, the Congress would determine the increase in national income during the prior calendar year. That percentage rise, in turn, would determine the maximum increase in receipts the government could collect for the coming fiscal year. If, say, national income rose 10 percent during the last calendar year, then receipts could rise by *no more than* 10 percent for the new fiscal year. Since outlays cannot exceed receipts (the budget must be balanced or in surplus), government spending could not rise by more than 10 percent. Sections 1 and 2, in conjunction, establish a *de facto* spending limit. Thus neither taxes nor spending can grow more rapidly than the economy.

The amendment permits federal spending to grow more rapidly than the economy *only* if Congress explicitly votes to allow receipts to rise more rapidly than the growth of the economy. It takes a direct vote of a constitutional majority of both Houses of Congress to permit the growth of federal spending to outpace the growth of the economy. Or, federal spending may outpace economic growth if Congress approves, by a three-fifths majority vote, a deficit in which outlays from year to year exceed economic growth rates. Thus the federal government is not hamstrung; it can meet what may be regarded as increased genuine needs of the people, if it also were prepared to vote on the record for higher taxes or deficits to finance higher spending.

Wartime Waiver

> *Section 3.* The Congress may waive the provisions of this article for any fiscal
> year in which a declaration of war is in effect.

In the event of a declaration of war, Congress has the discretionary authority to operate outside of the provisions of the amendment. Such a waiver would be on a year-to-year basis by concurrent resolution of Congress, as defined under Article 1, Section 8, of the Constitution. Congress would have to adopt annually a separate waiver for each fiscal year at issue.

Borrowing and Repayment of Debt

> *Section 4*. Total receipts shall include all receipts of the United States except
> those derived from borrowing and total outlays shall include all outlays of the
> United States except those for repayment of debt principal.

The purpose of Section 4 is to exclude the proceeds of debt issuance from
receipts. Thus, treasury notes and bonds would not count as receipts, but as the
proceeds of selling debt. Similarly, the term outlays is intended to include all
disbursements from the Treasury of the United States, both "on-budget" and
"off-budget," either directly or indirectly through federal or quasi-federal
agencies created under the authority of acts of Congress. Section 4 states that
funds used to repurchase or retire federal debt would not count as outlays. Interest
accrued or paid in conjunction with the debt obligation would, however, be
included in outlays.

The amendment permits Congress to plan for a budgetary surplus. Those
surplus receipts, subject to the increase limit of Section 2, used to repay
principal—that is, retire national debt—would not be counted as outlays. Should
the government fully retire the national debt, the amendment would still allow the
government to plan for an annual surplus, and even accumulate reserves. Interest
earned on these reserves, however, would be subject to the revenue limit.
(Admittedly, it would take generations for this scenario to develop.)

Date of Implementation

> *Section 5*. This article shall take effect for the second fiscal year beginning
> after its ratification.

Section 5 stipulates when the amendment would take effect. If ratification were
completed before September 30, 1985, the amendment would require Congress to
adopt its first balanced budget statement before September 30, 1986; if ratification was completed between October 1, 1985, and before September 30, 1986, the
first balanced budget adoption would be required by September 30, 1987, and so
on.

*Some Questions and Answers about the Balanced Budget-Tax
Limitation Amendment*

Q: Members of Congress face enormous pressures to increase spending. How
would the amendment be enforced to overcome these pressures?

A: While there are no sanctions contained expressly within S.J. Res. 58 for the
violation of any particular provision, the Congress and the President are expected
to act in accordance with the Constitution. By establishing a focus upon two or
three critical votes each year relating to the total level of taxation or the size of the
deficits, in place of the present piecemeal focus on hundreds of separate spending
measures, the amendment will enable the electorate to better identify those
members of Congress most responsible for higher levels of spending, taxing, and
deficits, with their harmful effects on inflation, interest rates, and unemployment.

Q: So far, Congress has disregarded those statutes that call for a balanced budget. Won't the Congress also find ways to circumvent the provisions of the amendment?

A: It is important to focus on the difference between an ordinary statute and a constitutional amendment. The reason that our civil rights have survived for 200 years is because they are expressly set forth in the Constitution. Without the protection of the Constitution, it is quite likely that many of our individual freedoms would have been eroded over time. Similarly, Congress will find it more difficult to flout the constitutional requirement of budget balance and tax limitation.

Q: Isn't it improper to read economic policy into the Constitution?

A: There are several answers to this question. First, the Constitution already contains numerous items which help formulate economic policy. Among these is the Sixteenth Amendment that made possible the income tax which has fueled rising levels of taxation and government spending. Secondly, the amendment does not dictate any given level of spending or taxing; it only overcomes the bias toward higher spending by eliminating the unlimited access to deficit spending and the availability of automatic tax increases. Under the amendment, Congress would have to vote explicitly to increase, decrease or maintain any given level of government spending. Finally, the amendment only seeks to reimpose prior constitutional limitations on deficits which constituted an "unwritten" rule of budget balance.

Q: Won't the amendment hamstring the ability of Congress to respond to urgent or genuine needs of the American people?

A: No. The amendment is automatically waived for one year in the event of a declaration of war. For other emergencies, the Congress can adopt by a three-fifths vote of the whole membership of both Houses a planned deficit, and, by a majority vote of the whole membership, higher taxes.

Q: Won't it be difficult to agree on the definition of national income and other economic concepts in the amendment?

A: No. The Congress may choose to rely on any of several measures of economic performance, so long as this economic indicator is used consistently from year to year, or that some transition period accompany the substitution of one indicator for another.

Q: S. J. Res. 58 is a balanced budget-tax limitation amendment. How does it work to limit spending?

A: First, the growth in planned receipts from the coming fiscal year cannot exceed the growth of national income for the prior calendar year. Second, the requirement that Congress adopt a "statement" in which outlays do not exceed receipts limits the rise in outlays to the growth rate of national income. Finally, since *actual* outlays cannot exceed *statement* outlays, government spending cannot grow more rapidly than the private economy.

Q: Isn't it impossible to balance the budget during the course of the fiscal year?

A: The amendment does not impose a requirement of actual balance during the fiscal year, only the adoption of a *planned* balanced budget. Although the amendment monitors the flow of actual outlays to insure that actual outlays do not exceed those set forth in the budget statement, actual receipts may exceed or fall below the level set forth in the statement. The amendment imposes no requirement that Congress react to the actual flow of receipts, only to the actual flow of outlays.

Q: Won't Congress just shift more and more of its spending policies "off-budget"?

A: No. Budget outlays include both "on-" and "off-budget" items. Section 4 states, "Total outlays shall include all outlays of the United States except for repayment of debt principal."

Note on Additional Reading

For a detailed statement on the legislative history of the Amendment and definitions of its terms and provisions, see the official Committee report: "Balanced Budget-Tax Limitation Constitutional Amendment," *Report to the Committee on the Judiciary*, United States Senate, 97th Congress, 1st Session, Report No. 97-151, Washington, D.C.: U.S. Government Printing Office, 1981.

Hazlitt sees a balanced budget amendment as too restrictive and believes that it does not get to the root of the deficit problem, excessive government spending. He favors a pair of constitutional amendments designed to rein in federal spending. The first would give the President a line-item veto, and the second would give the Senate authority to reduce, but not increase, appropriations approved by the House.

A PROPOSAL FOR TWO CONSTITUTIONAL AMENDMENTS

Henry Hazlitt

A growing number of people (only a handful of whom, unfortunately, seem to be in Congress) are at last recognizing the desperate urgency of balancing the budget. We have now had deficits for 45 out of the last 53 years, and nothing but deficits for the last 15 years. They keep accelerating in amount—from $60 billion in fiscal 1980, for example, the year before Ronald Reagan came to office, to more than $200 billion estimated for the current fiscal year. (Including "off-budget" expenditures, these deficits rose to $74 billion to $225 billion respectively.)

The deficits have been the direct and major cause of our inflation, which has led to an increase in average consumer prices of 193 per cent even since 1967, and of 656 per cent since 1933.

But the crucial role played by deficits was belittled, until recently, by the monetarists. They insisted, correctly enough, that the main (they insisted the sole) cause for the depreciation of the dollar was the increase in the money supply. But what they ignored was that the chronic deficit spending was the main reason the money supply was being so constantly increased.

The deficit spending has now been so long continued, the lack of fiscal responsibility in Congress is now so glaring, that the time for further appeals to congressional responsibility has obviously passed. There is no remedy but a constitutional change that would curb or otherwise alter the power of the purse. The crucial problem is to decide precisely what such a change should be.

In an otherwise excellent article in the May 1983 issue of *Inquiry*, Alvin Rabushka recognizes the peril of our chronic deficits, and the need of constitutional amendment to halt them. But he advocates, I fear, the wrong amendments.

Reprinted by permission of the publisher from *Human Events*, June 4, 1983, p. 478.

The first is that suggested by Thomas Jefferson in a letter of John Taylor in 1798—a constitutional amendment "taking from the federal government the power of borrowing." Notwithstanding its revered origin, I think most of us would regard such an amendment, if obtainable, as an appalling mistake. Such a blanket prohibition could prove fatal in a war or other emergency. And there is no need for it.

The other proposal that Rabushka supports is a direct provision for a balanced budget such as the National Taxpayers Union and the National Tax Limitation Committee have been recommending for the past eight years—and one which the U.S. Senate actually passed last year—that would have both required a balanced budget and limited the increase in taxes to the growth of national income. (This was passed by more than the necessary two-thirds vote, but the measure was bottled up in committee by the Democratic leadership in the House.)

The trouble with such an amendment is not merely that it would be too cumbersome and restrictive, but that it misses the real problem. The basic problem is not the deficit itself, but the excessive government spending that causes the deficit.

I confess that I myself became aware of this belatedly. Our chronic deficits began in 1931. It was after a series of such deficits that I first remember reading a column by Walter Lippmann demanding that Congress "become responsible" and balance the budget—by raising taxes! Not a word about cutting expenditures. Much later, I did clip a column from the New York Herald-Tribune, dated March 5, 1959, in which Lippmann returned to the same theme.

"Both parties are pretending that they are struggling to balance the budget. In fact, neither the Administration nor the Congress shows any sign of being willing to vote the taxes which are absolutely essential if the budget is to be balanced."

All the spending already being made, Lippmann implied, plus a good deal more, was absolutely necessary.

The result seems to show that he won the argument. In fiscal 1959 budget receipts were $79.2 billion and outlays were $92.1 billion, making the deficit $12.9 billion. In 1960 a small surplus of $269 million was achieved, in spite of an increase in expenditures, because revenues suddenly jumped to $92.4 billion. But the 1959 deficit had not been caused by any significant fall in revenues, which were $79.6 billion in 1958, but by the sharp increase in spending from $82.6 billion in 1958 to the $92.1 billion of 1959.

And this has in fact been the routine history of the 45 deficits in the last 53 years. All but eight of them have been accompanied by rising outlays over the year preceding. And in all but one of the five years in which a deficit has been followed by a surplus, it is because revenues have been raised, and not because outlays have fallen.

So unless anyone wants to maintain seriously that the almost uninterrupted 225-fold rise in spending from $3.6 billion in 1931 to $805.2 billion in 1983 has practically all been justified and necessary, it is clear that the solution to our deficit problem does not lie in the "courage" to impose ever more burdensome repressive taxation but in lower spending.

This goal could be achieved by two amendments to our Constitution, and perhaps even by the first alone. That would be an amendment to give the President power to veto or reduce any individual item in an appropriation bill. At present he has only the power of vetoing an entire bill. This in practice makes his veto power, on appropriation bills, unusable. For Congress is able consistently to circumvent the intention of this constitutional provision by combining in a single bill appropriations it knows the President won't like with appropriations it knows he must have. He cannot take the responsibility for vetoing these, so there is no way in which he can force Congress to omit the particular spending he objects to.

A constitutional amendment giving the President the power to reduce or veto individual items in appropriation bills would give him the real power to curb congressional spending that the framers of the Constitution intended him to have. It is a power already enjoyed, I believe, by the governors of more than three-quarters of the states. Seven Presidents have asked in vain that Congress submit an amendment giving them this power.

If such an amendment were adopted, it might be enough by itself to bring federal spending under control. Yet one additional amendment would assure such an end. This would be one to give the Senate the power to reduce but not to increase the spending of the House.

The framers of the Constitution seem to have had a similar purpose in the back of their minds. They did provide (Art. I, Sect. 7) that "all bills for raising revenue shall originate in the House of Representatives." There are strong reasons for suspecting that this wording was an error in drafting. It refers as drafted only to bills for imposing taxes, but the framers probably intended also to include appropriation bills. This is hinted in James Madison's Notes on Debates in the Federal Convention of 1787, where he consistently writes "money bills," not tax bills, when referring to this provision.

In any case, the provision as drafted is inadequate. The record shows that in departmental and other omnibus appropriation bills, the Senate in nearly every case increases the appropriations provided by the House. And the bills as they come out of conference usually retain at least part of the increase.

The solution seems to be a constitutional amendment that would take from the Senate any power to initiate appropriations or to increase an appropriation by the House, but to leave it the power to reduce or veto any appropriation by the House. The House would be allowed to override such a reduction or veto by a three-fifths majority.

Such an amendment, if it could be obtained, would make a profound difference in the budget. At the very least, it would prevent the Senate from continuously increasing federal expenditures.

Senators, no longer able to compete with House members in dreaming up new handouts to special groups, would take more seriously their power to relieve taxpayers or keep the budget in balance. A long-run effect would be to bring the country more economy-conscious senators. It would tend to turn them from spenders into watchdogs against excessive spending.

There need be no fear that such an amendment would leave the senators with too few powers. It would give them more power than they have now (or than the President has now, until he gets the power of item veto) to reduce federal expenditures. It would still leave the Senate with powers to control appointments, to ratify treaties, to try impeachments, and to share with the House all the other enumerated powers assigned by the Constitution to Congress as a whole.

Of course we cannot imagine the Senate voting to deprive itself of the power of initiating or increasing appropriations, and we cannot seriously expect the Senate to vote to submit such a constitutional amendment for ratification by the States. But it would still be possible to secure such an amendment by the second method proposed by the Constitution: ". . . or, on the application of the legislatures of two-thirds of the several states, shall call a convention for proposing amendments."

This method of application has never been resorted to, and for obvious reasons. No individual state legislature, let alone two-thirds of them, is likely to ask for such a convention because it has no idea of what would come out of it. But there is nothing in this amendment provision to prevent an individual state legislature, or two-thirds of them, from asking for a convention *for the sole purpose of proposing a specific amendment,* provided they are all asking for the same one. Congress would have no choice but to grant their request. The state legislatures would then need to send only one delegate each to such a "convention," instructed to vote for or against the amendment, and the convention need not last more than a day.

Such a procedure could be adopted either for a presidential item veto amendment, or for one changing the appropriation powers of the Senate, or for both. The first alone might be enough to solve the federal spending problem; the two together would be almost certain to do so. In that case, the problem of getting back to a balanced budget would probably solve itself.

But it is highly unlikely that any attempt to amend the Constitution to try to force a balanced budget directly would ensure a balance at a reasonably low level or succeed in bringing anything but hopeless complications or deadlocks. No Congress can know in advance what future emergency appropriations may be necessary, or exactly what revenues any given set of tax rates will produce. But if we can once control the spending spigot, adjustments can be made quickly.

Stein believes that balancing the budget is no longer politically feasible. He takes an extremely eclectic view, mixing Keynesian and monetarist policy prescriptions. "The desirable size of the surplus or deficit," he says, "is not fixed forever. That is why it should not be incorporated in a constitutional amendment. The choice of a surplus or deficit target is a political decision to be made from time to time in the light of long-run growth considerations."

THE SIGNIFICANCE OF BUDGET DEFICITS

Herbert Stein

Nothing better reveals the vacuum in economic policy than the gap between the nearly universal statements of aversion to budget deficits and the prospect of exceptionally large deficits for as far ahead as the eye can see. No one any longer talks about balancing the budget. There is a tacit agreement that the things that would have to be done to eliminate the deficit cannot be done—which means only that the necessary action is considered worse than the deficit.

But if zero has been abandoned as a goal for the size of the deficit no other goal has received any general support. Everyone in the political process wants to be known as supporting a lower deficit than his rivals, but hardly anyone tries to justify any particular size of the deficit as a proper target. All the participants are willing to do something to reduce the prospective deficits, but each is willing to do only things that he was willing to do anyway, without regard to the size of the deficit. The President is willing to cut social programs he wanted to cut even when the deficits did not loom so large. Many "liberals" are prepared to cut the defense program, or to raise taxes on the "rich," in order to reduce the deficit—never having felt much need for a large defense program or much concern about the after-tax incomes of the upper-income minority.

The fact is that talk about reducing the budget deficit has become largely a ritual. Everyone believes that there are other people out there who are greatly worried about budget deficits and it is therefore necessary to show that one shares that worry. But the reasons for the worry are not cogent or agreed-upon and do not lead to any clear idea about the proper size of deficit, if it is not zero, or to much action.

There are people who believe that deficits don't really matter. They believe that the size of government expenditures matters. Government spending subtracts from the output available for private use. They are concerned about that subtraction—mainly to keep it as low as possible. But whether that subtraction is financed by taxation or by borrowing seems to them of no great importance. This attitude leads to a certain anomaly. People who hold this view are usually reluctant to avow it when expenditure decisions are being considered. Wanting to hold expenditures down, they would like all decision-makers to believe that they should not spend money unless they raise taxes to pay for it. But the decision-makers are not likely to accept that discipline unless they see some reason why they should raise taxes, and they will not see that unless they think that the difference between taxing and borrowing matters.

Our present situation is that we talk as if deficits were terribly important, we act as if they didn't matter very much, and we really don't know what the nature and size of their effects are. It is not easy to be positive in laying down principles for deciding on policy toward deficits. All one can do is to try prudently to adapt policy to a rather cautious and moderate view of what the effects are.

In my opinion the present state of economic analysis tends to support this view of the effects of the size of the deficit: Short-run variations in the size of the deficit have short-run effects on nominal GNP, the price level, output and employment. That is, an exogenous increase in the deficit—one not resulting from a decline of the economy—will tend temporarily to raise the rate of increase of nominal GNP and the price level and also to raise output and employment. In the long run the size of the deficit—whether large or small—if it is stable will not affect nominal GNP or the price level or employment. It will, however, affect the long-term growth rate of output and of productivity, because the larger the deficit is in the long run the slower will be the growth of private productive investment.

The proposition about the short-run effect of the budget deficit does not contradict what has been said earlier about the dominant role of the money supply in determining the long-run behavior of nominal GNP and the price level. Even the most extreme monetarist would recognize that velocity can fluctuate in the short run, which means that the economy can fluctuate even if the money supply does not. Variations in the deficit or surplus are among the possible causes of variations in velocity.

The key question is whether this short-run influence of fiscal policy should be used actively or only passively in an effort to achieve desired behavior of the economy. Almost everyone will now agree on at least the passive use. That is, the variations in the size of the deficit or surplus that come automatically with variations of the economy will be accepted. To try to offset those automatic variations by changing tax programs or expenditure programs is disturbing to the planning of taxpayers and government agencies, and certainly not helpful to the stability of the economy. There are some economists who retain a longing for more than that—for varying the deficit in a countercyclical direction. They cling to the early Keynesian idea of cutting tax rates to stimulate the economy when it is depressed or, more realistically, is expected to be depressed, and vice versa. But the number who believe this with confidence has greatly diminished. The effort to stabilize the economy by variation of fiscal policy has a high risk of being destabilizing because of the difficulty of forecasting the economy accurately. This destabilizing effect is likely to have an inflationary bias, because of the short-run preoccupation with reducing unemployment. For the same reason the short-run decisions about the budget are likely in the long run to add up to larger deficits than would be desirable.

This comes down to a short-run policy of keeping the size of the deficit stable from year to year, or even for longer periods, except insofar as the size of the deficit responds automatically to variations of the economy. This leaves two problems. First, how are we to distinguish between the automatic, passive variations of the deficit, which are to be accepted, and the active, purposely generated variations of the deficit, which are to be ruled out by the policy? This distinction requires us to identify a condition of the economy at which the deficit will be kept constant and from which deviations can be observed and measured. The CED in 1947 identified this condition as "high employment" and said that taxes and expenditures should be such that they would yield a constant surplus when the economy was at high employment. (In 1947 one still talked of a surplus.) This prescription was deficient in several respects. No one really knew what "high employment" was, the definition used turned out, as might have been expected, to be more ambitious than could be actually achieved on the average, and the prescription did not recognize the importance of the price level as an aspect of the condition of the economy. But the "high employment" notion, although crude, did reflect the correct basic idea. This was that tax and expenditure programs should be set so that they would yield a stable and desirable surplus (or deficit) when the economy was in a desirable and, on the average, probable condition. If this is done, variations in the surplus resulting automatically from variations of the economy will help to keep the economy near its desirable condition. The long-run size of the surplus will probably be the desired size because the budget has been set to yield that surplus when the economy is in its long-run probable condition. In the past, "practical" conservative people tended to scoff at the idea of balancing the budget at high employment because it promised to balance the budget under hypothetical conditions which might not exist whereas they were interested in "actual" balance. But the valid interest in the actual size of the surplus or deficit is an interest in the actual size of the surplus or deficit over a period of years. If we aim to get the desired surplus or deficit when the economy is on its most probable path we will probably realize that actual surplus or deficit on the average over a period of years, although not in every year.

The desirable, feasible, and probable condition of the economy at which we should plan to get the target surplus or deficit is the level of nominal GNP at which monetary policy is aiming. I have suggested above that the Federal Reserve should try to control the money supply so that it will on the average achieve growth of nominal GNP that is low and predictable. That is the desirable path of the economy, because if it is achieved there will be little inflation and the economy will fluctuate moderately about a high employment level. It is a feasible path because monetary policy can on the average keep the economy on it. And it will be the probable path, about which the actual economy will fluctuate, if the monetary policy is directed to achieving it. Therefore, if tax rates and expenditure programs are set so that they would achieve the desired surplus or deficit when the economy is on the target path, the actual surplus or deficit over a moderate number of years will be the desired one.

This implies that it should be the responsibility of the administration to submit an annual budget that would achieve the desired surplus or deficit when the economy is on the nominal GNP path set by the Federal Reserve. The present system in which the administration submits a five-year budget based on economic assumptions that the Federal Reserve may not share and to which it has no commitment is unsatisfactory. It encourages irresponsible window-dressing by the administration in making up its assumptions and permits anyone to challenge the policy by making up his own assumptions. Moreover, if it is not known whether the budget assumptions conform to the Federal Reserve's intentions no one can tell whether or not the budget describes the probable outcome for the deficit or surplus.

The interaction between monetary and fiscal policy would work something like this: The Federal Reserve would be directed to submit to the Congress each year its targets for nominal GNP for the next five years and its plan for the money supply in the next year to keep the economy on that path. Presumably the Fed will discuss these plans with the administration before it submits them to Congress. Congress can, if it wishes, comment on the Fed's plans. In extreme circumstances Congress could enact legislation which would instruct the Fed to do something different. This is quite unlikely to happen, however. Although many members of Congress like to be able to criticize the Fed, few Congressmen have shown any disposition to accept the responsibility for managing monetary policy. The administration would submit a budget for the next five years that would yield the desired surplus or deficit when the economy is on the Fed's target path. The desired surplus or deficit should be stable from year to year, so that variations of the size of the surplus or deficit will not disturb the economy from the path the Fed is seeking to maintain.

This brings us to the second question. What is the desirable size of the surplus or deficit, on the average, aside from cyclical fluctuations? That depends, of course, on what the effects of surpluses or deficits are. This has been the subject of much controversy over the years. Argument over this issue has, I believe, now properly led to the conclusion that the important effect of the absolute size of the deficit or surplus is the effect on private investment. That is, I think, the view now held by most, although not all, economists.

The argument is simple. Private savings equal the sum of private investment plus the government deficit. Private saving is totally absorbed in these two uses. The larger the government deficit is, the smaller private investment will be—unless the larger government deficit is matched by an equally larger total of private savings. There is some debate over this qualification. That is, there are people who contend that an increase in the deficit will be matched by an increase in private saving and so will not reduce private investment. There have been three kinds of argument for this position. The Keynesian argument is that the increase in the deficit will increase the national income and so increase saving enough not only to finance the deficit but possibly also to finance an increase in private investment. Hardly anyone would hold to that as a long-run proposition anymore. An older view recently revived is that if the deficit is increased people will realize that they will have to pay more taxes in the future and they will save to be able to pay those future taxes. But no one has been able to verify that people do respond in that way. The third argument is part of supply-side economics. This holds that if the deficit is higher because taxes are lower the after-tax return to saving will be higher and people will save more. There is probably something in that. But estimates of how much an increase in the after-tax return will increase saving do not come close to showing that the increase of saving would be as large as the increase of the deficit.

So while some uncertainty must be recognized, the most probable basis for thinking about the absolute size of the deficit or surplus over a period of time is that the primary effect is on the cumulative amount of private investment over that period. This effect on private investment is a matter of serious concern because the amount of private investment over time affects the level of total output and productivity.

One may ask why it is any business of the government to try to influence the rate of economic growth by a decision about the size of the government surplus or deficit. The national rate of economic growth is the statistical summation of the results of the decisions and efforts of millions of individuals and households, each seeking to manage its affairs so as to achieve the rate of personal income growth that seems feasible and desirable. There is no reason for the government to have a goal about that except to create conditions in which individuals can freely make their own choices. Therefore the government should only choose some arbitrary goal for the size of the deficit or surplus—like zero—and leave the private parties free to make whatever adjustment they like to that decision. If the private parties on the whole feel that the rate of their personal income growth is too low under these conditions, they can work more, save more, study more or do whatever else they think worthwhile. No one could say that the resulting rate of economic growth would be "wrong."

This is a conceivable position, and indeed I took this position about twenty years ago.[1] It does not seem to me a reasonable position today, however. Twenty years ago one might think that there was a position about the budget—namely, that it should be balanced—which although arbitrary had a great deal of public support. That satisfied the need for a standard to which politics would conform, and probably satisfied it better than any alternative that might seem less arbitrary. Also, twenty years ago one could be more complacent about the prospects for the growth of the American economy than one can be today—simply because our rate of productivity growth has fallen significantly.

The government does have to decide the size of the surplus or deficit. There is no free market solution for that. Neither is there any longer a traditional standard—like the balanced budget—for making the decision. A new standard has to be created and defended against alternatives, and it will have to be defended by showing that it has good effects. The most important of these effects is on the future rate of economic growth via the influence on the rate of private investment.

So it seems clear that in thinking about the desirable size of the deficit or surplus one should be thinking primarily about the desired rate of growth of national output and productivity. But once that has been said it is hard to say more. There is no objective way to determine how much the nation should forgo current government services and private consumption in order to make the future national income greater.

The problem is the same at the national level as at the household level. There is no objective way to determine how much a household should save in order to have more income in the future. One can list some things that the household should think about—the probable trend of its future income and the income prospects of its children, whether it has extraordinary expenses now or foreseeable in the future, what the costs of various levels of living after retirement would be and so on. But when all such information is assembled, different people will make different judgments about how much is to be saved. The best one can get is an informed feeling.

So at the national level all one can hope to achieve is a procedure in which a deliberate decision is made on the size of the surplus or deficit in the light of the relevant information by responsible people who represent the national feeling about the matter. The decision should be made for several years at a time—at least five. The effect of the budget decision on the stock of productive capital is very small in any one year, because the volume of investment in any one year is small relative to the capital stock. It is only the accumulated size of the deficit or surplus over a number of years that significantly affects the stock of capital and therefore the levels of output and productivity. Moreover, the considerations which affect what the size of the surplus or deficit should be will not ordinarily change much from one year to another, although they may change gradually over a longer period of time.[2]

Thus, one can visualize the administration in its annual budget setting a target for the size of the deficit or surplus in the ensuing five years. In deciding on this target it would take into account the recent and predicted trends of productivity growth. Even though one cannot objectively say what is the "proper" rate of productivity growth, forcing the population to adapt to a slowdown of real income growth relative to expectations is disruptive and should be avoided if possible. Therefore the case for a high surplus or low deficit will be strong if needed to prevent a slowdown of productivity growth. If current expenditure requirements are exceptionally high, as in a period of defense buildup, the case for deficits is strong, to avoid the necessity for tax rates which raise difficult questions of incentives and equity. This is traditionally recognized in wartime, of course. The composition of the budget may also make a difference in the decision. That is, the more the expenditure side of the budget provides for growth-promoting programs, like research, the more justification there is for borrowing rather than taxing.

The important point is that the decision about the deficit or surplus should be regarded as a decision about the allocation of the national output, like other decisions in the federal budget. Federal expenditures influence how much of the national output is devoted to defense and research and education and highways and so on. There are no precise objective formulas by which to determine the right amount in any of these cases. But we seek informed and responsible judgments. So the decision about the size of the surplus or deficit is a decision, positive or negative, about the share of the national output that goes to private investment, and it should be made and explained in that way.

In 1983 one could see the beginnings of thinking about the deficit in this way. The deficits in prospect were large by historical standards, but no one any longer took seriously the notion of balancing the budget. How big should the deficit be? Three considerations seemed to provide an answer. The growth of productivity in the 1970s had been disappointingly low. It was important to stop that trend of deterioration and if possible to reverse it. This pointed to the desirability of seeing that the deficits were at least no larger relative to GNP than they had been in the previous decade—about 2-1/2 percent of GNP—rather than the 6 percent experienced in 1983. On the other hand, we were planning an increase of defense spending relative to GNP, which meant that to get the deficit down below 2-1/2 percent of GNP would require high marginal tax rates that might endanger economic efficiency. Moreover, to avoid disturbing the economy's recovery from the recession it would be desirable that the reduction of the deficit should come gradually. This combination of factors led to the recommendation that the deficit be reduced gradually to 2-1/2 percent of GNP by 1988. The Reagan budget issued in January contained such a recommendation, and some of the foregoing argument was implicit in the report of the President's Council of Economic Advisers at that time.[3]

In circumstances different from those of the early 1980s a different conclusion about the desirable size of the deficit might be reached. If, for example, defense requirements should diminish, because the rebuilding of the armed forces had been completed or for some other reason, it might be appropriate to aim for a smaller deficit or even for a balanced budget. A radical change in the rate of productivity growth would also affect the surplus-deficit target. The desirable size of the surplus or deficit is not fixed forever. That is why it should not be incorporated in a constitutional amendment. The choice of a surplus or deficit target is a political decision to be made from time to time in the light of long-run growth considerations. The problem, of course, is to get them made in this way, rather than for short-run political expedience. There is no alternative to trying to develop understanding of the need for this, in the government and in the public. This should be one of the main objectives of the national reconsideration of economic policy that is now required.

Notes

1. Herbert Stein, comment on paper "Economic Growth as an Objective of Government Policy" by James Tobin, Proceedings of American Economic Association, December 27–29, 1963 (published May 1964), pp. 24–27.

2. In thinking about the proper size of deficits it is necessary to look out even beyond the five-year period suggested here for setting targets. The deficits run during one five-year period will determine the size of the debt with which the next five-year period begins, and that will affect the difficulty of holding deficits in that next five-year period to a level that may be consistent with national growth objectives. This only means that it is desirable to avoid deficits of a size that, although tolerable or helpful today, excessively limit the freedom of action of future generations.

3. A more explicit use of this reasoning to arrive at this recommendation appeared in an article by Cagan, Fellner, Penner and Stein, "Economic Policy for Recovery and Growth," *AEI Economist*, January 1983.

Chapter 6: LEGISLATIVE REFORM

Based on an analysis of spending and revenue trends, plus interviews in 1984 with administration officials, Clark concludes that future efforts to reduce the deficit will have to lean much more heavily on tax increases than on spending cuts. Neither Republican nor Democratic administrations have been able to control spending, leaving tax increases as the only way out.

STIFF TAX HIKES WILL BE KEY TO FUTURE EFFORTS TO CLOSE THE BUDGET DEFICIT

Timothy B. Clark

Although the architects of this year's "down payment" to reduce the government's budget deficits are searching for a delicate balance between spending cuts and revenue increases, installments in future years will concentrate much more heavily on taxes.

This conclusion emerges from an analysis of government spending and revenue trends over two decades, interviews with high-level Reagan Administration officials and a review of congressional attitudes toward budget options. It derives in part from an extensive historical review of the budget completed by the Office of Management and Budget (OMB) during the past six months and released in February and April.

The general conclusion that taxes must increase significantly if the budget is to move closer to being balanced is supported by a set of subordinate conclusions:

 • The explosion of domestic spending that began under President Johnson is as much a creature of Republican Administrations as Democratic. Indeed, the "Great Society" programs initiated by Johnson have not been the major force behind the domestic spending boom; the major expansion occurred under Presidents Nixon and Ford.

 • The huge social insurance programs that have driven that growth are essentially off-limits to budget cutters. In the past three years, a bipartisan consensus has emerged that social security and other retirement programs, which are almost entirely self-financed through payroll taxes, can be modified only to ensure their solvency but not to cut deficits.

 • Republicans have almost reached the limit of their willingness to countenance other domestic budget cuts. GOP committee chairmen in the Senate and ranking minority members of House committees and subcommittees were

Reprinted with permission of the publisher from *National Journal*, April 21, 1984, pp. 752–57.

present at the creation of many of the programs that have been the target of Administration budget cutters, and they are resisting further reductions.

• The Administration itself is reluctant to keep pushing members of its own party for domestic cuts they don't want to make. Deep cuts demanded in 1981 have given way to lesser demands as OMB has recognized the futility of repeating requests that have already been denied. OMB calculates that the Administration has asked Congress to make cuts totaling $570 billion in fiscal 1982–86 and that Congress has approved $288 billion, or 51 per cent.

• Defense cuts cannot be expected to contribute much to deficit reduction. Decisions made in 1981–82 have sent the military budget on an upward path that would be difficult to curb even for a Democratic President.

The obstacles to further deep spending cuts are already evident this year as Congress wrestles to produce a "down payment" on the deficit. Even if enacted, the package would leave cumulative deficits in the next three years of more than $500 billion.

In budget documents released this year, OMB has gloated about the "dramatic halt in domestic spending growth" that has occurred during the Reagan Administration. Measured in constant dollars that eliminate the distortion of inflation, domestic spending doubled from 1954–61, doubled again by 1971 and nearly doubled again by 1981. But "after an era in which the real cost of government doubled three times in less than three decades, the shift in national policy inaugurated by the Reagan Administration will result in a decade-long domestic real spending freeze," the February budget document said. Even if modest additional spending restraints requested in the new budget are not enacted, real spending for domestic programs will rise only 6 per cent from 1981–89, it added.

By documenting the domestic spending explosion that occurred under Republican Presidents during the 1970s and by outlining the spending slowdown already achieved during the Reagan Administration, OMB's two reports this year imply that little more can be done easily to curb spending growth. A further conclusion that is strongly implied but not openly stated is that tax increases are the only way out of the sea of red ink stretching through the end of the decade.

This conclusion is shared by some high-level Administration officials, including OMB director Dave Stockman, according to associates. Stockman, who ordered and personally directed the four-month OMB review of budget history, all but said as much in an interview with *Fortune* published on Feb. 6. "We have gone through a great testing process for three years, and that defines the financing requirements of the government," he said. "Now we have to figure out how to pay our bills."

For a long time, Stockman and Council of Economic Advisers chairman Martin S. Feldstein have reportedly advocated substantial tax increases to close the deficit. But this view has not carried the day within the Administration. Treasury Secretary Donald T. Regan, Reagan's chief economic spokesman, has continually raised his voice against tax increases of a magnitude that would be needed to make serious inroads against the deficits, and President Reagan has listened to him.

A few straws in the wind, however, seem to indicate that Regan and the President may come to the view that taxes must play a prominent role in a post-election deficit reduction drive. In budget briefings for congressional Republicans on March 21, Reagan acknowledged the possibility that new taxes might be needed if government spending could not be reduced enough to produce a balanced budget, although he added, "I happen to believe that there's a good chance that will not be necessary if we do what we should do with regard to shrinking the cost of government."

Regan has been taking a similar line. His department is now conducting a broad study of options for simplifying the tax code. Although Regan has said the options are designed to be "revenue-neutral," there is no reason why the study could not be used as a springboard for revenue-raising proposals.

Lawrence A. Kudlow, who served as Stockman's chief economist at OMB until last year and keeps up his contacts within the Administration, believes that the fierce resistance to new taxes from supply-siders and others in Cabinet and sub-Cabinet posts is slowly melting away. "Privately, inside the government, there is less disagreement than meets the eye" on the need for new taxes, Kudlow said, in large part because substantial additional savings in domestic programs are not politically attainable.

Yet other seasoned political observers do not agree that the limits of domestic budget cutting have been reached. Former deputy Treasury secretary Charles E. Walker, for example, believes there is a constituency in Congress for curtailing growth of the entitlement programs, including social security. "If we were not in an election year, and if [last year's] social security rescue legislation were not of such recent vintage, you could see legislation to hold cost-of-living increases 2-3 percentage points below the increase in inflation," Walker said. He predicts entitlements will be curtailed during the first three months of 1985 as part of a package that would also increase taxes.

Dimensions of the Problem

Rudolph G. Penner, director of the Congressional Budget Office (CBO), has served this year as a principal bearer of bad tidings on the budget. Not only has he supplied Congress with astronomical projections of rising deficits through the rest of the decade, but his agency also has thrown damp towels over various plans to stem the flow of red ink by challenging sponsors' claims of savings.

In February, the CBO sent Congress a report estimating that if nothing were done, the budget deficit in fiscal 1989 would reach $308 billion. From fiscal 1985–89, the agency said, accumulating deficits would add a bit more than $1.2 trillion to the national debt, which now stands at almost $1.5 trillion.

For fiscal 1985, which begins next Oct. 1, and the two following years, CBO now estimates that deficits will total $712 billion if nothing is done to change tax or spending policies. The Administration's original budget would cut the three-year tide of red ink to $627 billion, the agency says. The "Rose Garden" version of Reagan's budget—agreed to by the Senate Republican leadership on March 16 and approved by the Senate Budget Committee on April 11—would result in $570 billion in new debt in the next three years. And the House Democratic budget, passed on April 5, would produce deficits totaling $530 billion in fiscal 1985–87.

These numbers emphasize the modest nature of the deficit down payment now being discussed in Congress. The Rose Garden plan would reduce the three-year accumulation of debt by just 20 per cent, and the House plan by 25 per cent.

Thus not much of a dent will be made in the deficit even if the down payment is approved by Congress. Three years from now, the deficit will have gone up, not down, at least in terms of current dollars. Under the House plan, the deficit in 1987 would be $182 billion, $10 billion larger than in 1986. The Rose Garden package would produce a deficit of $204 billion in 1987, nearly $20 billion more than in 1986.

It's a safe bet that the balance due on deficit reduction will preoccupy the President and the Congress that take office next January.

The Long View

The judgment that further spending cuts will not contribute a great deal to next year's deficit reduction installment rests on a long view of budget history and politics.

Since shortly after World War II, the budget has divided the government's activities into functions and subfunctions that are based on 1,100 appropriations accounts that correspond to lines in the 13 appropriations bills Congress considers each year. Before this year, the budget functions had not been updated since the Congressional Budget Act became law in 1974.

Stockman wanted a more detailed and updated series of budget categories that would ease his task of historical analysis and make the budget more accessible to laymen.

First, he subdivided some of the 1,100 appropriations accounts, creating about 100 more, and then he combined all of the accounts into 430 new units that the OMB staff calls "building blocks." These were then combined into larger groupings that Stockman believed were more analytically meaningful, including "low-income benefit programs," "social insurance programs" and "national interest programs" such as Energy Department research on nuclear weapons technology, foreign military assistance and the space program.

Stockman also insisted that budget data stretching back more than two decades be plugged into these new categories. He wanted the ability to compare spending trends after eliminating distortions resulting from changing economic conditions, shifts in accounting or technical conventions and legislative melding of programs into block grants. Thus he was creating what some of his colleagues called a "who struck John" budget whose essential purpose was to chart spending and taxing changes attributable only to political choices made by Congresses and Presidents in the past two decades.

The principal conclusions of Stockman's work were presented in Part 3, "Budget Program and Trends," of the fiscal 1985 budget released on Feb. 1. They were elaborated on in a 591-page book, *Major Themes and Additional Budget Details,* that OMB released on April 11.

The Defense Pillar

Members of Congress, especially Democrats who are searching for ways to make good on the balance due after this year's deficit down payment, inevitably will turn their attention to defense spending. Unlike the beneficiaries of social security, medicare or unemployment insurance, the generals and weapons makers who spend the Pentagon dollar are not entitled to quasi-automatic appropriations mandated by law. The defense function of the budget includes more discretionary spending than any other.

Yet there seems little prospect of sharply slowing the defense buildup that started at the beginning of the decade; Reagan would resist it, and even the House Democrats do not seem inclined to approve huge cuts.

Stockman takes the long view to justify the Administration's defense program, emphasizing that its claim on the economy is modest when compared with the past. "The needed Defense budget growth launched on a bipartisan basis by Congress in 1980 and accelerated during the Reagan Administration does not come close to imposing the burden on the U.S. economy experienced during earlier periods," said the latest OMB book.

As a share of gross national product (GNP), it notes, defense spending averaged 8.6 per cent from 1954–70. In 1968, at the peak of the Vietnam war, the military was spending 9.9 per cent of GNP. But then defense spending, measured in constant dollars, declined for nearly a decade, reaching a low point of 5.5 per cent in 1976. The Administration's defense program for fiscal 1985 would put spending at 7 per cent of GNP, which OMB argued "can hardly be considered excessive" in a "difficult and threatening world" and represents "no more than a midpoint between the normal burden prior to the 1970s and the temporarily depressed levels of the mid and late 1970s."

OMB is accurate in its assertion that the defense buildup was launched under President Carter with bipartisan support. Although many Democrats in Congress now complain that Reagan has pushed ahead too fast, the argument is about the pace, not the direction. The Democratic budget passed by the House would shave a little more than 10 per cent from Reagan's proposed defense outlays during the next three years but still would increase the defense budget by 3.5 per cent above inflation. Outlays would be only $26.5 billion less in 1987 than under the Rose Garden budget.

The need for sustained growth in military outlays thus is a key pillar of the budget analysis supporting the conclusion that deficits cannot be eliminated through spending cuts.

Social Insurance

The analysis rests on another important conclusion about budget trends: that domestic spending programs undertaken during the 1970s with bipartisan support have been curtailed nearly as much as Congress will allow.

As the February budget notes, domestic spending measured in constant dollars will grow hardly at all during the rest of the decade, even if spending reductions proposed this year are not approved by Congress. This means that domestic outlays will shrink as a share of GNP. Domestic spending equaled only 4 per cent of GNP in 1954; it had grown to 7.3 per cent, by 1961, to 10.5 per cent by 1971 and to 15 per cent by 1981.

On the basis of legislation already enacted, domestic spending's share of GNP will drop to 14 per cent this year, according to the February budget, and to 12.6 per cent in 1989, even if other proposed spending reductions are not enacted. OMB boasts that "this reversal is nearly without precedent among major industrial democracies."

As Stockman recast the budget categories, he grouped domestic spending programs into three major categories: social insurance and pensions, low-income benefits, and discretionary items. The social insurance grouping was by far the largest, spending a projected $306 billion in fiscal 1985, or 58 per cent of domestic outlays, which totaled $525 billion. The category includes social security, medicare, federal retirement, unemployment insurance, railroad retirement, black lung benefits and insurance for private pensions. In general, said OMB, the programs "are financed by dedicated revenues, chiefly payroll taxes, which gives them their 'insurance' character."

For two decades, the social insurance and pension programs grew faster than any other category of the budget. From 1966–75, spending for these programs grew by an annual average of 12.5 per cent above the inflation rate as Congress widened eligibility and sweetened benefits and as the retired population increased. From 1962–81, these programs grew from 2.9 per cent of GNP to 7.6 per cent, accounting for the entire increase in the government's claim on the economy.

This "era of legislative expansion" gave way to an "era of bipartisan restraint" that began with enactment of social security reforms in 1977, the budget documents say. Four essential principles emerged during the second era, in OMB's view:

- a "commitment to maintaining the basic structure of universal protections against the risks of unemployment, retirement, old age, sickness and disability that emerged" over four decades;

- a recognition that program benefits and coverage could not be liberally expanded as in the 1960s and 1970s;

- a rejection of "massive general fund subsidies" to remedy the financing shortfalls of various trust funds in favor of " 'solvency plans' that reinforced the essential social insurance character" of the programs through mandatory savings made through the payroll tax;

- adoption of solvency formulas based on shared sacrifice by taxpayers and beneficiaries.

Just as strong bipartisan majorities in Congress voted to liberalize the social insurance programs in the late 1960s and early 1970s, so the two parties have joined in curtailing their growth during the past seven years. Legislation in 1977, 1980 and 1983 raised social security retirement taxes and curbed benefits. The 1981 Budget Reconciliation Act included provisions to shore up the unemployment insurance program. The 1982 Tax Equity and Fiscal Responsibility Act limited hospital reimbursements under medicare, and in 1983, a prospective medicare reimbursement system for hospitals was enacted. In 1983, too, the solvency of the railroad retirement program was restored by increasing taxes and shaving benefits.

The financial condition of the social insurance and pension trust funds dipped to a low point in 1983, when receipts of $209 billion equaled only 76 per cent of outlays, and the deficit reached $67 billion. But their financial condition will improve steadily during this decade: in 1989, receipts will equal 95 per cent of outlays, the budget estimates.

If it is true that the financing problems of the social insurance programs must be addressed by ensuring the "solvency" of the trust funds that support them, then these programs are off limits to deficit reduction plans. Reagan's 1981 proposal to cut social security benefits received a hostile reaction, and his budget now emphasizes that the social security problem has been solved. Similarly, House Democrats, in their budget, declared that there was nothing more to do on social security. Administration officials predict that a "solvency solution" will be found for the huge financing gap that will confront the medicare program in the 1990s.

Reforms enacted in recent years have dramatically slowed the growth of the social insurance programs. Real (after inflation) growth slowed to an annual average of 5 per cent from 1976–80 and will slow further under existing law, to 3.2 per cent from 1985–89 or to 2.6 per cent if Administration proposals are enacted. Rises in the beneficiary population and technical factors will account for all of the new growth.

The social insurance programs' drain on the economy thus will decline during the rest of the decade. Their share of GNP peaked at 8.6 per cent in 1983 and will drop about a point by 1989.

Low-Income Benefits

If the huge social insurance category is off limits, low-income benefit programs seem no more susceptible to budget cuts because their growth has been slowed more dramatically.

In fiscal 1985, under the Administration's budget, $66 billion will be spent for this grouping of programs, which includes such major means-tested entitlements as aid to families with dependent children (AFDC), supplemental security income, medicaid and child nutrition and such discretionary programs as housing aid, low-income energy assistance and nutrition assistance to pregnant women and small children. In constant dollars, outlays will remain about the same throughout the 1980s.

From 1954–81, the cost of these programs, not counting inflation, increased eleven-fold, the budget documents say. From 1970–81, the cost more than tripled. Now, OMB says, "unsustainable, unnecessary and socially counterproductive expansion has been stopped." But, it concludes, the "social safety net is as strong today as it was in 1981 as measured by constant dollars of budget resources."

The social insurance and low-income benefit categories have suffered no real erosion under the Reagan Administration, but that is not true for nonentitlement domestic outlays. Discretionary outlays have been cut by 24 per cent in real (inflation-adjusted) terms since 1978. In 1984, these programs will spend $158 billion, down from $208 billion (in constant 1985 dollars) from six years earlier.

The "major themes" budget book includes a roster of successful Administration sorties against the discretionary programs. Some of these budget reductions are found in the category of "human development and services," which includes aid for elementary, secondary and higher education, employment and training activities, health services (but not financing) and services for such groups as young children, older Americans, Indians and the handicapped. The purchasing power of programs in this cluster has eroded by more than 25 per cent since it peaked in 1979. In 1984, the programs will spend $32 billion.

With the exception of aid to colleges and college students, the Administration has succeeded in cutting education, training, health and social services programs to at least 20 per cent below their peak levels, in constant dollars. The largest savings have come in public employment and job training services, most of which were provided under the since-repealed Comprehensive Employment and Training Act (CETA). From a 1978 peak of $17 billion (in 1985 dollars), spending has declined by 70 per cent, to $5.3 billion this year and $4.8 billion proposed for next year.

A cluster of human development programs that includes foster care, head start, rehabilitation and social services for the elderly and other groups will spend $6.8 billion this year, down 20 per cent from the 1979 peak.

Health and mental services programs, with $3 billion in outlays this year, have declined 37 per cent in purchasing power from their 1976 peak.

"Community development and economic subsidies," another of Stockman's large program clusters, have been cut in half, from a peak of $48 billion (in constant dollars) in 1980 to $24 billion in 1984. Such programs as community development block grants, aid to Appalachia and Economic Development Administration grants and loan guarantees have been substantially curtailed. Trade adjustment assistance for workers and firms hurt by imports has been slashed from $2.1 billion in 1980 (in 1985 dollars) to $64 million this year. Maritime and rail subsidies have declined, as have housing programs.

Cuts in many other small programs throughout the budget contribute to the Administration's remarkable success in eroding the buying power of the government's discretionary spending programs.

Growth

For many years, Republicans have been campaigning against the perceived excesses of the "Great Society" initiated by President Johnson. The famous 89th Congress (1965–66) did indulge in a program creation spree that helped push domestic spending from 7.3 per cent of GNP in 1961 to 10.5 per cent in 1971.

But OMB's analysis indicates that programs initiated during Johnson's term did not grow much during the 1970s. They did increase enough to offset the effects of inflation, but their real purchasing power stayed about the same.

So congressional expansion of the original Great Society programs cannot explain the rise in domestic spending's share of GNP to 15 per cent by 1981—50 per cent higher than 10 years earlier.

What happened, OMB says, was that pre-Great Society programs were greatly expanded and new ones initiated. Within OMB, this era is called "Great Society II."

Few Members of Congress today were present when the original Great Society programs were created. Only 11 current Senators were in the Senate at the beginning of the 89th Congress. But many more Members were there during the 1970s spending boom, and their allegiance to the new programs has blocked half of the spending cuts Reagan has advocated since he took office in 1981.

Repeatedly, OMB's analysis of budget trends emphasizes that the biggest boom in domestic spending came in the 1970s, chiefly under Presidents Nixon and Ford.

From 1970–76, for example, the cost of the social insurance and retirement category doubled in real terms, from about $100 billion to $200 billion in 1985 dollars. Social security spending grew significantly, in part because of retirement benefit increases of 10 per cent in 1971 and 20 per cent in 1972. Medicare's cost, in constant dollars, more than tripled from 1970–82, and pensions for retired federal workers, which now cost about $23 billion, nearly tripled during the same period.

The community development and economic subsidies category, though smaller than social insurance, grew even more dramatically in the early 1970s. Its real cost increased fourfold during the first half of the decade, to more than $40 billion in 1985 dollars.

Most of the growth in low-income benefits also occurred from 1970–76, when the cost of these programs more than doubled in constant 1985 dollars. This growth, said the OMB book, was "primarily the result of a flurry of legislative expansions during the years 1970–75." Growth slowed during the second half of the decade, but still, the document said, from 1970–81, a "19 per cent annual compound growth rate in outlays far outstripped the rate of inflation, causing constant dollar expenditures to more than triple. Throughout the 1970s, low-income benefit programs were the fastest rising segment of the federal budget."

Resistance Movement

Reagan has railed against federal spending for many years, and, if reelected, will certainly be inclined to push for a new round of program reductions. But the depth of the cuts he suggests and the vigor with which he pursues them will just as surely be tempered by the knowledge that Republicans in Congress are reluctant to keep making cuts.

Their reluctance stems both from pride of authorship and personal commitment to the programs and from more parochial concerns about the economic well-being of their states and districts.

Robert Dole, R-Kan., chairman of the Senate Finance Committee and second-ranking member of the Agriculture, Nutrition and Forestry Committee, is one senior Republican who has resisted some Administration proposals for spending cuts. As a junior Senator in the early 1970s, he joined then-Sen. George McGovern, D-S.D., in building the case for nutrition assistance to the poor. It was during those years that the greatest increases for food stamps and other nutrition programs occurred. The food stamp program peaked at about $13 billion in 1981. Reagan asked Congress to trim it to $9 billion in 1981, but Dole would only go to $11 billion. The Administration is no longer advocating deeper cuts. Dole has also rejected other cuts that have come before the Finance Committee.

Sen. John Heinz of Pennsylvania has led Republican opposition this year to an Administration plan to reduce the medicare financing gap by increasing the premiums retired people pay. And Heinz, along with Sen. William S. Cohen, R-Maine, is leading a drive to curb Administration efforts to save money by dropping people from the social security disability rolls.

In the House, Administration proposals to cut back education and child nutrition programs have run into opposition from Rep. William F. Goodling of Pennsylvania, the senior Republican on the Education and the Labor Subcommittee on Elementary, Secondary and Vocational Education. Goodling, third in seniority on the full committee, has fought to keep subsidies for reduced-priced school lunches higher than the Administration proposed on the ground that entire school districts would drop out of the program if the subsidy were cut too much.

Goodling, a former teacher, has fought education cuts because he believes it is unfair for the government to mandate programs without helping to pay for them and because he thinks it is irresponsible to reduce assistance "at the same time the Administration has made education such a big issue."

"A lot of us feel that we can't go much further" in cutting discretionary spending, Goodling said, while adding that he would support some form of spending freeze to reduce the budget deficits.

On a more parochial level, the Administration has encountered opposition in its attempts to cut federal payroll costs from Rep. Marjorie S. Holt, R-Md., whose district includes large numbers of federal workers. And Republicans from farm states have resisted cuts in farm programs.

Unwilling to put Republicans such as Goodling through the wringer again for a losing cause, the Administration has moderated its requests for spending cuts. In 1981, for example, it asked Congress to cut Job Corps spending from $853 million to $392 million, but Congress refused to approve that and the request for fiscal 1985 is for $599 million. Similarly, the 1985 request for compensatory education is $3.4 billion, $1 billion less than at the end of the Carter Administration but twice the level requested in 1981.

If deep spending cuts are impossible to achieve, the large deficits will continue unless taxes are raised.

Time for Taxes?

Advocates of substantial revenue increases cite two trends in tax policy to help build their case.

One has been the huge rise in payroll taxes to finance the social insurance programs. Paralleling the rise in social insurance outlays, these taxes have grown from 2 per cent of GNP in the mid-1950s to 6.6 per cent in 1984.

The other has been the steady erosion of other sources of revenue, particularly the income tax. In 1954, these other revenue sources totaled 17.2 per cent of GNP, but today they are under 12 per cent.

Analysts who segregate the social insurance programs from the rest of the budget because they are self-financing conclude that the budget deficit is entirely attributable to the other functions of government. And this leads to the conclusion that government is borrowing about $200 billion a year to help finance such key programs as defense, space and infrastructure and transfer programs such as welfare and food stamps. The distasteful idea of floating debt to pay for these kinds of activities helps build the case for tax increases.

All of this is not to say that major tax increases necessarily lie in the future. Quite possibly, deficits do instead.

The CBO's Penner often hears, when talking to groups of congressional constituents on Capitol Hill, that "the public doesn't like deficits, doesn't like taxes and wants to cut spending," he said in a recent interview. But, he continued, the groups never want to cut defense or social security or medicare, and, of course interest on the national debt cannot be avoided. "They are always amazed when I tell them that these four categories of the budget will eat up 95 per cent of the revenues that the current tax system will raise in the next five years," he said. "The public is furious about welfare and foreign aid, but that's not where the money goes."

Penner, for one, fears that these attitudes will lead to deficits continuing at an unacceptably high level for the foreseeable future.

In Feldstein's view, current deficits constitute a serious economic problem but are not likely to lead to economic chaos. He rules out permanent tax increases, stating that the key to deficit reduction lies in keeping pressure on the administration and Congress to cut nondefense spending. Feldstein was willing to stretch out the third year of the President's tax cut, but he would retain tax bracket indexing at all costs.

THE JOB OF REDUCING THE FEDERAL DEFICIT

Martin Feldstein

Speculating about the President's reaction to the budget advice of his economic counselors is such an absorbing activity that it's easy to forget that the administration's proposals are only the first step in the budget process. Congress will ultimately determine the shape of the budget for 1983 and beyond. Because both taxes and spending are in transition, it is particularly important that Congress make its budget decision as part of a long-term strategy.

The immediate focus in Congress will be on controlling the federal deficit. Only a few months ago, the administration shocked many people by acknowledging that tax rules and spending patterns imply a 1984 deficit of $160 billion. Such a deficit would be about 4% of 1984's $4 trillion gross national product, or about twice the rate of fiscal 1981. How did the prospective deficit get so large? And what will be done to reduce it?

It would be wrong to say that the 1984 deficit figure is due to a massive cut in personal tax rates. The 25% reduction that Congress enacted will be just about enough to prevent bracket creep from raising the share of income that is taken in taxes. It would also be wrong to say that the prospective deficit is due to a major rise in defense spending since the 7% a year real increase that the President has called for would raise defense spending only from 5.5% of GNP in 1980 to 6.5% in 1984.

Roots of the Deficit

The main reason that the prospective 1984 deficit is 4% of GNP is that the administration inherited a deficit that had grown over the past decade to 2% of GNP. The increase in defense spending over four years will add an additional 1% of GNP to the 1984 deficit. The business tax reductions (primarily the accelerated

---

Reprinted with permission of the author from *The Wall Street Journal*, January 19, 1982, p. 28.

cost recovery system) and the personal tax cuts (including the bracket reductions, the saving incentives and the end of the marriage penalty) each increase the 1984 deficit by about 0.75% of GNP. Offsetting these increases are the spending cuts enacted in 1981 that, by 1984, will reduce outlays by about 0.5% of GNP. Combining the inherited deficit with these changes in taxes and spending implies a 1984 deficit of 4% of GNP, or $160 billion.

Some analysts have overreacted to this figure, saying that such deficits would cause financial chaos. Some administration spokesmen and their outside friends have overreacted in the opposite direction and said such deficits don't matter. Neither extreme position is correct. Large deficits in 1983 and beyond wouldn't cause financial chaos but they would be a very serious economic problem.

Continued deficits put pressure on product markets that makes prices increase faster than they otherwise would. Though the Fed may be able to prevent a significant rise in inflation by allowing high real interest rates to crowd out private spending, large deficits surely put the Fed's monetarist determination to a severe test. Moreover, such a policy could strain Congress' tolerance of high interest rates to the point where it forces the Fed back to the inflationary accommodation policies of the past decade.

But even if their inflationary effect is small, sustained deficits would be pernicious by crowding out private investment. In recent years, net private investment has been only 6% of gross national product. A rise of the deficit by another 2% of GNP could reduce net private investment by one-third of its current value to just 4% of GNP.

Of course the tax incentives enacted this year may raise total saving and increase the flow of saving into business investment by enough to permit the government deficit to rise substantially without reducing the current ratio of business investment to GNP. But even if that occurs, it wouldn't change the fact that the deficit would have prevented the increased capital formation that would otherwise have occurred.

It would surely be unfortunate if the important new tax incentives for saving and investment serve only to prevent our rate of investment from becoming lower than it has been in recent years.

What then should be done to decrease the deficit? The key is reducing federal nondefense spending. The overgrowth of government spending that has occurred in the past two decades would deserve substantial pruning even if there were no deficit. Much of the increase in government spending during these years has been due to the introduction and expansion of programs that are wasteful and are the source of serious distortions in economic incentives.

The issue is whether Congress and the administration will have the political fortitude to make the necessary legislative changes, especially in Social Security and the other "entitlement" or cash-transfer programs. Every proposed spending cut brings howls from those who would lose benefits and from the industries and professional groups that serve them. Moreover, the status quo acquires such an appearance of legitimacy that many others also rush to defend every existing program. But this plethora of programs cannot be legitimized by reference to their history.

Anyone contemplating the possibility of major reductions in government spending should recognize just how recently many of the spending programs were created or expanded. In 1960, federal civilian spending accounted for 9% of gross national product. That increased to 13% by 1970 and 17% by 1980. Returning such spending to 1970's share of GNP—hardly back to the Dark Ages in terms of economic and social spending—would reduce outlays by 4% of GNP or $160 billion at the 1984 level, enough to eliminate the entire deficit.

Though such a reduction of the federal government's share in GNP will not occur by 1984, it could be achieved over a somewhat longer period. If the growth of federal civilian spending were slowed to 2% less than the inflation rate, the share of such spending would be reduced to 1970's 13% in less than six years. Slowing the growth of spending in this way would obviously be politically difficult. But the existing legislative commitment to future tax cuts and the justifiable dislike of budget deficits may together provide the political pressure that Congress needs to enact this spending slowdown.

Canceling the personal tax cuts or increasing other taxes at the present time would reduce this pressure on Congress and thereby make it more difficult to achieve desirable cuts in government spending. Nevertheless, the failure to raise taxes implies larger deficits in the next few years and therefore more undesirable crowding out of private investment. How should this dilemma be resolved?

It is clear that if Congress is never going to get the spending share down to match the tax revenue that current tax rules imply, the tax rules must be changed to provide more revenue. Repealing the 1983 tax cut of 10% would add 1984 revenue of about $40 billion or 1% of GNP as a permanent tax increase. Similarly, the changes in excise taxes and other tax rules that the administration has discussed could permanently add some $30 billion to future tax revenue.

It would be wrong, however, to assume that the administration and Congress will lack the courage to control the growth of spending. Making such an assumption and therefore voting a permanent tax increase now would, by reducing the political pressure that a prospective deficit provides, make it more difficult for Congress to continue to slow the growth of spending.

My preference would therefore be to avoid a permanent tax increase but to obtain a temporary increase in tax revenue by stretching out the personal tax cut. For example, the 10% rate cut scheduled for July 1983 could be postponed until July 1984 or even divided between 1984 and 1985. Such a stretch-out would reduce the crowding out of investment during the next few years while the spending reductions bring total outlays into line with the tax structure.

Bracket Indexing Vital

It is crucial for Congress to remain committed to both the series of personal tax rate cuts and the bracket indexing that together will keep the tax share from being increased by inflationary bracket creep. Because bracket indexing is scheduled to begin only in 1985 and is still not widely understood, it is vulnerable to the political pursuit of additional tax revenue. The abandonment of bracket indexing would virtually guarantee a return to spiraling increases in taxes and government spending.

Any extra tax receipts that result from raising excise tax rates or from other changes in tax rules should be only a temporary revenue increase designed to limit crowding out during transition to a lower government spending level. It would be appropriate therefore for Congress to vote in 1982 to return any such revenue in future years by gradually increasing the $2,000 IRA deduction limit or by making other tax changes designed to encourage saving.

In short, the legitimate fear of a permanent deficit cannot justify a reversal of the 1981 tax cuts or a permanent increase in taxes from other sources. Even more important, a desire to eliminate the deficit should not be used as a rationale for undoing the structural tax changes that were enacted to stimulate saving and business investment. If that were to happen, the favorable long-term consequences of the 1981 tax changes would be destroyed.

Deficits do matter, Rivlin maintains, because they put upward pressure on interest rates, stunt economic growth, and intensify the international debt crisis. She calls for a series of political compromises to eliminate the deficit, centering on across-the-board reductions in spending and increased taxes.

WHY AND HOW TO CUT THE DEFICIT

Alice M. Rivlin

A drastic change is needed in U.S. economic policy—and needed quickly. High deficits in the federal budget, and the high interest rates that go with such deficits, are endangering the future growth of the U.S. economy and crippling the ability of American industry and agriculture to compete in world markets. If we continue on our present course, we will be using much of our national saving to finance the government rather than to increase investment, devoting a rapidly rising fraction of our resources to servicing the federal debt, and burdening our children with costly repayments of our debts to foreigners.

We need to summon the political will to reduce the deficit—substantially and soon. This article proposes a program—of immediate actions and longer-term reforms—that would bring the budget into approximate balance by fiscal year 1989. The proposed changes would be painful and unpopular. There is no painless way to reduce a large deficit. But this plan is designed to be evenhanded in its distribution of sacrifice and politically realistic in its scope and pace.

The plan presented here is discussed at greater length in a new book, *Economic Choices 1984*. It was hammered out by a team of Brookings researchers—Henry J. Aaron, Barry P. Bosworth, Linda Cohen, Harvey Galper, William W. Kaufmann, Lawrence B. Krause, Robert Z. Lawrence, Robert H. Meyer, Louise B. Russell, and myself. Over a period of several months, we discussed options and argued about priorities. In the end our plan, like all serious deficit reduction plans, involved compromise. Not all of us are enthusiastic about all parts of it. But we believe it is a feasible and fair proposal to solve a crucial policy problem.

The Outlook: High Deficits and High Interest Rates

For the last several years, monetary and fiscal policies—the two principal instruments by which the federal government affects the overall state of the

From *The Brookings Review*, Summer 1984. Copyright © 1984 by the Brookings Institution, Washington, D.C.

economy—have worked at cross-purposes. Monetary policy has been predominantly restrictive, while fiscal policy has been mainly stimulative. The results have been high deficits and high interest rates that will continue for the forseeable future unless policies are changed.

Beginning in 1979, the monetary authorities, concerned about the high inflation of the late 1970s, assiduously restricted growth in the money supply. Interest rates rose to extremely high levels, and the economy went into a deep and lengthy recession from which it did not begin to recover until the end of 1982. Not surprisingly, the interest-rate-sensitive sectors of the economy were especially hard hit. Unemployment jumped to over 10 percent, and inflation dropped dramatically.

Meanwhile, fiscal policy was dominated by the large personal and corporate income tax reductions enacted in 1981. The resulting shrinkage in revenue was not matched by cuts in spending; only the mix of spending changed, shifting away from domestic programs and toward defense and interest payments on the rising debt. As a result of both the recession and the enactment of massive tax cuts without corresponding reductions in total spending, the federal deficit soared to $193 billion, or 6 percent of the gross national product, in fiscal year 1983.

Since the end of 1982, the economy has been experiencing a healthy recovery. But even if the economy continues to grow, the deficit will not decline under current policies. Indeed, although revenues will rise as the economy expands, spending will rise even faster—and so the deficit will actually continue to increase. This prospect of a rising deficit in an improving economy makes the present situation very unusual; since World War II, high deficits have ordinarily been associated with recession, not recovery.

The projected deficits are not attributable to the social security and medicare trust funds. Taken together, these funds are expected to be roughly in balance through 1989—thanks to recent increases in payroll taxes. The shortfall will be in the rest of the budget. Spending for programs other than medicare and social security will total about 17.2 percent of GNP in 1985 and will rise slightly faster than GNP, with defense and interest payments accounting for most of the increase. Revenues, however, which were sharply reduced by the income tax cuts passed in 1981, will be only about 12.7 percent of GNP in 1985 and will rise slightly slower than GNP. So it is that we will be facing a large and widening gap.

Government borrowing to finance the deficit is contributing to high interest rates and can be expected to exert more upward pressure on them in the near future as private credit demands increase. As workers and factories become more fully employed, the monetary authorities will have to keep a tight rein on credit to avoid a reescalation of inflation. The conflict between a stimulative budget policy and a restrictive monetary policy will intensify, and interest rates are likely to rise further.

Why Policies Must Be Changed

Large deficits are bad news for America. They are enemies of economic growth, impediments to American competitiveness in the international marketplace, and aggravators of the increasingly grave international debt problem.

Effects on Growth

Sustained economic growth should be a high priority of public policy. We should aim for an economy in which average incomes rise gradually over the years so that more is available for the satisfaction of both public and private needs. In a growing economy, public choices are less agonizing and divisive, because an increase in the resources devoted to one objective does not automatically decrease the resources available for other purposes. Growth also cushions the impact of economic change, making it easier for workers in declining industries to find new jobs and for new firms to spring up to replace those that are in decline. Moreover, the experience of the postwar period indicates that overall economic growth is a powerful force for the reduction of poverty. Programs of education and training for low-income people have little chance of success if there are few jobs available. Even if some proportion of those in poverty cannot be expected to participate in income growth, the provision of resources for their support is easier in a growing economy.

Budget deficits in the anticipated range will absorb about two-thirds of the net private savings expected to be available; this will leave less for the capital formation necessary for continued economic growth. Examination of the past yields little hope that private saving will rise enough to offset federal dissaving of such unprecedented magnitudes. Far more likely is fierce competition for limited savings, resulting in higher interest rates.

High deficits and high interest rates do not necessarily mean immediate disaster for the economy. The deficits will continue to stimulate the economy generally, while the high interest rates will tend to slow particular types of spending, especially housing and business investment. High deficits and high interest rates affect the *mix* of total spending—with more resources going to consumption and less to housing and investment than would be the case if we had lower deficits and lower interest rates. A low level of investment in plant and equipment is likely to reduce productivity increases and hamper economic growth in the longer run. Penalizing investment is borrowing from the future to increase consumption now.

Effects on American Competitiveness

High interest rates have already had a devastating impact on the ability of U.S. industry to compete in world markets. These rates have attracted a large inflow of capital from abroad. The foreign capital has helped to finance the federal deficit as well as private investment, but it has added to the demand for dollars on foreign exchange markets. The exchange value of the dollar has risen sharply in the last several years, making U.S. exports more expensive for foreigners and foreign goods and services cheaper for Americans. As a result, the United States has been running a huge deficit in its balance of trade, and output and employment in industries facing foreign competition have suffered. Borrowing from abroad is also borrowing from the future to fund current consumption, since the debts incurred will have to be repaid, with interest, out of future national production.

Effects on International Debt

High interest rates in the United States lead to high interest rates around the world and greatly aggravate the precarious international debt situation. As interest rates rise, third world countries find it increasingly difficult to make the interest payments on their debts to U.S. banks. Severe balance-of-payments difficulties have led the largest of the borrowing countries to adopt restrictive domestic economic policies in efforts to reduce import requirements. These problems of debt financing are especially serious in Latin America, the Philippines, and Africa.

The Future is Now

We cannot continue putting off action on the budget deficit. The time for temporizing is past; delay in grappling with the deficit not only augments the problems described above, but it increases the costs of taking the steps that we will need to take sooner or later.

At high interest rates, the rising debt adds rapidly to the interest costs of the federal government. Each year that the United States postpones action on its deficit adds $200 billion to the debt and increases required annual interest payments by about $20 billion. Thus, the longer we procrastinate, the more taxes will have to be raised or spending cut—and that is a permanent cost to current and future generations.

On the other hand, prompt action sharply reduces the magnitude of the changes required to bring the budget into balance. For example, at current interest rates of 10 percent, because of the compound effect of interest financing a $1 billion expenditure cut would reduce the annual budget deficit after five years by a total of $1.7 billion—a figure that reflects an additional savings of $0.7 billion in interest payments.

The Need for Political Compromise

The economy would benefit greatly from major shifts in monetary and fiscal policies to reduce deficits and interest rates. Those changes will not be easy to bring about, however. While concern about the deficits is widely expressed, specific proposals to raise taxes or cut domestic or defense programs are likely to encounter far more opposition than support. It will take political courage, ingenuity, and vision to fashion a deficit reduction plan than can garner broad support even though specific elements of it would be painful.

Not only will compromise within Congress and between it and the president be required to effect a successful switch of policies, but also an unusual degree of coordination between monetary and fiscal decision-makers will be essential. If the switch is to be made without slowing the economy unduly as the deficit falls, monetary authorities will have to permit substantial reductions in interest rates and the exchange value of the dollar.

The need to reduce the federal deficit is pressing, and much is riding on the decisions that are made, or fail to be made, in the short term. But we should not lose sight of the opportunities that this need creates. We can use this juncture to reexamine government priorities and the effectiveness of specific programs. And we can seize the chance to reform the federal tax system as we raise more revenue through it; indeed, tax increases without reform would magnify the inequities and inefficiencies of the present system.

A Compromise Plan

The plan offered here represents an attempt by a group of economists to construct a feasible, fair blueprint for bringing the federal budget close to balance by 1989. It reflects a recognition that the deficits are so large that we must proceed on all fronts in doing battle with them; thus, it incorporates proposals for reduction in the growth of both domestic and defense spending and for increases in revenue. The plan is intended to be realistic about timing as well. Action to reduce the deficit must be taken soon; we cannot allow the pursuit of fundamental reforms to block short-term steps in the right direction. Therefore, the package involves a set of simple, evenhanded measures to be taken quickly—and to be followed by more thorough efforts at reform.

Our objective was to design a plan that would bring the federal budget into approximate balance by 1989. Hence the task was to agree on a set of legislative proposals to cut spending or raise revenues that, together with the attendant reductions in federal interest costs, would save about $300 billion in 1989. The plan we developed would do just that—by reducing domestic expenditures $46 billion in that year, lopping another $46 billion off the CBO baseline projection for defense spending, increasing tax revenues $108 billion, and yielding $88 billion of interest savings.

The individual pieces of the plan would not necessarily be endorsed by every member of the research team. Some of the elements are desirable in themselves; others can be defended only as part of a compromise plan to cut the deficit. Indeed, virtually all of them would face strong political opposition from some quarter or another. But we believe that cutting the deficit is so important that normal political differences must be submerged in a common effort to achieve a goal that will benefit the economy and the country.

Reductions in Domestic Spending

Spending on domestic programs rose from less than 8 percent of GNP in fiscal 1962 to about 15 percent in 1980 as the federal government took on new responsibilities and expanded existing programs. Since 1980 this growth has slowed because of substantial cuts made in many programs. By the end of this decade, as the cuts continue to take effect and the economy recovers, domestic spending is expected to fall to about 13 percent of GNP. Nevertheless, domestic spending must be reviewed again if the budget is to be brought into balance by 1989.

We propose a two-stage program to restrain domestic spending. The first stage is a one-year freeze in 1985, during which cost-of-living increases in benefits paid to individuals would be omitted unless prices rose more than 5 percent; appropriations for most other programs would be held at 1984 levels. Programs for low-income people would be exempted from the freeze. This modified freeze is a relatively simple and evenhanded way to reduce spending quickly, while allowing time for debate over the longer-term restructuring of domestic programs. The proposed freeze would save about $15 billion in 1985 if the CBO's most recent projection of the inflation rate (5.2 percent for fiscal 1985) is accurate. Since the one-year freeze would lower the base from which future increases are computed, saving would continue into the future—at a rate of more than $20 billion annually in 1986–89.

The second stage would require more fundamental changes in domestic spending programs. The Brookings team identified four major areas of domestic spending in which reforms would produce substantial savings:

—The automatic growth in social security spending should be reduced somewhat in order to give the political system more flexibility in its allocation of resources between social security benefit increases and other federal activities. Reductions should be achieved through changes in initial benefits, not in the cost-of-living adjustment.

—The new system of prospective rates for paying hospitals under medicare should be used to restrain the growth in costs to inflation plus 1 percent. Although this policy should be adequate for the next few years, further changes may be required in benefits or revenues if projections continue to predict large deficits in the medicare trust fund by the mid-1990s.

—Both the civil service and military retirement systems should be changed to bring them more in line with private-sector pension plans. For future retirees, initial benefits should be reduced somewhat and full benefits should be made available only to those sixty-two years of age or older. Benefits for current and future retirees should be only partially indexed for inflation.

—Agricultural programs should be geared toward the stabilization of prices around long-term market-clearing levels. Deficiency payments should be ended for all crops.

Savings could be achieved in other programs by imposing user charges for services that the federal government now provides without charge or below cost (for example, maintenance of the canal system at little cost to commercial shippers); by reducing subsidies for some activities; or by eliminating programs that have outlived their rationales.

Reductions in Defense Spending

Because defense outlays account for about 30 percent of all federal spending and are rising faster than other spending, they are an obvious source of possible deficit reductions. Such reductions, however, must not endanger national security. The nation needs and can afford a strong defense, but the rapid defense buildup advocated by the Reagan administration is both unjustified and unwise. A more moderate and balanced growth could meet the administration's defense objectives more efficiently. Indeed, forces appropriate to an even higher level of perceived threat and a need for more immediate readiness could be purchased for less money than the administration is proposing to spend.

Simple percentage reductions in appropriations will not ensure that the remaining dollars are spent wisely and may in fact merely exacerbate some of the imbalances in the Reagan defense plan by preventing neglected categories of expenditure from receiving their due. What would make more sense is a program of targeted reductions, with three major emphases. First, the expensive duplication that results from an undisciplined planning process and fierce interservice rivalry should be reduced. Several big-ticket weapons systems—including the MX missile, the B1B bomber, the Army's AH-64 attack helicopter, and the Navy's F-15 fighter aircraft—largely duplicate the capabilities of other systems. Trimming such redundancy could save about $23 billion in fiscal year 1985 and more in subsequent years. Second, substantial savings could be achieved by replacing the current costly rush to modernize with a more orderly and sustainable long-term investment strategy. Third, even larger spending cuts could be made by abandoning some objectives for which there is little convincing rationale. For example, there is no need to engage in rapid modernization of North American defenses against bombers when the main threat to the United States is from Soviet ballistic missiles. Similarly, the costly addition of three carrier battle groups to the twelve already available appears to be without serious military justification. In sum, the level of national security sought by the Reagan administration is achievable at substantially lower spending levels.

Increases in Tax Revenues

To bring the budget into approximate balance by 1989 would require substantial additions to revenues; if the spending cuts contemplated by the Brookings package were to be effected, a revenue increase of about $100 billion would be required to close the remaining budgetary gap. Thorough reform of the current tax system is clearly indicated. The corporation and individual income taxes are riddled with provisions that treat taxpayers inequitably and needlessly reduce economic efficiency. Raising revenue simply by raising tax rates would aggravate these problems.

Various approaches to reform are possible. Some would broaden the base of the individual income tax by ending most exclusions and deductions in order to obtain additional revenue without increasing tax rates. Others would shift part of the revenue structure from income taxation to the taxation of consumption through a value-added tax or national sales tax. The Brookings proposal combines both ideas: broadening the base and taxing spending rather than income. Both the individual income tax and the estate and gift tax would be replaced by an individual cash flow tax on income from all sources minus net saving. With this base, reduced rates of 5 to 32 percent would impose burdens on each economic class similar to those entailed by the current income and estate taxes. Somewhat higher rates—ranging up to 38 percent—would be needed to achieve a balanced budget in 1989. The corporation income tax would be replaced by a cash flow tax on corporate receipts minus current expenses (including investment). This new tax system would not be free of problems—no perfect tax exists—but it would be fairer, simpler, and more favorable to growth than the present system, while not shifting tax burdens among economic classes.

Such a major change in tax laws could not be put in place quickly enough to produce the added revenue needed to bring down the deficit in the next two or three years. Some immediate steps to broaden the tax base, coupled with a temporary income tax surcharge, would help to reduce the deficit during this interim period. A variety of short-term base-broadening measures are possible—from repealing the 15 percent interest exclusion to eliminating the availability of tax-exempt bonds for private purposes.

A cash flow tax on individuals and corporations would go farther than commonly proposed alternatives to the current structure toward achieving simultaneously all the goals of a desirable tax system. It would impose tax burdens based on each person's lifetime command over resources. It would terminate the current capricious variations in business tax rates that distort investment decisions. It would reduce the potential for tax avoidance through tax shelters. It would ease compliance for those who face the greatest difficulty in determining their tax liabilities under current law. Finally, it would provide a consistent, logical framework for assessing tax burdens.

The plan set forth here—and, in greater detail, in *Economic Choices 1984*—is offered in the hope that it will stimulate both debate and action. It is, of course, not the only possible path to a balanced budget. What is of paramount importance is that we choose a plan to reduce the deficit and get on with the job. If we act quickly to bring down the deficit and interest rates, there is a good chance that the next few years will see healthy, balanced growth in the U.S. economy and improvement in America's ability to compete in world markets.

Cutting the federal budget is politically difficult, Butler argues, because the benefits from spending programs go to concentrated special interest groups while the costs are spread out over all taxpayers. Privatization of federal services can both reduce the budget and create coalitions of interest groups dedicated to maintaining and expanding privatization.

PRIVATIZATION: THE ANTIDOTE TO BUDGET-CUTTING FAILURES

Stuart M. Butler

One could almost feel the shell shock in Washington as Pres. Reagan presented a budget request to Congress based on a cumulative deficit for 1981–85 of $728,000,000,000—more than half the cumulative deficit rung up by all presidents since World War II. Despite coming to power as a budget balancer and an advocate of smaller government, Reagan has presided over runaway deficits and a level of Federal spending that now consumes nearly three per cent more of the nation's income than was the case under Jimmy Carter.

The rhetoric is still tough, but Administration officials and the President's Congressional supporters have seemingly all but conceded that the Federal budget cannot be cut. David Stockman calls "dreamers" those who still press for major cuts in social programs. The initial Reagan target of cutting Federal spending to 19% of GNP should be revised, said the Office of Management and Budget director in a recent *Fortune* interview: "The minimum size of government achievable appears to be 22% to 23%."

Stockman's weary assessment seems to be shared by his friends on Capitol Hill. "If you cannot touch Social Security, and you cannot touch entitlements, and you cannot cut defense, and you cannot control interest payments," asked Senate Finance Committee Chairman Robert J. Dole (R.-Kans.) at hearings late in 1983, "what can you cut?"

The Administration's failure to reduce Federal spending does not stem from any shortcomings of philosophy or enthusiasm. It derives instead from a deep failure to understand the political dynamics of budget growth. This failure has dogged the Reagan team ever since it arrived in town. The Great Communicator has managed to score some stunning legislative victories when he could draw his opponents into the open in a well-publicized battle, but in the trench warfare of the budget, his forces are constantly in disarray. They keep forgetting that programs grow because narrow interest groups have much to gain from increased spending, while the cost is thinly spread over all taxpayers.

When their pet programs are threatened, these groups make every effort to defeat reductions; yet, the potential tax savings are unlikely to be of any significance whatever to the average taxpayer. This means the political contest turns out to be very one-sided. While program supporters fight tooth-and-nail to keep their benefits, John Q. Public does not get excited about saving a few cents of his taxes—and so does not demand cuts with nearly the same enthusiasm.

The solution to the Administration's budget-cutting malaise lies in recognizing these dynamics and creating a "mirror image" movement to urge the delivery of services by the private sector. The answer to Dole's question—"what can be cut?"—is, in fact, not even to think in terms of denying programs to beneficiaries, but to develop strategies to *divert* the demand for government services into the private sector. In short, to "privatize" these services.

The Federal ratchet

Federal programs tend to grow according to a pattern. The first step is usually the creation of a small program to provide assistance or benefits to a limited group. This may not even involve a comprehensive program of cash benefits; it might simply be a demonstration project or a study. Normally, the budget allocation is so small that the taxpayer can feel that a need has been met with no identifiable extra tax burden on himself. Once this initial funding has been voted and the program created, however, a coalition consisting of three elements begins to form:

Beneficiaries and "near" beneficiaries. New programs rarely satisfy the expectations of the targeted beneficiaries, so it is not usually very long before beneficiary organizations emerge to mobilize political support for increased funding. Moreover, there are inevitably those who just fall outside the criteria set for inclusion in the program. These "near" beneficiaries, like the actual beneficiaries, have every incentive to press for an ever-larger program.

Administrators. More Federal spending means more jobs and promotion opportunities for the Federal staff administering programs. Administrators also have every incentive, therefore, to join in the coalition pressing for more funding. Just as business executives are on the lookout for new market opportunities, Federal workers tackling one problem always try to identify new problems—real or perceived—that could be treated by expanding the program.

Service providers. Even private-sector providers of Federally funded services have the incentive to jump aboard the Federal spending bandwagon. Housing contractors, for instance, have everything to gain from urging more spending on Federal housing, just as professional social workers gain from more welfare spending and aircraft manufacturers from a defense buildup. So, segments of the private sector, conscious of their own self-interest, are inevitably drawn into the coalition lobbying for an expansion of the initial program.

This coalition provides the underlying momentum to expand Federal spending. Each element of the coalition has much to gain or lose from program changes. Consequently, there is a strong incentive to press for additional funding and to resist cuts. When a program obtains an increase in funds, the benefits to individual coalition members are likely to be significant. At the same time, the costs are spread over 100,000,000 taxpayers, and so the cost to any one particular taxpayer is likely to be trifling. A taxpayer may complain about taxes and spending in the aggregate, but any particular program imposes no discernible burden on him. Therefore, the taxpayer does not have a strong vested interest to oppose an increase in funding for a specific program, while the coalition member has every reason to mount a well-organized, politically powerful, and expensive campaign to win Congressional approval.

This momentum, of course, only works in the direction of increased Federal spending. When reductions in spending are under consideration, the coalition has much to lose and works to frustrate the would-be budget cutters. "Studies" are produced on the calamitous results that would surely follow spending cuts, distraught witnesses are brought to well-publicized hearings, and carefully designed lobbying campaigns are set in motion. One need only pause to consider the onslaught against the Reagan welfare reduction proposals to see just how much political damage can be inflicted on those attempting to cut spending. Despite his reputation as an enemy of the poor, the President has hardly dented the growth of total entitlement and safety net programs.

The reason he hasn't is that the potential savings would be spread very thinly across all taxpayers. Few Americans really have much stomach for denying assistance to people who seem to be in need, when all they might gain is a dollar or two less in taxes each year.

The privatization strategy recognizes the existence of the Federal spending ratchet and seeks to replace it with a private ratchet. Instead of trying to win an unwinnable war of attrition on the budget, privatization calls for the government to become a "facilitator," rather than a provider, of goods and services for society. It does not deny that government has an obligation to ensure that goods and services are provided for certain public projects, or to help citizens in need. However, a distinction is drawn between the government raising taxes and providing services itself, and the government requiring or encouraging those services to be provided by others.

The Federal government would, in some instances, retain its function of delivery of services. Privatization means that government would, in many other cases, create incentives for people to demand them from nongovernment providers, and ultimately cease to deliver them itself. Privatization, in other words, would mean transferring programs into the private sector, using the carrot of incentives, rather than the stick of cutbacks. It would mean *deflecting* the demand for services into the non-government sector, not trying to halt that demand. As the demand for Federal services declined, so the political resistance to conventional budget cuts would weaken.

Deflecting demand is only one part of a two-part strategy. The other part involves the conscious creation of coalitions of beneficiaries, providers, and administrators to press for an expanded private-sector role in delivering services, just as the public-sector coalitions now lobby for increased Federal spending.

These private-sector coalitions—a mirror image of the public-sector coalitions—are the keystone of the privatization strategy. The political dynamics of the groups, according to the approach, would lead to a "privatization ratchet" in opposition to the current Federal ratchet. By providing a targeted benefit (such as a tax incentive) only to those who choose a private option, the rewards for members of the private-sector coalition can be considerable. They can be expected to press for deeper incentives. Yet, the tax "cost" is spread widely and thinly.

Moreover, the "near" beneficiaries (those who just fail to qualify for the incentives) can be expected to campaign for an expansion of the private sector, such that they are included. So, the pressure for an ever-wider private option is likely to overwhelm the resistance of those who carry the tax cost of the incentives.

Privatization thus stands conventional political dynamics on its head. Each element of the coalition has much to gain from the growth of the private-sector option, and thus will press for more incentives. Every legislative success won by the coalition only strengthens that coalition, adding to its capacity to achieve further concessions and political power. Just as the conventional coalitions backing Federal programs gain from a political ratchet effect whenever their programs are attacked, so the privatization coalition can use the same ratchet process in reverse to protect its private alternative.

If the privatization strategy sounds like an interesting but purely academic exercise in political science, consider the case of IRA's and Social Security. Not only does the IRA case show how the dynamics of privatization can be set in motion, it also shows just how powerful and irreversible the process may be.

Social Security is a classic example of how a relatively modest Federal program takes on a life of its own. Enacted in 1935 to provide a modest supplementary retirement income, Social Security has mushroomed into an enormous program that includes disability income, hospital insurance, spousal benefits, and even allowances for students. The system has been shown to be in serious financial difficulties, yet, the political power of the coalition behind the system is such that even minimum economies have been achieved only after the shedding of much political blood. Absorbing more than one-quarter of all Federal outlays, Social Security has been a perfect example of the Federal ratchet in operation.

Almost as an afterthought, however, Congress attached a provision to the 1981 tax act, allowing all working Americans to open tax deductible IRA's. In so doing, Congress planted the seeds of a private Social Security alternative. It was not long before the political dynamics of privatization began to be felt. Even before the new law went into effect, banks and other financial institutions began a massive campaign to encourage the public to open IRA's. The privatization coalition was born.

The new political power of this coalition is clear from the fact that the tax cost of the deduction has been many times that originally expected. When the legislation was before Congress, Treasury estimates put the 1982 cost of the deduction at about $3,000,000,000; it turned out to be nearer to $10,000,000,000. Yet, despite the enormous Federal budget deficit facing Congress, repealing or reducing the deduction is politically unthinkable. Indeed, there is every likelihood that politicians will have to commit themselves to expanding IRA's to a critical group of "near" beneficiaries—non-working spouses.

The reason that this coalition has grown so large and formidable in such a short time is that many Americans see IRA's as a preferable retirement option to Social Security. In short, the incentive has served to divert demand pressure from the publicly provided service (Social Security) into the privately provided substitute (IRA's). If the coalition succeeds in winning more extensions of the IRA alternative, as seems likely, the option will become even more attractive. That, in turn, will increase the size of the coalition and its political power, and so enhance its capacity to win further coalition-building legislative changes.

From the budget-cutter's point of view, the growth of this privatization coalition offers a real hope for spending reductions in Social Security. The more the public sees IRA's, rather than Social Security, as its primary pension vehicle, the less will be the resistance to sensible restructuring of the runaway Social Security program.

Implementing the strategy

The IRA alternative to Social Security is just one—albeit very important—way in which the privatization strategy could be used to dismantle the Federal budget ratchet. There are many other areas of the budget in which the strategy could be used.

Robert Woodson, of the Washington-based National Center for Neighborhood Enterprise, says that many studies have shown that low-income city residents prefer local, volunteer social services to those provided through expensive Federal programs. Yet, he notes, restrictive licensing and regulations have prevented neighborhood organizations from delivering many basic community services at significant savings. If these restrictive rules were simplified and incentives for corporate support of groups expanded, argues Woodson, privatization would mean the creation of a strong constituency for non-government "safety net" services, thus enabling the government to cut outlays while improving services.

World Bank scholar Gabriel Roth and others have applied the same reasoning to the multi-billion-dollar mass transit and highway programs of the Federal government. Roth points out that the combination of Federal transit subsidies, underpricing, and restrictions on private alternatives discourages more efficient private mass systems (such as minibus and subscriber bus services). If the Administration were to press for the removal of barriers to competition, and for the introduction of cost-based pricing—rather than simply trying vainly to win Congressional approval of cuts—it would sow the seeds of a potent private mass transit coalition.

Johns Hopkins University economist Steve Hanke has explored the privatization approach in the case of another unlikely element of the Federal budget—the

$2,000,000,000 wastewater grant program. The structure of the program leads U.S. cities to spend billions on Federally subsidized sewage disposal plants. However, government-built and -operated plants, discovered Hanke, cost 20-50% more to construct and operate than private plants. Moreover, EPA rules tend to hold back cost-cutting design innovations and profitable uses for plant products. If these rules were to be amended, and if creative financing techniques (such as lease-back arrangements) are kept on the statute book, Hanke is convinced that many more cities would begin to switch to completely private wastewater systems—cutting Federal and city outlays while improving efficiency.

If the Reagan Administration is to have any success in cutting Federal spending, and thereby reducing the looming budget deficits, it must review Federal services to identify programs that might be privatized in this way. In view of the success of the Grace Commission in discovering methods of improving efficiency in government, a presidential task force on privatization might be the best method of determining the best targets for privatization and the most appropriate methods of shifting those Federal functions into the private sector.

By adopting the privatization strategy, the President could achieve his objective of reducing permanently the size of the Federal government while turning the political flank of those who now condemn him for cutting back on necessary programs. By shifting programs into the private sector and creating a vested interest coalition around those privatized programs, the Administration would set in motion the necessary political dynamics both to prevent the erosion of cuts already achieved and to win further reductions by diverting demand to the private sector. However, if Reagan persists in a head-to-head confrontation with the interest groups, it will be back to business as usual as soon as he leaves the White House. His Administration will have merely won a short pause in the inexorable growth of government.

Economists have historically believed that some goods and services can be provided only by the government. The traditional theory, Boettke and Ellig suggest, does not mean that we know for certain which specific goods those are in the real world. They propose allowing the market to decide what private enterprise can or cannot do by allowing private firms to compete with the government in the production of public goods, including the monetary system. As the scope of government activity shrinks, so, of course, will deficits.

THE BUSINESS OF GOVERNMENT AND GOVERNMENT AS A BUSINESS

Peter Boettke and Jerome Ellig

A football coach at a midwestern high school was frequently asked what his team had to do to win Friday night's game. His response was always the same. "That's easy," he said. "All we have to do is score more points than the other team."

The cause of the current deficit dilemma can be explained in a similarly accurate, but uninformative, fashion. The U.S. government is spending more money than it takes in in taxes and fees; hence, it must make up the difference by issuing debt. That debt is either monetized by the Federal Reserve System or purchased by individuals and organizations in place of private investments.

The Deficit Problem is an Expenditure Problem

Traditional fiscal theory called for the government to maintain a balanced budget except in time of emergency, most notably war. This view, which held sway until the Keynesian revolution of the 1940s, was aptly summarized by Adam Smith:

> When war comes, there is no money in the treasury but what is necessary for carrying on the ordinary expence of the peace establishment. In war an establishment of three or four times that expence becomes necessary for the defence of the state, and consequently a revenue three or four times greater than the peace revenue. . .
>
> But the moment in which war begins, or rather the moment in which it appears likely to begin, the army must be augmented, the fleet must be fitted out, the garrisoned towns must be put into a posture of defence; that army, that fleet, those garrisoned towns must be furnished with arms, ammunition, and provisions. An immediate and great expence must be incurred at the moment of immediate danger, which will not wait for the gradual and slow

returns of the new taxes. In this exigency government can have no other
resource but in borrowing.[1]

The only non-emergency exception to this rule was government expenditures on
projects such as highways which required a large initial outlay but yielded benefits
for a number of years into the future. These capital expenditures were to be
accompanied by an amortization schedule coinciding with the productive life of
the asset.[2] Up to the time of the Great Depression and World War II, the U.S.
government consciously followed a policy of paying off its debts incurred during
wars and other emergencies.[3]

The Keynesian revolution, and specifically Abba Lerner's development of the
concept of "functional finance,"[4] provided intellectual justification for abandon-
ing the balanced budget orthodoxy. With the acceptance of this new view, deficit
financing came to be regarded as a tool for demand management instead of the
result of budgetary mismanagement. Keynesianism reached the height of its
political influence in the 1960s.

The simultaneous experience of high inflation and high unemployment in the
following decade, however, dethroned Keynes without unambiguously indicating
a successor. The growing deficit and its corresponding consequences for the
economy have led to serious reconsideration of what had become the new orthodoxy in fiscal theory. James Buchanan and Richard Wagner assert that at least
part of the failure of Keynesianism is due to the fact that it ignored the nature of the
democratic political process.[5] Like many economists, Keynes assumed that the
government he was advising was run by a benevolent despot who was genuinely
concerned with promoting the common good. In reality, budgetary policy is
shaped by the tug and pull of special interests. Federal programs often benefit
well-organized factions at the expense of unorganized voters. The abolition of any
one program has little impact on any one individual's tax bill, but each program
will be virulently defended by one or many special interest groups. The resulting
natural tendency toward ever-increasing government spending was held in check
as long as the unwritten "fiscal constitution" mandating budget balance held
sway. Removal of this constraint has led to a ballooning public sector and a
stagnating economy.

On the microeconomic level, government spends money for two main purposes.
First, it provides goods and services, ranging from national defense to interstate
highways to satellite launches. Second, it redistributes income—sometimes from
rich to poor, sometimes from poor to rich, and most frequently from the unorganized to the organized. Many government activities accomplish both of these
objectives. Education, for instance, though formally a service, is often utilized as a
means of income redistribution. Aid to Families With Dependent Children, on the
other hand, is almost a pure transfer program, but it can also be viewed as a service
to the extent that upper- and middle-income people desire to redistribute income
and choose to use government for this purpose.[6]

Recognition that the deficit problem is an expenditure problem suggests that a
critical re-evaluation of government's role in the provision of public goods is in
order. Any proposals to cut government spending, however, are superfluous in

the absence of a political strategy for their implementation. Drastic cuts will not occur until it becomes in someone's political interest to make them. One particular reform, extensive privatization of government activities, offers perhaps the most realistic chance of reducing the deficit in today's economic and political climate.

A Workable Political Strategy

Taxpayers are dispersed, unorganized, and uninformed. Special interests are concentrated and well-organized. This combination has never proved to be a particularly effective recipe for deficit reduction. The way out of the dilemma is to create political coalitions who will find it in their interest to push for lower spending. "What is . . . required," the Heritage Foundation's Stuart Butler notes, "is a set of tactics designed to discourage demand for public sector services, while making private sector alternatives more attractive."[7]

Most discussion of privatization has concentrated on identifying programs which are good candidates for privatization. Butler, in fact, has proposed a presidential commission for precisely that purpose.[8] While a commission and the implementation of its findings would be a welcome first step, there is another, complementary means of pursuing privatization which should not be neglected. A commission composed of fallible individuals will likely identify many of the more obvious opportunities for privatization of federal services. However, the vast majority of such opportunities are not so obvious. No board or committee can say with certainty that the market will not provide some service if government does not, because no board or committee can possibly predict what services entrepreneurs will discover how to provide if given the freedom to do so. If America is to reap the full benefits of privatization, government services should be thrown open to competition from the private sector. To the extent that profit-seeking entrepreneurs and nonprofit organizations find ways to provide them, the government will be relieved of additional financial burdens. If, on the other hand, some services are not supplied by the private sector, government can continue to do so (or, of course, reexamine their desirability entirely) and nothing will have been lost. Let the market—that is, consumers—decide who is best able to provide which services.

Government Expenditures and Public Goods

The above suggestion may sound a bit unusual to anyone familiar with the economist's concept of public goods. Certain kinds of goods and services will not be provided by private enterprise, the theory goes, so government must step in and provide them. However, economists' traditional theoretical justification for government provision of public goods becomes less convincing when one attempts to combine that theory with an analysis of economic and political processes. One cannot determine whether or not a good is "public" independently of its institutional context. A brief reexamination of public goods theory lends support to the suggestion that buyers and sellers in the market should be relied upon to decide which public goods the market is capable of providing.

The Classic Definition of Public Goods

One of the two defining characteristics of a public good, nonrivalrous consumption, was provided by Paul Samuelson in 1954.[9]

In addition to nonrival consumption, public goods are also often assumed to possess the characteristic of nonexcludability. That is to say, once the good is provided for paying customers, nonpayers cannot be prevented from simultaneously consuming the good. (This is implicit in Samuelson's mathematical definition.) Here a definitional quirk emerges. Some economists regard any good possessing just the first characteristic as a public good, preferring to call a good which possesses both by some other name, such as a "collective good." Thus Demsetz[10] argues that "public goods" can be provided privately as long as nonpayers can be excluded. Examples of this type of good abound; movies, sporting events, and schooling are three. Browning and Browning,[11] on the other hand, state that a public good is one which is characterized by both nonexcludability and nonrival consumption. For the sake of simplicity, this paper will employ Browning and Browning's terminology.

Authors generally agree that the market, on its own, is not likely to provide public goods. "No decentralized pricing system," Samuelson states, "can serve to determine optimally these levels of collective consumption."[12] To see why, it is useful to examine one classic case of a public good, construction of a dam. Assume that a community of ten people wishes to construct a dam at a cost of $5000. Each person believes that the flooding thus prevented will save him $1000 in damages; it is in everybody's interest to have the dam built. Once it is built, though, it is difficult to exclude anyone from enjoying the benefits. Any one citizen has an incentive to refuse to help finance the project, "free riding" on the efforts of the rest of the community.[13] Now, when there are only ten people in the community, it is likely that each person will realize that if anyone does not pay, the dam will not be built. In a large group, however, one person's refusal to pay will not prevent the dam from being built. In such cases, it is perfectly rational for anyone—and hence everyone—to seek to be a free rider.[14] "Because this is true for every person, no one will contribute, and the good will not be provided."[15]

Why Give Government a Monopoly?

The free rider problem suggests that the market may not supply some public goods. It does not, though, imply that government need become a monopoly producer of any good, public or otherwise. Friedrich von Hayek, for example, says that in some cases "it is either technically impossible, or would be prohibitively costly, to confine certain services to particular persons, so that these services can be provided only for all (or at least will be provided more cheaply and effectively if they are provided for all) . . . In many instances the rendering of such services could bring no gain to those who do so, and they will therefore not be provided by the market."[16] While small groups may be able to overcome the free rider problem, larger communities are forced to use the government's power to tax to ensure that everyone pays. Hayek grants government the exclusive right to employ coercion for the provision of public goods, but he does not permit government to use coercion to prevent the private sector from trying to provide them:

> This ought not to mean, however, that the right of providing such services should be reserved to government if other means can be found for providing them . . . [t]he current distinction between the government and the private sector is sometimes erroneously taken to mean that some services beyond the enforcement of rules of just conduct should be reserved to the government by law. There is no justification for this. Even if in given circumstances only government is in fact able to supply particular services, this is no reason for prohibiting private agencies from trying to find methods of providing these services without the use of coercive powers.[17]

The Publicness of a Good Depends on Its Institutional Context

Many economists simply accept the definition of public goods advanced by Samuelson even though that definition has little to say about the actual conditions under which such goods are provided. This habit leads naturally to the conclusion that those goods which are assumed in economists' models to possess the characteristics of nonrival consumption and nonexcludability in fact do possess them in the real world.

In actuality, publicness or privateness are not attributes of particular economic goods. Rather, they depend on the institutional setting and conditions of production of the good under examination. "For instance," Tyler Cowen suggests, "a road in a community with very little traffic could be considered a public good since when one person drives on the road he does not prevent anyone else from driving on the road at the same time. However, we can introduce a number of 'institutional' changes, each of which is sufficient to turn 'roads' into a private good."[18] The most obvious change is simply an increase in traffic. At some point, a sufficiently large amount of traffic increases congestion to such an extent that an additional person driving on the road will indeed interfere with others' opportunity to "consume" its services.[19]

A public good can also be turned into a private good, and vice versa, by varying the size of the marginal unit. National defense, for example, is usually viewed as a public good.[20] This view, however, is due to the more or less arbitrary decision to regard the entire defense system as the marginal unit. If a single missile is chosen as the marginal unit, that missile is not a public good from the point of view of the entire nation. "The same missile cannot protect both New York and San Francisco, so consumption is neither joint nor non-rivalrous. The more limited and narrow our perception of what the relevant marginal unit of the good is, the closer it approaches being a private good."[21] A single government-owned pistol may not be considered a public good at all.

The above examples were presented as a critique of the jointness criterion. Similar criticisms can be leveled against the non-excludability criterion. Home-owners' property can be protected by either burglar alarms or police patrols; the former method allows for exclusion, while the latter does not.[22] Thus, Cowen concludes that the definition of public goods is, in reality, not nearly as un-ambiguous at it seems:

Although certain imagined methods of exclusion may seem economically or sociologically absurd at the moment, this may only be the case because of certain institutional structures or barriers—barriers which are not immune to change. Even if an exclusion method is not easily imaginable, this may simply be because the good has been produced by the public sector for so long that there has been no incentive for the private sector to develop exclusion mechanisms.[23]

Why Government Can't Be Run as a Business

Although government provides public goods, there are fundamental differences between the way in which it does so and the way in which private businesses serve their customers. The private sector can make profits only by catering to the desires of consumers. Individuals and businesses earn only what others are willing to pay for their products.[24]

Government, on the other hand, is coercive. It levies taxes, and the manner in which the proceeds are spent is determined by some mechanism of *collective* choice in place of *individual* choice. Of course, one purpose of democracy is to maximize individuals' input into collective decisions. Nevertheless, these decisions are made by some form of majority rule, which guarantees that at least a minority is likely to disagree with whatever action is taken.[25] Unless everyone in the United States unanimously agrees on the proper level of defense spending, for example, the actual level decided upon will be too high for some people and too low for others. In addition, the defense budget is but one component of a larger total federal budget which must be approved by Congress and the president in its entirety. In the market, there is a direct link between payment for and consumption of a specific product. Government provision of goods and services breaks this link, for "[p]ayment is made . . . not by users on the basis of their voluntary purchases, but by a coerced levy on the taxpayers. A basic split is effected between payment for and receipt of service."[26]

Government provision of education provides an excellent example of the effects of this split. Recent intense debate over prayer in public schools demonstrates that some parents want their children to have the prayer option while others do not. If the market were relied upon to provide schooling, this difference of opinion would be resolved relatively easily: parents would send their children to whichever school met their approval. The decision over prayer in government-run schools, though, has to be made via the political process, which means that one decision must be made binding upon all. In such a case, conflict over values means that government must impose one group's values on society. This problem has been particularly acute throughout the history of public education. The extensive system of Catholic parochial schools in the United States today owes its existence partially to the fact that nineteenth century Catholics saw public school systems as an attempt to impose nondenominational Protestantism on their children.[27]

Breaking the consumption-payment link also reduces the incentive to provide services efficiently. For a private business, the standard of success is profit and loss. Profit means that the businessman has succeeded in pleasing consumers; losses tell him that he has failed. Government agencies have to meet a different standard. Their employees are directly responsible not to the consumer but rather to the politicians who make budget decisions. Since politicians, in turn, have the power to tax, they are only loosely constrained by the requirement that the government provide services which are worth more to taxpayers than they cost. Some opponents of "big" government suggest that if businessmen—or home-makers—were placed in charge of the bureaucracy, government could be run as efficiently as any business or household. This proposal fails to get at the root of the problem. Government workers are not lazy or incompetent. They merely face a different set of incentives than businesses and individuals in the market. They do not bear the monetary risks of their decisions; taxpayers do:

> The free market provides a "mechanism" for allocating funds for future and present consumption, for directing resources to their most value-productive uses for all people. It thereby provides a means for businessmen to allocate resources and to price services to insure such optimum use. Government, however, has no checkrein on itself, i.e., no requirement for meeting a profit-and-loss test of valued service to consumers, to enable it to obtain funds. Private enterprise can get funds only from satisfied, valuing customers and from investors guided by profits and losses. Government can get funds literally at its own whim.[28]

The government cannot be run "as if" it were a business because it is not a business.[29]

A firm which ignored the signals of profit and loss would be driven out of business by competitors. Government, on the other hand, can and frequently does outlaw competition, as in the case of the U.S. Postal Service. Monopolization allows the government to restrict output and charge a price for its services higher than that which would prevail under competition. Lack of competition also permits the government to lower the quality of its services.

Though government monopolization can occur, it is not a necessary condition for government provision of public goods. In addition, the degree of publicness of a good depends on particular circumstances of time, place and technology. These insights, along with the distinction between government and business, are important to keep in mind when considering deficit reduction plans.

Proposed Deficit Remedies

Tax Increases Only Exacerbate the Problem

In spite of the fact that the deficit is primarily an expenditure problem, one of the most commonly proposed methods of reducing it is tax increases. Experience has demonstrated, however, that tax increases do little to reduce deficits. Instead, they merely reduce the incentive to cut spending by increasing the resources at government's disposal. Since 1969, the last year in which a budget surplus occurred, the trends in federal receipts, expenditures and deficits have all moved in the same direction—up. (See table.)

In addition to encouraging spending, tax increases are harmful in their own right. As supply-side economists and politicians are fond of saying, "When you tax something you get less of it; when you subsidize something you get more of it."

U.S. GOVERNMENT BUDGET, 1940–86 (in $billions)

(Including outlays off-budget under current law, which are proposed to be on-budget)

	Receipts	Outlays	Surplus or deficit (−)	Federal deficit as % of GNP
1940	6,548	9,468	− 2,920	− 3.1
1941	8,712	13,653	− 4,941	− 4.5
1942	14,634	35,137	− 20,503	− 14.8
1943	24,001	78,555	− 54,554	− 30.8
1944	43,747	91,304	− 47,557	− 23.5
1945	45,159	92,712	− 47,553	− 21.9
1946	39,296	55,232	− 15,936	− 7.9
1947	38,514	34,496	4,018	1.8
1948	41,560	29,764	11,796	4.8
1949	39,415	38,835	580	0.2
1950	39,443	42,562	− 3,119	− 1.2
1951	51,616	45,514	6,102	2.0
1952	66,167	67,686	− 1,519	− .4
1953	69,608	76,101	− 6,493	− 1.8
1954	69,701	70,855	− 1,154	− .3
1955	65,451	68,444	− 2,993	− .8
1956	74,587	70,640	3,947	1.0
1957	79,990	76,578	3,412	0.8
1958	79,636	82,405	− 2,769	− .6
1959	79,249	92,098	− 12,849	− 2.7
1960	92,492	92,191	301	0.1
1961	94,388	97,723	− 3,335	− .7
1962	99,676	106,821	− 7,146	− 1.3
1963	106,560	111,316	− 4,756	− .8
1964	112,613	118,528	− 5,915	− 1.0
1965	116,817	118,228	− 1,411	− .2
1966	130,835	134,532	− 3,698	− .5
1967	148,822	157,464	− 8,643	− 1.1
1968	152,973	178,134	− 25,161	− 3.0
1969	186,882	183,640	3,242	0.4
1970	192,812	195,649	− 2,837	− .3
1971	187,139	210,172	− 23,033	− 2.2
1972	207,309	230,681	− 23,373	− 2.1
1973	230,799	245,707	− 14,908	− 1.2
1974	263,224	269,359	− 6,135	− .4
1975	279,090	332,332	− 53,242	− 3.6
1976	298,060	371,779	− 73,719	− 4.5
TQ	81,232	95,973	− 14,741	− 3.4
1977	355,559	409,203	− 53,644	− 2.9
1978	399,740	458,729	− 58,989	− 2.8
1979	463,302	503,464	− 40,161	− 1.7
1980	517,112	590,920	− 73,808	− 2.9
1981	599,272	678,209	− 78,936	− 2.7
1982	617,766	745,706	− 127,940	− 4.2
1983	600,562	808,327	− 207,764	− 6.4
1984	666,457	851,781	− 185,324	− 5.2
1985 estimate	736,859	959,085	− 222,226	− 5.7
1986 estimate	793,729	973,725	− 179,996	− 4.3

Source: Executive Office of the President, Office of Management and Budget, *Historical Tables: Budget of the United States Government*, Fiscal Year 1986 (U.S. Government Printing Office, 1985), Tables 1.1 and 1.2

Individuals respond to incentives. Tax increases reduce the rewards to work, saving and innovation, reducing the tax base. In the long run, higher taxes reduce economic growth. In the short run, they may even increase the deficit as the tax base shrinks.

One myth which ought to be laid to rest is that current budget deficits are due to the Reagan administration's 1981 25 percent tax cut, which was projected to amount to $960 billion between 1982 and 1987. According to former Assistant Secretary of the Treasury Paul Craig Roberts, previously scheduled Social Security tax increases and bracket creep cancelled out $660 billion before the bill was even signed. The administration's Tax Equity and Fiscal Responsibility Act of 1982, the largest peacetime tax increase in America's history, raised taxes by $229 billion for the period. The subsequent five cents a gallon increase in the federal gasoline tax left only $55 billion of the original tax cut intact, and accelerated FICA tax increases eliminated that amount.[30] The only permanent accomplishment of the original Reagan tax reduction bill, it seems, was indexing of tax rates to prevent inflation from pushing citizens into higher tax brackets each year. The tax cut has vanished, but the deficit remains. Increasing taxes has only encouraged Congress and the administration to spend more, just as congressional opponents of the 1982 tax increases had predicted.[31]

Constitutional Reform

Of the many proposed solutions to the current fiscal crisis perhaps constitutional reform has most successfully sparked the imaginations of scholars. A balanced-budget amendment may, at first glance, seem desirable, but there are problems associated with its implementation. Many government expenditures occur in what is known as the "off-budget sector." Off-budget operations allow the elected official "to preach fiscal conservatism to his constituents while simultaneously increasing the size and scope of the public sector."[32] Off-budget enterprises (OBEs) enable officials to pursue their personal political goals more effectively than would be possible if constitutional limits on debt were strictly enforced.[33]

Of course, it would be political suicide for anyone running for election or re-election to admit publicly to such motivation. As a result, a good deal of time and money are spent trying to convince voters that off-budget activity is actually in the public interest. The sub-discipline of economics known as public choice, however, has called into question the public interest view of government. Instead, government officials are seen as self-interested individuals intent on maximizing their utility, just like other agents in society. Individuals respond to incentives in the voting booth and Congress as well as in the job market and in the grocery store. Politicians promote off-budget spending not because it is in the public interest but because it is in their own interest. They do so not because they are evil, but because they are rational.

Even if there were such a thing as "the public interest" independent of the actions of voters and their representatives, off-budget enterprises would still give rise to a contradiction:

> Undoubtedly, off-budget activities were undertaken because certain goals
> could be better achieved through back-door finance and spending than

through the normal agencies of government. The issue is whether the interests of the taxpayers or the interests of the politicians are enhanced more by the operation of OBEs. The statutory and constitutional restraints on government that OBEs are able to bypass were instituted originally to protect the taxpayer from the profligate proclivities of politicians to borrow and spend excessively. There is ample evidence that such constraints are needed; calls for a Constitutional amendment requiring a balanced budget are based on a widely accepted view that neither Congress nor the administration in power can put that nation's fiscal affairs in order without a constitutional directive. Thus, restraints on public sector fiscal activities have long been viewed as in the public interest. Is it then reasonable to argue that strategies intended to evade these restraints can simultaneously be in the public interest?[34]

Though passage of the balanced-budget amendment may be a necessary condition for fiscal reform, it is certainly not a sufficient one. Another possible constitutional reform which has received attention would put limits on federal taxation.[35] Although this proposal would probably help reduce government expenditures, it still leaves open a rather wide avenue for politicians who wish to spend: money creation.

Money Creation: An Indirect Tax, and Then Some

Even if a tax limitation amendment is passed, politicians can still pressure the Federal Reserve into creating money to finance federal programs. If both balanced-budget and tax limitation amendments are enacted, the Fed could still monetize existing government debt, freeing up tax revenues for expenditure programs. The hidden tax of inflation could be substituted for overt taxation. Constitutional fiscal reform will not bring public sector spending under control unless it is accompanied by monetary reform.

By inflating the money supply, government does not increase the actual amount of goods and services produced. Instead, inflation merely enables the government to bid resources away from others. Inflation is an indirect tax. As new money spreads throughout the economy, prices rise. The "price" of the dollar in terms of goods—that is, the amounts of various goods one dollar can buy—falls. These changes in the price level do not affect everyone equally. Workers signed to long-term contracts lose because their wages do not rise to keep pace with prices. Creditors lose because debts are paid back in dollars which will buy less than they could when they were borrowed. Until tax rate indexing was enacted in 1981, taxpayers were penalized doubly because rising nominal incomes put them in higher tax brackets even as real incomes fell.

These price level effects are by now widely recognized.[36] However, inflation does not just raise the price level; it also distorts *relative* prices. This occurs because new money enters the economy at specific points and only gradually spreads throughout the entire system. Since someone receives the new money first, the prices of the goods he or she buys will rise before the prices of other goods do. The next people to receive the money bid up the prices of the goods they buy, and so on, until the money works its way through the economy and most prices rise by some amount. Since the inflation process has redistributed wealth to those who were originally given the new money, there is no guarantee that the new set of relative prices will be identical to the old. The important point to note is that a purely *monetary* event can indeed alter the *real* pattern of economic activity.[37]

In the United States today, new money enters the economy through the banking system. The Federal Reserve System expands the money supply by purchasing government debt from banks, allowing banks to extend more loans than they otherwise would. A greater supply of funds in the loan market lowers the rate of interest. Many previously unprofitable investments now appear profitable. Investment increases. The new money pulls economic resources, including workers, toward capital goods industries, altering the previous structure of the economy.

This part of the process looks like prosperity, but it merely sets the stage for a recession. In the simplest case, a one-time increase in the money supply, the market rate of interest falls only temporarily. When money creation stops, the interest rate rises back toward its previous level. The prices which businessmen must pay for inputs, meanwhile, have risen as the new money makes its way through the economy, bidding up prices as it goes. Those investments which were undertaken only because the interest rate fell are now no longer profitable. They will be discontinued; the workers they had previously employed will lose their jobs.

The Fed cannot prevent this unemployment by increasing the money supply at some constant rate. A constant rate of money growth leads to continually rising prices. People will learn to expect prices to increase at some rate in the future, and market interest rates will have to rise to compensate savers for their loss of purchasing power. In addition, producers realize that not every observed price change represents a true signal from consumers. They decline to respond as quickly or as vigorously to any given price change; consequently, larger distortions in relative prices are necessary to induce them to maintain employment at some level. A constant rate of money growth, therefore, also results in unemployment as soon as savers' and producers' price expectations adjust.

Once the Fed embarks on money creation, then, it can only prevent the resulting recession by increasing the money supply at an ever-increasing rate. This kind of policy, of course, cannot continue for very long. As money's value falls at faster rates, people substitute other nations' currencies and tangible goods as stores of value. Ever-accelerating money growth leads ultimately to hyperinflation and establishment of a new monetary standard. Monetization, like increasing taxes, essentially defeats its original purpose of reducing the federal deficit. It is often considered an attractive option, though, because its benefits are immediate and quite obvious while its costs are distant and less obvious.

Monetary Reform

Perhaps the most well-known proposal to curb government's abuse of the power of money-creation is the adoption of a money growth rule. Growth of the money supply is to be limited to some annual rate, such as five percent. Some observers, in fact, believe that the Fed has been trying to follow some such money growth rule for the past six years, with a dubious degree of success. In any case, money growth rules are hampered by the implicit theoretical assumption that money influences only the general level of prices and not the structure of the economy. A money growth rule might restrict government's ability to create money to pay its bills, but it would not prevent the boom-bust business cycle.

Another proposal, advocated by some conservatives, is a return to the gold standard. Like a money growth rule, the gold standard would be an improvement over the present situation. It would restrict government's power to create money to an even greater extent than a money growth rule. Fluctuations in gold production, though, could still cause business cycles.

There is another serious criticism of a government-established gold standard which is much more in the spirit of previous privatization proposals: How do we know that gold is the best money? It is true that the market often chose gold (and/or silver) as money on those occasions in the past when it was free to do so, but there is no guarantee that the market would make this same choice in the future. In the choice of a monetary standard as in anything else, the competitive process is a discovery procedure which reveals important information only as competition takes place. There is no way of knowing that gold is the best form of money for the future unless we observe that individuals in the market freely choose it as such. "[T]he monopoly of government of issuing money," Hayek notes, "has not only deprived us of good money but has also deprived us of the only process by which we can find out what would be good money."[38]

Free Market Money

Most privatization proposals are directed at cutting government spending. Privatization of money issue is aimed at a somewhat different goal. A free market in money provides the ultimate check on government's ability to finance expenditures through the indirect tax of money creation. It allows the money supply to expand only in response to increasing money demand, eliminating money-induced business fluctuations.[39]

The idea of opening up government's money monopoly to competition is neither new nor untested. Between 1700 and 1845, Scotland developed a highly stable free banking system. There was no central bank, no monetary policy, little government regulation of banking, free entry into the industry, and a universal right of note issue. Banks chose to redeem their notes in specie.[40]

The Scottish system evolved into a complex order in which many competing banks each issued their own notes. Though these bank notes did not have legal tender status, they were widely accepted throughout the country. All banks of issue participated in a note exchange system. Competition between note issuers provided a more rapid and direct check on overissues than is available in a central banking system in which the central bank has a monopoly on note issue.[41] If citizens began to doubt one bank's solvency, they could always substitute the notes of a higher-quality competitor. In addition, unlimited liability meant that any bank which increased its note issue beyond what was necessary to meet an increase in demand for its notes ran the risk of losing both its specie and its stockholders' assets. This internal check on overissuance vastly reduced money supply-induced business fluctuations. It kept banks from overexpanding the money supply but maintained flexibility of note issue. During the period of Scottish free banking, the local economy remained relatively stable and demonstrated a rapid ability to adjust to changing conditions.[42]

The crash of the poorly managed Ayr Bank in 1772 demonstrates particularly well how profit-seeking banks find it in their interest to counteract the adverse effects of overissue by any one bank. When the Ayr Bank went under, the Bank of Scotland and the Royal Bank announced that they would accept its notes. Doing so enabled them to maintain confidence in the monetary system as a whole, but it also brought more immediate pecuniary advantages. The two banks were able to attract new depositors and widen the circulation of their own notes. The cost to them of accepting Ayr Bank notes was small because Scottish banks were subject to unlimited liability. "Despite their magnitude," Lawrence White notes, "the Ayr Bank's losses were borne entirely by its 241 shareholders. The claims of its creditors, including note holders, were paid in full."[43]

Both unscrupulous and recklessly-managed banks were thus driven out of business by the competitive process. The Scottish system afforded few opportunities for profit through fraud because of the short average circulation period, which made the detection of bad notes likely. The government could prosecute bank note fraud just as it could prosecute any other form of fraud.

In the United States, Congress established the Federal Reserve System because it recognized the need for an "elastic" money supply, one which could readily expand in response to increased money demand. The crises the Fed was designed to prevent were the result of an inelastic supply of bank notes, not an inelastic supply of bank reserves (gold or "legal tender").[44] The Fed's power to create bank notes is sufficient to cope with fluctuating money demand. However, the Fed also has the power to augment commercial bank reserves. It has in its hands a tremendous capacity for inflation.

An American free banking system would combine Milton Friedman's proposal for freezing the U.S. monetary base[45] with the flexibility of free entry and competitive note issue. A practical program for the implementation of free banking would allow commercial banks to issue currency redeemable in base money. Banks could choose to employ whatever kind of base money consumers are willing to accept—Federal Reserve Notes, gold, other nations' currencies, etc.[46] Consumers would determine the success or failure of banks of issue by deciding which bank notes to hold. After the right of note-issue is restored, the supply of Federal Reserve Notes would be frozen at its then-current level.[47] Restoration of private note issue combined with elimination of the Fed's money-creation power would insulate the money supply from capricious government manipulation while still providing an elastic supply of currency.

Free banking can eliminate monetary disturbances by taking the monopoly over money away from the government. In addition, it would prevent the government from raising funds through the hidden tax of inflation. The government would have to obtain funds through direct taxation or borrowing. Since it would no longer be able to lower the real value of the public debt through inflation, government would have to take full account of the market rate of interest in deciding between borrowing and taxation. To the extent that the current fiscal crisis is the result of government's monopoly over the currency, eliminating that monopoly forces government to tighten its belt.

Conclusion

The deficit problem is fundamentally an expenditure problem. However, no single reform can guarantee that expenditures will be reduced. If the deficit is to be brought under control, all possible avenues for increased taxation and spending must be closed off. A balanced budget-tax limitation amendment to the Constitution will have to be accompanied by institutional changes which give politicians strong incentives to follow the spirit as well as the letter of the law. Privatization of federal government services creates new interest groups who benefit from reduced federal spending. In addition, privatization of the monetary system deprives government of the ability to finance its operations by creating money.

Notes

1. Adam Smith, *An Inquiry Into the Nature and Causes of the Wealth of Nations*, E. Canaan, Ed. (Chicago: Univ. of Chicago Press, 1976 [1776]), p. 444.

2. For a history of this "classical" theory of public finance and the effects of the Keynesian revolution, see James M. Buchanan and Richard E. Wagner, *Democracy in Deficit: The Political Legacy of Lord Keynes* (New York: Academic Press, 1977).

3. *Ibid.*, pp. 11–14.

4. Abba Lerner, "Functional Finance," *Social Research* 10 (Feb. 1943), pp. 38–51.

5. This is, in fact, a central theme of Buchanan and Wagner, *Democracy in Deficit.*

6. Of course, majority rule means that taxpayers who either do not want to give to the poor or do not view government as the best means of doing so are coerced. This is a problem inherent in the provision of any good or service through a political process operating under a less-than-unanimous voting rule, as we shall see below. For a more detailed analysis of the political process, see James Buchanan and Gordon Tullock, *The Calculus of Consent* (Ann Arbor: Univ. of Michigan Press, 1962).

7. Stuart M. Butler, "For Serious Action on Privatization," *The Journal of The Institute for Socioeconomic Studies* 10, No. 2 (Summer 1985), p. 18.

8. Stuart M. Butler, "Privatization: The Antidote to Budget-Cutting Failures," *USA Today* (July 1984), p. 24.

9. Paul Samuelson, "The Pure Theory of Public Expenditure," *Review of Economics and Statistics* 36 (Nov. 1954), p. 387.

10. Harold Demsetz, "Private Production of Public Goods," *Journal of Law and Economics* 13 (Oct. 1970).

11. Edgar K. Browning and Jacqueline M. Browning, *Public Finance and the Price System* (New York: Macmillan Publishing Co., Inc., 1979), pp. 21–25.

12. Samuelson, "Pure Theory," p. 388.

13. Browning and Browning, *Public Finance*, p. 24.

14. James M. Buchanan, *The Demand and Supply of Public Goods* (Chicago: Rand McNally, 1968), Ch. 5.

15. Browning and Browning, *Public Finance*, p. 25.

16. Friedrich Hayek, *Law, Legislation, and Liberty, Vol. 3: The Political Order of a Free People* (Chicago: Univ. of Chicago Press, 1979), p. 44.

17. *Ibid.*, p. 47.

18. Tyler Cowen, "A Public Goods Definition and Their Institutional Context: A Critique of Public Goods Theory," *Review of Social Economics* 43, No. 1 (April 1985), p. 55.

19. *Ibid.*, p. 55.

20. Some have argued that excessive defense spending is a "public bad," but that is an entirely different issue from the one considered here.

21. Cowen, "Public Goods," pp. 56–57.

22. *Ibid.*, p. 59.

23. *Ibid.*, p. 62.

24. Murray Rothbard, *Power and Market* (Kansas City: Sheed Andrews and McMeel, 1977), p. 169.

25. We say at least, because logrolling makes possible the enactment of legislation favored only by a minority which has traded its votes on some other issue.

26. Rothbard, *Power,* p. 173.

27. See Jack High and Jerome Ellig, "The Private Supply of Education: Some Historical Evidence," in Tyler Cowen, Ed., *The Theory of Market Failure: A Critical Examination* (Washington, D.C.: Cato Institute, forthcoming.)

28. Rothbard, *Power,* p. 176.

29. See Ludwig von Mises, *Bureaucracy* (Cedar Falls, IA: Center for Futures Education, 1983), esp. pp. 60–63.

30. Joe Stilwell, "Deficits and the Economy," *The Journal of Social, Political, and Economic Studies* 8, No. 2 (Summer 1983), p. 176.

31. Shortly before the House vote on the Tax Equity and Fiscal Responsibility Act of 1982, Congressman Jack Kemp (R-NY) stated:

> Fifty years ago Congress faced a similar choice. There was high unemployment, a huge deficit, the president wanted a tax increase, and the Congress went along blindly with it. Interestingly enough, interest rates did not go down, they went up; unemployment did not go down, it went up; and the deficit grew and the recession deepened into the Great Depression.

Quoted in Paul Craig Roberts, *The Supply-Side Revolution: An Insider's Account of Policymaking in Washington* (Cambridge, MA: Harvard Univ. Press, 1984), p. 244.

32. James T. Bennett and Thomas J. DiLorenzo, *Underground Government* (Washington, D.C.: Cato Institute, 1983), p. 33.

33. *Ibid.*, p. 52.

34. *Ibid.*, p. 55.

35. See Alvin Rabushka, *A Compelling Case for a Constitutional Amendment to Balance the Budget and Limit Taxes* (Washington, D.C.: Taxpayer's Foundation, 1984 [1982]).

36. See Reuben Kessel and Armen Alchian, "Effects of Inflation," *Journal of Political Economy* 60, No. 6 (Dec. 1962).

37. Monetarists concentrate almost exclusively on the previously-mentioned price level effects and downplay the importance of these injection effects. For a seminal formulation of this theory, see Friedrich Hayek, *Prices and Production,* 2nd revised and enlarged edition (New York: Augustus M. Kelley, 1967 [1935]) and *Monetary Theory and the Trade Cycle* (New York: Harcourt Brace Jovanovich and Co., Inc., 1933). For a less technical explanation, see Ludwig von Mises et al., *The Austrian Theory of the Trade Cycle and Other Essays* (Washington, D.C.: The Ludwig von Mises Institute for Austrian Economics, Inc., 1983).

38. Friedrich Hayek, "Toward a Free Market Money," *Journal of Libertarian Studies* 3, No. 1 (1979), p. 5.

39. George Selgin, "The Case for Free Banking: Then and Now," Cato Institute *Policy Analysis* No. 60, Oct. 21 1985.

40. Lawrence White, *Free Banking in Britain* (New York: Cambridge University Press, 1984), p. 23.

41. *Ibid.*, p. 18.

42. *Ibid.*, pp. 44–49.

43. *Ibid.*, p. 32.

44. Selgin, "The Case," p. 11.

45. Milton Friedman, "Monetary Policy Structures," in *Candid Conversations on Monetary Policy* (Washington: House Republican Research Committee, 1984); and "Monetary Policy for the 1980's," in John H. Moore, Ed., *To Promote Prosperity: U.S. Domestic Policy in the mid-1980's* (Stanford: Hoover Institution Press, 1984).

46. Selgin, "The Case," p. 12.

47. *Ibid.*, p. 15.

Chapter 7: THE WASHINGTON SCENE

This chapter highlights the current "battle of the budget" in Washington. Orzechowski and Conda review the history of the federal budget process since passage of the Budget and Impoundment Control Act of 1974, which shifted power over the budget away from the President and toward Congress. Rising federal spending has fueled interest in balanced budget and tax limitation amendments; this chapter identifies the major elected leaders and political organizations which have lined up on either side of the balanced-budget constitutional amendment issue.

THE FUTURE OF FEDERAL BUDGET REFORM

William P. Orzechowski and Cesar V. Conda

I. Introduction

It took 160 years for federal spending to claim 10 percent of America's Gross National Product (GNP), which it did in 1940. Since that time, federal spending has risen to nearly 25 percent of GNP. The acceleration of federal spending was lauded by many economists who failed to consider the serious disincentive effects associated with such a trend. They held that increasing government spending, by adding to the overall demand for goods and services, would actually stimulate real economic growth. However, as tax rates rose to finance such expenditure, the returns to work, saving and investment fell. As a consequence, economic growth declined.[1]

The American public has come to realize that economic growth is dependent upon incentives to work, save and invest. Robust economic growth cannot be sustained when such rewards crumble in the wake of rising government expenditures and taxation. Europe, for example, has pushed government spending as a percentage of national income (approximately 50 percent of Gross Domestic Product) far beyond the share that all levels of government take of the national income of the United States (approximately 38 percent of GDP). The results have been disastrous; Europe has been mired in a prolonged state of economic stagnation.[2]

As the American people have become more wary of big government, they have demanded a smaller role for government. They even elected a president who holds this view. However, history shows that reducing public spending is much easier said than done. While the public clamors for spending control it also demonstrates an obstinate refusal to cut back popular federal programs. There have been many attempts to untie this Gordian knot, usually without much success.

In what follows, federal budget trends are used to illustrate major flaws in the federal budget process. Strategies to curtail government growth are outlined. While many of these proposals are potent devices to control spending, a great deal of enthusiasm and legislative effort will be needed to secure their passage. Consequently, it is important to explain the role of concerned citizens groups and the business community. Many of these groups have mounted lobbying campaigns in recent years on behalf of fiscally responsible measures. However, they face formidable odds in the myriad of Washington's special interest groups that continually lobby for more spending. An assessment of the role of political interest groups is thus critical to an understanding of the future development of the federal budget.

II. The Failure to Control Public Spending

Evidence from around the World

Over the last century, U.S. public spending has been rising at an annual rate almost two to three times faster than the Gross National Product (GNP). While this trend is noteworthy in itself, its ramifications can be shocking. According to some estimates, if we extrapolate the historical trend of federal expenditures into the future, federal expenditures as a percentage of GNP will approach 40 percent by the year 2000 and 100 percent by 2036. By this timetable, the actual percentage of federal expenditures for fiscal year 1985 would be in the neighborhood of 24 percent, which means that the actual 1985 share of 24.5 percent is right on schedule!

One only has to take a look at modern Europe to see how difficult it is to stop the trend toward big government.[3] By any measure, most European nations have clearly overstepped the bounds of fiscal responsibility. Table I reveals the massive and relentless rise of the European public sector.

Just two decades ago, the size of the public sector in Europe was moderate by today's standards. At that time, total government revenues and expenditures as a percentage of GDP averaged 32.7 percent and 32.5 percent respectively, similar to the rates now prevailing in Japan and Switzerland. By 1982, these percentages had grown to 45.7 percent and 50.9 percent, with several governments spending in excess of 60 percent of GDP.

Table II reveals the effects of the public-sector boom in Europe. Though Europeans could brag about brisk economic growth during the 1960s and early 1970s, their economies now breed stagnation. With a smaller public sector, real economic growth in Europe averaged 4.4 percent from 1965 to 1969 and 4.1 percent from 1970 to 1974. A burgeoning public sector, however, was accompanied by a fall in average real economic growth to 2.5 percent for the 1975–79 period. In the 1980–84 period, real economic growth plummeted to less than one percent. While other factors, such as increased energy prices and the world recession, have certainly affected European economies, the persistence of economic deterioration in Europe long after the advent of vigorous recoveries in the less heavily taxed United States and East Asian countries suggests that government absorption of resources and high marginal tax rates are indeed the primary problem.

TABLE I
REVENUES AND GOVERNMENT EXPENDITURES
AS A PERCENTAGE OF GDP

	Revenues		Public Spending	
	1962	1982	1962	1982
United States	27.0	32.0	28.8	37.6
Japan	21.6	30.2	19.0	34.5
West Germany	36.6	45.3	35.6	49.6
France	36.6	46.9	37.0	50.7
United Kingdom	33.1	43.7	34.2	47.4
Italy	29.1	41.1	30.5	53.7
Canada	27.0	39.0	30.0	45.8
Austria	34.0	46.7	33.6	50.3
Belgium	29.2	45.4	30.5	56.6
Denmark	28.2	50.7	28.1	60.7
Finland	30.1	39.7	27.4	41.3
Netherlands	34.4	55.8	35.6	63.7
Sweden	35.5	59.7	32.4	67.3
Switzerland	23.9	33.2	18.5	30.0
OECD EUROPE*	32.7	45.7	32.5	50.9

Explanation: Revenues include tax receipts and fees from all levels of government.

*OECD-Europe—includes the following: Austria, Belgium, Denmark, Finland, France, West Germany, Greece, Ireland, Iceland, Luxembourg, Netherlands, Norway, Portugal, Spain, Sweden, Switzerland, and the United Kingdom.

Source: *OECD Economic Outlook, December, 1984*

TABLE II
AVERAGE REAL GDP GROWTH
FOR OECD EUROPE

Period	Annual Average (%)
1965–69	4.42
1970–74	4.14
1975–79	2.50
1980–84	0.96

Source: *OECD Economic Outlook, October, 1984*

The European experience should provide a valuable lesson for policymakers in the United States. However, if recent experience is any guide, it looks as though we may be travelling down the same path.

The Breakdown of the Congressional Budget Reform Act of 1974

The Congressional Budget and Impound Control Act of 1974 established the current budget process, which wrested budgetary power from the president and concentrated it in Congress.[4] The act created the budget committees, the Congressional Budget Office (CBO), budget resolutions, and the reconciliation process. Proponents believed that they had created an effective mechanism for budget control. But the evidence since 1974 demonstrates otherwise. Federal spending has more than tripled, from $267 billion in 1974 to $950 billion in 1985. Inflation-adjusted spending increased at a 17.5 percent rate over the four years of the Carter administration and at the same rate during the first Reagan term.

In fact, in the past five fiscal years, Congress has surpassed its own budget resolution by an average of $28 billion a year (see Chart I). Although actual outlays remained just within the resolution's targets in fiscal 1984, this by no means suggests that Congress has regained budget control. Actual outlays for 1985 are running about $10 billion over the fiscal 1985 resolution, and the budget resolution for 1986 is in the process of being dismantled.

CHART I

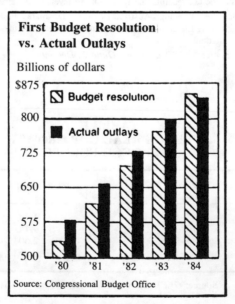

First Budget Resolution vs. Actual Outlays

Billions of dollars

Budget resolution

Actual outlays

Source: Congressional Budget Office

Errors in forecasting business cycles and the consequent changes in entitlement programs, such as unemployment insurance, account for some of the overruns in each year. However, since variations in economic activity tend to offset one another, the five-year average of $28 billion is due mostly to a congressional bias toward spending.

III. How Budget Resolutions are Broken

Like a magician distracting an audience away from the real action, Congress often fools the public by focusing attention on the wrong point. In congressional budgeting, the public's attention is often focused on the formation of a budget resolution. This document sets forth spending priorities for all of Congress's authorization and appropriations committees for the coming fiscal year. Over 80 percent of the year is taken up with such deliberations. In this process, the budget committees appear to wield enormous power since it is their responsibility to set such priorities. However, as all Washington "insiders" know, the real spending action goes on behind the scenes in the authorization and appropriations committees. Using "covert" budget techniques, these committees often go on spending as if the budget resolution hardly mattered. This is the primary reason why budget resolutions are breached by an average of $28 billion per year.

Like any good magician, Congress is reluctant to reveal its methods. Some of the more popular techniques to conceal spending include the following:

Underestimating Program Costs

Special interests must deal with the charge that their spending programs would "break the bank" and breach the budget resolution's targets. In response, unreasonably low cost estimates are employed to keep programs within the resolution's target. Supplemental, or additional funding beyond the amount set at the beginning of the fiscal year, is required later in the year when the higher-than-expected program costs begin to emerge. Once the program's constituency identifies itself closely with this spending, the higher-than-expected program costs are no longer a political barrier.

Underfunding a Mandatory Program

One variation of the underestimation theme is underfunding a mandatory program to give the illusion of budget cuts. For example, in the 1983 budget resolution Congress agreed to the president's food stamp cuts, but it did not enact the legal changes that would have made them possible. Consequently, funding ran out in nine months, and the president was forced to agree to a supplemental appropriation to sustain the program.

Fund Transfers

The illusion of budget cuts is sometimes achieved by transferring funds from one government account to another and counting the transfer as a spending cut even though total spending remains the same.

Out-Year Spending Reductions

The resolution's targets can often be avoided by planning for reductions in out-year spending. These "savings," however, tend to disappear by the end of the year in question. Congress simply restores spending because the resolution's out-year targets are nonbinding and subsequent budget resolutions often overturn changes made in the past. For example, actual spending levels were $39 billion higher on average for fiscal years 1982, 1983, and 1984, compared with the limits set for these years in the resolutions prepared in 1980, 1981, and 1982.

Stacking Low-Priority Spending Bills

Congressional enforcement mechanisms only apply to the aggregate levels set forth by a budget resolution. However, these levels are made up of 21 budget functions that in turn are made up of thousands of programs. This allows Congress to present or stack low priority bills early in the budget process when spending is below the resolution. Popular or high priority programs are held back until late in the session, when media and constituent pressure can be used to generate political support even though these programs, combined with low priority bills, breach the budget resolution.

Postponing Payments

Illusory budget cuts are often achieved by postponing payments made at the end of one fiscal year to the beginning of the next fiscal year.

The Fall of the 1986 Budget Resolution

The 1986 budget resolution passed by both houses of Congress is a prime example of how budget resolutions are broken.[5] It proposes to reduce the deficit by $56 billion in fiscal year 1986 and $277 billion over the next three years. Defense spending reductions and minor revenue increases comprise over 50 percent of the proposed savings in fiscal year 1986. Unlike the Senate's original plan, the compromise budget fails to incorporate important structural changes, such as a freeze on Social Security and other retirement cost-of-living adjustments and a wide range of program terminations. Instead, the compromise budget substitutes mild spending freezes and loosely defined spending reductions for the hard programmatic spending cuts in the Senate's original budget.

Progress on the 1986 budget has followed a familiar pattern. As of this writing, the House has completed action on its 13 appropriations bills; it has failed to enact over half of the budget resolution's proposed domestic spending reductions. Out of a scheduled $22 billion in non-defense spending cuts for 1986, nearly $14 billion has been lost to fiscal irresponsibility.

Either through outright disregard of the resolution's ceilings or through deceptive budgeting, Congress is breaking its own budget. Some congressmen have tried to keep some of these spending bills from reaching the floor. An amendment by Representative Gradison (R-OH) that would have brought the Ways and Means Committee spending bill within budget was submitted to the House Rules Committee. The Gradison amendment prompted the Rules Committee to send the bill back to Ways and Means committee with a recommendation to propose more reasonable spending levels before sending the bill to the House floor.

Another example is the House agriculture authorization bill, which sets U.S. farm policy for the next five years. As currently drafted, the legal requirements for farm programs in the bill will necessitate spending far beyond the limits incorporated in this year's budget. The major cause of this overspending is the use of outdated estimates of farm crop prices. In determining the level of funding for agricultural price supports and deficiency payments, the committee used the January 1985 farm crop price estimates assumed in the budget resolution. However, crop prices dropped precipitously during the summer of 1985. Consequently, spending for price supports will be much higher. Using up-to-date crop prices, the Department of Agriculture estimates that the agriculture bill will exceed the budget mark set by the budget resolution by approximately $5 billion in fiscal year 1986 and as much as $21 billion over the next three years. The agriculture committees were fully aware of this problem but refused to incorporate the new crop estimates, claiming that the January estimates assumed in the budget are binding on appropriations.

Another $3.3 billion in budget savings over three years will be achieved by postponing advanced deficiency payments after October 1 of each fiscal year. All this does is slightly delay the pay-out of agriculture subsidies in order to shift payments into the next fiscal year. The House Agriculture appropriations committee intentionally underfunded a mandatory program by transferring $39 million from Food Stamps to another agricultural account and counting the transfer as a cut in Food Stamps.

In the House-passed Energy and Water Appropriation Bill, a spending cut of $217 million for energy supply research and development was assumed by transferring $217 million of balances to other accounts. In the House-passed Housing and Urban Development appropriations bill, the subcommittee underfunded by $1.1 billion the mandatory General Revenue Sharing program and used these funds to increase discretionary programs. Supplemental funding will be required later in the fiscal year. The House Labor/Health and Human Services/Education appropriations bill underfunds several mandatory programs in the bill by at least $2.3 billion. This is achieved by deferring action on appropriations for the programs awaiting authorizing legislation and providing insufficient funds for student financial assistance programs authorized under current law.

Fiscal discipline faded in nearly every area of the budget. The Senate Budget Committee has estimated that the House-passed appropriations bills, excluding farm support arguments, have breached the 1986 budget resolutions by at least $4.2 billion. Further, domestic spending programs within the jurisdiction of the House Ways and Means Committee are almost $1 billion over budget. Moreover, the Senate has historically tended to add more spending to the House's appropriations bills. It all adds up to another chapter in our long history of broken budget resolutions.

IV. Future Strategies to Control Federal Spending

Few Americans believe that their government will ever claim over 50 percent of the nation's output, but this is precisely the case in nearly other major industrial country. At 38% of GDP, total government spending in the U.S. is not far behind the trend established throughout much of Europe. Given the lax attitude of our Congress toward budget control, there is much room for future concern.

Any strategy to reduce the deficit must hold the line against tax increases. There have been few nations in recent history that have solved their fiscal problems with higher taxes. Instead, higher taxes have slowed economic growth and have provided the fuel for further expansions of government spending. For example,

Europe has tried to bring its deficits down with higher taxes. But after thirty years of tax increases, European deficits have constantly increased as a percentage of GNP—from balanced budgets in the 1950s to deficits that now take up close to five percent of GNP.

Without exception, Europe's experiment with increased taxation has led to an explosion in public expenditures. As the European tax burden has accelerated, so has government spending. This should stand as a lesson to those in this country who believe that fiscal discipline requires increased taxation. The truth of the matter is that you do not control a big spender (i.e. government), by raising its allowance (taxes). Moreover, higher taxation would dampen the supply-side incentive effects unleashed by the Kemp-Roth tax reductions, thereby slowing economic growth.

There are a number of strategies and proposals that may yet reduce the growth of federal spending.

First, spending reduction can be achieved to some extent through the budget resolution and appropriations process. In the budget resolution process, across-the-board approaches to reduce spending are politically attractive and thus have the best chances of being approved by Congress. In the appropriations process, amendments to strike specific measures in appropriations bills can serve as a congressional line-item veto.

Second, the tax limitation/balanced budget constitutional amendment provides, in the view of many, a potent device to control federal spending. Given the failed statutory attempts to limit expenditure growth, it is believed that constitutional fiscal norms are needed to restore fiscal discipline.

The first section of the amendment requires that Congress plan for a balanced budget and that Congress and the president ensure that actual spending does not exceed planned spending. Nothing is said in this section about assuring that actual receipts equal (or exceed) planned receipts. This is because an administration has some control over spending, but it cannot exercise the same degree of control over receipts, which are affected much more by cyclical conditions in the economy. If a boom develops, actual receipts will exceed planned receipts; in a recession, receipts will drop. The first section does not rule out such automatic surpluses or deficits. This is one of the most important subtleties of the amendment. It avoids a rigidity that would be intolerable and harmful. It requires no year-by-year budget balance, but balance over the length or course of business cycles. By itself, the first section would not directly limit the growth of government. It would simply require that taxes and spending go up together.

The second section contains a firm restraint on Congress's ability to raise taxes. It provides that planned tax receipts may not increase from one year to the next by a greater percentage than the growth of the economy unless approved by a majority of both houses of Congress. Under section one, planned spending must be less than or equal to planned receipts, and actual spending must be less than or equal to planned spending. Hence, limiting tax receipts limits spending.

Politically, legislators will find it in their interest to honor the amendment. As it now stands, legislators have no effective political defense against special interest lobbies urging more spending. With the balanced budget amendment they can say: "Your program is an excellent one; I would like to support it but the total amount we can spend is fixed. To get funds for your program, we shall have to cut elsewhere. Where should we cut?" In the words of Milton Friedman, the effect is to force special interests to compete against one another rather than against the amorphous and poorly represented body of taxpayers.[6]

Third, the president's power in budgetary matters could be restored. The most popular proposal to enhance presidential power is the line-item veto. Currently, the president's veto is an all-or-nothing tool. Congress has responded to this situation by loading appropriations bills with "pork barrel" projects, knowing that the president will find it difficult to veto entire appropriations bills. As a consequence, the president's constitutional veto power has been diminished.

To complement the item veto, the president's rescission powers could be enhanced. Under current law, the president has the authority to "rescind" previously appropriated budget authority. This request must be affirmatively approved by Congress within 45 days. Congress can simply do nothing, and the president must spend the money. In fiscal 1983, Mr. Reagan proposed rescissions totaling $1.58 billion. All of these rescissions were blocked through congressional inaction. To reverse the bias in the current system, rescissions should take effect after 45 days unless specifically allowed by Congress. This would force Congress to make some tough decisions rather than reject savings by inaction.

Fourth, there have been a large number of proposals that would modify the current budget process. These run the gamut from a radical restructuring of the present system, as proposed in the Gramm-Rudman Balanced Budget and Emergency Deficit Control Act of 1985, to relatively minor alterations, such as improved budgetary information. The Gramm-Rudman approach offers a procedural mechanism which would force spending reductions. It would achieve a balanced budget in 1991 by mandating deficit reductions of approximately $36 billion per year over the next five years. It contains a novel feature that would empower the president to cut most federal spending programs across-the-board during a fiscal year if the actual deficit breaches the deficit limit for that particular fiscal year. The Gramm-Rudman approach, like the line-item veto, restores budgetary power to the Executive.

Finally, there are a host of technical procedures that could be used to improve the existing budget process. For example, the budget resolution should be enforced through congressional rules at the committee and subcommittee levels (in technical language, "binding 302 allocations"). In this way, it should be possible to reduce the incentive for stacking low priority bills early in the session in the hope that they will ride along with high priority bills in the end. Out-year budget targets should also be binding in order to prevent Congress from pushing deficits into the future. Finally, in order to prevent the problem of underestimation of budgetary costs, there should be a statute requiring the appropriations committees to make compensating reductions within the committee's allocation if actual costs turn out to be greater than estimated costs. This would encourage Congress to propose more accurate program costs.

V. The Politics of Federal Budget Reform

The growth in the number of special interest groups has coincided with the relentless growth in federal spending. Since 1971, the number of interest groups headquartered in the Washington, D.C. metropolitan area has increased 135 percent, from 817 in 1971 to about 2000 today. Within this same period, domestic spending as a percentage of Gross National Product has grown from a 9.4 percent average in the years 1950 to 1972 to 17.6 percent in 1985. For every federal spending program, there is a well-organized interest group lobbying for more federal funds: the American Association of Retired Persons (AARP) for Social Security and Medicare, the National Rural Electric Cooperative Association (NRECA) for federal subsidies to rural electric cooperatives, the National Education Association (NEA) for federal education programs, the American Federation of State, County and Municipal Employees (AFSCME) for federal assistance to the states with programs like revenue sharing, the AFL-CIO for the range of federal programs affecting unionized labor, and so on.

There have been several reasons for the success of special interests in expanding domestic programs. First, they have had the advantage of focusing their efforts on one or two specific programs. Second, because of the fiscal bifurcation of spending and tax decisions, beneficiaries of public spending rarely pay the specific tax costs associated with their programs. Instead, the costs of their programs are spread over the entire set of federal taxpayers and onto future generations through debt creation. Third, until recently, there has been a general absence of counterveiling forces lobbying for fiscal discipline.

In response to these alarming trends, the business community and concerned citizens groups have marshalled forces in recent years to lobby for fiscally responsible measures. While these groups do not share identical federal budget methodologies, they are generally united by concern over the growth of federal spending and deficits. The leading organizations involved include the following:

Major Business Groups

Chamber of Commerce of the United States. Founded in 1912, the Chamber is the world's largest federation of business companies and associations. The Chamber's members are predominantly small business firms. Yet, virtually all of the nation's largest companies are also active members. In addition to its Washington headquarters, the Chamber maintains six regional offices throughout the country. While the Chamber has 60 registered lobbyists, the Chamber's lobbying strength lies in its grassroots membership. The Chamber is involved in over 120 different legislative issues with the most important being tax, budget, domestic, and international issues.

National Association of Manufacturers. The NAM represents 13,500 manufacturing firms. The NAM was founded in 1895 to promote American commerce, especially international trade.[7] In addition to its Washington office, NAM has four regional offices across the country. The NAM, like the U.S. Chamber, draws its lobbying strength from its grassroots membership. The NAM is vitally concerned with tax and budget issues.

Other business groups. Aside from the Chamber and the NAM, other business organizations representing more specific interests have played leading roles in the fight to control the budget. These include the Business Roundtable, which represents 200 major corporations and is the major voice for big business; the National Association of Wholesaler-Distributors, which represents about 15,000 distributors nationwide; the National Federation of Independent Business, which represents more than 500,000 small businesses and is one of the major voices for small business; the American Business Conference, which represents high growth firms; and the American Electronics Association, which represents hi-tech firms.[8]

Citizens and Taxpayer Groups

National Taxpayers Union. Founded in 1969, the National Taxpayers Union, with its 150,000 members, is the leading voice for American taxpayers. The Tax Limitation/Balanced Budget Constitutional Amendment is NTU's chief legislative issue. Since 1975, NTU has been instrumental in the drive to enact the amendment. In addition, NTU is actively involved in enacting tax simplification and cutting government spending.

National Tax Limitation Committee. NTLC was founded in 1975 to press for constitutional control over growth of spending and taxes. It is supported by thousands of individuals, companies, and trade associations across the nation. NTLC was instrumental in drafting the tax limitation section of the balanced budget constitutional amendment. The National Taxpayers Union and the NTLC have been the leaders in the drive to enact the amendment on both the state and national levels.

Other citizens and taxpayer groups. Aside from the NTU and the NTLC, other citizens groups have been involved in the fight to control spending. These include Citizens for a Sound Economy, which advocates market-oriented solutions to government spending. Citizens for a Sound Economy, which was founded in 1983, has blossomed from a relatively small membership to an organization of over 200,000 members. Its dynamic growth is a reflection of the public's desire to control government growth. Citizens for a Sound Economy is fast becoming an emerging force within the Washington "scene." The Competitive Enterprise Institute, which advocates free market approaches to economic issues, has had success in a number of areas. Other groups include Free the Eagle Citizens Lobby, which lobbies against excessive government bailouts; Citizens Choice, which is an individual-membership arm of the U.S. Chamber of Commerce; and "new right" conservative groups such as Paul Weyrich's Coalitions for America and Howard Phillips's Conservative Caucus, which lobbies to "defund the left."

Riding the crest of the perceived Reagan mandate to reduce government spending, the business community and citizens groups, working individually and through coalitions, have supported the balanced budget amendment, the Senate Republican budget cuts of 1985, the Gramm-Rudman balanced budget bill of 1986, the line item veto, the 1981 Gramm-Latta budget cuts and several smaller initiatives to cut specific programs.

While these alliances are united behind the general concept of balanced budgets and deficit reduction, there are two distinct economic philosophies concerning the methods to achieve these goals. Many of these organizations believe that deficit reduction is the most important goal of economic policy. As a consequence, they are willing to accept tax increases combined with spending cuts as a viable means to achieve this goal. The other view holds that deficit reduction should come entirely from spending restraint and economic growth. In essence, proponents of the latter view agree with Nobel prize-winning economist Milton Friedman that the true cost of government is the level of government expenditure itself. Switching the method of finance from deficits to taxes will not reduce the burden of government, since taxes are associated with rather costly disincentive effects. Moreover, as Friedman argues, raising taxes leads to more public spending.

The 1982 fight over The Tax Equity and Fiscal Responsibility Act (TEFRA), which proposed a combination of spending cuts and major tax increases to reduce the deficit, highlighted these two philosophies and temporarily severed the business alliance. However, these groups have since come together to form coalitions to reduce the growth of federal spending and deficits.

The Major Issues

Tax Limitation/Balanced Budget Coalition. In the early 1980s, the National Taxpayer's Union and the National Tax Limitation Committee led an ad hoc coalition of groups to lobby for the Tax Limitation/Balanced Budget Constitutional Amendment. The coalition provided an informal but effective working arrangement between NTU, NTLC, the U.S. Chamber of Commerce, the American Farm Federation Bureau, the National Association of Realtors, and the National Federation of Independent Business. Opposition to the amendment was led by the AFL-CIO and AFSCME. These groups opposed the amendment because it imposed severe restrictions on Congress's taxing authority, which in turn would limit spending for their domestic programs. The opposition characterized the coalition and the amendment effort as the "radical right wing's" agenda to eliminate government.

Despite the opposition's extensive grassroots campaign, the coalition's efforts led to a victory in 1982, with the U.S. Senate approving the Tax Limitation/Balanced Budget Amendment by a vote of 69 to 31. The amendment passed the House by a majority but failed to achieve the two-thirds majority necessary to amend the Constitution.

With the setback on the national level, the coalition focused its efforts on the constitutional convention drive to enact the amendment. In 1985, 32 of the required 34 states had passed resolutions calling for a constitutional convention.

This year, the coalition strengthened its operations by acquiring the services of former White House lobbyist Wayne Valis. Under Valis's leadership, the Tax Limitation/Balanced Budget Coalition, as it is formally titled, has grown from roughly eight members to its current membership of 41 business organizations, individual companies, and taxpayer organizations. Some of the new members include TRW Inc., American Mining Congress, Amway Corporation, Citizens for a Sound Economy, and United Telecommunications, Inc. The coalition specifically supports S.J. Res. 13, the tax limitation/balanced budget amendment. However, a competing version of the amendment has been introduced by Senator Paul Simon (D-IL). This balanced budget amendment—S.J. Res. 225—does not limit Congress's authority to raise taxes. As in the 1982 TEFRA battle, the Simon version might cause the coalition to review its positions.

Budget resolution battles and the Deficit Reduction Coalition. In 1981 and 1985, the business community united behind budget resolutions that proposed drastic cuts in the growth of government spending. The 1981 Gramm-Latta budget proved that spending can be reduced, to a limited extent, through the budget process. In terms of the magnitude of budget cuts and lobbying activity by the business community, the 1985 budget battle took on historic proportions. The White House/Senate Republican budget proposed an unprecedented $57 billion spending reduction by freezing defense, freezing Social Security cost-of-living increases, and eliminating 13 government programs. The Deficit Reduction Coalition, originally formed by the U.S. Chamber of Commerce, National Association of Wholesaler-Distributors, American Business Conference, National Federation of Independent Business, National Association of Realtors, and National Association of Manufacturers, grew to almost 400 participating business organizations, individual corporations, and citizens groups.

The Senate passed the budget the coalition favored by a vote of 50 to 49. However, this was a short-lived victory. Using Social Security as a political issue to attack the Republicans, House Democrats pressured the president to withdraw his support from the Senate plan. As mentioned earlier, the resulting compromise budget resolution for fiscal 1986 failed to make a substantial dent in government spending, leaving $200 billion annual deficits for the foreseeable future.

Gramm-Rudman Balanced Budget/Emergency Deficit Control Act and the Budget Control Working Group. The startling emergence of the Gramm-Rudman bill underscored the growing political strength of budget reduction issues. The law establishes a deficit reduction schedule which would eliminate the federal budget deficit by 1991. Congress is required to reduce the deficit by $36 billion for each of the next five years. If Congress falls short of the target in any year, the president is authorized to make across-the-board spending cuts which would affect virtually all programs except Social Security.

The U.S. Chamber of Commerce took the lead in promoting Gramm-Rudman in the business community and among the members of a coalition known as the Budget Control Working Group. The group was formed shortly before the first inauguration of President Reagan, and it also lobbied for the Gramm-Latta budget proposals in 1981 and 1982. Its members include most of the major taxpayer and business groups described above, plus over 50 other individual corporations, trade associations, and public interest organizations.

Many of these groups will lend support to Congressman Dick Armey's (R-TX) "Budget Commando" group that will monitor the appropriations process for appropriations items that they see as fiscally irresponsible or in violation of the budget resolution.

The business community and the fiscally conservative citizens groups have become more effective in lobbying for fiscal responsibility. Coalitions like the Deficit Reduction Coalition and the Tax Limitation/Balanced Budget Coalition have proven to be powerful vehicles in mobilizing large-scale cooperative efforts and grassroots campaigns. Innovative ideas such as privatization have put fiscal conservatives on the intellectual high ground by promoting positive ideas to reduce the budget. And finally, poll after poll indicates that the American people want the deficit reduced through spending cuts—not tax increases. The will of the American people is the ultimate weapon on the side of fiscal discipline.

VI. Conclusion

In 1980, when the United States first gave serious consideration to substantial tax cuts and firmer limitations on government spending, proponents of this course of action had to rely on the logic of their arguments and the instincts of the electorate to win their case. Now, five years later, there is considerably more evidence, albeit largely anecdotal, that economic performance varies inversely with the size of government. The key to economic growth, many believe, lies not in big government but in government restraint in taxation and spending. Recent events in federal budgeting suggest that this message is being ignored by Congress. The budget process is in a shambles. Federal spending continues to rise. But as spending grows, budget reform and tax and spending reduction measures gain visibility and credibility in the eyes of the American public.

Notes

1. A historical review of the incentive effects of taxation is contained in Robert E. Keleher and William P. Orzechowski, "Supply-Side Fiscal Policy: An Historical Analysis of a Rejuvenated Idea" in *Supply-Side Economics: A Critical Appraisal*, Ed. Richard H. Fink (Frederick, Maryland: University Publications of America, 1982).
2. Ronald D. Utt and William P. Orzechowski, "International Perspectives on Economic Growth," *Cato Policy Report* (July/August 1985).
3. See Utt and Orzechowski, "International Perspectives."
4. William P. Orzechowski and Cesar V. Conda, "How to Break a Budget Resolution," *Wall Street Journal* (August 7, 1985).
5. William P. Orzechowski and Cesar V. Conda, "Will Another Budget Resolution be Broken," *Economic Outlook* (Washington: U.S. Chamber of Commerce, October, 1985).
6. Milton Friedman and Rose Friedman, *Free to Choose* (New York: Harcourt Brace Jovanovich, 1980), p. 301.
7. Norman J. Ornstein and Shirley Elder, *Interest Groups, Lobbying, Policymaking* (Washington: Congressional Quarterly Press, 1978), pp. 38–40.
8. Ibid., pp. 38–40.